HIGH COURT CASE SUMMARIES

CORPORATIONS

Keyed to Hamilton and Macey's
Casebook on Corporations,
10th Edition

THOMSON

WEST

Mat #40737579

TEXT IS PRINTED ON 10% POST
CONSUMER RECYCLED PAPER

Table of Contents

Page

CHAPTER TWO. The Partnership — 1
Richert v. Handly — 5
Richert v. Handly — 7
Bane v. Ferguson — 9
National Biscuit Co. v. Stroud — 11
Smith v. Dixon — 13
Rouse v. Pollard — 15
Roach v. Mead — 17
Meinhard v. Salmon — 19
Collins v. Lewis — 21
Cauble v. Handler — 23
Adams v. Jarvis — 25
8182 Maryland Associates, Limited Partnership v. Sheehan — 27
Lampert, Hausler & Rodman, PC v. John F. Gallant, et al. — 29
Gibbs v. Breed, Abbott & Morgan — 31
Bohatch v. Butler & Binion — 33
Martin v. Peyton — 35
Smith v. Kelley — 37

CHAPTER THREE. The Limited Partnership: With Special Reference to Federal Income Taxation — 39
In re USACafes, L.P. Litigation — 41
In re Spree.com Corp. — 43

CHAPTER FOUR. Limited Liability Companies — 45
Blackmore Partners, L.P. v. Link Energy LLC — 47
Elf Atochem North America, Inc. v. Jaffari and Malek LLC — 49
Abry Partners V, L.P. v. F & W Acquisition LLC — 53
Poore v. Fox Hollow Enterprises — 55
Marie L. Kasten v. Doral Dental USA, LLC — 57

CHAPTER FIVE. The Development of Corporation Law in the United States — 59
Louis K. Liggett Co. v. Lee — 61

CHAPTER SIX. The Formation of a Closely Held Corporation — 63
711 Kings Highway Corp. v. F.I.M.'s Marine Repair Serv., Inc. — 65
Sullivan v. Hammer — 67
Stanley J. How & Assoc., Inc. v. Boss — 69
Robertson v. Levy — 71
Frontier Refining Company v. Kunkel's, Inc. — 75

CHAPTER SEVEN. Disregard of the Corporate Entity — 77
Bartle v. Home Owners Co-op. — 79
DeWitt Truck Brokers v. W. Ray Flemming Fruit Co. — 81
Baatz v. Arrow Bar — 83
Radaszewski v. Telecom Corp. — 85
Fletcher v. Atex, Inc. — 87
United States v. Bestfoods — 89
Stark v. Flemming — 93
Roccograndi v. Unemployment Comp. Bd. of Review — 95
Cargill, Inc. v. Hedge — 97
Pepper v. Litton — 99
Nissen Corp. v. Miller — 101

CHAPTER EIGHT. Financial Matters and the Corporation — 105
Hanewald v. Bryan's Inc. — 107
Torres v. Speiser — 109

	Page
S.E.C. v. Ralston Purina Co.	111
Smith v. Gross	113
Stokes v. Continental Trust Co. of City of New York	115
Katzowitz v. Sidler	117
Lacos Land Company v. Arden Group, Inc.	121
Gottfried v. Gottfried	123
Dodge v. Ford Motor Co.	125
Wilderman v. Wilderman	127
Donahue v. Rodd Electrotype Co.	129

CHAPTER NINE.   Management and Control of Corporation — **131**

McQuade v. Stoneham	135
Galler v. Galler	137
Zion v. Kurtz	139
Matter of Auer v. Dressel	141
Salgo v. Matthews	145
Humphrys v. Winous Co.	147
Ringling Bros.–Barnum & Bailey Combined Shows v. Ringling	151
Brown v. McLanahan	153
Lehrman v. Cohen	155
Ling and Co. v. Trinity Sav. and Loan Ass'n	157
Gearing v. Kelly	159
In re Radom & Neidorff, Inc.	161
Davis v. Sheerin	165
Abreu v. Unica Indus. Sales, Inc.	167
In the Matter of Drive-In Dev. Corp.	169
Lee v. Jenkins Bros.	171
DeBaun v. First Western Bank and Trust Co.	173
Perlman v. Feldmann	177

CHAPTER TEN.   Control and Management in the Publicly Held Corporation — **179**

Studebaker Corp. v. Gittlin	181
In the Matter of Caterpillar, Inc.	183
J.I. Case Co. v. Borak	187
TSC Indus., Inc. v. Northway, Inc.	189
Virginia Bankshares, Inc. v. Sandberg	191
Rauchman v. Mobil Corp.	195

CHAPTER ELEVEN.   Duty of Care and the Business Judgment Rule — **197**

Litwin v. Allen	199
Shlensky v. Wrigley	203
Smith v. Van Gorkom	205
In re Caremark Intern. Inc. Derivative Litigation	209
Stone v. Ritter	211
Malone v. Brincat	213
Gall v. Exxon Corp.	215
Zapata Corp. v. Maldonado	217
Aronson v. Lewis	221
In re Oracle Corp. Derivative Litigation	225
Cuker v. Mikalauskas	227

CHAPTER TWELVE.   Duty of Loyalty and Conflict of Interest — **229**

Marciano v. Nakash	231
Heller v. Boylan	233
Brehm v. Eisner	235
Brehm v. Eisner	239
Sinclair Oil Corporation v. Levien	241
Weinberger v. UOP, Inc.	243
Northeast Harbor Golf Club, Inc. v. Harris	245

CHAPTER THIRTEEN.   Transactions in Shares: Rule 10b–5, Insider Trading and Securities Fraud — **247**

In Re Enron Corporation Securities, Derivative & ERISA Litigation	249
Securities and Exchange Comm'n v. Texas Gulf Sulphur Co.	253
Chiarella v. United States	257
United States v. O'Hagan	261

	Page
Dirks v. Securities and Exchange Commission	265
United States v. Chestman	269
Basic, Inc. v. Levinson	273
MDCM Holdings, Inc. v. Credit Suisse First Boston Corporation	277
CHAPTER FOURTEEN. Indemnification and Insurance	**281**
Merritt-Chapman & Scott Corp. v. Wolfson	283
McCullough v. Fidelity & Deposit Co.	285
CHAPTER FIFTEEN. Takeovers	**287**
CTS Corporation v. Dynamics Corp. of America	289
Moran v. Household International, Inc.	293
Mentor Graphics v. Quickturn Design Systems, Inc.	295
International Brotherhood of Teamsters v. Fleming Companies	297
CHAPTER SIXTEEN. Corporate Books and Records	**299**
Thomas & Betts Corporation v. Leviton Manufacturing Co., Inc.	301
Saito v. McKesson HBOC, Inc.	303
Parsons v. Jefferson-Pilot Corp.	305

*

Alphabetical Table of Cases

Abreu v. Unica Indus. Sales, Inc., 224 Ill.App.3d 439, 166 Ill.Dec. 703, 586 N.E.2d 661 (Ill.App. 1 Dist.1991), 167
Abry Partners V, L.P. v. F & W Acquisition LLC, 891 A.2d 1032 (Del.Ch.2006), 53
Adams v. Jarvis, 23 Wis.2d 453, 127 N.W.2d 400 (Wis.1964), 25
Aronson v. Lewis, 473 A.2d 805 (Del.Supr.1984), 221
Auer v. Dressel, 306 N.Y. 427, 118 N.E.2d 590 (N.Y.1954), 141

Baatz v. Arrow Bar, 452 N.W.2d 138 (S.D.1990), 83
Bane v. Ferguson, 890 F.2d 11 (7th Cir.1989), 9
Bartle v. Home Owners Co-op., 309 N.Y. 103, 127 N.E.2d 832 (N.Y.1955), 79
Basic Inc. v. Levinson, 485 U.S. 224, 108 S.Ct. 978, 99 L.Ed.2d 194 (1988), 273
Bestfoods, United States v., 524 U.S. 51, 118 S.Ct. 1876, 141 L.Ed.2d 43 (1998), 89
Blackmore Partners, L.P. v. Link Energy LLC, 864 A.2d 80 (Del.Ch.2004), 47
Bohatch v. Butler & Binion, 977 S.W.2d 543 (Tex.1998), 33
Brehm v. Eisner, 746 A.2d 244 (Del.Supr.2000), 235
Brown v. McLanahan, 148 F.2d 703 (4th Cir.1945), 153

Caremark Intern. Inc. Derivative Litigation, In re, 698 A.2d 959 (Del.Ch.1996), 209
Cargill, Inc. v. Hedge, 375 N.W.2d 477 (Minn.1985), 97
Caterpillar, Inc., In the Matter of, Admnistrative Proceeding File No. 3–7692, SEC Rel. No. 34–30532 (Admin. Proceeding 1992), 183
Cauble v. Handler, 503 S.W.2d 362 (Tex.Civ.App.-Fort Worth 1973), 23
Chestman, United States v., 947 F.2d 551 (2nd Cir.1991), 269
Chiarella v. United States, 445 U.S. 222, 100 S.Ct. 1108, 63 L.Ed.2d 348 (1980), 257
Collins v. Lewis, 283 S.W.2d 258 (Tex.Civ.App.-Galveston 1955), 21
CTS Corp. v. Dynamics Corp. of America, 481 U.S. 69, 107 S.Ct. 1637, 95 L.Ed.2d 67 (1987), 289
Cuker v. Mikalauskas, 547 Pa. 600, 692 A.2d 1042 (Pa.1997), 227

Davis v. Sheerin, 754 S.W.2d 375 (Tex.App.-Hous. (1 Dist.) 1988), 165
DeBaun v. First Western Bank & Trust Co., 46 Cal.App.3d 686, 120 Cal.Rptr. 354 (Cal.App. 2 Dist.1975), 173
DeWitt Truck Brokers, Inc. v. W. Ray Flemming Fruit Co., 540 F.2d 681 (4th Cir.1976), 81
Dirks v. S.E.C., 463 U.S. 646, 103 S.Ct. 3255, 77 L.Ed.2d 911 (1983), 265
Dodge v. Ford Motor Co., 204 Mich. 459, 170 N.W. 668 (Mich.1919), 125
Donahue v. Rodd Electrotype Co. of New England, Inc., 367 Mass. 578, 328 N.E.2d 505 (Mass.1975), 129
Drive–In Development Corp., In re, 371 F.2d 215 (7th Cir. 1966), 169

8182 Maryland Associates, Ltd. Partnership v. Sheehan, 14 S.W.3d 576 (Mo.2000), 27
Elf Atochem North America, Inc. v. Jaffari, 727 A.2d 286 (Del.Supr.1999), 49
Enron Corp. Securities, Derivative & ERISA Litigation, In re, 235 F.Supp.2d 549 (S.D.Tex.2002), 249

Fletcher v. Atex, Inc., 68 F.3d 1451 (2nd Cir.1995), 87
Frontier Refining Co. v. Kunkel's, Inc., 407 P.2d 880 (Wyo. 1965), 75

Gall v. Exxon Corp., 418 F.Supp. 508 (S.D.N.Y.1976), 215
Galler v. Galler, 32 Ill.2d 16, 203 N.E.2d 577 (Ill.1964), 137
Gearing v. Kelly, 227 N.Y.S.2d 897, 182 N.E.2d 391 (N.Y. 1962), 159
Gibbs v. Breed, Abbott & Morgan, 271 A.D.2d 180, 710 N.Y.S.2d 578 (N.Y.A.D. 1 Dept.2000), 31
Gottfried v. Gottfried, 73 N.Y.S.2d 692 (N.Y.Sup.1947), 123

Hanewald v. Bryan's Inc., 429 N.W.2d 414 (N.D.1988), 107
Heller v. Boylan, 29 N.Y.S.2d 653 (N.Y.Sup.1941), 233
Humphrys v. Winous Co., 165 Ohio St. 45, 133 N.E.2d 780 (Ohio 1956), 147

In re (see name of party)
International Broth. of Teamsters General Fund v. Fleming Companies, Inc., 975 P.2d 907 (Okla.1999), 297
In the Matter of (see name of party)

J. I. Case Co. v. Borak, 377 U.S. 426, 84 S.Ct. 1555, 12 L.Ed.2d 423 (1964), 187

Katzowitz v. Sidler, 301 N.Y.S.2d 470, 249 N.E.2d 359 (N.Y. 1969), 117

Lacos Land Co. v. Arden Group, Inc., 517 A.2d 271 (Del.Ch. 1986), 121
Lampert, Hausler & Rodman, PC v. Gallant, 18 Mass. L. Rptr. 614, 2004 WL 3120801 (Mass.Super.2004), 29
Lee v. Jenkins Bros., 268 F.2d 357 (2nd Cir.1959), 171
Lehrman v. Cohen, 43 Del.Ch. 222, 222 A.2d 800 (Del. Supr.1966), 155
Ling & Co., Inc. v. Trinity Sav. & Loan Ass'n, 482 S.W.2d 841 (Tex.1972), 157
Litwin v. Allen, 25 N.Y.S.2d 667 (N.Y.Sup.1940), 199
Louis K. Liggett Co. v. Lee, 288 U.S. 517, 53 S.Ct. 481, 77 L.Ed. 929 (1933), 61

Malone v. Brincat, 722 A.2d 5 (Del.Supr.1998), 213
Marciano v. Nakash, 535 A.2d 400 (Del.Supr.1987), 231
Marie L. Kasten v. Doral Dental USA, LLC, 2006 WL 861382 (Wis.App.2006), 57
Martin v. Peyton, 246 N.Y. 213, 158 N.E. 77 (N.Y.1927), 35
McCullough v. Fidelity & Deposit Co., 2 F.3d 110 (5th Cir. 1993), 285
McQuade v. Stoneham, 263 N.Y. 323, 189 N.E. 234 (N.Y. 1934), 135
MDCM Holdings, Inc. v. Credit Suisse First Boston Corp., 216 F.Supp.2d 251 (S.D.N.Y.2002), 277
Meinhard v. Salmon, 249 N.Y. 458, 164 N.E. 545 (N.Y.1928), 19
Mentor Graphics Corp. v. Quickturn Design Systems, Inc., 728 A.2d 25 (Del.Ch.1998), 295
Merritt–Chapman & Scott Corp. v. Wolfson, 321 A.2d 138 (Del.Super.1974), 283
Moran v. Household Intern., Inc., 500 A.2d 1346 (Del. Supr.1985), 293

National Biscuit Co. v. Stroud, 249 N.C. 467, 106 S.E.2d 692 (N.C.1959), 11
Nissen Corp. v. Miller, 323 Md. 613, 594 A.2d 564 (Md.1991), 101
Northeast Harbor Golf Club, Inc. v. Harris, 661 A.2d 1146 (Me.1995), 245

O'Hagan, United States v., 521 U.S. 642, 117 S.Ct. 2199, 138 L.Ed.2d 724 (1997), 261

Oracle Corp. Derivative Litigation, In re, 824 A.2d 917 (Del. Ch.2003), 225

Parsons v. Jefferson–Pilot Corp., 333 N.C. 420, 426 S.E.2d 685 (N.C.1993), 305

Pepper v. Litton, 308 U.S. 295, 60 S.Ct. 238, 84 L.Ed. 281 (1939), 99

Perlman v. Feldmann, 219 F.2d 173 (2nd Cir.1955), 177

Poore v. Fox Hollow Enterprises, 1994 WL 150872 (Del.Super.1994), 55

Radaszewski by Radaszewski v. Telecom Corp., 981 F.2d 305 (8th Cir.1992), 85

Radom & Neidorff, Inc., In re, 307 N.Y. 1, 119 N.E.2d 563 (N.Y.1954), 161

Rauchman v. Mobil Corp., 739 F.2d 205 (6th Cir.1984), 195

Richert v. Handly, 53 Wash.2d 121, 330 P.2d 1079 (Wash. 1958), 7

Richert v. Handly, 50 Wash.2d 356, 311 P.2d 417 (Wash. 1957), 5

Ringling Bros.–Barnum & Bailey Combined Shows v. Ringling, 29 Del.Ch. 610, 53 A.2d 441 (Del.Supr.1947), 151

Roach v. Mead, 301 Or. 383, 722 P.2d 1229 (Or.1986), 17

Robertson v. Levy, 197 A.2d 443 (D.C.App.1964), 71

Roccograndi v. Unemployment Compensation Bd. of Review, 197 Pa.Super. 372, 178 A.2d 786 (Pa.Super.1962), 95

Rouse v. Pollard, 18 A.2d 5 (N.J.Ch.1941), 15

Saito v. McKesson HBOC, Inc., 806 A.2d 113 (Del.Supr.2002), 303

Salgo v. Matthews, 497 S.W.2d 620 (Tex.Civ.App.-Dallas 1973), 145

Securities and Exchange Commission v. Ralston Purina Co., 346 U.S. 119, 73 S.Ct. 981, 97 L.Ed. 1494 (1953), 111

Securities and Exchange Commission v. Texas Gulf Sulphur Co., 401 F.2d 833 (2nd Cir.1968), 253

711 Kings Highway Corp. v. F.I.M.'s Marine Repair Service Inc., 51 Misc.2d 373, 273 N.Y.S.2d 299 (N.Y.Sup.1966), 65

Shlensky v. Wrigley, 95 Ill.App.2d 173, 237 N.E.2d 776 (Ill. App. 1 Dist.1968), 203

Sinclair Oil Corp. v. Levien, 280 A.2d 717 (Del.Supr.1971), 241

Smith v. Dixon, 238 Ark. 1018, 386 S.W.2d 244 (Ark.1965), 13

Smith v. Gross, 604 F.2d 639 (9th Cir.1979), 113

Smith v. Kelley, 465 S.W.2d 39 (Ky.1971), 37

Smith v. Van Gorkom, 488 A.2d 858 (Del.Supr.1985), 205

Spree.com Corp., In re, 2001 WL 1518242 (Bkrtcy.E.D.Pa. 2001), 43

Stanley J. How & Associates, Inc. v. Boss, 222 F.Supp. 936 (S.D.Iowa 1963), 69

Stark v. Flemming, 283 F.2d 410 (9th Cir.1960), 93

Stokes v. Continental Trust Co. of City of New York, 186 N.Y. 285, 78 N.E. 1090 (N.Y.1906), 115

Stone ex rel. AmSouth Bancorporation v. Ritter, 911 A.2d 362 (Del.Supr.2006), 211

Studebaker Corp. v. Gittlin, 360 F.2d 692 (2nd Cir.1966), 181

Sullivan v. Hammer, 1990 WL 114223 (Del.Ch.1990), 67

Thomas & Betts Corp. v. Leviton Mfg. Co., Inc., 681 A.2d 1026 (Del.Supr.1996), 301

Torres v. Speiser, 268 A.D.2d 253, 701 N.Y.S.2d 360 (N.Y.A.D. 1 Dept.2000), 109

TSC Industries, Inc. v. Northway, Inc., 426 U.S. 438, 96 S.Ct. 2126, 48 L.Ed.2d 757 (1976), 189

United States v. ______ (see opposing party)

USACafes, L.P. Litigation, In re, 600 A.2d 43 (Del.Ch.1991), 41

Virginia Bankshares, Inc. v. Sandberg, 501 U.S. 1083, 111 S.Ct. 2749, 115 L.Ed.2d 929 (1991), 191

Walt Disney Co. Derivative Litigation, In re, 906 A.2d 27 (Del.Supr.2006), 239

Weinberger v. UOP, Inc., 457 A.2d 701 (Del.Supr.1983), 243

Wilderman v. Wilderman, 315 A.2d 610 (Del.Ch.1974), 127

Zapata Corp. v. Maldonado, 430 A.2d 779 (Del.Supr.1981), 217

Zion v. Kurtz, 428 N.Y.S.2d 199, 405 N.E.2d 681 (N.Y.1980), 139

CHAPTER TWO

The Partnership

Richert v. Handly

Instant Facts: A partner in a logging venture claimed that he was entitled to reimbursement for his capital contribution when the partnership proved unsuccessful.

Black Letter Rule: Upon termination of a partnership where one partner has contributed capital and another partner has contributed only services, the capital contribution must be reimbursed unless the parties intended otherwise.

Richert v. Handly

Instant Facts: After two men entered into a partnership under which one would outlay capital and the other contribute services, the capital contributing partner brought suit seeking a contribution for his capital outlay when the partnership incurred a net loss.

Black Letter Rule: A partner who contributes services to a partnership rather than capital is, nevertheless, required to contribute toward capital losses sustained by the partnership according to his share in the profits.

Bane v. Ferguson

Instant Facts: A retired attorney sued his former partners for their alleged negligent mismanagement which caused the firm to dissolve, resulting in a loss of pension benefits for retired partners.

Black Letter Rule: A law firm is not liable to a former partner for negligent mismanagement that affects the retired partner's non-contractual pension benefits.

National Biscuit Co. v. Stroud

Instant Facts: A partner in a grocery store sought to avoid liability for purchases of bread made by his copartner on the ground that he had informed the store's creditor that he would not be liable for purchases made by his copartner.

Black Letter Rule: A partner in a general partnership cannot deny his liability for the debts of the partnership by informing creditors that he is not liable for a copartner's purchases occurring in the ordinary course of business.

Smith v. Dixon

Instant Facts: A partnership sought to revoke a contract for the sale of land on the ground that the managing partner did not have the authority to sell the land for the price of the contract.

Black Letter Rule: A partnership's express limitation on a particular member's power to bind the partnership is insufficient to avoid liability for contracts made with third parties who were unaware of such a limitation and reasonably believed that the partner had the authority to act.

Rouse v. Pollard

Instant Facts: A woman who was defrauded by her attorney sought to recover against the attorney's former partners.

Black Letter Rule: A law firm may not be held vicariously liable for a partner's fraud in connection with investment advice given to clients.

Roach v. Mead

Instant Facts: An attorney sought to avoid vicarious liability for his law partner's negligence by claiming that the loan transaction conducted between the negligent partner and the injured client was outside the scope of the partnership's business.

Black Letter Rule: A law firm may be held liable for a partner's failure to advise his client to seek independent legal advice when the partner enters into a business transaction with the client.

Meinhard v. Salmon

Instant Facts: When a partnership is offered a profitable lease, one partner accepts it for himself, prompting the other to demand participation.

Black Letter Rule: Partners' fiduciary duties of loyalty forbid appropriating opportunities offered to the partnership.

Collins v. Lewis

Instant Facts: A partner in a cafeteria business sought to have a court dissolve the partnership after the cafeteria initially proved unprofitable.

Black Letter Rule: A court will not grant dissolution to a partner who has failed to perform his obligations under the partnership agreement.

Cauble v. Handler

Instant Facts: When the surviving partner in a furniture store continued to operate the business after a suit for an accounting was filed by the deceased partner's estate, the administartrix claimed the estate had a right to share in the profits of the continuing business.

Black Letter Rule: The representative of the estate of a deceased partner has a right to share in the profits if the other partner continues to operate the business after dissolution.

Adams v. Jarvis

Instant Facts: A doctor in medical partnership sought to claim his statutory share in the partnership's accounts receivable upon his withdrawal, even though the partnership agreement provided that accounts receivable were to remain property of the partnership upon the withdrawal of any partner.

Black Letter Rule: If a partnership agreement provides for continuation, sets forth a method of paying the withdrawing partner his agreed share, and does not jeopardize the rights of creditors, the agreement is enforceable.

8182 Maryland Associates, Limited Partnership v. Sheehan

Instant Facts: After its tenant, a law firm, filed for bankruptcy, a landlord filed suit against all of the firm's current and former partners, claiming that each was personally liable for damages resulting from breach of the lease.

Black Letter Rule: When a partnership signs a lease, the existing partners remain liable for rent even after their withdrawal, unless the lessor agrees otherwise.

Lampert, Hausler & Rodman, Pc v. John F. Gallant, Et Al.

Instant Facts: A law firm sued its former partner for breach of fiduciary duty to collect legal fees from unfinished business after the partner's resignation.

Black Letter Rule: A lawyer may not participate in offering or making an agreement in which a restriction on the lawyer's right to practice is part of the settlement or controversy.

Gibbs v. Breed, Abbott & Morgan

Instant Facts: Two law firm partners sent their new firm a memo setting forth the salaries, bonuses, billable rates, billable hours, and educational backgrounds of partnership employees they wished the new firm to hire.

Black Letter Rule: Withdrawing partners may not disclose confidential partnership information without notifying the partnership.

Bohatch v. Butler & Binion

Instant Facts: An attorney filed suit against the law firm which terminated her for reporting her suspicion that a partner was overbilling clients, alleging that expulsion from a partnership for whistle-blowing constituted a breach of fiduciary duty.

Black Letter Rule: The fiduciary relationship between partners in a law firm does not give rise to a duty not to expel a partner who reports suspected overbilling by another partner.

Martin v. Peyton

Instant Facts: Lenders investing in a near-bankrupt partnership were granted profit sharing and some management rights until they were repaid. When the partnership defaulted on debts, a creditor sued the lenders, contending their rights made them partners and personally liable for partnership debts.

Black Letter Rule: Even partnership creditors who are granted a share of profits and some management control are not necessarily deemed partners if other factors indicate contrary intent.

Smith v. Kelley

Instant Facts: The former employee of an accounting firm brought suit for a partnership accounting, claiming that he became a partner by estoppel because he was held out to the public as a partner in the firm.

Black Letter Rule: The mere fact that one is held out to the public as a partner in a firm does not mean the such person is a partner for intra-firm purposes.

Richert v. Handly

(Capital Contributing Partner) v. *(Services Contributing Partner)*

50 Wash.2d 356 (1957)

THE INTENT OF THE PARTNERS GOVERNS HOW PROFITS AND LOSSES ARE TO BE BORNE

■ **INSTANT FACTS** A partner in a logging venture claimed that he was entitled to reimbursement for his capital contribution when the partnership proved unsuccessful.

■ **BLACK LETTER RULE** Upon termination of a partnership where one partner has contributed capital and another partner has contributed only services, the capital contribution must be reimbursed unless the parties intented otherwise.

■ **PROCEDURAL BASIS**

Appeal to the Supreme Court of Washington challenging the trial court's finding that a capital contributing partner was not entitled to reimbursement from partnership revenues upon termination of the partnership.

■ **FACTS**

C.C. Handly (D) and Mr. Richert (P) entered into a partnership under which Richert (P) agreed to purchase a stand of timber for $26,842 and Handly (D) agreed to log the timber and manage the business. The venture suffered a loss of $9,825.12, a net amount which included $10,000 drawn by Richert (P) and $7,016.88 drawn by Handly (D) from the proceeds of sales. Although the agreement provided that the partners were to share equally in profits and losses, it failed to specify the basis upon which losses were to be shared or whether Richert (P) was to be reimbursed prior to the sharing of profits. The trial court found that the $17,016.88 drawn by the partners were "unexpended revenues," which were to be divided equally. The trial court held that Richert (P) was liable to Handly (D) for $1,491.59, one-half the difference between the amounts drawn by each. The court also held that Richert (P) was not entitled to reimbursement from Hadley (D) for his contribution of capital.

■ **ISSUE**

Are losses to be divided between a partner who contributes only services and one who contributes capital without a reimbursement to the capital contributing partner?

■ **DECISION AND RATIONALE**

(Rosellini, J.)   No. Upon termination of a partnership where one partner has contributed capital and another partner has contributed only services, the capital contribution must be reimbursed unless the partners intended otherwise. The fact that Handly (D) was not personally liable to Richert (P) for his losses does not mean that Richert (P) was not entitled to a reimbursement out of partnership proceeds. Implicit in the court's holding is that the services provided by Handley (D) were worth the $26,842 contribution made by Richert (P), yet the court failed to make such a finding. Furthermore, there is no evidence showing that the parties did not intend for Richert (P) to be reimbursed. In such a case, the court is required to determine the basis upon which losses are to be shared and whether the claims of one partner are to take priority over another; the amount contributed, either in capital or

---

services, by each partner; the total receipts and authorized disbursements; the amounts which each partner has received; and the amount due each partner as per their agreement. Reversed.

Analysis:

This case illustrates the contractual nature of partnership agreements and the importance of establishing the precise manner in which profits and losses are to be shared in a partnership agreement. Note that the court's opinion is devoid of any reference to statutes or case law, which should not be taken to mean that the court was "winging it." Instead, the court wanted a clearer finding as to the intent of the parties. The trust of the court's opinion was that the intent of the parties should govern when a service-partnership agreement fails to provide a method for the sharing of profits and losses. Consequently, the trial court's error was that it failed to determine what the parties intended with respect to reimbursement for Richert's (P) capital contribution, the value of Handly's (D) service and the manner in which profits and losses were to be split.

Richert v. Handly

(Capital Contributing Partner) v. *(Services Contributing Partner)*

53 Wash.2d 121 (1958)

WHERE A PARTNERSHIP AGREEMENT FAILS TO PROVIDE THE BASIS FOR SHARING LOSSES, THE UPA CONTROLS, REQUIRING A SHARE IN LOSSES EQUAL TO THE SHARE IN PROFITS

■ **INSTANT FACTS** After two men entered into a partnership under which one would outlay capital and the other contribute services, the capital contributing partner brought suit seeking a contribution for his capital outlay when the partnership incurred a net loss.

■ **BLACK LETTER RULE** A partner who contributes services to a partnership rather than capital is, nevertheless, required to contribute toward capital losses sustained by the partnership according to his share in the profits.

■ **PROCEDURAL BASIS**

Appeal to the Supreme Court of Washington challenging the trial court's judgment dismissing the parties' complaints.

■ **FACTS**

C.C. Handly (D) and Mr. Richert (P) entered into a partnership under which Richert (P) agreed to purchase a stand of timber for $26,842 and Handly (D) agreed to log the timber and manage the business [sound familiar?]. Although the agreement provided that the partners were to share equally in profits and losses it failed to specify the basis upon which losses were to be shared or whether Richert (P) was to be reimbursed prior to the sharing of profits. For use of Handly's (D) logging, the partnership paid nearly $18,000. During that time Richert (P) drew $10,000 from the partnership. The partnership eventually failed, realizing a net loss of $12,121.78. Richert (P) sought reimbursement from Handly (D) equal to one half the capital contribution less one half of the net losses. On remand, the trial court held that Richert (P) was not entitled to judgment because the agreement did not specify the basis upon which the capital losses were to be borne.

■ **ISSUE**

Must a partner who only contributes services to the partnership bear any capital losses in proportion to his share of the profits?

■ **DECISION AND RATIONALE**

(Hunter, J.) Yes. A partner who contributes to a partnership services rather than capital is, nevertheless, required to contribute toward capital losses sustained by the partnership according to his share of the profits. Since Handly (D) and Richert (P) did not specify the basis upon which losses where to be shared or that the claims of one partner were to take priority over the claim of another, the provisions of the Uniform Partnership Act (UPA) are controlling. Section 18(a) of the UPA specifically provides that each partner must contribute towards the losses, capital or otherwise, sustained by the partnership according to his share in the profits. The UPA also provides that a partner is not entitled to compensation for acting in the partnership business, yet the record discloses that Handly (D) was paid

---

for the logging services he provided. Because he drew $10,000 from the partnership, Richert's (P) capital losses amounted only to $16,842. Furthermore, Richert's (P) one-half share of the net losses equals $6,060.89. Therefore, Handly (D) must reimburse Richert (P) $10,781.11 for the latter's capital losses. Reversed and remanded.

Analysis:

The question presented by *Richert* is whether in a service-partnership (in which one partner contributes capital while the other partner merely contributes services) the service-only partner is monetarily liable for the capital contribution of the other partner. The express language of the UPA seemingly requires such a contribution. Section 18 of the UPA expressly provides that a partner is to be repaid for his *capital* contribution to the partnership. There is no corresponding requirement for the contribution of services. In fact, the UPA provides that a partner is not entitled to compensation for his services. Reading these provisions in conjunction, the court here holds that a service-only partner is to reimburse the capital partner for his contribution to the extent necessary to equalize total losses. Other courts, however, disagree with this position. In their view, such a reading of the statute is a clear frustration of the intent of the parties. ... These polar views notwithstanding, one could read *Richert v. Handly* to require only that a reimbursement of capital is required when the service-only partner is paid for his services.

Bane v. Ferguson

(*Retired Partner*) v. (*Partners*)

890 F.2d 11 (7th Cir. 1989)

PARTNERS IN A LAW FRIM ARE NOT LIABLE TO RETIRED PARTNERS FOR NEGLIGENT MISMAN-AGEMENT CAUSING A LOSS IN PENSION BENEFITS

■ **INSTANT FACTS** A retired attorney sued his former partners for their alleged negligent mismanagement which caused the firm to dissolve, resulting in a loss of pension benefits for retired partners.

■ **BLACK LETTER RULE** A law firm is not liable to a former partner for negligent mismanagement that affects the retired partner's non-contractual pension benefits.

■ **PROCEDURAL BASIS**

Not provided.

■ **FACTS**

Upon his retirement from the law firm of Isham, Lincoln & Beale (Isham Lincoln), Charles Bane (P), a former partner in Isham Lincoln, began to draw pension payments under the firm's retirement plan. The plan provided every retiring partner with a pension, the amount of which depended on the partner's earnings prior to retirement. By its terms, the plan was to cease when the firmed dissolved without any successor entity. Several months after Bane's (P) retirement, Isham Lincoln merged with another firm. After proving a total failure, the merged firm dissolved, causing the pension benefits to cease. Bane (P) brought a suit against a group of former partners (Partners) (D) alleging negligent mismanagement.

■ **ISSUE**

May a retired attorney sue his former partners for their negligent mismanagement that causes the cessation of non-contractual pension benefits?

■ **DECISION AND RATIONALE**

(Posner, Cir. J.) No. A law firm is not liable to a former partner for negligent mismanagement that affects the retired partner's non-contractual pension benefits. An allegation of negligent mismanagement is insufficient to support such a claim under any theory of liability. First, Section 9(3)(c) of the Uniform Partnership Act (UPA), which provides that no partner has the authority to do any act which would make it impossible to carry on ordinary business, does not support liability in this case because the section is aimed at protecting partners, which Bane (P) ceased to be upon retirement. Second, Bane (P) cannot recover under a breach of fiduciary obligations theory. A partnership does not owe retired partners any fiduciary duty; and even if they did, the business judgment rule would shield them from liability. Nor can Bane (P) recover under a contractual theory because the plan specifically provided that it would cease upon dissolution. Bane's (P) claim in tort is that the managers of a failed enterprise owe a duty to those who are harmed by the failure. Although this presents an interesting theory, we find no authority to support it. Affirmed.

Analysis:

Judge Posner's opinion in *Bane v. Ferguson* limits the fiduciary duty owed to former partners. First, Judge Posner suggests that no fiduciary duty is owed by the partnership to its former members. Second, the opinion suggests that even if such a duty were owed, it would not be a broad one. In Judge Posner's view, the *business judgment rule* would shield the partnership from liability for mistakes in management, just as the rule protects directors of corporations from liability to shareholders. If Bane (P) had alleged fraud, self-dealing, or intentional misconduct, however, such allegations, if provable, would be sufficient to pierce the business judgment rule and require the partners to explain their decisions.

National Biscuit Co. v. Stroud

(Partnership Creditor) v. *(Partner)*

249 N.C. 467 (1959)

A PARTNER'S AUTHORITY TO BIND THE PARTNERSHIP CAN BE LIMITED ONLY BY AGREEMENT OF THE PARTNERS

■ **INSTANT FACTS** A partner in a grocery store sought to avoid liability for purchases of bread made by his copartner on the ground that he had informed the store's creditor that he would not be liable for purchases made by his copartner.

■ **BLACK LETTER RULE** A partner in a general partnership cannot deny his liability for the debts of the partnership by informing creditors that he is not liable for a copartner's purchases occurring in the ordinary course of business.

■ **PROCEDURAL BASIS**

Not provided.

■ **FACTS**

C.N. Stroud (D) and Earl Freeman (D) entered into a general partnership to operate a grocery store. The partnership agreement in no way limited the power of either to bind the partnership. In February of 1956, Stroud (D) informed the National Biscuit Co. (Nabisco) (P) that he would not be personally liable for any bread sold to the grocery store. Nevertheless, Nabisco (P) continued to sell bread to the store, which incurred a debt totaling $171.04. Nabisco (P) then sought to recover this amount from Stroud (D).

■ **ISSUE**

May a partner disclaim liability for the debts of the partnership by informing the creditors that he is not liable for the acts of his copartner?

■ **DECISION AND RATIONALE**

(Parker, J.) No. A partner in a general partnership cannot deny his liability for the debts of the partnership by informing a creditor that he is not liable for the acts of his partners occurring in the ordinary course of business. Stroud's (D) notice to Nabisco (P) was insufficient to relieve himself from liability for partnership debts. The Uniform Partnership Act provides that each partner is jointly and severally liable for the debts of the partnership. Furthermore, it is well settled that each partner's acts occurring in the ordinary course of business bind the partnership, unless the partnership agreement states otherwise. This power can only be limited by the express will of a majority of the partnership. Where the partnership is composed of two members, the majority necessarily consists of both partners. Because the purchases of bread were in the ordinary course of the grocery store's business, Stroud (D) is liable for the cost thereof. Affirmed.

Analysis:

Section 9 of the UPA provides each partner with full authority to bind the partnership. In other words, partners are liable for the debts and obligations arising out of a copartner's transaction with third parties for purposes of the partnership's business. This type of authority to bind is knows as "actual authority." UPA § 9 notwithstanding, a partner's actual authority may be limited by an agreement of the partnership. When a third party reasonably believes that the partner is empowered to act for the partnership, the partner is said to act with "apparent authority," regardless of whether the partner has actual authority or not. Usually a partner acts either with both actual and apparent authority, or only with apparent authority if the partnership agreement limits his actual authority. Because Nabisco (P) had been warned that Freeman (D) "lacked" the ability to bind Stroud (D), Freeman (D) was acting with only actual authority. It is an unusual circumstance that a partner has actual but not apparent authority. Yet, as this case shows, a partner who acts with actual authority may bind the partnership, a lack of apparent authority notwithstanding.

Smith v. Dixon

(Partnership) v. *(Lessee)*
238 Ark. 1018 (1965)

A PARTNERSHIP IS BOUND BY A PARTNER WHO TRANSACTS WITH THIRD PARTIES WHO ARE UNDER THE IMPRESSION THAT THE PARTNER HAS AUTHORITY TO ACT

■ **INSTANT FACTS** A partnership sought to revoke a contract for the sale of land on the ground that the managing partner did not have the authority to sell the land for the price of the contract.

■ **BLACK LETTER RULE** A partnership's express limitation on a particular member's power to bind the partnership is insufficient to avoid liability for contracts made with third parties who were unaware of such a limitation and reasonably believed that the partner had the authority to act.

■ **PROCEDURAL BASIS**

Appeal to the Supreme Court of Arkansas challenging the trial court's decision to award the plaintiff special damages.

■ **FACTS**

As managing partner of E.F. Smith & Sons (D), W.R. Smith (D) entered into a contract with Mr. Dixon (P) for the lease and sale of land owned by the partnership (D). When the partnership (D) refused to convey the land as recited in the contract, Dixon (P) instituted a suit for specific performance. The trial court denied specific performance and awarded special damages. The partnership (D) claimed that it was not bound by the acts of W.R. Smith (D) because, although he was authorized to negotiate the sale, he had no authority to accept a price less than $225,000.

■ **ISSUE**

Is a partnership bound by the acts of a partner who acts with apparent authority?

■ **DECISION AND RATIONALE**

(Holt, J.) Yes. A partnership is bound by the acts of a partner who acts with apparent authority. In addition to cases establishing this proposition, sections 9 and 10 of the Uniform Partnership Act (1914) also hold that a partnership is bound to a contract for the sale of land entered into by any partner acting with apparent authority. In this case, it was customary for the partnership (D) to rely on W.R. Smith (D) to transact the business of the partnership (D). Therefore, W.R. Smith (D) was acting with apparent authority that is sufficient to bind the partnership (D). Affirmed.

Analysis:

Whereas in *National Biscuit v. Stroud*, 249 N.C. 467 (1959), the partner sought to escape liability for his partner's purchases by informing the creditor that he would not be personally liable for the purchases, the E.F. Smith & Sons (D) partnership claimed it was not liable to perform the contract because it had effectively limited W.R. Smith's (D) authority to act. Therefore, *National Biscuit* was a case of a partner acting with actual but not apparent authority, and this was a case where the partner acted with apparent but not actual authority. When read in conjunction, the cases establish that a partner may bind the partnership if he acts with either apparent or actual authority. The court here held that Smith (D) acted with apparent authority because the limitation placed on his actual authority had not been communicated to Dixon (P), who reasonably relied on the fact that Smith (D) always conducted business for the partnership (D).

Rouse v. Pollard

(*Client*) v. (*Law Firm Partners*)

129 N.J.Eq. 47 (Ch. 1941)

A PARTNERSHIP IS NOT LIABLE FOR THE MALFEASANCE OF A PARTNER WHOSE ACTS OCCUR OUTSIDE THE SCOPE OF THE PARTNERSHIP'S BUSINESS

■ **INSTANT FACTS** A woman who was defrauded by her attorney sought to recover against the attorney's former partners.

■ **BLACK LETTER RULE** A law firm may not be held vicariously liable for a partner's fraud in connection with investment advice given to clients.

■ **PROCEDURAL BASIS**

Decision of the New Jersey Court of Chancery dismissing a cause of action for failure to state a claim.

■ **FACTS**

Mrs. Rouse (P) was a client of Thomas Fitzsimmons, a partner in the law firm of Riker & Riker. Fitzsimmons had induced Rouse (P) to sell her securities and have Fitzsimmons invest the proceeds in mortgages. For almost ten years Fitzsimmons made biannual interest payments to Rouse (P). In the meantime the firm of Riker & Riker had dissolved. In 1938, Fitzsimmons was arrested for embezzlement and sentenced to prison. The other partners in Riker & Riker (Partners) (D) were neither aware of Fitzsimmons' investment activities nor his fraudulent activity. The Partners' (D) ignorance notwithstanding, Rouse (P) sought to recover from them on the theory that they were liable for Fitzsimmons' professional activities.

■ **ISSUE**

Are the partners in a law firm liable for another partner's misfeasance in connection with investment activities that are not a part of the law firm's usual business?

■ **DECISION AND RATIONALE**

(Bigelow, V.C.) No. A law firm may not be held vicariously liable for a partner's fraud in connection with investment advice given to clients. As a general matter, the receipt of money for the purpose of investing it is not part of the practice of law. It is well settled that, although a partner's acts are binding upon the partnership, one partner's acts occurring outside the scope of the partnership's business cannot bind the partnership. The same is true for fraudulent acts. Although some lawyers indeed receive money from clients for general investment, such is not the normal practice. Furthermore, there is nothing establishing that the firm of Riker & Riker engaged in such activities. Therefore, the Partners (D) are not answerable for fraudulent acts of Fitzsimmons. The complaint is dismissed.

Analysis:

Under the principles of agency, a person is vicariously liable for the negligent or intentional tortious acts of his partner. As this case makes apparent, a partner is *not* liable for acts occurring outside the scope of the partnership's business. Thus, the court's holding turns on whether general investment advice is within the scope of a law firm's business. The court's focus on the "scope of business" requirement is now embodied in UPA § 14. That provision provides, "a partnership is bound to make good the loss...where a partner acting within the scope of his apparent authority receives money or property of a third person and misapplies it." This case might be decided differently today, because § 14 requires only that the partner have acted with "apparent authority."

Roach v. Mead

(Client) v. *(Attorney)*
301 Or. 383 (1986)

A PARTNER'S NEGLIGENT ACTS ARE WITHIN THE SCOPE OF THE PARTNERSHIP'S ORDINARY COURSE OF BUSINESS IF AN INJURED THIRD-PARTY COULD REASONABLY BELIEVE THE ACTS WERE WITHIN SUCH SCOPE

■ **INSTANT FACTS** An attorney sought to avoid vicarious liability for his law partner's negligence by claiming that the loan transaction conducted between the negligent partner and the injured client was outside the scope of the partnership's business.

■ **BLACK LETTER RULE** A law firm may be held liable for a partner's failure to advise his client to seek independent legal advice when the partner enters into a business transaction with the client.

■ **PROCEDURAL BASIS**

Appeal to the Supreme Court of Oregon challenging the decision of the Court of Appeals holding that an attorney was liable for the negligence of his partner.

■ **FACTS**

Kenneth Mead (D) was the attorney for William Roach (P) in connection with traffic violations, business dealings and income tax filings. When Roach (P) asked Mead (D) for advice on investing a portion of the proceeds from the sale of his business, Mead (D) told Roach (P) that he would take the proceeds. Mead (D) then executed a promissory note payable within two years at 15 percent interest. Mead (D) offered to secure the loan with a second mortgage on his home, but Roach (P) left the decision up to Mead (D), who left the loan unsecured. Roach (D) testified he believed the transaction to be legal advice. Mead (D) never repaid the money and was declared bankrupt. Roach (P) subsequently sued Mead (D) and his partner, David Berentson (D), alleging that the partnership failed to: *(1)* disclose the conflict of interest; *(2)* advise Roach (D) to seek independent counsel; *(3)* inform Roach (D) of the risks involved; and *(4)* advise Roach (D) that the loan was usurious and unenforceable. Berentson (D) moved to dismiss on the ground that the loan was outside the partnership's business. The trial court denied the motion and ordered damages in the amount of the initial loan. The Court of Appeals affirmed.

■ **ISSUE**

May a law firm be held liable for a partner's failure to render legal advise to a client with whom the partner enters into a private transaction with?

■ **DECISION AND RATIONALE**

(Jones, J.) Yes. A law firm may be held liable for a partner's failure to advise his client to seek independent legal advice when the partner enters into a business transaction with the client. The Uniform Partnership Act (1914) provides that partners are jointly and severally liable for the tortious acts of other partners if the acts are committed in the ordinary course of the business of the partnership. We have held that if a third person reasonably believes that the services rendered by a member of a professional partnership are part of the partnership's business, the partnership may be bound for negligence incident to those services. As usual, the reasonableness of the third party's belief is a question of fact. Roach (P) does not argue that solicitation of loans from clients was partnership business. Instead, Roach (P) claims that he believed he was getting investment advice from Mead (D) and that advice on the legal aspects of loans and investments in general is a normal part of the practice of law. Mead's (D) failure to advise of Roach's (P) need to seek independent legal counsel, to secure the loan and check Mead's (D) credit, and inform Roach (P) that the loan was unenforceable as being usurious constituted negligence within the scope of the partnership's business. Therefore, Berentson (D) is vicariously liable for Mead's (D) negligent acts. Affirmed.

Analysis:

Together, UPA §§ 13 and 15 make the partnership jointly and severally liable for the negligence of other partners acting "in the ordinary course of the business of the partnership." The court's holding suggests that what is in the ordinary course of a partnership's business is dependent on the reasonable beliefs of the injured third party. Therefore, Berentson (D) was held liable for Mead's (D) acts because Roach (P) thought that he was getting legal advice when he made the loan. Holding Berentson (D) liable was probably the correct outcome, but also for other reasons beyond the court's analysis. The court expressly points out that Roach (P) was not claiming that investment advice was part of the firm's business. Instead, the court interpreted Roach's (P) claim to allege that he believed Mead (D) was giving legal advice. The issue then becomes whether Mead (D) and Roach (P) were in an attorney-client relationship when the loan was made. If such a relationship existed, Mead (D) would have been required to render the advice. The failure to do so would constitute negligence for which Berentson (D) would be liable.

Meinhard v. Salmon

(Partner) v. *(Partner)*
249 N.Y. 458, 164 N.E. 545 (Ct. App. 1928)

PARTNERS HAVE A FIDUCIARY DUTY TO SHARE BUSINESS OPPORTUNITIES

■ **INSTANT FACTS** A partnership is offered a profitable lease and one partner accepts it for himself, prompting the other to demand participation.

■ **BLACK LETTER RULE** Partners' fiduciary duties of loyalty forbid appropriating opportunities offered to the partnership.

■ **PROCEDURAL BASIS**

Appeal from appellate court judgment modifying and affirming a judgment for plaintiff, founded on referee's report, in contract action seeking declaratory judgment and equitable relief.

■ **FACTS**

Salmon (D), a real estate broker, leased a hotel from Gerry for 20 years, planning to convert it into shops, and took on Meinhard (P), a wool merchant, as his silent partner. [Yet it was Salmon who pulled the wool over Meinhard.] Their agreement provided that (i) Meinhard (P) would provide half the cost of leasing, maintaining and converting the hotel, (ii) Meinhard (P) would be paid 40% of the net profits for the first 5 years and 50% each year thereafter, and (iii) Salmon (D) alone was to manage the building. After 20 years, during which both partners earned rich returns, Gerry offered Salmon (D) a long-term lease on the building at favorable terms. Salmon (D), without telling Meinhard (P) about the offer, accepted it for himself alone through his controlled company. Meinhard (P), upon learning of the deal, demanded to be allowed to participate in the offer. When Salmon (D) refused, Meinhard (P) sued, contending that Salmon (D), as his partner, had a duty to offer him participation in the lucrative opportunity. Salmon (D) apparently contended that (i) Gerry offered the lease to him individually, (ii) since the partnership's original 20-year term was near its end, he was again free to act in his own interests, and (iii) Meinhard (P) effectively waived rights to the new lease because he never mentioned his interest in renewing. At trial, the referee found for Meinhard (P), but gave him only a 25% share in the new lease, because the 25% in the new, more profitable lease was calculated to have the same monetary value as his original 50% share in the old lease. On cross-appeal, the appellate court affirmed the decision for Meinhard (P) and modified it to award him a 50% share. Salmon (D) appealed.

■ **ISSUE**

As a joint venture terminates, can partners individually accept opportunities offered that relate to the partnership?

■ **DECISION AND RATIONALE**

(Cardozo, J.) No. Partners' fiduciary duties of loyalty forbid appropriating opportunities offered to the partnership. Their agreement made Salmon (D) and Meinhard (P) coadventurers (partners), since they had agreed to share profits and losses. Thus, as partners they owed each other duties of loyalty. Salmon (D) had an even greater duty, as both partner and manager. The duty of loyalty is fiduciary, so partners as fiduciaries owe each other the very highest standard of loyalty, honesty, and honor. Since partners are "held to something stricter than the morals of the marketplace," their fiduciary duty may prohibit them from performing business acts which are otherwise legal, and arguably moral. Thus, here, Salmon (D) had a duty to inform Meinhard (P) of the lease offer, to at least allow him a chance to compete for it. We will not rule on the issue of whether Salmon (D), had he won this competition, would then be required to continue the partnership by granting Meinhard (P) participation. That the lease was offered by Gerry to Salmon (D) personally is irrelevant. Although Gerry may not have known Salmon (D) represented a partnership, Salmon (D) was a partnership agent and bound to represent the partnership faithfully in accepting. Also, there is no proof that Gerry intended to offer the lease only to Salmon (D), and would not have offered it to Meinhard (P). That Meinhard (P) did not propose a lease extension is also irrelevant, since he had no obligation to monitor matters which Salmon (D) handled exclusively as manager. We do not find that Salmon (D) intended to defraud Meinhard (P). It is likely he assumed in good faith that, since the partnership was ending, he was free to take the new lease for himself. This act would be proper for a competitor, but not for a managing coadventurer, whose duty of loyalty must be supreme, and here included bringing related opportunities to his partner's attention. The rule may be different if one partner is offered an opportunity unrelated to his position as a partner/manager. Here, however, the new opportunity was an extension of the old one, so Salmon (D) should have expected reproach for appropriating it. As for the proper relief, the court previously held that the new lease should be held in trust by Salmon (D) and his company for Meinhard (P), but we find this inefficient, since it restricts Salmon (D) from selling his portion. Partitioning the building itself would be impractical. Instead, we order that the new lease be divided into shares, and that Salmon (D) be awarded 50% plus one share, with Meinhard (P) taking the rest. This slight majority allows Salmon (D) to continue exercising control during the new lease, as he exercised during the old one, and as he would reasonably expect if the partnership continued.

■ DISSENT

(Andrews, J.) The opinion would be correct if applied to a general partnership, but not to the instant agreement, which was a joint venture with a limited objective and time.

Analysis:

Generally, partners' and agents' fiduciary duty of loyalty prohibits them from appropriating for themselves profitable opportunities offered to the partnership/principal. The policy reasons are obvious, but the extent of the rule is not. This case leaves open the issue of whether opportunities seemingly unrelated to the partnership/agency properly belong to it. The holding that partners owe to each other the utmost duty and honor makes it difficult to limit a partnership's term or scope, even by explicit agreement. This may create uncertainty about how partners can provide for their future as a partnership is dissolving. For instance, consider a law firm/partnership that is dissolving, intentionally or not. Once the partnership terminates, the former partners will revert to competitors. In the meantime, it is likely the partnership still has continuing clients, which each partner would like to appropriate for his own later practice. To forbid any partner from soliciting them seems a waste of goodwill, but under the default rules set by *Meinhard v. Salmon,* it is unclear whether any of the partners can solicit them without violating his or her broad duty to other partners.

■ CASE VOCABULARY

FIDUCIARY: Relationship by which one is required to act in another's best interest, esp. an agent, partner, or legal guardian.

JOINT VENTURE: a.k.a. "joint adventure." A partnership with a specified aim or project.

Collins v. Lewis

(Partner) v. *(Partner)*
283 S.W.2d 258 (Tex. Civ. App. 1955)

A PARTNER WHO CHOOSES TO UNILATERALLY DISSOLVE THE PARTNERSHIP MAY BE HELD LIABLE FOR A BREACH OF THE PARTNERSHIP AGREEMENT

■ **INSTANT FACTS** A partner in a cafeteria business sought to have a court dissolve the partnership after the cafeteria initially proved unprofitable.

■ **BLACK LETTER RULE** A court will not grant dissolution to a partner who has failed to perform his obligations under the partnership agreement.

■ PROCEDURAL BASIS

Appeal from the judgment of the trial court denying the dissolution of a partnership.

■ FACTS

John Lewis (D) and Carr Collins (P) formed a partnership to establish and operate a cafeteria. Under the partnership agreement, Lewis (D) was to provide the lease and management experience, while Collins (P) would furnish the money. The partners' undertaking encountered innumerable difficulties requiring Collins (P) to advance funds in excess of $600,000, twice the amount originally contemplated by Lewis (D) and Collins (P). These setbacks notwithstanding, the partners continued with their venture and, eventually, the cafeteria opened for business. When the cafeteria initially proved unprofitable, Collins (P) demanded that Lewis (D) restore the business to profitability. The relationship then became acrimonious. Collins (P) filed suit seeking a dissolution of the partnership. At trial, the jury, paradoxically, found: (1) Lewis (D) was capable of running the business at a profit; (2) the business had no reasonable expectation of profit while Lewis (D) continued to manage it; and (3) Collins' (P) interference made it impossible for the cafeteria to earn a profit. Based on those findings, the trial court entered a judgment denying Collins (P) relief. Collins (P) appealed, positing, among other arguments, that there is no such thing as an indissoluble partnership and that the right to dissolution exists whenever the partnership has no reasonable expectation of profit.

■ ISSUE

Does a partner always have the right to a dissolve a partnership?

■ DECISION AND RATIONALE

(Hamblen, J.) No. A court will not grant dissolution to a partner who has failed to perform his obligations under the partnership agreement. We agree with the proposition that there is no such thing as an indissoluble partnership. But the fact that a partner has the power to dissolve the partnership does not mean he has a legal right to do so. The legal right to dissolution is an equitable right. In this case, the jury found that it was Collins' (P) conduct that made the business unprofitable. We know of no rule which grants a partner who had failed to perform his obligations under the partnership the right to dissolve the partnership. The Supreme Court has held that a court of equity will not assist a partner in breach of the agreement to procure a dissolution. That is not to say, however, that the parties must endure a venture with no expectation of profit. Either may dissolve the partnership at any time. The partner who chooses to do so may be liable for damages flowing from a breach of contract. Affirmed.

Analysis:

A partnership is a contractual relationship. As such, the contracting parties—the partners—have the power to terminate the relationship. But the unilateral exercise of that power may effect a breach of contract. The court here holds that a partner does not always have a right—contractual or statutory—to dissolution of the partnership. It is difficult to say whether the case would come out differently under the UPA. Certainly, the UPA provides that a partner may dissolve a partnership that has an indefinite term. Because this case was decided prior to Texas' enactment of the UPA, the court fails to discuss whether the partnership was indefinite.

Cauble v. Handler

(Estate of Deceased Partner) v. (Surviving Partner)

503 S.W.2d 362 (Tx. App. 1973)

A RETIRED PARTNER OR THE ESTATE OF A DECEASED PARTNER HAS A RIGHT TO SHARE IN THE PROFITS OF THE PARTNERSHIP IF THE BUSINESS CONTINUES TO OPERATE AFTER DISSOLUTION

■ **INSTANT FACTS** When the surviving partner in a furniture store continued to operate the business after a suit for an accounting was filed by the deceased partner's estate, the administratrix claimed the estate had a right to share in the profits of the continuing business.

■ **BLACK LETTER RULE** The representative of the estate of a deceased partner has a right to share in the profits if the other partner continues to operate the business after dissolution.

■ PROCEDURAL BASIS

Appeal from the trial court's decision entering a judgment in the amount of $20.95 for the deceased partner's estate.

■ FACTS

Tom Handler (D) and Thomas Cauble (P) were equal partners in a furniture and appliance store. After Cauble's (P) death, the administratrix of Cauble's (P) estate brought suit against Handler (D) for an accounting of the partnership's assets. Handler (D), who took an inventory of the partnership's assets upon Cauble's (P) death, continued to operate the business after the partner's death, making a profit of $40,163.42. In determining the value of the partnership's assets, the trial court relied on Handler's (D) inventory which used the book value. Instead of awarding Cauble's (P) estate a share of the profits from Handler's (D) operation of the business, the trial court awarded an interest in the amount of $3,764.89, taxing to the estate the full cost of the auditor's fee.

■ ISSUE

Does the estate of a deceased partner have the right to share in the profits of the business if the surviving partner elects to carry on the business after dissolution?

■ DECISION AND RATIONALE

(Brewster, J.) Yes. If he so elects, the representative of the estate of a deceased partner has a right to share in the profits when the other partner continues to operate the business after dissolution. The Uniform Partnership Act (1914) (UPA) gives the estate of a deceased partner (or a retiring partner) several options upon dissolution. First, he can force the partnership's assets to be liquidated, its debts paid, and his share in the surplus paid to him in cash. Cauble's (P) administratrix did not make this election. If the business continues, the estate has two primary options. It may force a liquidation and take its part of the proceeds, sharing in the profits and losses after dissolution. The estate may also elect to permit the business to continue and claim as creditor the value of its interest at dissolution. If the estate takes this latter route, the estate may choose to receive either the value of its interest upon dissolution or the profits attributable to the use of his interest in the partnership. The facts establish that Cauble's (P) estate elected to have the value of Cauble's (P) interest at dissolution ascertained and to receive an amount equal to the value of that interest, plus the profits attributable to his right in the property of the dissolved partnership. It was error for the court to refuse to allow Cauble's (P) administratrix a share in the profits made by Handler (D) by continuing the partnership business between the date of dissolution and the date of judgment. It was also error for the court to rely on the book value of the inventory for determining the value of the partnership's assets. The court should have used the market value of that inventory. Finally, the court erred in taxing the auditor's fee entirely to the Cauble's (P) estate. One partner should not have to rely on the adverse party's word for the state of the partnership's account. Thus such fees are paid out of the partnership's assets. Reversed and remanded.

Analysis:

This case illustrates the confusion that can result from the death or retirement of a partner when the partnership agreement does not provide its own process for dealing with such an event. The UPA controls when the partnership agreement is silent on this point. Often the business of a partnership will continue after the death or retirement of one or more partners. After all, the business is, most likely, the source of livelihood for the remaining partners. When the business is continued, UPA § 42 gives a retired partner (or a deceased partner's estate) two options. First, the partner can have the value of his interest in the partnership as of the date of dissolution. As have most courts, the Texas Court of Appeals held that a partner's interest is to be determined based on the fair market value of the partnership's assets. In lieu of that interest, the retired partner may elect to share in the profits attributable to the use of his interest. Essentially, he can share in the profits without the risk of any losses. The reason for giving this generous option to retired partners is to compel the remaining partners to wind up the partnership as soon as possible.

■ CASE VOCABULARY

BOOK VALUE: The value at which an asset is carried on a company's balance sheet.

Adams v. Jarvis

(Withdrawing Partner) v. *(Remaining Partners)*

23 Wis.2d 453 (1964)

A PARTNERSHIP MAY AGREE TO ITS OWN RULES OUTLINING THE RIGHTS AND OBLIGATIONS OF A WITHDRAWING PARTNER

■ **INSTANT FACTS** A doctor in medical partnership sought to claim his statutory share in the partnership's accounts receivable upon his withdrawal, even though the partnership agreement provided that accounts receivable were to remain property of the partnership upon the withdrawal of any partner.

■ **BLACK LETTER RULE** If a partnership agreement provides for continuation, sets forth a method of paying the withdrawing partner his agreed share, and does not jeopardize the rights of creditors, the agreement is enforceable.

■ **PROCEDURAL BASIS**

Appeal from the trial court's conclusion that the withdrawal of a partner effected a statutory dissolution entitling the withdrawing partner to a liquidation.

■ **FACTS**

Dr. Adams (P) was a partner in The Tomahawk Clinic (D). The clinic's partnership agreement provided that the withdrawal of any partner would not terminate the partnership and established a method for paying any withdrawing partner his share of partnership assets. However, the agreement specifically excluded current accounts receivable from the withdrawing partner's share. Dr. Adams (P) filed suit, claiming that his withdrawal constituted a statutory dissolution of the partnership agreement, giving him the right to elect a liquidation of all assets, including the accounts receivable. The trial court agreed and concluded that Dr. Adams (P) was entitled to a one-third interest in the accounts receivable.

■ **ISSUE**

Does a withdrawal of a partner constitute a statutory dissolution of the partnership, notwithstanding a partnership agreement to the contrary?

■ **DECISION AND RATIONALE**

(Beilfuss, J.) No. If a partnership agreement provides for continuation, sets forth a method of paying the withdrawing partner his agreed share, and does not jeopardize the rights of creditors, the agreement is enforceable. Just because the Uniform Partnership Act (1914) (UPA) does not contemplate this type of withdrawal with a continuation of the business, its provisions should not be construed to invalidate an otherwise valid, enforceable contract. Nothing in the UPA expressly forbids partners from agreeing to their own withdrawal procedure. As to the accounts receivable, Dr. Adams (P) argues that the agreement effects a forfeiture and is violative of public policy. We disagree. Dr. Adams (P) was on equal bargaining ground when he entered into the agreement. Furthermore, the provision is designed for legitimate reasons. We do note, however, that because the liquidation of accounts receivable does impact year-end profits, to which Dr. Adams (P) is partly entitled, the remaining partners stand in a fiduciary relationship and must make good faith efforts to collect on the accounts. Reversed.

Analysis:

The UPA provisions regarding the rights of withdrawing, retiring, or deceased partners are not mandatory. The UPA gives partners a strong incentive to wind up the partnership after dissolution. Termination of the partnership, however, is not always desirable. The court here held that, even though a dissolution under the UPA had occurred, the provisions regarding the rights of a withdrawing partner need not supersede the partnership agreement. Accordingly, a partnership agreement can provide the partners respective rights upon dissolution. The policy behind the court's holding is that a partnership agreement is a contract, and contractual rights should not be interfered with unless there is a statutory mandate or some overriding public policy demanding that the agreement not be enforced.

8182 Maryland Associates, Limited Partnership v. Sheehan

(Landlord) v. *(Former Partners)*

14 S.W.3d 576 (Mo. 2000)

DISSOLUTION ALONE DOES NOT RELIEVE PARTNERS OF LIABILITY FOR THE DEBTS OF THE PARTNERSHIP

■ **INSTANT FACTS** After its tenant, a law firm, filed for bankruptcy, a landlord filed suit against all of the firm's current and former partners, claiming that each was personally liable for damages resulting from breach of the lease.

■ **BLACK LETTER RULE** When a partnership signs a lease, the existing partners remain liable for rent even after their withdrawal, unless the lessor agrees otherwise.

■ **PROCEDURAL BASIS**

Appeal to the Supreme Court of Missouri challenging the decision of the trial court granting summary judgment to the former members of a partnership, which had defaulted on its lease.

■ **FACTS**

In the spring of 1984, the general partnership of Popkin, Stern, Heifitz, Lurie, Sheehan, Reby, & Chervitz, a law firm, entered into a lease with 8182 Maryland Associates, Limited Partnership (8182 Maryland) (P). Richard Sheehan (D) and 13 other general partners signed the lease. The firm occupied office space under the lease with 8182 Maryland (P) from 1986 to 1991, at which point the firm defaulted on its lease. During that same period, Sheehan (D) withdrew from the partnership, the partnership changed its name to Popkin & Stern, and Timothy Noelker, Douglas Burdette, Barbara Lageson and Jeffrey Klar (Incoming Partners) (D) all joined the firm as partners, withdrawing prior to the firm's default. When the firm filed for bankruptcy 8182 Maryland (P) filed suit against all former and current partners, claiming each was personally liable on the lease. The trial court granted summary judgment to all former partners who had not been dismissed as defendants. 8182 Maryland (P) appealed.

■ **ISSUE**

Does the act of withdrawal relieve a partner of his obligation under a lease entered into by the partnership while he was a member?

■ **DECISION AND RATIONALE**

(Price, C.J.) No. When a partnership signs a lease, the existing partners remain liable for rent even after their withdrawal, unless the lessor agrees otherwise. Section 29 of the Uniform Partnership Act (UPA) expressly states that the withdrawal of one partner effects a dissolution of the partnership. The UPA goes on to provide that dissolution does not discharge the existing liability of any partner. Such liability may be discharged upon agreement of the partner, the partnership and the creditor whose rights are at issue. When the lease with 8182 Maryland (P) was signed by Sheehan (D) and his partners, they all became personally liable for its performance. Thus, Sheehan (D) remained liable on the lease until 8182 Maryland (P) agreed otherwise, which it did not. The fact that Sheehan (D) withdrew from the partnership prior to the firm's occupancy is immaterial because he became *jointly* and *severally* liable upon signing the lease. We also reject Sheehan's (D) argument that he was

---

absolved of liability because no breach occurred prior to his withdrawal. As we have stated, liability for partnership obligations does not cease simply by disassociating oneself from the partnership business. The issue of the personal liability of the Incoming Partners (D) presents a different issue. Although the UPA does not expressly make the admission of a new partner grounds for dissolution, it is generally agreed that any change in membership effects a dissolution. Thus, when the Incoming Partners (D) were admitted, the existing partnership was dissolved but never terminated. These "new" partnerships were liable for the lease because UPA § 41 provides that creditors of the old partnership also become creditors of the new partnership. Section 7, however, limits an incoming partner's liability for all preexisting obligations of the partnership to his interest in partnership property. This would seem to absolve the Incoming Partners (D) of liability. However, a lease obligation arises under theories of both contract and property. Under the doctrine of privity of estate, a lessee is liable for rents regardless of whether there exists a written contract. Thus the new partners were liable while they occupied the premises. When the Incoming Partners (D) withdrew, they were no longer in privity of estate with 8182 Maryland (P) and their obligations as tenants ceased. Therefore, the Incoming Partners (D) are not liable for breach of the lease because they performed their obligations while in possession of the premises. Reversed in part and affirmed in part.

Analysis:

Under the common law the withdrawal of a partner meant that the "old" partnership was dissolved and a "new" partnership was formed. However, the common law did not provide that the creditors of the old partnership were creditors of the new partnership. UPA § 41 changes this inequity by expressly treating all creditors alike, regardless of membership. Sheehan's (D) liability is expressly governed by UPA § 36(b), which provides that dissolution itself does not discharge a partner from his existing liability. Upon Sheehan's (D) withdrawal, a "new" partnership was formed, carrying with it the "old" partnership's obligations (including the lease) under UPA § 41. When the Incoming Partners (D) joined the firm, a new partnership was again formed, again taking with it the obligations of the "old" and "older" partnerships. But under UPA § 17, the incoming Partners (D) were liable for preexisting debts only to the extent of their interest in the partnership.

Lampert, Hausler & Rodman, PC v. John F. Gallant, et al.

(Law Firm) v. *(Former Partner)*

18 Mass. L. Rptr. 614, 2004 WL 3120801 (Super. Ct. 2004)

A LAW CORPORATION MAY AGREE TO SPLIT FEES FROM UNFINISHED BUSINESS

■ **INSTANT FACTS** A law firm sued its former partner for breach of fiduciary duty to collect legal fees from unfinished business after the partner's resignation.

■ **BLACK LETTER RULES** A lawyer may not participate in offering or making an agreement in which a restriction on the lawyer's right to practice is part of the settlement or controversy.

■ **PROCEDURAL BASIS**

Trial court consideration of the plaintiff's motion for partial summary judgment.

■ **FACTS**

Gallant (D) was a shareholder in a law firm formed as a professional corporation. The firm never memorialized in writing how legal fees from unfinished business or dissolution of the firm should be distributed. When Gallant (D) resigned, taking certain clients with him to his new competing firm located in the same town, the law firm (P) sued him for breach of fiduciary duty and recovery of the contingent fees from matters not completed at the time of resignation. Gallant (D) likewise filed a counterclaim for breach of fiduciary duty. The law firm (P) moved for partial summary judgment on the issue of breach of fiduciary duty.

■ **ISSUE**

May a law corporation enforce a fiduciary duty owed by a former partner in a way that restricts his ability to practice law?

■ **DECISION AND RATIONALE**

(Van Gestel, J.) No. Lawyers in a partnership owe their former partners a fiduciary duty not to improperly solicit clients. The Massachusetts Rules of Professional Conduct require that "[a] lawyer shall not participate in offering or making: (b) an agreement in which a restriction on the lawyer's right to practice is part of the settlement or controversy." The rule furthers clients' free choice of counsel and forbids restrictions on competition in all partnership agreements. However, a law firm is entitled to some measure of protection of its financial survival when a partner's departure strips the firm of substantial fees while leaving significant partnership debt. And although these important interests are not at stake here, the interests of clients and potential clients must also be protected. Lawyers cannot forsake the interests of their clients by enforcing a fiduciary duty to refrain from competition. Therefore, where an agreement to forfeit fees includes a restriction on a lawyer's ability to practice law, the agreement will be severed to eliminate the offending provisions and enforced to the extent capable under the law. This remedy recognizes the fiduciary duties owed among the former partners without sacrificing the clients' interests in retaining counsel of their choice. Accordingly, the motion for partial summary judgment is granted insofar as it does not restrict Gallant's (D) ability to practice law.

Analysis:

It is clear from the canons of ethics that the agreement involved here would not be permitted if the clients themselves were forbidden from choosing Gallant (D) as their attorney. A fee-splitting provision does not always, however, involve such a restriction. Agreements establishing the method for splitting fees upon a lawyer's resignation or the dissolution of a law firm are commonplace and enforceable when carefully drafted.

■ CASE VOCABULARY

FIDUCIARY: One who owes to another the duties of good faith, trust, confidence, and candor.

CLOSE CORPORATION: A corporation whose stock is not freely traded and is held by only a few shareholders (often within the same family).

Gibbs v. Breed, Abbott & Morgan

(*Former Partner*) v. (*Partnership*)

271 A.D.2d 180, 710 N.Y.S.2d 578 (App. Div. 2000)

WITHDRAWING PARTNERS MAY NOT DISCLOSE CONFIDENTIAL PARTNERSHIP INFORMATION WITHOUT NOTIFYING THE PARTNERSHIP

■ **INSTANT FACTS** Two law firm partners sent their new firm a memo setting forth the salaries, bonuses, billable rates, billable hours, and educational backgrounds of partnership employees they wished the new firm to hire.

■ **BLACK LETTER RULE** Withdrawing partners may not disclose confidential partnership information without notifying the partnership.

■ **PROCEDURAL BASIS**

Appeal of action for breach of fiduciary duty.

■ **FACTS**

Gibbs (P) and Sheehan (P) were partners in the trust and estate department of Breed Abbott & Morgan (BAM) (D). They left BAM in 1991 to join Chadbourne & Park (Chadbourne). After giving notice to BAM that they were leaving, Gibbs (P) and Sheehan (P) sent Chadboume a memo regarding the other personnel in BAM's (D) trust and estate department, including their salaries, billable hours, billable rate, and educational background. Gibbs (P) and Sheehan (P) had prepared the memo months earlier in anticipation of discussions with prospective firms. Chadbourne interviewed four BAM (D) employees before Gibbs (P) and Sheehan (P) left. Before Gibbs (P) and Sheehan (P) left BAM (D), they wrote letters to clients informing them that they were leaving and that other BAM (D) attorneys could serve them. Gibbs (P) and Sheehan (P) took their chronology files with them when they left. After they left, they began contacting former clients and several other BAM (D) employees left BAM (D) for Chadbourne. Gibbs (P) and Sheehan (P) sued BAM (D) for money they alleged were due them under their BAM (D) partnership. BAM (D) countersued, alleging that Gibbs (P) and Sheehan (P) breached their fiduciary duty to BAM (D). The trial court held that Gibbs (P) and Sheehan (P) breached their duty to BAM (D) when Gibbs (P) persuaded Sheehan (P) to leave BAM, when they gave Chadbourne the memo regarding BAM (D) employees, and when they took their chronological files. It ruled that Gibbs (P) and Sheehan (P) were jointly and severally liable for $1,861,045.

■ **ISSUE**

May withdrawing partners disclose confidential partnership information without notifying the partnership?

■ **DECISION AND RATIONALE**

(Mazzarelli, J.) No. Withdrawing partners may not disclose confidential partnership information without notifying the partnership. Partners owe each other a duty of loyalty and good faith. We agree that Gibbs (P) and Sheehan (P) breached their fiduciary duty by supplying Chadbourne with information about BAM (D) employees. However, we find no breach with respect to Gibb's (P) interactions with Sheehan (P) or with either partner's removal of their chronological files. Gibbs (P) testified that he refrained from telling one of his partners that he planned to recruit specific employees from BAM (D).

Pre-withdrawal recruitment is generally allowed only after the lawyer has given a firm notice of his or her withdrawal. The memo gave Chadbourne an unfair advantage in recruiting the employees. The breach occurred before Gibbs (P) and Sheehan (P) gave notice to BAM (D) of their intent to leave, and could not be cured by their after-the-fact notification. The memo, including the information regarding employee bonuses, was confidential. The dissent's statement that such information was known to headhunters is without foundation. The information in the memo went directly to the employees' value and were accessible only by BAM (D) partners.

■ CONCURRENCE AND DISSENT

(Saxe, J.) I disagree that Gibbs (P) and Sheehan (P) breached their duty of loyalty by sending the memo about BAM (D) employees to Chadbourne. Soliciting partnership employees is not the same as soliciting partnership clients. Soliciting clients may be prohibited because it competes with the partnership for business. There is no evidence that Gibbs (P) and Sheehan (P) gave the memo to Chadbourne before they gave notice to BAM (D). The salaries and bonuses of law firm employees is widely known outside the firms. It is not some sort of trade secret. I would reverse and dismiss the counterclaims in their entirety.

Analysis:

A partner's duty of loyalty to a partnership is quite broad. Under this duty, a partner may not avail himself of knowledge that is considered the partnership's property. The majority and the dissent agree regarding the existence and scope of this duty. They both agree that information, such as client lists, may be partnership property. They disagree over a factual question: whether the information contained in the memo Gibbs (P) and Sheehan (P) sent to Chadbourne was in fact partnership property or was publicly available.

■ CASE VOCABULARY

HEADHUNTER: Legal placement and recruitment firm.

Bohatch v. Butler & Binion

(Expelled Partner) v. *(Law Firm)*
977 S.W.2d 543 (Tex. 1998)

THE EXPULSION OF A PARTNER FOR ENGAGING IN WHISTLE-BLOWING ACTIVITIES DOES NOT CONSTITUTE A BREACH OF FIDUCIARY DUTY

■ INSTANT FACTS An attorney filed suit against the law firm which terminated her for reporting her suspicion that a partner was overbilling clients, alleging that expulsion from a partnership for whistle-blowing constituted a breach of fiduciary duty.

■ BLACK LETTER RULE The fiduciary relationship between partners in a law firm does not give rise to a duty not to expel a partner who reports suspected overbilling by another partner.

■ PROCEDURAL BASIS

Appeal to the Supreme Court of Texas challenging the decision of the court of appeals reversing the judgment of the trial court and holding that expulsion of a partner for whistle-blowing was not a breach of a fiduciary duty.

■ FACTS

Colette Bohatch (P), an attorney and partner in the firm of Butler & Binion (D), was expelled from the partnership after she reported her suspicion that another partner was overbilling a client. The client, however, found no irregularities and was satisfied with the reasonableness of the bills. One month later, Bohatch (P) was informed that an investigation revealed no basis for her allegations and that she should begin looking for other employment. Over the next year Bohatch (P) received no work from the firm and was denied a partnership distribution. A year after making her allegations, Butler & Binion (D) informed Bohatch (P) that she should vacate her office. Bohatch (P) subsequently filed suit; the firm voted to expel her shortly thereafter. After the jury found that the partners in Butler & Binion (D) had violated their fiduciary duty and breached the partnership agreement, the trial court entered a judgment for Bohatch (P). Finding no evidence of a breach of fiduciary duty, the court of appeals reversed in part.

■ ISSUE

Does the fiduciary relationship between and among partners create an exception to the at-will nature of partnerships giving rise to a duty not to expel a partner who reports her suspicion of overbilling by another partner?

■ DECISION AND RATIONALE

(Enoch, J.) No. The fiduciary relationship between partners in a law firm does not give rise to a duty not to expel a partner who reports suspected overbilling by another partner. Because neither the Uniform Partnership Act nor Butler & Binion's (P) partnership agreement address the issue of expulsion for an improper purpose, we must look to the common law to find the principles governing Bohatch's (P) claim that the firm breached a fiduciary duty. Several other states have held that a partnership may expel a partner for purely business reasons. Furthermore, it is well settled that the fiduciary duty partners owe to each other does not require a duty to remain partners. We are asked to create an

---

exception to this proposition which would require a partnership to retain a whistle-blower partner. Bohatch (P) argues that such an exception is necessary to prevent law firms from retaliating against an attorney who fulfills her ethical obligation to report overbilling. The argument has some merit, but we reject it nevertheless. The simple fact is that once charges of this kind are made, partners may find it difficult to continue to work together. We do not see how the trust relationship necessary for a law firm's existence and effective representation of clients can survive allegations of overbilling. We do realize that our decision may place attorneys in the difficult position of choosing between their careers and their ethical duties. However, the profession sometimes demands that such difficult decisions be made. The fact that ethical duties may create an irreparable schism within a partnership does not transform expulsion of whistle-blowers into a tort. As to Bohatch's (D) claim for breach of contract we find that the court of appeals correctly held that Butler & Binion (P) improperly withheld Bohatch's (D) monthly draw and tentative distribution.

■ CONCURRENCE

(Hecht, J.) Both the majority and the dissent see this case as presenting a choice between promoting the trust necessary to form a partnership and the duty of an attorney to report overbilling of clients. I believe that there is a middle ground, where some expulsions for reporting ethical violations are culpable while others are not. For example, I do not believe that a firm of five hundred attorneys would be as affected by such accusation as would a firm of only five attorneys. Furthermore, I believe that a firm can always expel a partner for exercising poor judgment, albeit in good faith. Therefore, I would hold that Butler & Binion (D) did not breach its fiduciary duty by expelling Bohatch (P) because her charges proved groundless and destroyed her relationship with the partners in the process.

■ DISSENT

(Spector, J.) I would hold that partners violate their fiduciary duty to one another by punishing compliance with the Disciplinary Rules of Professional Conduct. These rules should be incorporated into the fiduciary relationship among law partners. Although the evidence here is not conclusive, it is ample to support the jury's finding that Bohatch (P) made a good faith effort to comply with ethical rules and that Butler & Binion (D) retaliated against her for doing so. The Court's holding sends an inappropriate signal to lawyers and to the public that the rules of professional responsibility are subordinate to the firm's other interests.

Analysis:

The Supreme Court of Texas was the first high court of any state to decide whether there should be an exception to the at-will nature of partnerships to protect whistle-blowing attorneys. The argument for the exception was based on the Rules of Professional Responsibility, which require an attorney to report attorney misconduct, including overbilling. Nevertheless, the court was unwilling to create an exception, justifying its holding on the grounds that whistle-blowing often causes amongst partners an irreparable rift that affects both the conduct of business and the representation of clients. From the point of view of partnership law, the court's holding is correct, because partnerships are voluntary associations and a partner should not be forced to work with someone he does not trust.

Martin v. Peyton

(Partnership's Creditor) v. *(Alleged Partner)*
246 N.Y. 213, 158 N.E. 77 (Ct. App. 1927)

PARTIES MAY IMPLICITLY FORM A PARTNERSHIP THROUGH THEIR CONDUCT

■ **INSTANT FACTS** Lenders investing in a near-bankrupt partnership were granted profit sharing and some management rights until they were repaid. When the partnership defaulted on debts, a creditor sued the lenders, contending their rights made them partners and personally liable for partnership debts.

■ **BLACK LETTER RULE** Even partnership creditors who are granted a share of profits and some management control are not necessarily deemed partners if other factors indicate contrary intent.

■ PROCEDURAL BASIS

Appeal from appellate court judgment, based on referee's report, for defendants in contract action seeking damages [and possibly declaratory judgment].

■ FACTS

Knauth, Nachod & Kuhne ("K.N. & K.") (D), a banking and brokerage partnership, made speculative investments which nearly bankrupted it. Needing money to keep the firm operating, Hall (D), a partner, arranged for it to borrow from his friend Peyton (D) $500,000 in bonds to use as collateral for needed bank loans. Needing more, Hall (D) then arranged for it to borrow another $2,500,000 from Peyton (D), and Freeman (D) [and possibly Perkins (D) and his wife (D)] in exchange for (i) 40% of K.N. & K.'s (D) profits until repayment, with a minimum of $100,000 and a maximum of $500,000, (ii) an option to join the firm as partners within 3 months of repayment, and (iii) collateral consisting of K.N. & K.'s (D) own junk securities. This exchange was memorialized by 3 contemporaneous contracts—an "agreement," "indenture" and "option." The "agreement" labels Peyton (D) and Freeman (D) "trustees" and (i) protects their collateral from commingling, (ii) requires they be informed of all transactions affecting their collateral, (iii) allows them to inspect the firm's business records, (iv) grants them all revenues from the collateral or its sale, (v) allows them to veto any business they deem risky, (vi) requires they be "consulted" on important matters, (vii) assigns to them each existing partner's partnership interest, (viii) restricts the firm's loans and distributions to partners, (ix) allows Peyton (D), Freeman (D), and Hall (D) to assess the firm's value, (x) specifies Hall (D) is to run the firm until repayment, and (xi) requires Hall's (D) life be insured for $1,000,000, with the lenders named beneficiaries. The "indenture" mortgages the collateral. The "option" permits the lenders to (i) become partners within 3 months of repayment by buying a minority share from any partners at a set price, (ii) propose the partnership be reincorporated into a corporation, and (iii) force the resignation of any partner. Amazingly, this opinion fails to mention who the plaintiff is or why he sued, which would have been helpful. Presumably, the partnership failed to pay its creditor Martin (P), who sued Peyton (D) and Freeman (D) as personally liable for the partnership's debts, contending they were made *de facto* partners by the agreements, which gave them sufficient management powers and a share of profits sufficient to constitute a partnership interest. Peyton (D) contended the agreements merely constituted a loan, without making him a partner liable for the partnership's debts. The trial court found Peyton (D) and the other lenders (D) were not partners, and the appellate court affirmed.

■ ISSUE

Is a partnership creditor who is granted a share of profits and some management control deemed a partner?

■ DECISION AND RATIONALE

(Andrews, J.) No. Even partnership creditors who are granted a share of profits and some management control are not necessarily deemed partners if other factors indicate contrary intent. Under modern partnership law, only partners are liable for partnership debts, with few exceptions. Partnership may be inferred from an express or implied contract, written or verbal, which suggests a partnership. However, a contract denying a partnership is not necessarily dispositive, and may be voided as a sham if it disclaims a de facto partnership. An agreement to share profits should be given weight in determining whether a partnership was intended, but profit sharing alone is not decisive. The true test of whether a business association is a partnership comes from examining all facts and circumstances to determine whether there was an intent to do business as co-owners for profit. Here, the contractual rights granted to the lenders (D) were insufficient to make them partners. The "agreement's" provisions maintaining the value of the collateral do not indicate an intended partnership, since they are typical of loan agreements and intended to ensure repayment of the loan. Hall's (D) empowerment and insurance is not necessarily an indication to associate, since the lenders trusted Hall (D) and were justified in requiring his leadership to ensure the firm would return to profitability and repay their loan. The lenders' contractual veto power was not equivalent to a partner's stake, because they could not initiate transactions or bind the firm as partners could, and because veto power is deemed a proper precaution to their loan, since it allowed them to reduce speculative risks to their loan. For this precaution, it was also necessary they receive financial information about the firm. The "indenture" is basically a mortgage, and does not suggest the lenders were partners. The "option's" provision that the lenders may demand partners' resignations is somewhat unusual, but it was arguably justified to protect the lenders' loan against further speculation, and is not enough to prove an intent to make the lenders into partners. Judgment affirmed.

Analysis:

It is well settled that parties may inadvertently establish a partnership with each other based on their conduct. The determination of whether a partnership should be inferred from conduct is made on a case-by-case analysis, with no single factor dispositive. Although the court's opinion states that profit-sharing alone does not create a partnership, the UPA states that the sharing of profits is "prima facie evidence" of the existence of a partnership. This rule can wreak havoc when a financing arrangement gives a creditor a share in the profits and limited control over some management decisions. As this case shows, the question is one of degree.

■ CASE VOCABULARY

INDENTURE: A contract between multiple parties (possibly containing the terms and conditions concerning indebtedness).

OPTION: The right, but not obligation, to buy or sell a specified item at a specified price on/by a specified date.

REFEREE: A court-appointed official, usually a fact-finder or value assessor, authorized to prepare a report for the court.

Smith v. Kelley

(Accounting Firm Employee) v. *(Accounting Firm Partners)*
465 S.W.2d 39 (Ky. 1971)

A FORMATION OF A PARTNERSHIP SHOULD BE IMPLIED ONLY IF THERE IS EVIDENCE THAT THE PARTIES INTENDED TO FORM A PARTNERSHIP

■ **INSTANT FACTS** The former employee of an accounting firm brought suit for a partnership accounting, claiming that he became a partner by estoppel because he was held out to the public as a partner in the firm.

■ **BLACK LETTER RULE** The mere fact that one is held out to the public as a partner in a firm does not mean the such person is a partner for intra-firm purposes.

■ **PROCEDURAL BASIS**

Appeal to the Appellate Court of Kentucky challenging the decision of the Chancellor adjudging that no partnership existed.

■ **FACTS**

Smith (P) brought a suit for a partnership accounting against Kelley (D) and Galloway (D), partners in an accounting business. During his three years with the firm, Smith (P) drew a salary of $1,000 per month plus a small additional sum out of the profits of the business. In a contract entered into by Kelley (D), Galloway (D), Smith (P) and a third party, Smith (P) was identified as a partner in the business. Furthermore, Smith was listed as a partner in tax returns and a statement filed with the Board of Accountancy. These facts notwithstanding, there was never an agreement that Smith (P) would be a partner or that he had a right to share in the profits or losses. Smith (P) made no capital contribution and took no part in management.

■ **ISSUE**

Does the fact that an employee is held out to third parties as a partner create a partnership by estoppel giving the employee full rights as a partner?

■ **DECISION AND RATIONALE**

(Clay, Commissioner) No. The mere fact that one is held out to the public as a partner in a firm does not mean that such person is a partner for intra-firm purposes. A partnership is a contractual relationship and the intention to create it is necessary. As to third parties, a partnership by estoppel may arise from the conduct of the parties, a lack of intent notwithstanding. However, the issue here is different. For Smith (P) to be entitled to share in the profits he would have to show that the parties intended and did create a partnership. The Chancellor's finding that no such intent existed is fully supported by the record. Affirmed.

Analysis:

This case stands for the proposition that there must be an intent to operate the business as partners before a court will hold that an implied partnership has been formed. Section 16 of the Uniform

Partnership Act provides for a partnership by estoppel, but such a partnership pertains only to the rights of third parties (usually the creditors of the implied partnership). Thus, a partnership only as to third parties may exist without any intent to form a partnership. In this case, it is almost certain that the conduct of the parties created a partnership by estoppel as to third parties. However, the reason that such a partnership is not created for intra-firm purposes is that the parties are in a much better position to determine their own intentions than would be a third-party creditor.

CHAPTER THREE

The Limited Partnership: With Special Reference to Federal Income Taxation

In Re USACafes, L.P. Litigation

Instant Facts: A group of limited partners filed suit against the board of directors of the corporate general partner, alleging that the directors breached their fiduciary duties to the limited partnership when the directors received substantial side payments, inducing them to authorize the sale of the partnership's assets for a less than fair price.

Black Letter Rule: The directors of a corporate general partner stand in a fiduciary relationship with limited partners.

In Re Spree.com Corp.

Instant Facts: Breach of contract and breach of fiduciary duty claims were alleged by liquidation company (P) against investors (D) who spoke to press concerning bankrupt dot.com company.

Black Letter Rule: A general partner serving on the board of a portfolio company owes fiduciary duties to the company, and upon breach of the duty, damages are available.

In re USACafes, L.P. Litigation

(*Limited Partnership*)

600 A.2d 43 (Del. Chan. 1991)

THE DIRECTORS OF A CORPORATE GENERAL PARTNER OWE A FIDUCIARY DUTY TO THE LIMITED PARTNERS

■ **INSTANT FACTS** A group of limited partners filed suit against the board of directors of the corporate general partner, alleging that the directors breached their fiduciary duties to the limited partnership when the directors received substantial side payments, inducing them to authorize the sale of the partnership's assets for a less than fair price.

■ **BLACK LETTER RULE** The directors of a corporate general partner stand in a fiduciary relationship with limited partners.

■ **PROCEDURAL BASIS**

Decision of the Delaware Court of Chancery denying a motion to dismiss for failure to state a claim.

■ **FACTS**

When Metsa Acquisition Company (Metsa) purchased all of the assets of USACafes, L.P. (the Partnership) (D), the holders of limited partnership units in the Partnership (D) filed a class action suit against the directors of USACafes General Partner, Inc. (the General Partner) (D). The limited partners claimed that the directors of the General Partner (D) breached their duty of loyalty to the Partnership (D) when they authorized the sale of the Partnership's (D) assets at a low price. The limited partners specifically alleged that the directors, directly and indirectly, received over $15 million in payments from Metsa as inducements to refrain from searching for a better offer. The directors filed a 12(b)(6) motion to dismiss, claiming that the individual directors of a corporate general partner owe no fiduciary duties to limited partners.

■ **ISSUE**

Do the directors of a corporate general partner owe fiduciary duties to the limited partners?

■ **DECISION AND RATIONALE**

(Allen, C.) Yes. The directors of a corporate general partner stand in a fiduciary relationship with limited partners. The principle of fiduciary duty is that one who controls property of another may not, without implied or express agreement, intentionally use that property in a way that benefits the holder of the control to the detriment of the property or its owner. The issue raised here has been addressed in the area of trust law, where leading authority accepts the proposition that the directors and officers of a corporate trustee are under a duty to the beneficiaries of the trust not to cause the corporation to misappropriate the property held in trust. Recognizing that the directors of a corporate general partner owe a fiduciary duty to the limited partners is consistent with the idea of fiduciary duties. Of course, such a duty only extends to dealings with the partnership's property or business. Because the directors of the General Partner (D) were in control of the Partnership's (D) property, it is fair to impose upon them a fiduciary duty with respect to the limited partners.

Analysis:

This case illustrates one of the major differences between a limited partnership with a corporation as general partner and one with an individual as general partner. Under the latter form, there is no confusion as to the identity of those responsible for managing the partnership. In contrast, with a corporate general partner there is a corporate veil shielding the individuals responsible for the business of the partnership. It is the extent of this shield that is the issue in this case. As Chancellor Allen's opinion noted, a general partner, whether a corporation or individual, owes a fiduciary duty to limited partners. The question presented here was whether the same duty is owed by the directors of the corporate general partner. The case answers the question in the affirmative.

In re Spree.com Corp.

(Bankrupt Company) v. *(Bad-Mouthing Investors)*

2001 WL 1518242 (Bankr. E.D. Pa. 2001)

VENTURE CAPITAL LIMITED PARTNERSHIP AGREEMENTS GIVE RISE TO FIDUCIARY DUTIES AND CONFIDENTIALITY REQUIREMENTS BETWEEN THE VENTURE CAPITALISTS AND THE PORTFOLIO COMPANY

■ **INSTANT FACTS** Breach of contract and breach of fiduciary duty claims were alleged by liquidation company (P) against investors (D) who spoke to press concerning bankrupt dot.com company.

■ **BLACK LETTER RULE** A general partner serving on the board of a portfolio company owes fiduciary duties to the company, and upon breach of the duty, damages are available.

■ **PROCEDURAL BASIS**

Motion before trial court to dismiss causes of action of complaint in action for damages for breach of contract and breach of fiduciary duties.

■ **FACTS**

A liquidation company (P) brought suit against a venture capital fund—which was the corporate general partner of a limited partnership—and other investors (D) alleging that certain damaging statements made to a reporter from the Wall Street Journal resulted in the filing of bankruptcy protection by Spree.com Corp. [The bursting of the dot.com bubble may have had something to do with it as well!] The statements in question, made by Defendant investor, Mark Tesler—a member of the board of directors of Spree.com, were as follows: "What do we want to do with this puppy? The cash runs out soon." The complaint alleged that the damaging statements were made in breach of the venture capital limited partnership agreement ("the Agreement"), and in breach of the duties of confidentiality, loyalty, and due care. The confidentiality clause required the investors to keep information concerning Spree.com confidential, but "confidential material" did not include publicly available information. The issue before the trial court was whether the statements contained "confidential material" as defined in the Agreement, and whether the statements breached a fiduciary duty of care owed by the investors (D) to the company. The investors (D) claim that because Spree.com embarked on a "road show" to solicit additional investors before the statements were made, and presumably in so doing, discussed the company's financial condition, the disclosure to the reporter concerning the company's need for money was not confidential. The trial judge dismissed certain allegations, but ordered the investors (D) to answer the Complaint as to the tortious interference with prospective contract claims.

■ **ISSUE**

Does a corporate general partner, serving on the board of a portfolio company, owe duties of confidentiality and loyalty to the portfolio company?

■ **DECISION AND RATIONALE**

(Judge's name not given) Yes. Where, under the terms of a venture capital limited partnership agreement, a corporate general partner serves as a member of the board of the portfolio company, it owes duties of confidentiality and loyalty to the portfolio company. Since the alleged wrongful statement was made after the road show to solicit money, the disclosure to the reporter was not a breach of confidence. Pursuant to the terms of the confidentiality clause, any information that is or becomes publicly available other than through breach of the agreement is not "confidential material." Thus, the statement that Spree.com is "running out of cash" does not provide a claim for breach of contract. Use of the term "puppy" does not constitute a disclosure of any confidential material. The Fifth Claim of the Complaint pertains to tortious interference with prospective contracts with third parties. The facts pled in the complaint, if proven, would establish a lack of privilege or justification as to investor Tesler (D). The Complaint alleges the existence of a fiduciary duty of care by Tesler (D), which he breached by making statements to the press that he knew would and did indeed injure Spree.com by foreclosing prospective financing agreements being negotiated. The Fifth Claim is viable with respect to tortious interference with prospective agreements, but dismissed to the extent it alleges tortious interference with existing contracts.

Analysis:

The facts of this case demonstrate a "staged investment" approach in a business relationship between venture capitalists and portfolio companies. Generally, the venture capitalists do not initially invest enough money into the company in order for it to complete its business plan. Thus, if the company is not a good prospect or if there are problems with the company not cooperating, the venture capitalists need not make further investments. Without this "staged investment" arrangement, the company would generally proceed until the money was gone. Note that as in other limited partnership arrangements, the general partner of the venture capital limited partnership owes fiduciary duties to the limited partners.

■ CASE VOCABULARY

FIDUCIARY DUTY: The duty held by a "fiduciary" to a beneficiary, which requires the exercise of good faith, loyalty, honesty, and other methods of acting for the benefit of another.

JUDICIAL NOTICE: Where the court will accept something as already proven, without actually requiring its proof; usually where the matter is undisputable.

CHAPTER FOUR

Limited Liability Companies

Blackmore Partners, L.P. v. Link Energy LLC

Instant Facts: After Link (D) agreed to sell its assets and distribute all proceeds to its creditors, equity unit holders sued claiming breach of fiduciary duty.

Black Letter Rule: When the facts of a complaint, taken as true, sufficiently allege a breach of fiduciary duty, a motion to dismiss must be denied.

Elf Atochem North America, Inc. v. Jaffari and Malek LLC

Instant Facts: Two Delaware companies entered into a joint venture which contracted to resolve disputes only through arbitration in the state of California.

Black Letter Rule: Members of an LLC may alter the default jurisdictional provisions of a statute and contract away their right to file suit.

Abry Partners V, L.P. v. F & W Acquisition LLC

Instant Facts: Despite contractual language barring rescission claims, Abry Partners (P) filed suit to rescind its contract based on the defendant's material misrepresentations of fact.

Black Letter Rule: Contracts may not be rescinded based on misrepresentations made during negotiations unless one party to the contract made those misrepresentations to the other, knowing them to be false.

Poore v. Fox Hollow Enterprises

Instant Facts: The plaintiff moved to strike the defendant's answering brief in a lawsuit because the drafter of the brief was not an attorney.

Black Letter Rule: A member or manager of a limited liability company (LLC) may not appear in Court to represent the entity without representation by legal counsel.

Marie L. Kasten v. Doral Dental USA, LLC

Instant Facts: A limited liability company member demanded to inspect copies of draft agreements and email records between the company and potential purchasers.

Black Letter Rule: Under Wisconsin's Limited Liability Company Act, statutory rights to inspect company records are broad, subject to narrowing language contained in the company's operating agreement.

Blackmore Partners, L.P. v. Link Energy LLC

(*Equity Owners*) v. (*Limited Liability Company*)

864 A.2d 80 (Del. Ch. 2004)

THE BUSINESS JUDGMENT RULE PROTECTS BOARD ACTIONS TAKEN IN GOOD FAITH WITH DUE DILIGENCE

■ **INSTANT FACTS** After Link (D) agreed to sell its assets and distribute all proceeds to its creditors, equity unit holders sued claiming breach of fiduciary duty.

■ **BLACK LETTER RULE** When the facts of a complaint, taken as true, sufficiently allege a breach of fiduciary duty, a motion to dismiss must be denied.

■ **PROCEDURAL BASIS**

Chancery court decision on the defendant's motion to dismiss the plaintiffs' complaint.

■ **FACTS**

Emerging from Chapter 11 bankruptcy in 2002, EOTT Energy Partners, L.P. created Link Energy, LLC (D), a Delaware limited liability company, to assume and continue its business. As part of the Chapter 11 restructuring, EOTT's publicly traded common equity units were cancelled and its former unit holders received equity units in Link (D). Additionally, EOTT cancelled $235 million in outstanding 11% senior unsecured notes, for which their holders received 9% senior unsecured notes issued by Link (D) and a share of Link (D) equity units. Blackmore Partners, L.P. (P) obtained Link equity units as a result of the restructuring.

Following the restructuring, Link's (D) periodic statements indicated that the business was not meeting its economic forecasts and suffered from a high cost of capital. As a result, Link's (D) management began considering alternatives to continuing its operations. In March 2004, Link (D) disclosed an agreement to sell all of its assets and business for $290 million, announcing that it was unlikely that equity unit owners would receive any value for their units. As part of this agreement, Link (D) management dedicated $265 million to repay debt, including the 9% unsecured notes created during the restructuring. The remaining $25 million was also paid to the 9% note holders in exchange for a waiver of a covenant in the notes requiring the new purchaser to assume the obligation on the notes.

Link's (D) operating agreement authorized its board of directors to enter into the agreement without a vote of its unit holders. Nonetheless, Blackmore (P) and other unit holders filed suit in federal court alleging that the directors breached their fiduciary duties to the unit holders by agreeing to the sale. According to the complaint, Blackmore (P) approached the board following the announcement of the sale with an alternative proposal that would have potentially enabled the equity holders to realize some gain on their units. By declining to consider this proposal, Blackmore (P) alleged, the board placed the interests of the 9% note holders above the unit holders. Link (D) moved to dismiss the plaintiffs' complaint on the basis of an exculpatory clause contained in the operating agreement.

■ **ISSUE**

Does the complaint allege sufficient facts to support an inference that the board breached its fiduciary duties to the plaintiffs?

■ DECISION AND RATIONALE

(Lamb, Vice Ch.) Yes. When the facts of a complaint, taken as true, sufficiently allege a breach of fiduciary duty, a motion to dismiss must be denied. When a board of directors determines to sell a business's assets, the board has a duty to ensure the highest value reasonably attainable for its stockholders under the circumstances. If the circumstances indicate that the board acted in good faith and with due diligence, it will not have breached its fiduciary duties. Under those circumstances, the board's actions are protected by the business judgment rule. Additionally, an exculpatory clause in the operating agreement immunizes the directors from liability unless the plaintiff has demonstrated bad faith.

When considering a motion to dismiss, the court will consider the allegations in the complaint as true, granting the motion only if those allegations fail to establish an inference of liability. Here, the complaint alleges that the directors approved a transaction that was disadvantageous to the unit holders. Before the transaction, the units had considerable value, which disappeared after the transaction. These allegations permit the reasonable inference that Link (D) was not insolvent and was in no danger of returning to bankruptcy. The facts may demonstrate that the directors acted in good faith and, after reasonable investigation, made a business judgment that the company's long-term prospects were less advantageous than the sale of its assets. However, taken as true, the allegations of the complaint do state a claim for breach of fiduciary duty. The defendant's motion to dismiss is therefore denied.

Analysis:

The court speaks mostly of the duty of good faith and due diligence in making business decisions, and simply infers disloyalty from the allegations. When a board makes a good-faith informed business decision to place creditors' interests ahead of its owners' interests, however, the business judgment rule offers protection against liability for the apparent disloyalty. In matters such as these, the duty of good faith and the duty of loyalty often go hand in hand, for disloyalty frequently demonstrates a lack of good faith.

■ CASE VOCABULARY

BUSINESS JUDGMENT RULE: The presumption that in making business decisions not involving direct self-interest or self-dealing, corporate directors act on an informed basis, in good faith, and in the honest belief that their actions are in the corporation's best interest.

EXCULPATORY CLAUSE: A contractual provision relieving a party from any liability resulting from a negligent or wrongful act.

FIDUCIARY: One who owes to another the duties of good faith, trust, confidence, and candor.

LIMITED LIABILITY COMPANY: A company—statutorily authorized in certain states—that is characterized by limited liability, management by members or managers, and limitation on ownership transfer.

Elf Atochem North America, Inc. v. Jaffari and Malek LLC

(*Hazardous Chemical Manufacturer*) v. (*Environmentally Friendly Chemical Producer*)

727 A.2d 286 (Del. 1999)

ONLY WHERE AN AGREEMENT IS INCONSISTENT WITH MANDATORY STATUTORY PROVISIONS WILL THE AGREEMENT OF THE MEMBERS OF AN LLC BE INVALIDATED

■ **INSTANT FACTS** Two Delaware companies entered into a joint venture which contracted to resolve disputes only through arbitration in the state of California.

■ **BLACK LETTER RULE** Members of an LLC may alter the default jurisdictional provisions of a statute and contract away their right to file suit.

■ **PROCEDURAL BASIS**

Appeal from the grant of the defendant's motion to dismiss based on lack of subject matter jurisdiction.

■ **FACTS**

Elf Atochem (P) manufactures and distributes solvent-based maskants to the aerospace and aviation industries throughout the world. Jaffari (D), the president of Malek, Inc., had developed an innovative, environmentally-friendly alternative to the solvent-based maskants. Recently, the Environmental Protection Agency (EPA) classified solvent-based maskants as hazardous chemicals and air contaminants. To avoid conflict with EPA regulations, Elf (P) considered developing or distributing a maskant less harmful to the environment. Elf (P) approached Jaffari (D) and proposed investing in his product and assisting in its marketing. Jaffari (D) found the proposal attractive since his company, Malek, Inc., possessed limited resources and little international sales expertise. Elf (P) and Jaffari (D) agreed to undertake a joint venture that was to be carried out using a limited liability company as the vehicle. On October 29, 1996, Malek, Inc. caused to be filed a Certificate of Formation with the Delaware Secretary of State, thus forming Malek LLC (D), a Delaware limited liability company (LLC) under the Delaware Limited Liability Company Act ("Act"). Next, Elf (P), Jaffari (D), and Malek, Inc. entered into a series of agreements providing for the governance and operation of the joint venture. Of particular importance to this litigation, they entered into the Agreement, a comprehensive and integrated document setting forth detailed provisions for the governance of Malek LLC (D), which is not itself a signatory to the Agreement. The Agreement contains an arbitration clause covering all disputes. The clause, Section 13.8, provides that "any controversy or dispute arising out of this Agreement, the interpretation of any provisions hereof, or the action or inaction of any Member or Manager hereunder shall be submitted to arbitration in San Francisco, California. The Section further provides that no action shall be instituted in any court except to compel arbitration or to enforce an award obtained in an arbitration proceeding. The Agreement also contains a forum selection clause, Section 13.7, which provides that all members consent to "exclusive jurisdiction of the state and federal courts sitting in California in any action arising out of, under or in connection with this Agreement or the transactions contemplated by this Agreement, provided such claim is not required to be arbitrated pursuant to Section 13.8"; and personal jurisdiction in California. On April 27, 1998, Elf (P) sued Jaffari (D) and Malek LLC (D), individually and derivatively on behalf of Malek LLC, in the Delaware Court of Chancery, seeking equitable remedies. Among other claims, Elf (P) alleged that Jaffari (D) breached his fiduciary duty to Malek LLC (D), pushed Malek LLC (D) to the brink of insolvency by withdrawing funds for personal use, interfered with business opportunities, failed to make disclosures to Elf (P), threatened to make poor quality maskant and threatened to violate environmental regulations. Elf (P) also alleged breach of contract, tortious interference with prospective business relations, and (solely as to Jaffari (D)) fraud. The Court of Chancery granted Jaffari's (D) and Malek LLC's (D) motion to dismiss based on lack of subject matter jurisdiction. The court held that Elf's (P) claims arose under the Agreement, or the transactions contemplated by the Agreement, and were directly related to Jaffari's (D) actions as manager of Malek LLC (D). Therefore, the court found that the Agreement governed the question of jurisdiction and that only a court of law or arbitrator in California is empowered to decide these claims. Elf (P) appealed, claiming that the Court of Chancery erred in holding that the arbitration and forum selection clauses in the Agreement governed, and thus deprived that court of jurisdiction to adjudicate all of Elf's (P) claims, including its derivative claims made on behalf of Malek LLC (D). Elf (P) contends that, since Malek LLC (D) is not a party to the Agreement, it is not bound by the forum selection provisions. Elf (P) also argues that the court erred in failing to classify its claim as derivative on behalf of Malek LLC (D) against Jaffari (D) as manager. Therefore, Elf (P) claims that the court should have adjudicated the dispute. Finally, Elf (P) argues that the dispute resolution clauses of the Agreement are invalid under Section 109(d) of the Act, which, it alleges, prohibits the parties from vesting exclusive jurisdiction in a forum outside of Delaware.

■ ISSUE

May members of an LLC alter the default jurisdictional provisions of a statute and contract away their right to file suit?

■ DECISION AND RATIONALE

(Veasey, C.J.) Yes. The phenomenon of business arrangements using "alternative entities" has been developing rapidly over the past several years. Long gone are the days when business planners were confined to corporate or partnership structures. The basic approach of the Delaware Act is to provide members with broad discretion in drafting the Agreement and to furnish default provisions when the members' agreement is silent. The Act is replete with fundamental provisions made subject to modification in the Agreement (for example, "unless otherwise provided in a limited liability company agreement"). In general, only where the agreement is inconsistent with mandatory statutory provisions will the members' agreement be invalidated. Such statutory provisions are likely to be those intended to protect third parties, not necessarily the contracting members. As a framework for decision, we apply that principle to the issues before us, without expressing any views more broadly. In this case, the parties did not sign the Agreement until November 4, 1996. Elf (P) contends that Malek LLC (D) existed as an LLC as of October 29, 1996, but never agreed to the Agreement because it did not sign it. Because Malek LLC (D) never expressly assented to the arbitration and forum selection clauses within the Agreement, Elf (P) argues it can sue derivatively on behalf of Malek LLC (D). We are not persuaded by this argument. Malek, Inc. and Elf (P), the members of Malek LLC (D), executed the Agreement to carry out the affairs and business of Malek LLC (D) and to provide for arbitration and forum selection. Notwithstanding Malek LLC's (D) failure to sign the Agreement, Elf's (P) claims are subject to the arbitration and forum selection clauses of the Agreement. The Act is a statute designed to permit members maximum flexibility in entering into an agreement to govern their relationship. It is the members who are the real parties in interest. The LLC is simply their joint business vehicle. This is the contemplation of the statute in prescribing the outlines of a limited liability company agreement. We find no reason why the members cannot alter the default jurisdictional provisions of the statute and contract away their right to file suit in Delaware. We hold that, because the policy of the Act is to give the maximum effect to the principle of freedom of contract and to the enforceability of LLC agreements, the parties may contract to avoid the applicability of the Delaware statute. We therefore affirm the judgment of the Court of Chancery dismissing Elf Atochem's (P) amended complaint for lack of subject matter jurisdiction.

Analysis:

In this case, the Supreme Court of Delaware was required to determine whether an agreement concerning the governance and operation of the LLC was enforceable even though the LLC was not a party to the contract and the terms altered the default jurisdictional provisions of the state's LLC Act concerning Delaware as the proper forum. The court noted that the express policy of the Act was to give the maximum effect to the "principle of freedom of contract." The court held that the agreement was enforceable, even though the LLC was not a party to the agreement, because the Act defined an LLC agreement as "any agreement, written or oral, of the member or members as to the affairs of the limited liability company and the conduct of its business." Since the members of the LLC executed the agreement, it was enforceable notwithstanding the LLC's failure to sign. With respect to the arbitration and forum selection provisions of the agreement, the court held that they were enforceable, noting that there is nothing in the LLC Act that prohibits members of an LLC from altering the default jurisdictional provisions of the Act and contracting away their right to file suit in the State.

■ CASE VOCABULARY

ARBITRATION PROCEEDINGS: A process of dispute resolution in which a neutral third party (arbitrator) renders a decision after a hearing at which both parties have an opportunity to be heard.

DERIVATIVE SUIT: A suit by a shareholder to enforce a corporate cause of action, and the relief which is granted is a judgment against a third person in favor of the corporation.

FIDUCIARY DUTY: A duty to act for someone else's benefit, while subordinating one's personal interests to that of the other person.

FORUM SELECTION CLAUSE: A clause in a contract preselecting a particular forum, such as a given state, country, court or administrative proceeding, for the resolution of a dispute.

JOINT VENTURE: A legal entity in the nature of a partnership engaged in the joint undertaking of a particular transaction for mutual profit.

LIMITED LIABILITY COMPANY: Persons or entities ("members") which join together in an environment of private ordering to form and operate an enterprise under an agreement with tax benefits akin to a partnership and limited liability akin to the corporate form.

REAL PARTIES IN INTEREST: Persons who will be entitled to the benefits of an action if successful.

Abry Partners V, L.P. v. F & W Acquisition LLC

(Buyer) v. *(Seller)*

891 A.2d 1032 (Del. Ch. 2006)

BUSINESSES MAY CONTRACTUALLY LIMIT THEIR LIABILITY IN THE EVENT OF BREACH

■ **INSTANT FACTS** Despite contractual language barring rescission claims, Abry Partners (P) filed suit to rescind its contract based on the defendant's material misrepresentations of fact.

■ **BLACK LETTER RULE** Contracts may not be rescinded based on misrepresentations made during negotiations unless one party to the contract made those misrepresentations to the other, knowing them to be false.

■ PROCEDURAL BASIS

Chancery court consideration of the defendant's motion to dismiss.

■ FACTS

According to the plaintiff's complaint, Abry Partners (P) bargained with Providence Equity Partners (D) to purchase F & W Publications, a portfolio company in the publishing business, for ten times the company's $48 million cash flow over a twelve-month period ending on June 30, 2005, amounting to a $480 million sale price. The company, however, presented financial records that demonstrated expected cash flow of $51 million over that time period, and the parties ultimately agreed to a $500 million sale price.

After closing on the sale, the plaintiff learned that three monthly financial statements misrepresented the company's earnings for those periods by inflating revenues for new magazine subscriptions that had not yet begun, by failing to account for higher-than-normal book returns it reasonably anticipated, and by otherwise manipulating its financial data to appear to be more profitable before closing. As a result of these misrepresentations by the company, Abry (P) sued Providence (D) for rescission of the contract. Providence (D) moved to dismiss the case based on the terms of the Stock Purchase Agreement.

■ ISSUE

Does public policy forbid the contractual waiver of rescission claims based on material misrepresentations of fact?

■ DECISION AND RATIONALE

(Strine, Vice Ch.) No. Contracts may not be rescinded based on misrepresentations made during negotiations unless one party to the contract made those misrepresentations to the other, knowing them to be false. It is important to note that, as Abry (P) carefully alleges in its complaint, all misrepresentations at issue were made solely by the company, and not by the seller. This is important, because the terms of the Stock Purchase Agreement, in several places, demonstrate Abry's (P) agreement that it entered into the purchase transaction solely relying on the information and statements contained within the four corners of the agreement. While the agreement requires the company to warrant the veracity of its representations, Abry (P) is unjustified in relying upon any extra-contractual information. Accordingly, based on this fact alone, Abry (P) would have no cause of action against Providence (D) for misrepresentation.

However, Abry (P), as a sophisticated private equity firm, demanded in the agreement that Providence (D) certify that all closing conditions relating to the accuracy of both the seller's and the company's representations and warranties. Providence (D) issued such a certificate, confirming that each representation and warranty of the company was true and correct. This certification opens Providence (D) up to potential liability for any misrepresentations made by the company in the Stock Purchase Agreement. Accounting for this exposure, the Stock Purchase Agreement explicitly limits Abry's (P) remedies to an "Indemnity Claim"—an arbitration claim for damages not to exceed $20 million. Thus, the terms of the Stock Purchase Agreement forbid Abry's (P) claim of rescission.

Abry (P) seeks to avoid the contractual limitations, arguing that the Indemnity Claim provision applies to negligent, not intentional, misrepresentations, and that these contractual terms are void as against public policy. First, "misrepresentation" is a broad word commonly understood as "that act of making a false or misleading statement about something, [usually] with the intent to deceive." As written, it must be deemed to encompass both negligent and intentional acts. Second, the freedom to contract is deeply rooted in American law, giving great respect to bargained-for liability limitations. On the other hand, tradition abhors dishonesty and deceit in bargaining. Therefore, to avoid the limitations it agreed to in the Stock Purchase Agreement, Abry (P) must demonstrate that Providence (D) either knew that the representations in the company's financial statements were false or itself lied to the plaintiff in its Officer's Certificate. Any lesser showing is insufficient to avoid the Indemnity Claim provision. Motion granted in part, denied in part.

Analysis:

While the court's decision to enforce the limitation provisions against Abry (P) seems inequitable on the surface, keep the facts of the case in perspective. Abry (P) initially sought to purchase the company for $20 million less than the $500 million it eventually paid. When the company increased its cash flow value above that determined by Abry (P) after conducting its initial due diligence, it is very likely that Abry (P) itself insisted on that figure to protect its investment in the company, after thoroughly reviewing the company's revised financial statements. It is also likely that Abry (P) appreciated the risk of mistakes in these statements and took appropriate action.

■ CASE VOCABULARY

FRAUD: A knowing misrepresentation of the truth or concealment of a material fact to induce another to act to his or her detriment; a misrepresentation made recklessly without believe in its truth to induce another person to act; unconscionable dealing, especially in contract law; the unfair use of the power arising out of one of the parties' relative positions and resulting in an unconscionable bargain.

NEGLIGENT MISREPRESENTATION: A careless or inadvertent false statement in circumstances where care should have been taken.

RESCISSION: A party's unilateral unmaking of a contract for a legally sufficient reason, such as the other party's material breach.

Poore v. Fox Hollow Enterprises

(Plaintiff) v. *(Non-Represented LLC)*
1994 WL 150872 (Del. Super. 1994)

AN LLC REQUIRES REPRESENTATION BY LEGAL COUNSEL IN COURT PROCEEDINGS

■ **INSTANT FACTS** The plaintiff moved to strike the defendant's answering brief in a lawsuit because the drafter of the brief was not an attorney.

■ **BLACK LETTER RULE** A member or manager of a limited liability company (LLC) may not appear in Court to represent the entity without representation by legal counsel.

■ **PROCEDURAL BASIS**

The plaintiff filed a Motion to Strike the defendant's Answering Brief for failure to properly file an answer through counsel.

■ **FACTS**

Pursuant to Superior Court Civil Rule 12(f), Poore (P) filed a Motion to Strike Fox Hollow Enterprises' (D) Answering Brief for failure to file an answer in Superior Court through Delaware counsel. During the oral arguments concerning this Motion, Campbell admitted he drafted the answering brief himself. Although Campbell stated he did not have a license to practice law in Delaware, he believed that because Fox Hollow (D) is an LLC and not a corporation, he could represent this company in Superior Court without a Delaware licensed attorney [it's just a piece of paper anyway, right?].

■ **ISSUE**

May a member or manager of an LLC appear in Court to represent the entity without representation by legal counsel?

■ **DECISION AND RATIONALE**

(Steele, J.) No. The Court recognizes that the Delaware General Assembly enacted the Delaware LLC Act to serve as an alternative business entity which allows the combination of the best features of both partnerships and corporations. The Delaware statute treats a properly structured LLC as a partnership for federal income tax purposes while affording limited liability for members and managers similar to the limited liability afforded to shareholders and directors of a Delaware corporation. Although the statute treats an LLC as a partnership for federal income tax purposes, an LLC is largely a creature of contract—with management, economic, voting and other rights and obligations being primarily specified in the LLC agreement. Additionally, the interest of a member in the LLC is analogous to shareholders of a corporation. A member usually contributes personal property and has no interest in specific assets owned by the LLC. Moreover, a member or manager of an LLC cannot be held liable for the company's debts or obligations above his or her contribution to the company. The Court finds these aspects of the LLC constitute a distinct, but artificial entity under Delaware law. Because of the limited liability inherent in the LLC and the contractual nature of this entity, the Court finds the Delaware Legislature did not intend a member or manager of an LLC could appear in Court to represent the entity without representation by Delaware legal counsel. Because Fox Hollow (D) did not obtain Delaware

---

legal counsel to represent its interests in this appeal, the Court grants Poore's (P) Motion to Strike Fox Hollow's (D) Answering Brief pursuant to Superior Court Civil Rule 12(f).

Analysis:

An LLC can take on characteristics of both a partnership and a corporation. For instance, the benefits of limited liability associated with a corporation are enjoyed by an LLC, as are the benefits of pass-through taxation associated with a partnership. In this case, the court was faced with the issue of whether the LLC business entity should take on the characteristics of a partnership or a corporation with respect to legal representation. Recall that a corporation must be represented by an attorney or, put another way, it cannot represent itself in pro per. In reaching its decision, the court analyzed Delaware's LLC statute, noting that it was enacted to combine the best features of both partnerships and corporations. Its ultimate ruling declaring that a member or manager of a LLC cannot appear in court to represent the entity without being a licensed Delaware attorney was based upon the fact that an LLC has limited liability and is largely a creature of contract, thereby more closely resembling a corporation.

■ CASE VOCABULARY

CORPORATION: An association of persons created by statute as a legal entity which is distinct from the individuals who comprise it.

FICTIONAL ENTITY: An artificial person or legal entity contrived by the law to permit a court to dispose of a matter.

NATURAL PERSON: A human being.

PARTNERSHIP: A business owned by two or more persons that is not organized as a corporation.

Marie L. Kasten v. Doral Dental USA, LLC

(Member) v. *(Limited Liability Company)*

2006 WL 861382 (Wis. Ct. App. 2006)

STATUTORY INSPECTION RIGHTS MAY BE ALTERED BY AGREEMENT

■ **INSTANT FACTS** A limited liability company member demanded to inspect copies of draft agreements and email records between the company and potential purchasers.

■ **BLACK LETTER RULE** Under Wisconsin's Limited Liability Company Act, statutory rights to inspect company records are broad, subject to narrowing language contained in the company's operating agreement.

■ PROCEDURAL BASIS

On appeal to review a trial court decision denying the plaintiff's motion to compel production of company records.

■ FACTS

As part of a divorce settlement in 2001, Kasten (P) obtained a 23.1% membership interest in Doral Dental USA, LLC (D). In 2002 and 2003, Doral Dental (D) entered into various negotiations for the sale of the company. Fearful that the sale may affect her interest in the company, Kasten (P) began requesting various business documents, financial ledgers, and other records, including draft agreements negotiated with potential purchasers and email records. After Doral Dental (D) complied with only some of the requests, Kasten (P) filed suit to enforce her statutory and contractual rights to inspect and copy the business's records. On Kasten's (P) motion to compel production of the documents, the trial court ruled that she was not entitled to inspect any draft agreements or email records, but granted the motion with respect to other written correspondence.

■ ISSUE

Does Wisconsin's Limited Liability Company Law grant a broad right of member access to limited liability company records that embraces informal and nonfinancial records?

■ DECISION AND RATIONALE

(Snyder, J.) No. Under Wisconsin's Limited Liability Company Act, statutory rights to inspect company records are broad, but they are subject to narrowing language contained in the company's operating agreement. By statute, any member of a limited liability company may inspect and copy any enumerated record required by law to be held in the company's principal place of business and, "unless otherwise provided in an operating agreement, any other limited liability company record, wherever the record is located." Additionally, the defendant's operating agreement allows members a right to inspect all books of account "and all other Company records at all reasonable times." Doral Dental (D) contends that the Limited Liability Company Law borrows significantly from Wisconsin's Uniform Limited Partnership Act and Business Corporation law, each of which limits inspection rights to certain designated records. However, as Kasten (P) argues, neither of those acts incorporated terms similar to the "any other limited liability company record" language adopted in the Limited Liability Company Law. This statutory language demonstrates that the members' rights to inspect company records were intended to be broad, leaving it to the company's operating agreement to appropriately tailor the right of inspection. Whether such rights encompass email records, which often carry a frank, conversational tone that would not ordinarily be memorialized in a formal business document, must be determined by the Wisconsin Supreme Court.

Analysis:

On certification, the Wisconsin Supreme Court determined that Kasten (P) was entitled to access to the draft agreements and emails at issue. *See Kasten v. Doral Dental USA, LLC*, 733 N.W.2d 300 (Wis. 2007). However, the court issued its decision without establishing as a matter of law that such informal and nonfinancial records were subject to inspection under Wisconsin statutes. Instead, the court concluded that the common meaning of a "document"—the term used in the Doral Dental operating agreement—is broader than the meaning of a "record"—the term used in the inspection statute. Therefore, the court limited its holding to the facts of the case, concluding that the operating agreement, not the statute, demanded Kasten's limited access to the draft documents and emails sought.

■ CASE VOCABULARY

INSPECTION RIGHT: The legal entitlement in certain circumstances to examine articles or documents, such as a consumer's right to inspect goods before paying for them.

CHAPTER FIVE

The Development of Corporation Law in the United States

Louis K. Liggett Co. v. Lee
Instant Facts: Not Stated
Black Letter Rule: Not Stated

Louis K. Liggett Co. v. Lee

(*Not Stated*) v. (*Not Stated*)

288 U.S. 517, 548–65, 53 S.Ct. 481, 490–96, 77 L.Ed. 929, 944–54 (1933)

THE REMOVAL OF THE LIMITATIONS UPON THE SIZE AND POWERS OF BUSINESS CORPORA-
TIONS APPEARS TO HAVE BEEN DUE TO THE CONVICTION THAT IT WAS FUTILE TO INSIST UPON
THEM BECAUSE LOCAL RESTRICTION WOULD BE CIRCUMVENTED BY FOREIGN INCORPORATION

■ **INSTANT FACTS** Not Stated

■ **BLACK LETTER RULE** Not Stated

■ **PROCEDURAL BASIS**

Not Stated

■ **FACTS**

Not Stated

■ **ISSUE**

Not Stated

■ **DECISION AND RATIONALE**

Not Stated

■ **DISSENT**

(Brandeis, J.) Limitation upon the amount of the authorized capital of business corporations was long universal. The maximum limit frequently varied with the kinds of business to be carried on, being dependent apparently upon the supposed requirements of the efficient unit. Although the statutory limits were changed from time to time, this principle of limitation was long retained. Limitations upon the scope of a business corporation's powers and activity were also long universal. At first, corporations could be formed under the general laws only for a limited number of purposes—usually those which required a relatively large fixed capital, like transportation, banking and insurance, and mechanical, mining, and manufacturing enterprises. Permission to incorporate for ''any lawful purpose'' was not common until 1875, and even then the powers which the corporation might exercise in carrying out its purposes were sparingly conferred or strictly construed. The removal by the leading industrial states of the limitations upon the size and powers of business corporations appears to have been due not to their conviction that maintenance of the restrictions was undesirable in itself, but to the conviction that it was futile to insist upon them because local restriction would be circumvented by foreign incorporation. The economic and social results of removing all limitations upon the size and activities of business corporations and of vesting in their managers vast powers once exercised by stockholders were long unsuspected. Size alone gives to giant corporations a social significance not attached ordinarily to smaller units of private enterprise. Through size, corporations, once merely an efficient tool employed by individuals in the conduct of private business, have become an institution which has brought such concentration of economic power that so-called private corporations are sometimes able to dominate the state. Ownership has been separated from control, and this separation has removed many of the checks which formerly operated to curb the misuse of wealth and power. And, as ownership of the shares becomes continually more dispersed, the power which formerly accompanied ownership becomes increasingly concentrated in the hands of a few. The changes thereby wrought in the lives of the workers, of the owners and of the general public are so fundamental and far-reaching as to lead scholars to compare the evolving "corporate system" with the feudal system.

Analysis:

This case illustrates the general principle that, originally, corporations were chartered (authorized) only subject to severe restrictions. These limitations include allowing incorporation only for public works (to restrict the number of corporations), limiting their corporate powers and lines of industry (to prevent their competition with unincorporated competitors), and capping their maximum capital (to keep them from out-spending smaller businesses). This principle was long-standing in England and early America, but is now outdated. After industrialization and commerce intensified in America, corporations were increasingly tolerated as necessary for expansion, and all the restrictions mentioned here were eventually lifted. However, the underlying policy concern—corporations' ability to dominate smaller competitors, labor, and even state government by virtue of their size and capitalization—endures today.

■ CASE VOCABULARY

FEUDAL SYSTEM: A political and social system which prevailed throughout Europe during the eleventh, twelfth, and thirteenth centuries, which formed the entire basis of the real-property law of England in medieval times.

MONOPOLY: A form of market structure in which one or only a few firms dominate the total sales of a product or service.

MORTMAIN: A term applied to denote the alienation of lands or tenements to any corporation.

CHAPTER SIX

The Formation of a Closely Held Corporation

711 Kings Highway Corp. v. F.I.M.'S Marine Repair Serv., Inc.

Instant Facts: Property to be used only as a movie theater was leased to a boat builder, who was not permitted to conduct such operations under its corporate charter.

Black Letter Rule: Except in the three stated situations set forth in Section 203 of the New York Business Corporation Law, ultra vires may not be invoked as a sword in support of a cause of action any more than it can be utilized as a defense.

Sullivan v. Hammer

Instant Facts: Shareholders brought a derivative action against the corporation, challenging a charitable contribution.

Black Letter Rule: To determine whether a settlement is reasonable, a court looks to the probable validity of the claims; the apparent difficulties in enforcing the claims through the courts; the collectibility of any judgment recovered; the delay, expense and trouble of litigation; the amount of the compromise compared to the amount and collectibility of the judgment; and the views of the parties involved.

Stanley J. How & Assoc., Inc. v. Boss

Instant Facts: An architect sued to recover payment on a contract for architectural services performed.

Black Letter Rule: A promoter, though he may assume to act on behalf of the projected corporation and not for himself, will be personally liable on his contract unless the other party agreed to look to some other person or fund for payment.

Robertson v. Levy

Instant Facts: A man is suing the person who bought his business before the man had completed the process of incorporating for failure to make the required installment payments after the new business went under.

Black Letter Rule: An individual who incurs statutory liability on an obligation because he has acted without authority, is not relieved of that liability where, at a later time, the corporation does come into existence.

Frontier Refining Company v. Kunkel's, Inc.

Instant Facts: When a defectively incorporated company's manager bought oil before incorporating, the seller sued his absentee associates as partners

Black Letter Rule: A defectively incorporated business's members are jointly and severally liable for its debts only if (i) they represented themselves as incorporated, or authorized an agent to do so (implicitly or explicitly), (ii) the debt was incurred in the corporation's name, and (iii) granting personal liability would be equitable.

711 Kings Highway Corp. v. F.I.M.'s Marine Repair Serv., Inc.

(Landlord) v. *(Tenant)*

51 Misc.2d 373, 273 N.Y.S.2d 299 (1966)

THE DOCTRINE OF ULTRA VIRES MAY NOT BE INVOKED TO AVOID A CONTRACT

■ **INSTANT FACTS** Property to be used only as a movie theater was leased to a boat builder, who was not permitted to conduct such operations under its corporate charter.

■ **BLACK LETTER RULE** Except in the three stated situations set forth in Section 203 of the New York Business Corporation Law, ultra vires may not be invoked as a sword in support of a cause of action any more than it can be utilized as a defense.

■ **PROCEDURAL BASIS**

Defendant's motion for judgment dismissing the plaintiff's complaint for legal insufficiency or in the alternative for summary judgment.

■ **FACTS**

The plaintiff, 711 Kings Highway Corp. (P), leased premises to F.I.M.'s Marine Repair Service (D) under a written agreement for a period of 15 years. With the exception of a $5,000 security deposit paid by F.I.M.'s (D), the lease remains wholly executory. Under the terms of the agreement, the premises were to be used as a motion picture theater, however F.I.M. (D), as set forth in its certificate of incorporation, is restricted generally to marine activities, including marine repairs and building and equipment of boats and vessels. The complaint filed by 711 (P) alleges that the execution of the lease calling for F.I.M.'s (D) use of the premises as a motion picture theater, and the conduct and operation of a motion picture theater business by F.I.M. (D) are acts which fall completely outside the scope of the powers and authority conferred by F.I.M.'s (D) corporate charter, thereby rendering invalid the lease agreement entered into by the parties [then why did they lease the property in the first place?]. The complaint then prays for a declaratory judgment declaring the lease to be invalid, or in the alternative for rescission. Further, the complaint prays that F.I.M. (D) be enjoined from performing, or exercising any rights under the lease.

■ **ISSUE**

Is it beyond the powers of a corporation authorized to provide marine repairs to lease and operate real property as a motion picture theater?

■ **DECISION AND RATIONALE**

(Anfuso, J.) No. In the opinion of this Court, Section 203 of the New York Business Corporation Law embraces the situation presented by the factual allegations of the complaint and requires a dismissal of the complaint for failure to state a cause of action. This section provides as follows: That no act of a corporation and no transfer of property to or by a corporation, otherwise lawful, shall be invalid by reason of the fact that the corporation was without capacity or power to do such act or engage in such transfer except that such lack of capacity or power may be asserted (1) in an action brought by a shareholder to enjoin a corporate act or (2) in an action by or in the right of a corporation against an incumbent or former officer or director of the corporation or (3) in an action or special proceeding

---

brought by the Attorney General. It is undisputed that the present case does not fall within the stated exceptions contained in Section 203. Thus, it is accordingly clear that there is no substance to 711's (P) argument, which is predicated on a want of corporate power to do an act or enter into an agreement beyond the express or implied powers of the corporation conferred by the corporate charter. Neither is there merit to 711's (P) contention that Section 203 applies only where ultra vires is raised as a defense. Except in the three stated situations set forth in the section, which are not applicable to the instant case, ultra vires may not be invoked as a sword in support of a cause of action any more than it can be utilized as a defense. To hold otherwise would render meaningless those provisions in Section 203 which permit ultra vires to be invoked in support of the actions or proceedings set forth as exceptions to the general language of this section. Finally, 711's (P) contention that the ultra vires doctrine still applies fully to executory contracts must be rejected. By virtue of Section 203, the doctrine may not be invoked even though the contract which is claimed to be ultra vires is executory, as in the instant case. Accordingly, F.I.M.'s (D) motion for summary judgment dismissing the complaint for insufficiency is granted.

Analysis:

This otherwise unexceptional case illustrates the *ultra vires* doctrine and the policy reasons why many courts struggle to find ways to avoid it. In principle, *ultra vires* is useful for helping shareholders void unauthorized (and often self-serving) actions taken by corporate managers. However, while applying this doctrine may protect shareholders, it often cheats people who enter into contracts with the corporation in good faith, who have no reason to believe the transaction is unauthorized. To avoid these unjust consequences, courts usually found pretexts to avoid applying *ultra vires* doctrine, including estoppel, unjust enrichment, quasi-contract, and waiver.

■ CASE VOCABULARY

DECLARATORY JUDGMENT: A binding adjudication of the rights and status of litigants even though no consequential relief is awarded.

ENJOIN: To require a person to perform, or to abstain or desist from, some act.

ESTOPPEL: The party is prevented by his own acts from claiming a right to the detriment of another party who was entitled to rely on such conduct and has acted accordingly.

EXECUTORY: That which is yet to be fully executed or performed.

LEGAL INSUFFICIENCY: Not supported by competent, pertinent evidence.

QUASI-CONTRACT: An obligation which the law creates in the absence of an agreement.

SUMMARY JUDGMENT: Procedural device available for the prompt and expeditious disposition of a controversy without a trial when there is no dispute as to a material facts, or if only a question of law is involved.

ULTRA VIRES: An act which is beyond the scope of the powers of a corporation, as defined by its charter or laws of state incorporation.

UNJUST ENRICHMENT: Occurs when a person has and retains money or benefits which in justice and equity belong to another.

Sullivan v. Hammer

(*Shareholder*) v. (*Director*)

1990 WL 114223 (Del. Ch. Ct. 1990)

THE BUSINESS JUDGMENT RULE DETERMINES THE REASONABLENESS OF SETTLEMENTS

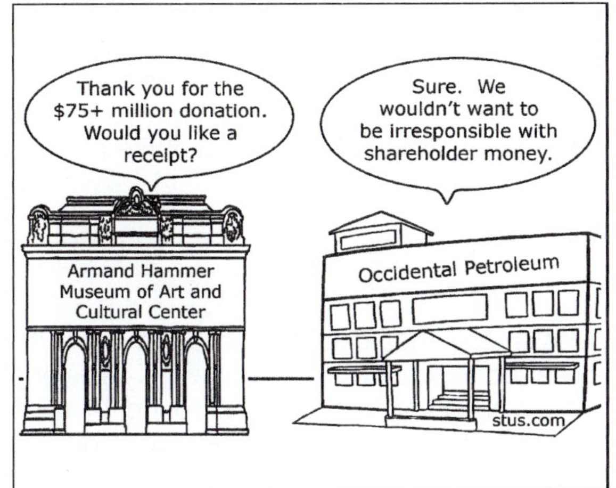

■ **INSTANT FACTS** Shareholders brought a derivative action against the corporation, challenging a charitable contribution.

■ **BLACK LETTER RULE** To determine whether a settlement is reasonable, a court looks to the probable validity of the claims; the apparent difficulties in enforcing the claims through the courts; the collectibility of any judgment recovered; the delay, expense and trouble of litigation; the amount of the compromise compared to the amount and collectibility of the judgment; and the views of the parties involved.

■ **PROCEDURAL BASIS**

Chancery court consideration of the parties' proposed settlement agreement.

■ **FACTS**

Occidental Petroleum Corporation (D) delivered proxy statements to its shareholders for its annual meeting, reporting that a special committee had approved a proposal to financially support the construction of the Armand Hammer Museum of Art and Cultural Center to be built adjacent to the corporation's headquarters. The proxy statement noted that the corporation would provide $50 million in construction costs with a thirty-year rent-free lease to the museum, a $24 million annuity for the museum's benefit, and an option to purchase the museum at the end of the lease for its estimated fair-market value. The proxy statement also indicated that the corporation would pay Dr. Hammer (D) a salary to operate the museum at a rate seven times his prior year's earnings. The shareholders brought a derivative suit against the corporation for waste and Dr. Hammer (D) for breach of the duty of loyalty. After settlement discussions, the parties agreed to resolve the claims subject to the defendants' disclosure of other charitable contributions they had made. After receiving the supplemental disclosures, the parties entered into a written settlement agreement. The agreement was presented to the special committee for approval. After consulting with independent counsel and reexamining its proposal to fund the museum, the special committee approved the settlement as in the best interests of the corporation. The proposed settlement agreement was submitted for court approval.

■ **ISSUE**

Is a settlement proposal that confers some benefit upon the shareholders in the face of weak legal claims reasonable?

■ **DECISION AND RATIONALE**

(Hartnett, Vice Ch.) Yes. In reviewing a proposed settlement, a court must determine whether the terms of the settlement comply with state law, view the facts and circumstances upon which the claims are based and any possible defenses, and then exercise its business judgment to determine whether the settlement is reasonable. In exercising this judgment, the court looks to the probable validity of the claims; the apparent difficulties in enforcing the claims through the courts; the collectibility of any judgment recovered; the delay, expense and trouble of litigation; the amount of the compromise compared to the amount and collectibility of the judgment; and the views of the parties involved.

The business judgment rule "is a presumption that in making a business decision the directors of a corporation acted on an informed basis, in good faith and in the honest belief that the action taken was in the best interests of the company." Against this presumption, the plaintiffs have offered very little to demonstrate that the directors acted out of self-interest or dishonesty. The directors' actions would therefore be presumed valid. Likewise, the museum qualifies as a charity and the proposed contributions are reasonable. The plaintiffs' claims are therefore comparatively weak. Given the weakness of the claims, the benefits received by the class of shareholders from the settlement require its approval. The settlement ensures that the corporation will receive considerable good will and the right to use the museum in advertising its business. These benefits, when viewed against the weakness of the plaintiffs' claims, are sufficient to approve the settlement.

Analysis:

As the opinion suggests, when considering whether a settlement should be approved, the court is obliged to view it by its business judgment, not whether the judge would find the board's decision a wise choice if he were a shareholder. Thus, if board action is within the board's sound business judgment, it should be approved so long as it confers some benefit to the shareholders, regardless of whether the judge would approve the action himself.

■ CASE VOCABULARY

BUSINESS–JUDGMENT RULE: The presumption that in making business decisions not involving direct self-interest or self-dealing, corporate directors act on an informed basis, in good faith, and in the honest belief that their actions are in the corporation's best interest.

CHANCERY: A court of equity; collectively, the courts of equity.

ULTRA VIRES: Unauthorized; beyond the scope of power allowed or granted by a corporate charter or by law.

Stanley J. How & Assoc., Inc. v. Boss

(Architect) v. *(Corporations Promoter)*

222 F.Supp. 936 (S.D. Iowa 1963)

A PERSON WHO SIGNS A CONTRACT FOR A NONEXISTENT CORPORATION WILL BE PERSONALLY LIABLE

■ **INSTANT FACTS** An architect sued to recover payment on a contract for architectural services performed.

■ **BLACK LETTER RULE** A promoter, though he may assume to act on behalf of the projected corporation and not for himself, will be personally liable on his contract unless the other party agreed to look to some other person or fund for payment.

■ **PROCEDURAL BASIS**

Action to recover on a contract for the performance of architectural services.

■ **FACTS**

Stanley J. How & Assoc. (P) entered into an agreement with Boss (D), a promoter of a corporation, to provide architectural services. The original contract contained a signature line for "Boss Hotels Co., Inc.," however when the contract was presented to Boss (D), he erased those words and inserted the language "By: Edwin A. Boss, agent for a Minnesota corporation to be formed who will be the obligor." He then asked Mr. How (P) if the change was acceptable, How (P) said it was, and the contracts were then signed by the two men. Boss (D) caused an Iowa corporation named Minneapolis-Hunter Hotel Co. to be formed to construct the project. The checks sent to Stanley How (P) for partial payments under the contract bore the name of this corporation. The project was ultimately abandoned after a substantial amount of architectural work had been performed under the contract. Stanley How (P) alleged that it had performed the required services and was entitled to a fee of $38,250, of which it had received only $14,500. How (P) seeks to collect the difference from Boss (D).

■ **ISSUE**

Will a promoter, who assumes to act on behalf of a corporation to be formed in the future and not for himself, be personally liable on his contract for payment?

■ **DECISION AND RATIONALE**

(Hanson, D.J.) Yes. There really is not much debate as to what the law is on the questions raised. A promoter, though he may assume to act on behalf of the projected corporation and not for himself, will be personally liable on his contract unless the other party agreed to look to some other person or fund for payment. This is a situation where the parties used ambiguous words to describe their intentions. To solve this ambiguity, it is helpful to resort to the usual rules of interpretation of ambiguous contracts. Mr. How's (P) testimony and his business records show that he did not intend that the new corporation was the sole obligor on the contract. He states that he believed Boss Hotel Co., Inc. or Boss Hotels was liable on the contract. This is not inconsistent with thinking that Mr. Boss (D) was liable on the contract, but it is inconsistent with intending that the new corporation was to be solely liable on the contract. Promoters other than the one signing the contract may be liable on the contract also. In this case, Boss Hotel Co., Inc. was not made a party, but this does show a reason why Mr. How (P) might state that he felt Boss Hotel Co., Inc. was liable on the contract. The oral testimony on this point was only generally to the effect that the parties agreed that the contract was all right as written, but did tend to support the conclusion that Mr. Boss (D) was intended to be the present obligor on the contract. It might well be that the parties were thinking about an understanding wherein there would be a future novation. However, Boss (D) didn't feel this was the situation. He did not plead or argue novation or agreement to that effect. Therefore, the only issue was whether the contract was a continuing offer to the then nonexistent corporation, or was an agreement that Mr. Boss (D) was a present obligor. While the agreement was not completely clear, the words "who will be the obligor" are not enough to offset the rule that the person signing for the nonexistent corporation is normally to be personally liable. This is especially true when considered in the light of other circumstances of this case and would be true even without the inference that the law puts on this situation. At the time the specifications and drawings were completed, the amount owed Mr. How (P) was $38,250. Mr. How (P) has already been paid $14,500, leaving an amount of $23,750 due to Mr. How (P). Accordingly, the court concludes that Stanley J. How & Assoc. (P) should have and recover judgment against Edwin Boss (D) in the amount of $23,750, with interest and costs and, accordingly, a judgment will be entered.

Analysis:

Although the problem in this case may have been avoided by the use of clearer language, even with clearer language, what was truly required was the formal assumption of the agreement by the corporation and a writing acknowledging that assumption signed by all, including the corporation. To what extent the Minneapolis-Hunter Hotel Co. actually came into being is not clear in the record. No corporate charter, by-laws, or resolutions were offered into evidence. At any rate, even if this new corporation existed, there were no assets in it to pay the amount due on the contract. In the present case, the contract was signed: "Edwin A. Boss, agent for a Minnesota corporation to be formed who will be the obligor." Boss (D) argued that this is an agreement that the new corporation is solely liable. The problem here is to determine what is the import of the words "who will be the obligor." It says nothing about the present obligor. The words "will be" connote something which will take place in the future.

■ CASE VOCABULARY

BY-LAWS: Regulations, ordinances, rules or laws adopted by an association or corporation or the like for its internal governance.

CORPORATE CHARTER: Document issued by state agency or authority granting a corporation legal existence and right to function as a corporation.

NOVATION: A type of substituted contract that has the effect of adding a party, either as obligor or obligee, who was not a party to the original duty.

OBLIGEE: The party to whom someone else is obligated under a contract.

OBLIGOR: The person who has engaged to perform some obligation.

PROMOTOR: The persons who, for themselves or others, take the preliminary steps to the founding or organization of a corporation or other venture.

RESOLUTIONS: Formal documentation of an action taken by the board of directors of a corporation.

Robertson v. Levy

(*Original Business Owner*) v. (*Purchaser of Plaintiff's Business*)

197 A.2d 443 (D.C. App. 1964)

THERE CAN BE NO LIMITED LIABILITY FOR CORPORATE SHAREHOLDERS BEFORE A CERTIFICATE OF INCORPORATION IS FILED

■ **INSTANT FACTS** A man is suing the person who bought his business before the man had completed the process of incorporating for failure to make the required installment payments after the new business went under.

■ **BLACK LETTER RULE** An individual who incurs statutory liability on an obligation because he has acted without authority, is not relieved of that liability where, at a later time, the corporation does come into existence.

■ **PROCEDURAL BASIS**

Appeal from the trial court's decision in favor of the defendant.

■ **FACTS**

On December 22, 1961, Martin Robertson (P) and Eugene Levy (D) entered into an agreement whereby Levy (D) was to form a corporation, Penn Ave. Record Shack, Inc., which was to purchase Robertson's (P) business. Levy (D) submitted articles of incorporation on December 27, 1961, but no certificate of incorporation was issued at this time. Pursuant to the contract, an assignment of lease was entered into on December 31, 1961, between Robertson (P) and Levy (D), the latter acting as president of Penn Ave. Record Shack, Inc. On January 2, 1962, the articles of incorporation were rejected by the Superintendent of Corporations [oops!], but on the same day Levy (D) began to operate the business under the name Penn Ave. Record Shack, Inc. Robertson (P) executed a bill of sale to Penn Ave. Record Shack, Inc. on January 8, 1962, disposing of the assets of his business to that "corporation" and receiving in return a note providing for installment payments signed "Penn Ave. Record Shack, Inc. by Eugene M. Levy, President." The certificate of incorporation was issued on January 17, 1962. One payment was made on the note, presumably after the certificate of incorporation was issued. Penn Ave. Record Shack, Inc. ceased doing business in June 1962 and is presently without assets [that was quick]. Robertson (P) sued Levy (D) for the balance due on the note as well as for additional expenses incurred in settling the lease arrangement with the original lessor. In holding for the defendant, the trial court found that Robertson (P) was estopped to deny the existence of the corporation.

■ **ISSUE**

Can the president of an "association" which filed its articles of incorporation, which were first rejected but later accepted, be held personally liable on an obligation entered into before the certificate of incorporation has been issued?

■ **DECISION AND RATIONALE**

(Hood, C.J.) Yes. On this appeal, we are concerned with an interpretation of sections 50 and 139 of the 1950 Model Act. A search of the case law convinces us that these particular sections of the corporation acts have never been the subject of a reported decision. The first portion of section 50 sets

---

forth a sine qua non regarding compliance. No longer must the courts inquire into the equities of a case to determine whether there has been "colorable compliance" with the statute. The corporation comes into existence only when the certificate has been issued. Before the certificate issues, there is no corporation de jure, de facto or by estoppel. After the certificate is issued under section 50, the de jure corporate existence commences. Only after such existence has begun can the corporation commence business through compliance with section 48 of the MBCA (1950) by paying into the corporation the minimum capital, and with section 51 of that Act, which require that the capitalization be no less than $1,000. These latter two sections are given further force and effect by a non-Model Act section which declares that directors of a corporation are jointly and severally liable for any assets distributed or any dividends paid to shareholders which renders the corporation insolvent or reduces its net assets below its stated capital. The authorities which have considered the problem are unanimous in their belief that MBCA (1950) sections 50 and 139 have put to rest de facto corporations and corporations by estoppel. The portion of section 50 which state that the certificate of incorporation will be "conclusive evidence" that all conditions precedent have been performed eliminates the problems of estoppel and de facto corporations once the certificate has been issued. The existence of the corporation is conclusive evidence against all who deal with it. Under section 139, if an individual or group of individuals assumes to act as a corporation before the certificate of incorporation has been issued, joint and several liability attaches. We hold, therefore, that the impact of these sections, when considered together, is to eliminate the concepts of estoppel and de facto corporateness. It is immaterial whether the third person believed he was dealing with a corporation or whether he intended to deal with a corporation. The certificate of incorporation provides the cut off point; before it is issued, the individuals, and not the corporation, are liable. Turning to the facts of this case, Penn Ave. Record Shack, Inc. was not a corporation when the original agreement was entered into, when the lease was assigned, when Levy (D) took over Robertson's (D) business, when operations began under the Penn Ave. Record Shack, Inc. name, or when the bill of sale was executed. Only on January 17 did Penn Ave. Record Shack, Inc. become a corporation. Levy (D) is subject to personal liability because, before this date, he assumed to act as a corporation without any authority to do so. Nor is Robertson (P) estopped from denying the existence of the corporation because after the certificate was issued he accepted one payment on the note. An individual who incurs statutory liability on an obligation under section 139 because he has acted without authority, is not relieved of that liability where, at a later time, the corporation does come into existence by complying with section 50. Subsequent partial payments by the corporation does not remove this liability. The judgment appealed from is reversed with instructions to enter judgment against Levy (D) on the note and for damages proved to have been incurred by Robertson (P) for breach of the lease.

Analysis:

In early common law times, private corporations were looked upon with distrust and disfavor. The distrust of the corporate form for private enterprise was eventually overcome by the enactment of statutes that set forth certain prerequisites before the status was achieved, and by court decisions that eliminated other stumbling blocks. Problems soon arose, however, when there was substantial compliance with the prerequisites of the statute, but not formal compliance. Thus the concepts of de jure corporations, de facto corporations, and "corporations by estoppel" came into being. A de jure corporation results when there has been conformity with the mandatory conditions precedent (as opposed to merely directive conditions) established by the statute. A de jure corporation is not subject to direct or collateral attack either by the state in a quo warranto proceeding or by any other person. A de facto corporation is one that has been defectively incorporated and thus is not de jure. A de facto corporation is recognized for all purposes except when there is a direct attack by the state in a quo warranto proceeding. The concept of de facto corporation has been roundly criticized. Cases continued to arise, however, where the corporation was not de jure, where it was not de facto because of failure to comply with one of the four requirements above, but where the courts, lacking some clear standard or guideline, were willing to decide on the equities of the case. Thus another concept arose, the so-called "corporation by estoppel." One of the reasons for enacting modern corporation statutes was to eliminate problems inherent in the de jure, de facto, and estoppel concepts. Thus, as the Court applies the law to the facts of this case, liability is imposed on all persons who assume to act as a corporation.

■ CASE VOCABULARY

ARTICLES OF INCORPORATION: The basic instrument filed with the appropriate governmental agency on the incorporation of a business.

COLLATERAL ATTACK: An attack on a judgment in any manner other than by action or proceeding, whose very purpose is to impeach or overturn that judgment.

CORPORATION BY ESTOPPEL: A corporation which comes about when parties, by their agreements or conduct, estop themselves from denying the existence of the corporation.

DE FACTO CORPORATION: An association claiming to be a legally incorporated company, and exercising the power and functions of a corporation, but without actual lawful authority to do so.

DE JURE CORPORATION: That which exists by reason of full compliance by incorporators with requirements of an existing law permitting organization of such corporation.

JOINT AND SEVERAL LIABILITY: A creditor may demand payment or sue one or more of the parties to such liability separately, or all of them together at his option.

QUO WARRANTO: A common law writ designed to test whether a person exercising power is legally entitled to do so.

Frontier Refining Company v. Kunkel's, Inc.

(Creditor) v. *(Defectively Incorporated Business and Members)*

407 P.2d 880 (Wyo. 1965)

DEFECTIVE CORPORATION'S INVESTORS ARE NOT LIABLE FOR CORPORATE DEBT IF THEY ARE IGNORANT AND PASSIVE

■ **INSTANT FACTS** When a defectively incorporated company's manager bought oil before incorporating, the seller sued his absentee associates as partners.

■ **BLACK LETTER RULE** A defectively incorporated business's members are jointly and severally liable for its debts only if (i) they represented themselves as incorporated, or authorized an agent to do so (implicitly or explicitly), (ii) the debt was incurred in the corporation's name, and (iii) granting personal liability would be equitable.

■ **PROCEDURAL BASIS**

In suit to recover business debt, appeal from judgment for defendants.

■ **FACTS**

Businessman Kunkel (D) wanted to buy a gas station from owner Frontier Refining Company (P). To raise the money, Kunkel (D) approached investors Mr. Fairfield (D) and Mr. Beach (D) for money. (It is unclear whether he requested a loan, partnership, or corporation). Fairfield (D) and Beach (D) agreed, but only if the venture was incorporated. They understood that Kunkel (D) would operate the station. Fairfield (D) and Beach (D) expected Kunkel (D) to also have the business incorporated, and told Kunkel (D) not to operate before incorporating. The incorporation was forgotten. Frontier's (P) inspector Warren visited the premises. He came away believing the station was a corporation, Kunkel's, Inc. (D), with Fairfield (D) and Beach (D) as officers. (Warren claims Fairfield (D) told him so.) Simultaneously, Kunkel (D) purchased leases and supplies from Frontier (P) over 30 days, sometimes signing contracts "Kunkel DBA Kunkel's, Inc.," but usually just signing his name without mentioning Kunkel's, Inc. (D). Apparently, Fairfield (D) and Beach (D) were unaware that Kunkel (D) had started doing business, and still had not incorporated. Kunkel (D) ended up owing Frontier (P) $5,000. Wyoming's statutes provided, "All persons who assume to act as a corporation without authority . . . shall be jointly and severally liable for all debts . . . incurred . . . thereof." Frontier (P) sued Kunkel (D), Fairfield (D), and Beach (D) personally, claiming Kunkel's, Inc. (D) was a partnership, with each partner personally liable. Fairfield (D) and Beach (D) denied any partnership, claiming Kunkel (D) was doing business as an individual. At trial, the court held for the defendants, finding no partnership existed. Frontier (P) appeals, citing the general rule that businesspeople who let their agents hold themselves out as corporate representatives are personally liable, jointly and severally.

■ **ISSUE**

If a defectively incorporated firm's agent incurs debt, and its members are unaware of the debt and defect, are they personally liable for the debt?

■ DECISION AND RATIONALE

(Gray, J.) No. A defectively incorporated business's members are jointly and severally liable for its debts only if (i) they represented themselves as incorporated, or authorized an agent to do so (implicitly or explicitly), (ii) the debt was incurred in the corporation's name, and (iii) granting personal liability would be equitable. The court's conclusion—that, under general legal principles, the defendants cannot be treated as partners—is supported. The court can infer that any representations about incorporation made to Frontier (P) were made by Kunkel (D) alone, without authorization (express or implied) by Fairfield (D) and Beach (D). Thus, if Fairfield (D) and Beach (D) did not hold themselves out as a corporation, they are not personally liable under the general rule. Also, the court could conclude that the debt was incurred in the name of Kunkel (D) individually rather than for a corporation, because when Frontier (P) first did business with Kunkel (D), it knew no corporation was yet formed, and was willing to transact with Kunkel (D) as an individual. We note Frontier's (P) position is inconsistent. In a companion case, Frontier (P) sued in replevin to repossess the property, and won on the inference that Kunkel (D) was operating as an individual. (To do that, Frontier (P) had Kunkel (D) sign a chattel mortgage on the gas station's equipment, as an individual.) To permit Frontier (P) to disavow such judgment, and now also recover from Fairfield (D) and Beach (D), would be unconscionable and inequitable. Judgment for defendants affirmed.

Analysis:

This case illustrates that "defective incorporation" cases tend to be decided inconsistently. They often blur the doctrines of "de facto" and "de jure" corporations, and incorporation by estoppel. Also, they often combine or choose rules from the law of agency and the law of partnership, which often yield different outcomes. Even when standards are prescribed by statute, they are still subject to broad judicial interpretation, and judges still tend to include other considerations. (E.g., here, the judge also considered "equity" as a factor.) Basically, this case is important to show that, since such matters are decided inconsistently, corporate investors should ensure than papers are filed properly, to avoid personal liability.

■ CASE VOCABULARY

CHATTEL MORTGAGE: A mortgage for goods, authorizing the seller to seize the goods if the buyer does not pay.

DBA: "Doing business as." Connotes that an individual or company is conducting business under an assumed name. Usual written d/b/a.

REPLEVIN: Lawsuit to recover property held wrongfully by another, usually a debtor.

CHAPTER SEVEN

Disregard of the Corporate Entity

Bartle v. Home Owners Corp.

Instant Facts: Bankruptcy trustee, Bartle (P), sought to pierce the corporate veil of Westerlea, in order to hold the parent corporation, Home Owners Corp. (D), liable for Westerlea's debts.

Black Letter Rule: The doctrine of "piercing the corporate veil" is used to hold the shareholders of a corporation liable in order to prevent fraud or to achieve equity.

Dewitt Truck Brokers v. W. Ray Flemming Fruit Co.

Instant Facts: Sole shareholder (D1) of company was sued individually for corporation's debt based upon his siphoning funds from company for himself and promises to personally pay debt.

Black Letter Rule: Sole shareholder of corporation may be held individually liable for corporate debts by piercing the corporate veil where, combined with other facts supporting disregard of the corporate fiction, fundamental equity and fairness dictate disregarding the corporate shield.

Baatz v. Arrow Bar

Instant Facts: Individual shareholders (D2) were sued because their corporation, a bar, negligently served drunken patron who caused an automobile accident injuring Baatz (P).

Black Letter Rule: The corporate veil will not be pierced to impose tort liability on individual shareholders merely because they personally guaranteed corporate contracts.

Radaszewski v. Telecom Corp.

Instant Facts: Radaszewski (P), an injured motorist, could not pierce the corporate veil of driver's corporate employer because corporation maintained adequate liability insurance.

Black Letter Rule: Piercing the corporate veil of a subsidiary corporation is not proper in a tort action where the subsidiary had liability insurance, even though the plaintiff is unable to recover under that insurance.

Fletcher v. Atex, Inc.

Instant Facts: Injured computer users sued Kodak, the parent corporation, claiming subsidiary computer keyboard manufacturer was its was alter ego, and parent should be held liable.

Black Letter Rule: In order to hold a parent corporation liable for its subsidiary's conduct on an alter ego theory, the two must operate as a single economic entity and an overall element of injustice or unfairness must be present.

United States v. Bestfoods

Instant Facts: Government sued parent corporation under federal statute for clean up costs of contamination caused by subsidiary that operated the polluting plant.

Black Letter Rule: A parent corporation that actively participates in, and exercises control over, the operations of a subsidiary, as is normally done by a parent corporation, without more, may not be held liable as an operator of a polluting facility owned or operated by the subsidiary. But, if the parent corporation takes more of an active role in the operations of the subsidiary, the parent may be liable under federal pollution control laws.

Stark v. Flemming

Instant Facts: Stark (P) placed her property in a corporation and drew a small salary, on which she claimed social security benefits.

Black Letter Rule: The federal government must recognize a properly formed corporation operating under normal corporate routines.

Roccograndi v. Unemployment Comp. Bd. of Review

Instant Facts: Corporate officers of family wrecking business who were systematically laid off when it was their turn sought unemployment benefits as employees of corporation.

Black Letter Rule: Corporate status will be disregarded if corporate officers asserted corporate status for a purpose used to defeat public policy.

Cargill, Inc. v. Hedge

Instant Facts: Hedge (D) tried to claim a homestead exemption for corporate-owned farm property to save it from an execution sale.

Black Letter Rule: When a corporation acts as the alter ego of its shareholders, the corporate veil may be reverse pierced to further strong public policy interests.

Pepper v. Litton

Instant Facts: Bankruptcy court disallowed the claim of owner shareholder of corporation for back salary to prevent fraud and unfairness to the other creditors.

Black Letter Rule: Bankruptcy court may use its equitable powers to disallow either as a secured or as a general or unsecured claim a judgment obtained by the dominant and controlling stockholder of the bankrupt corporation.

Nissen Corp. v. Miller

Instant Facts: Brandt purchased a treadmill marketed by American Tredex Corporation, which then sold its assets to Nissen Corporation. Subsequently, Brandt was injured by an alleged defect in the treadmill and now seeks to sue Nissen Corp., as successor in interest to American Tredex.

Black Letter Rule: A corporation acquiring all or a portion of the assets of another corporation does not also acquire that corporation's liabilities and debt except where: (1) such is expressed or implied in the agreement; (2) the acquisition actually amounts to a merger or consolidation; (3) the successor corporation is actually a continuation of the predecessor corporation or entity; or (4) the agreement was fraudulent, lacked good faith, or was made with inadequate consideration.

Bartle v. Home Owners Co-op.

(Bankruptcy Trustee) v. *(Parent Corporation)*

309 N.Y. 103, 127 N.E.2d 832 (Ct. App. 1955)

IN CERTAIN SITUATIONS, COURTS MAY "PIERCE THE CORPORATE VEIL" OF A CORPORATE ENTITY AND HOLD THE OWNERS LIABLE FOR CORPORATE DEBTS

■ **INSTANT FACTS** Bankruptcy trustee, Bartle (P), sought to pierce the corporate veil of Westerlea, in order to hold the parent corporation. Home Owners Corp. (D), liable for Westerlea's debts.

■ **BLACK LETTER RULE** The doctrine of "piercing the corporate veil" is used to hold the shareholders of a corporation liable in order to prevent fraud or to achieve equity.

■ **PROCEDURAL BASIS**

Appeal to State Supreme Court from affirming of judgment in action by bankruptcy trustee to pierce the corporate veil of a wholly owned subsidiary corporation.

■ **FACTS**

Bartle (P), as trustee in the bankruptcy matter of Westerlea Builders, Inc. (Westerlea), filed suit against Home Owners Coop. (Home) (D) in an attempt to hold Home (D) liable for the contract debts of its wholly owned subsidiary, Westerlea. Westerlea was organized for the purposes of being the building contractor corporation for Home (D), a builder of low-cost housing for its stockholder members. After experiencing financial difficulties, the creditors took over Westerlea's construction responsibilities, and four years later, the company was adjudicated a bankrupt. [In other words, the creditors are out of luck and there are no assets to collect from.] Bartle (P) contended that Home (D) should be liable for Westerlea's contract debts because the houses Westerlea built would be sold to Home's (D) shareholders in amounts fixed to so that Westerlea would never make a profit. The trial and appellate courts refused to pierce the corporate veil of Westerlea's corporate existence and Bartle (P) appealed.

■ **ISSUE**

May shareholders of a corporation ever be held liable for the corporation's debts?

■ **DECISION AND RATIONALE**

(Froessel, J.) Yes. Under the doctrine of "piercing the corporate veil," shareholders of a corporation may be held liable in order to prevent fraud or to achieve equity. Home (D), as owner of the stock of Westerlea, controlled its affairs. During the time the creditors extended credit to Westerlea, the outward indicia of the two separate corporations was always maintained and the creditors were not misled. There was no fraud, nor did Home (D) perform an act that caused injury to Westerlea's creditors by depletion of assets or otherwise. [It just set up a corporate entity that could never make a profit!] The law permits the incorporation of a business for the very purpose of escaping personal liability. In this case, there has been no fraud, misrepresentation, or illegality. Thus, invoking the doctrine of "piercing the corporate veil" would not be appropriate. Home's (D) purpose in placing its construction operation into a separate corporation was clearly within the limits of our public policy. Affirmed.

DISSENT

(Van Voorhis, J.) Not only is Westerlea a wholly owned subsidiary of Home (D), having the same directors and management, but also, and of primary importance, business was done on such a basis that Westerlea could not make a profit. Westerlea was organized as a builder corporation to erect homes for the stockholders of Home (D). The prices of the homes were fixed by Home's (D) price policy committee in such amounts as to make no allowance for profit by Westerlea. The object was to benefit Home's (D) stockholders by enabling them to obtain their houses at cost, with no builder's profits. The law has held a parent corporation liable where its subsidiary had, to begin with, nothing, made nothing, and could only end up with nothing. Even if Westerlea had been successful, it would not make a profit, and would just break even. The benefit to Home's (D) stockholders was a benefit to Home (D) as a corporation. Home (D) should be rendered liable for Westerlea's debts.

Analysis:

This case examines the doctrine of "piercing the corporate veil." As the court noted, the law permits incorporation for the very purpose of escaping personal liability. However, under certain situations courts permit the "piercing of the corporate veil" in order that the shareholder of the corporation, in this case Home (D), is held liable for the corporation's debts. The goals of piercing the corporate veil are to "prevent fraud" and to "achieve equity." Note that the following facts were *not* sufficient to permit the piercing of Westerlea's corporate veil: (1) it was wholly owned by Home (D), having the same directors and management; (2) Home (D) controlled Westerlea's affairs; (3) Home (D) contributed to Westerlea its original capital plus additional sums; (4) Westerlea's business was done on such a basis that it could not make a profit; (5) Westerlea was organized to build homes on Home's (D) land; and (6) the homes were sold by Home (D) to its stockholders at a price fixed by it making no allowance for profit by Westerlea. The decision to deny piercing was supported by these factors: (1) maintaining the indicia of two separate corporations; (2) creditors were not misled; (3) lack of fraud; and (4) no act by Home (D) causing injury to the creditors.

■ CASE VOCABULARY

COOPERATIVE CORPORATION: A corporation that is primarily organized for the purpose of providing services and profits to its members, rather than for corporate profit.

DOCTRINE OF UNJUST ENRICHMENT: One may not profit or enrich himself at the expense of another which is contrary to justice and equity.

EXTENSION AGREEMENT: One which gives additional time to perform the underlying agreement.

PARENT CORPORATION: A corporation that owns in excess of 50% of the stock of another company, called the "subsidiary."

PIERCE THE CORPORATE VEIL: Court disregards the cloak of officer and shareholder immunity from liability for corporate conduct, such as where fraud or inequity exits, thereby holding officers or shareholders liable for corporate obligations.

TRUSTEE IN BANKRUPTCY: The person assigned the duty of taking control of the debtor's estate in order to collect assets, bring suit on claims, defend actions against the debtor, and generally administer the estate while the debtor is in bankruptcy proceedings.

WHOLLY OWNED SUBSIDIARY CORPORATION: Where another corporation known as the parent corporation owns all of the shares and has control.

DeWitt Truck Brokers v. W. Ray Flemming Fruit Co.

(Produce Trucker) v. *(Shareholder)*

540 F.2d 681 (4th Cir. 1976)

ALTER EGO AND *MERE INSTRUMENTALITY* ARE CONCEPTS USED TO DETERMINE WHETHER TO PIERCE THE CORPORATE VEIL

■ **INSTANT FACTS** Sole shareholder (D1) of company was sued individually for corporation's debt based upon his siphoning funds from company for himself and promises to personally pay debt.

■ **BLACK LETTER RULE** In general, a court will pierce the corporate veil only reluctantly and cautiously, but will do so where the dominant owner of a closely held corporation treats the corporation as an alter ego or mere instrumentality and there is some element of injustice or fundamental unfairness.

■ **PROCEDURAL BASIS**

Appeal from judgment in action on debt seeking piercing of corporate veil.

■ **FACTS**

DeWitt Truck Brokers (DeWitt) (P) brought action against Mr. Ray Flemming (D1), the individual president of W. Ray Flemming Fruit Co. (Fruit Co.) (D2), seeking individual liability on the corporation's debt by piercing the corporate veil of Fruit Co. (D2). Fruit Co. (D2) was in the business of a commission agent, selling fruit produce for the account of growers of farm products. DeWitt (P) was the trucking company that hauled the products. Fruit Co. (D2) was to remit to the grower the full sale price, less any transportation costs incurred in transporting the products from the growers' farm or warehouse to the purchaser and its sales commission. Fruit Co. (D2) had as it operating funds only the commissions and amount of DeWitt's (P) transportation charges. In the accounting with the growers, Mr. Flemming (D1) represented he had paid DeWitt (P) the transportation charges. Mr. Flemming (D1) was withdrawing funds from Fruit Co. (D2) in the sum of at least $15,000 annually. The amount due DeWitt (P) in transportation costs was approximately the same as the $15,000 minimum annual salary Mr. Flemming (D1) was paid by Fruit Co. (D2). [What a coincidence!] The trial court imposed individual liability and Mr. Flemming (D1) appealed.

■ **ISSUE**

Can a sole shareholder of a corporation be held individually liable for corporate debts by piercing the corporate veil if there is a disregard of the corporate fiction?

■ **DECISION AND RATIONALE**

(Russell, J.) Yes. We hold that a sole shareholder of a corporation may be held individually liable for corporate debts by piercing the corporate veil where, combined with other facts supporting disregard of the corporate fiction, fundamental equity and fairness dictate disregarding the corporate shield. A corporation's debts are generally not the individual indebtedness of its stockholders. However, courts will decline to recognize the concept of separate entity whenever recognition of the corporate form would extend the principle of incorporation beyond its legitimate purposes and would produce injustices or inequitable consequences.   Thus, in the appropriate case, the corporate veil will be pierced and the corporation and its stockholders will be treated as identical.   Proof of plain fraud is not a necessary element to disregard the corporate entity.   However, when substantial ownership of all the stock of a corporation in a single individual is combined with other facts supporting disregard of the corporate fiction on grounds of fundamental equity and fairness, courts will apply an alter ego or instrumentality theory in order to disregard the corporate shield and impose liability on the individual stockholder.   Facts that should be given substantial weight, particularly in the case of the one-man or closely-held corporation, are whether the corporation was grossly undercapitalized for the purposes of the corporate undertaking, the failure to observe corporate formalities, non-payment of dividends, the insolvency of the debtor corporation, siphoning of corporate funds by the dominant stockholder, non-functioning of other officers or directors, absence of corporate records, and the corporation being merely a facade for the operations of the dominant stockholder.   Disregarding the corporate entity may not rest on a single factor, but must involve a number of factors.   In addition, it must present an element of injustice or fundamental unfairness.   The facts of this case show that the Fruit Co. (D2) was a one-man corporation.   At incorporation, 5,000 shares were issued for a consideration of one dollar each.   The corporate formalities were not observed.   Although there was one other director, he was nothing more than a figurehead who had not attended directors meetings, and had never received any fee or reimbursement of expenses or salary of any kind from the corporation.   There were no corporate records of real directors' meetings, and there was never a stockholders' meeting.   The payments to Mr. Flemming (D1), as the sole beneficiary of the corporation's operations, were not authorized by any resolution of the board of directors.   The corporation was obviously undercapitalized, evidenced by years of inability to pay a dividend.   Equity and fundamental justice support individual liability of Mr. Flemming (D1) for DeWitt's (P) transportation charges, payment which he asserted had been paid. Moreover, Mr. Flemming (D1) told DeWitt (P) that he would take care of the charges personally, if Fruit Co. (D2) failed to do so.   On this assurance, DeWitt (P) continued to haul for Fruit Co. (D2).   When one, who is the sole beneficiary of the corporation's operations and who dominates it, induces a creditor to extend credit to the corporation on such assurance as given here, that is a sufficient basis for piercing the corporate veil.   Affirmed.

Analysis:

In this case, the concepts of *alter ego or mere instrumentality* are introduced.   The court listed various factors that should be considered in deciding whether to pierce the corporate veil based on these concepts.   The facts in this case showed an improper diversion of corporate assets, i.e., the $15,000 salary paid to Mr. Flemming (D1), which in effect prevented the company from paying DeWitt (P).   The accounting showed that the money was to go to DeWitt (P), yet Mr. Flemming (D1) siphoned off the money to pay himself instead.   In addition, Mr. Flemming (D1) promised DeWitt (P) that he would be personally responsible for the transportation charges if the company could not pay.   This action could be construed as tricking or misleading DeWitt (P) into continuing to haul for the corporation.   These factors are sufficient to allow individual shareholder liability.

■ CASE VOCABULARY

ALTER EGO: Referring to the doctrine of "alter ego" whereby corporate entity is disregarded and stockholders are liable for the corporate debts and obligations.

INSTRUMENTALITY THEORY: A rule similar to "alter ego" but disregarding the corporate entity of a subsidiary corporation and holding the parent corporation responsible for the subsidiary's debts and obligations.

SUI GENERIS: Latin for "of its own kind or class."

Baatz v. Arrow Bar

(Injured Parties) v. *(Incorporated Bar)*

452 N.W.2d 138 (S.D. 1990)

PIERCING THE CORPORATE VEIL IN TORT ACTIONS REQUIRES MORE THAN PERSONALLY GUAR-
ANTEEING CORPORATE OBLIGATIONS

■ **INSTANT FACTS** Individual shareholders (D2) were sued because their corporation, a bar, negligently served drunken patron who caused an automobile accident injuring Baatz (P).

■ **BLACK LETTER RULE** The corporate veil will not be pierced to impose tort liability on individual shareholders merely because they personally guaranteed corporate contracts.

■ **PROCEDURAL BASIS**

Appeal from summary judgment dismissing individual defendants in action for negligence seeking damages for personal injuries.

■ **FACTS**

Kenny and Peggy Baatz (collectively Baatz) (P) were injured in an automobile/motorcycle accident with an uninsured and judgment proof individual named McBride. Baatz (P) sued Arrow Bar, Inc. (D1) and three individual shareholders, the Neuroth's (D2), for negligence in serving alcohol to the already intoxicated McBride. Edmond and La Vella Neuroth (D2) formed the Arrow Bar, Inc. (D) and contributed money for its initial capitalization. Thereafter, they purchased the Arrow Bar business with a $5,000 down payment and personally guaranteed the balance of the purchase price in the sum of $150,000. Three years later, the corporation obtained bank financing to pay off the purchase agreement and Edmond and La Vella Neuroth (D2) again personally guaranteed payment of the corporate debt. Edmond Neuroth (D2) was the president and Jacquette Neuroth (D2) was the manager of the business. The trial court originally entered summary judgment in favor of Arrow Bar (D1) and the Neuroths (D2), but the judgment was reversed and remanded back for trial. Shortly before the trial date, the Neuroths (D2) moved for and obtained summary judgment dismissing them as individual defendants. Baatz (P) appealed contending that it was error to not permit Arrow Bar's (D1) corporate veil to be pierced and to not hold the Neuroths (D2), as shareholders, individually liable for the corporation's negligence.

■ **ISSUE**

Can the corporate veil be pierced to impose tort liability on individual shareholders where the individual shareholders personally guaranteed corporate contracts?

■ **DECISION AND RATIONALE**

(Sabers, J.) No. The corporate veil will not be pierced to impose tort liability on the individual shareholders merely because they personally guaranteed corporate contracts. Factors that indicate injustices and inequitable consequences, and which allow a court to pierce the corporate veil are: 1) fraudulent representation by corporation directors; 2) undercapitalization; 3) failure to observe corporate formalities; 4) absence of corporate records; 5) payment by the corporation of individual obligations; or 6) use of the corporation to promote fraud, injustice or illegalities. Baatz (P) contends that the corporate veil should be pierced on various grounds. [Unfortunately, Baatz (P) doesn't have the evidence to prove the contentions asserted.] First, they argue that since Edmond and LaVella (D2) personally guaranteed corporate obligations, personal liability should be imposed. This argument is rejected because the personal guarantee of a loan is a contractual agreement and cannot be enlarged to impose tort liability. Second, they argue that the corporation is the alter ego of the Neuroths (D2) and the corporate veil should be pierced. However, they fail to show how Neuroths (D2) were transacting personal business through the corporation. Third, Baatz (P) contends that the corporation is undercapitalized because it started with only $5,000 in borrowed capital. However, they did not explain how that amount failed to equip the corporation with sufficient capital, and they fail to consider the personal guarantees to pay off the purchase contract. The final [rather desperate] argument asserts that the corporation failed to observe corporate formalities because the business signs and advertising failed to indicate that it was a corporation. This argument is rejected because the name of the business—Arrow Bar, Inc.—includes the abbreviation of the word incorporated. Even if it did not, this alone would not be sufficient to pierce the corporate veil. Affirmed.

■ DISSENT

(Henderson, J.) The corporation has no separate existence and it is the instrumentality of the three shareholders, officers, and employees. Arrow Bar, Inc. (D1) is being used to justify wrongs perpetrated by the incorporators in their individual capacity. Fraud is perpetrated upon the public. Edmond Neuroth (D2), the president of the company, testified that the reason for the incorporation was to shield against individual liability. The corporation was undercapitalized because the Neuroths (D2) borrowed $5,000 in capital. A corporation conceived in undercapitalization as a shield should not be used as an artifice to avoid the intent of the law that makes it unlawful for a licensed bar to sell an alcoholic beverage to an obviously intoxicated person.

Analysis:

This case deals with whether the corporate veil may be pierced to hold individual shareholders liable for the *torts* of the corporation. When a tort is involved, the third party does not deal with the corporation "voluntarily," and a *nonconsensual transaction* exits. The court was unwilling to extend tort liability to the individual shareholders merely because they personally guaranteed corporate loans. The case also examined other factors that may result in piercing the corporate veil, such as undercapitalization, failure to observe corporate formalities, and payment of individual obligations by the corporation. Even though this court did not allow piercing of the corporate veil, it should be noted that legal commentators have said that nonconsensual tort situations make a stronger case for piercing the veil due to the third party's lack of voluntariness.

■ CASE VOCABULARY

AFFIDAVIT: A written statement declaring, by oath or affirmation, the truth of the matters contained therein.

DRAM SHOP: A place where alcohol is sold to be drunk on the premises, such as a bar.

GENUINE ISSUES OF MATERIAL FACT: Also referred to as a triable issue of fact or question of fact, which will defeat a motion for summary judgment, so that the matter may proceed to trial.

JUDGMENT PROOF: Those persons who for various reasons it is not possible to collect on a judgment, such as bankrupts, insolvents, or exempt from levy.

LICENSEE: One who has a license to do something.

STOCK SUBSCRIPTION AGREEMENT: A contract whereby one agrees to buy stock.

Radaszewski v. Telecom Corp.

(Injured Tort Victim) v. *(Parent Corporation)*

981 F.2d 305 (8th Cir. 1992)

UNDERCAPITALIZATION MAY RESULT IN PIERCING THE CORPORATE VEIL IN TORT ACTIONS

■ **INSTANT FACTS** Radaszewski (P), an injured motorist, could not pierce the corporate veil of driver's corporate employer because corporation maintained adequate liability insurance.

■ **BLACK LETTER RULE** Piercing the corporate veil of a subsidiary corporation is not proper in a tort action where the subsidiary had liability insurance, even though the plaintiff is unable to recover under that insurance.

■ PROCEDURAL BASIS

Appeal from judgment dismissing complaint for personal injuries sustained in automobile collision.

■ FACTS

Radaszewski (P) was injured in an automobile accident when a truck driven by an employee of Contrux, Inc., a subsidiary of Telecom Corporation (D), struck the motorcycle he was riding. Contrux had liability insurance for its vehicles but [unfortunately for Radaszewski (P)] the insurance company became insolvent. [Not willing to give up,] Radaszewski (P) sued Telecom Corporation (D), and sought to pierce the corporate veil of its subsidiary, Contrux, Inc. in order to hold Telecom (D) liable for the conduct of Contrux's employee. The District Court held that it lacked jurisdiction. Radaszewski (P) appealed. The issue on appeal concerned whether it was proper to pierce the corporate veil of the admittedly undercapitalized Contrux even though it had obtained adequate liability insurance, albeit through a carrier that subsequently became involved two years after the accident.

■ ISSUE

Is piercing of the corporate veil of a subsidiary corporation proper in a tort action where the subsidiary had liability insurance but the plaintiff is unable to recover under that insurance?

■ DECISION AND RATIONALE

(Arnold, J.) No. Piercing the corporate veil of a subsidiary corporation is not proper in a tort action where the subsidiary had liability insurance, even though the plaintiff is unable to recover under that insurance. There are exceptions to the general rule that someone injured by the conduct of a corporation or one of its employees can look only to the employee or employer corporation for recovery. In Missouri, the following three elements must be shown in order to pierce the corporate veil: (1) Control in the form of complete domination of the finances, policy and business practice in respect to the particular transaction so that the corporate entity had no separate mind, will or existence of its own; (2) Such control must have been used by the defendant to commit fraud or wrong, to perpetrate the violation of a statutory or other positive legal duty, or perpetrate a dishonest and unjust act in contravention of plaintiff's legal rights; and (3) The aforesaid control and breach of duty must proximately cause the injury or unjust loss of which a plaintiff complains. *Undercapitalization* of a subsidiary, which means creating it and putting it in business without sufficient money will meet the requirement of element number (2) above. Thus, the existence of a corporate entity that is operated

---

while undercapitalized will be disregarded because of the inference that the parent is either deliberately or recklessly creating a business that will not be able to pay its bills or satisfy judgments against it. It is conceded that Contrux was undercapitalized, since the money contributed to its operation by Telecom (D) was in the form of loans, not equity, and when Contrux first went into business, Telecom (D) did not pay for all of the stock that was issued to it, a classic example of watered stock. [Sounds like Radaszewski (P) is about to win, until you read further.] We accept Telecom's (D) assertion that the inadequate capitalization does not matter because Contrux had significant liability insurance to pay judgments like the one that Radaszewski (P) hopes to obtain, even though the carrier subsequently became insolvent. The amount of insurance maintained by Contrux exceeded federal requirements. If a subsidiary is financially responsible, whether by means of insurance or otherwise, the policy behind the second element of the piercing the corporate veil test is met. The doctrine of limited liability would be destroyed if a parent corporation could be held liable simply based on errors in business judgment. Something more is required and there are no facts here to show something more. [Radaszewski (P) is about to lose.] We affirm the judgment dismissing the complaint for want of jurisdiction, but modify the judgment to provide that it is with prejudice as to Radaszewski's (P) complaint against Telecom (D). [This mean Radaszewski (P) has no chance in the future either.]

DISSENT

(Heaney) Contrux's liability insurance is a relevant factor to be considered, but after a trial a fact finder might find that this factor alone does not require a verdict for the defendant.

Analysis:

This case involves a tort, as opposed to a consensual transaction such as a contract dispute between the parties. The issue of piercing the corporate veil is examined with respect to the element of undercapitalization. There was no dispute that the subsidiary, Contrux, was undercapitalized. Rather, the issue involved whether adequate liability insurance was sufficient to offset the company's undercapitalization. The court in effect held that adequate insurance coverage, that was supposed to provide funds to an injured tort victim such as Radaszewski (P), amounted to capital that would prevent piercing the corporate veil of an otherwise undercapitalized corporation. The court held that since Contrux had adequate insurance coverage in accordance with federal requirements, it was sufficient to deny piercing of the corporate veil. Note that had there been no insurance policy, the result would have been different because undercapitalization would have allowed the piercing of Contrux's corporate veil.

■ CASE VOCABULARY

DOCTRINE OF LIMITED LIABILITY: As used herein, the law that limits the liability of the parent corporation for acts by its subsidiary.

WITH PREJUDICE: Dismissal of an action with no ability to re-file a complaint.

Fletcher v. Atex, Inc.

(Injured Computer Users) v. *(Subsidiary Manufacturer)*

68 F.3d 1451 (2nd Cir. 1995)

THE CORPORATE VEIL OF A COMPANY MAY BE PIERCED WHERE IT IS THE ALTER EGO OF ITS OWNER

■ **INSTANT FACTS** Injured computer users sued Kodak, the parent corporation, claiming subsidiary computer keyboard manufacturer was its alter ego, and parent should be held liable.

■ **BLACK LETTER RULE** In order to hold a parent corporation liable for its subsidiary's conduct on an alter ego theory, the two must operate as a single economic entity and an overall element of injustice or unfairness must be present.

■ **PROCEDURAL BASIS**

Appeal from dismissal of action following entry of summary judgment in action for damages for personal injuries.

■ **FACTS**

Fletcher (P) and other plaintiffs sued Atex, Inc. (D1) and its parent, Eastman Kodak Company (Kodak) (D2) for repetitive stress injuries caused by their use of computer keyboards manufactured by Atex (D1). [Watch out for those monster keyboards.]   Atex (D1) was the wholly owned subsidiary of Kodak (D2) for a number of years, although its name was changed a number of times throughout the years. Fletcher (P) sought to pierce Atex's (D1) corporate veil and hold its owner, Kodak (D2), liable on the ground that Atex (D1) was the alter ego of Kodak (D2) and the two operated as a single economic entity.   [In other words, they wanted to get at Kodak's (D2) assets.]   Summary judgment was entered dismissing Kodak (D2) and Fletcher (P) appealed.

■ **ISSUE**

Can a parent corporation be held liable for its subsidiary's conduct on an alter ego theory if the two operate as a single economic entity and an overall element of injustice or unfairness is present?

■ **DECISION AND RATIONALE**

(Cabranes, J.) Yes.   In order to hold a parent corporation liable for its subsidiary's conduct on an alter ego theory, there must be a showing that (1) the parent and the subsidiary operated as a single economic entity and that (2) an overall element of injustice or unfairness is present.   The factors that must be considered in determining whether or not the parent and subsidiary are operating as a single economic entity are adequate capitalization, solvency, payment of dividends, keeping corporate records, properly functioning officers and directors, observing corporate formalities, siphoning of corporate funds by dominant shareholder, functioning as a facade for the dominant shareholder. Fletcher (P) asserts that there was domination by Kodak (D2) because of: (1) use of a cash management system; (2) control of major expenditures, and sales of stock and assets; (3) a dominating presence on the board of directors; (4) brochures and literature describing the relationship between the two companies; and (5) Atex's (D1) assignment of a former officer's mortgage to Kodak (D2).   These elements are insufficient to establish the degree of domination necessary to pierce Atex's

---

(D1) corporate veil. With respect to Kodak's (D2) use of a cash management system, this is indicative of the usual parent-subsidiary relationship. There are no facts showing a system of complete commingling of funds or a means by which Kodak (D2) siphoned all of Atex's (D1) revenue into its own account. With respect to control and approval of expenditures and sales, this type of conduct is typical of a parent corporation. The domination of Atex's (D1) board of directors fails in that parents and subsidiaries frequently have overlapping boards while maintaining separate business operations. The statements in literature referring to a business unit, merger, acquisition, etc. between the companies and use of the Kodak (D2) logo are not evidence that the two operated as a single economic entity. Finally, we hold that even if there were a factual question regarding Kodak's (D2) domination of Atex (D1), summary judgment would still be appropriate because Fletcher (P) offered no evidence of an "overall element of injustice or unfairness" that would result from respecting the two companies' corporate separateness. [The court must be saying that Fletcher (P) has absolutely no chance of prevailing.]

Analysis:

This case looks at the doctrine of alter ego as a means of piercing the corporate veil of a subsidiary company. Note that a showing of fraud is not necessary. The requirements are that the parent and subsidiary "operate as a single economic entity" and that there is an overall element of injustice or unfairness. If a business is just a division or department, the parent may be held liable, but if the business is a true subsidiary, the parent generally will not be liable. Finally, it is interesting to note that the law of Delaware applied because it was the state of Atex's (D1) incorporation. The Delaware law concerning piercing the corporate veil is pro-defendant, probably because so many companies choose to incorporate there.

■ CASE VOCABULARY

CASH MANAGEMENT SYSTEM: Accounting method whereby the records always reflect the indebtedness of one entity to another.

United States v. Bestfoods

(Government) v. *(Parent Corporation)*

524 U.S. 51, 188 S.Ct. 1876, 141 L.Ed.2d 43 (1998)

A PARENT CORPORATION MAY BE DIRECTLY LIABLE UNDER FEDERAL LAW FOR ITS OWN CONDUCT INVOLVING A FACILITY CONTROLLED BY ITS SUBSIDIARY, OR INDIRECTLY LIABLE UNDER THE COMMON LAW DOCTRINE OF PIERCING THE CORPORATE VEIL

■ **INSTANT FACTS** Government sued parent corporation under federal statute for clean up costs of contamination caused by subsidiary that operated the polluting plant.

■ **BLACK LETTER RULE** A parent corporation that actively participates in, and exercises control over, the operations of a subsidiary, without more, may not be held liable as an operator of a polluting facility owned or operated by the subsidiary. But, if the parent corporation takes more of an active role in the operations of the facility, the parent may be liable under federal pollution control laws.

■ **PROCEDURAL BASIS**

Certiorari granted by United States Supreme Court from judgment after partial trial in action to recover cost of contamination clean up pursuant to federal statute.

■ **FACTS**

The United States Government (P) sued Bestfoods, previously known as CPC International Inc. and hereinafter referred to as CPC (D), and other entities for the cost of cleaning up hazardous substances generated by a chemical manufacturing plant that caused soil and ground water pollution. After various cases were consolidated for trial, the liability phase of the trial occurred focusing on the issue of whether CPC (D) and another entity, as the parent corporations of two subsidiary companies, had "owned and operated" the plant within the meaning of the Comprehensive Environmental Response, Compensation, and Liability Act of 1980 (CERCLA) [Federal statute that imposes responsibility for clean up and response costs on owners and operators of hazardous waste disposal sites]. The district court held that operator liability may attach to a parent corporation both directly, when the parent itself operates the facility, and indirectly, when the corporate veil can be pierced under state law. The district court held that CPC (D) and the other entity were liable as operators, especially since CPC (D) selected the subsidiary's board of directors and populated its executive ranks with CPC (D) officials, and that one CPC (D) official played a significant role in shaping the subsidiary's environmental policy. The Court of Appeals reversed in part and, after granting rehearing en banc, vacated the panel decision, and again reversed the district court in part. The court of appeals held that whether the parent will be liable as an operator depends upon whether the degree of control of the subsidiary, and the extent and manner of involvement of the facility, constitute an abuse of the corporate form warranting piercing the corporate veil. The court of appeals held that CPC (D) was not liable for controlling the actions of its subsidiaries, since the parent and subsidiaries maintained separate personalities and the parent did not utilize the subsidiary corporate form to perpetrate fraud or subvert justice. The United States (P) [wanting to be reimbursed the millions of dollars it spent cleaning up the toxic waste] petitioned the Supreme Court and it granted certiorari to resolve a conflict among the circuit courts regarding the extent to which parent corporations may be held liable under CERCLA for operating facilities ostensibly under the control of their subsidiaries.

■ ISSUE

May a parent corporation that actively participated in, and exercised control over, the operations of a subsidiary, without more, be held liable as an operator of a polluting facility owned or operated by the subsidiary?

■ DECISION AND RATIONALE

(Souter, J.) No. We hold that a parent corporation that actively participated in, and exercised control over, the operations of a subsidiary, without more, may not be held liable as an operator of a polluting facility owned or operated by the subsidiary, unless the corporate veil is pierced. However, a corporate parent that actively participated in, and exercised control over, the operations of the facility itself may be held directly liable in its own right as an operator of the facility. There is nothing in the enactment of CERCLA law preventing the application of state corporations law, which allows piercing the corporate veil when the corporate form would be misused to accomplish wrongful purposes, such as fraud on the shareholder's behalf. Thus, the court of appeals was correct [at least in one area] in holding that when (but only when) the corporate veil may be pierced, a parent corporation may be charged with derivative CERCLA liability for its subsidiary's actions. CERCLA liability may also turn on ownership, and there is nothing in the statute that bars a parent corporation from direct liability for its own actions in operating a facility owned by its subsidiary. The fact that a corporate subsidiary happens to own a polluting facility operated by its parent does nothing to displace the rule that the parent corporation is itself responsible for the wrongs committed by its agents in the course of its business. CERCLA's "operator" provision is concerned primarily with direct liability for one's own actions, as opposed to derivative liability that results from piercing the corporate veil. Thus any person who operates a polluting facility is directly liable for the clean up costs, regardless of whether that person is the facility's owner, the parent corporation or business partner. If the act of operating a subsidiary's facility is done on behalf of the parent corporation, the existence of the parent-subsidiary relationship is irrelevant to the issue of direct liability. We must consider what actions are sufficient to constitute direct parental "operation." We hold that an operator must manage, direct, or conduct operations specifically related to pollution, that is, operations having to do with the leakage or disposal of hazardous waste, or decisions about compliance with environmental regulations. We believe that the court of appeals correctly rejected the district court's analysis of direct liability. However, we also believe that the appeals court erred in limiting direct liability under CERCLA to a parent's sole or joint venture operation, so as to eliminate any possible finding that CPC (D) is liable as an operator. [This was the area that caused the vacating of the appeals court decision.] The question to be considered is not whether the parent operates the subsidiary, but rather whether it operates the facility and that operation is evidenced by participation in the activities of the facility, not the subsidiary. Control of the subsidiary, if extensive enough, gives rise to indirect liability under the piercing doctrine, not direct liability under the statutory language of CERCLA. The district court was therefore mistaken to focus on CPC's (D) relationship with the subsidiary, premising liability on little more that CPC's (D) 100 percent ownership of the subsidiary and CPC's (D) active participation and control over the subsidiary's board of directors. [Thus, both lower courts were wrong in certain areas.] The analysis should have been on the relationship between CPC (D) and the polluting facility itself. The district court failed to recognize that it is entirely appropriate for directors of a parent corporation to serve as directors of its subsidiary, and that fact alone may not serve to expose the parent corporation to liability for its subsidiary's acts. This is not enough to establish liability. The district court made no inquiry as to whether, contrary to the norm, the officers and directors were acting in their capacities as CPC (D) officers and directors, and not as officers and directors of the subsidiary, when they committed their actions. By focusing on the relationship between the parent and subsidiary (rather than the parent and the polluting facility), the district court erroneously treated CERCLA as though it displaced or altered common law standards of limited liability. We agree with the court of appeals that looking to the parent's supervision over the subsidiary cannot be used to identify operation of the facility resulting in direct parental liability. But the court of appeals stopped short [looks like they were wrong again!] by confining direct parental operation to its own exclusive operation in the stead of its subsidiary or alongside it in some sort of joint venture, and declined to find at least the possibility of direct operation by CPC (D). Activities that involve the facility but which are consistent with the parent's investor status, such as monitoring of the subsidiary's performance, supervision of the subsidiary's finance and capital budget decisions, and articulating of general policies and procedures, should not give rise to direct liability. The question is whether the actions directed to the facility by an agent of the parent alone are eccentric under accepted norms of parental oversight of a subsidiary's facility. The evidence here shows that CPC (D) engaged in some degree of this activity at the plant. An agent of CPC (D) alone played a conspicuous part in dealing with the toxic risks emanating from the operation of the plant. One G. Williams worked only for CPC (D), and was not an employee, officer or director of the subsidiary. Thus, his actions were of necessity taken only on behalf of CPC (D). The district court found that CPC (D) became directly involved in environmental and regulatory matters through the work of Williams, CPC's (D) governmental and environmental affairs director. He actively participated in and exerted control over a variety of the subsidiary's environmental matters, and he issued directives regarding the subsidiary's responses to regulatory inquiries. We think that these findings are enough to raise an issue of CPC's (D) operation of the facility through William's actions. We therefore remand, on the theory of direct operation, for reevaluation of William's role, and of the role of any other CPC (D) agent who might be said to have had a part in operating the facility. We vacate and remand.

Analysis:

This case illustrates that there may be a basis, other than the common law, for effectively piercing the corporate veil, such as when specific statutes so mandate. This United States Supreme Court opinion involves, in part, the ability to pierce the corporate veil where enforcement of a federal statute is sought. The Court examined the theory of *direct liability* of CPC (D) as an "operator" under CERCLA and held that there might be evidence to support such a theory. The Court held that a parent corporation must do more that participate in, and exercise control over, the subsidiary in order to be held liable as an "operator" of a facility owned or operated by the subsidiary. The Court also acknowledged that *indirect liability* could arise under the piercing of the corporate veil doctrine if there was evidence of extensive control of the subsidiary by the parent. However, this indirect liability would be based upon the state's common law regarding corporate piercing, as opposed to direct liability under the statutory language of CERCLA as an operator or owner. The opinion is significant in that it resolved a conflict among various circuit courts concerning liability of parent corporations under CERCLA for operating facilities ostensibly under the control of their subsidiaries. However, the opinion did not resolve whether piercing in CERCLA cases should be governed by federal or state law.

■ CASE VOCABULARY

CONSOLIDATED: Combing two or more different cases for trial at the same time before the same judge.

CONTRIBUTION CLAIM: Seeking to recover reimbursement from others who are liable, an aliquot share of the judgment imposed for the damage or loss.

COUNTER-CLAIM: Federal court pleading, like a complaint, by defendant against plaintiff or others.

CROSS-CLAIM: A pleading, like a complaint, by a defendant against co-defendant arising out of the same transaction or occurrence.

DERIVATIVE LIABILITY: As used herein, seeking to have liability imposed on a parent corporation for a wrong done by its subsidiary.

DIRECT LIABILITY: As used herein, seeking to have liability imposed against parent corporation for a wrong done by the parent through its personnel and management.

EN BANC: Where all members of the appellate court for a particular district or circuit hear a case on review, rather than just the limited quorum members initially assigned to hear the case.

Stark v. Flemming

(*Social Security Applicant*) v. (*Social Security Representative*)
283 F.2d 410 (9th Cir. 1960)

A CORPORATION OWNER'S SALARY MUST BE REASONABLE

■ **INSTANT FACTS** Stark (P) placed her property in a corporation and drew a small salary, on which she claimed social security benefits.

■ **BLACK LETTER RULES** The federal government must recognize a properly formed corporation operating under normal corporate routines.

■ **PROCEDURAL BASIS**

On appeal to review a decision of a federal district court denying the plaintiff benefits.

■ **FACTS**

Stark (P) formed a corporation to hold her farm and duplex house. From the corporation, she drew a monthly salary from which she sought to increase the amount of social security benefits to which she was entitled. The Secretary of Health, Education and Welfare ruled that Stark (P) was not entitled to old age benefits because the corporation was a sham, and the district court affirmed.

■ **ISSUE**

Can the federal government disregard a corporate structure if it was designed to increase a social security applicant's old age benefits?

■ **DECISION AND RATIONALE**

(Per curiam.) No. Under the statutory social security structure, Congress did not prohibit the organization of a corporate entity to obtain social security benefits. Stark (P) appears to have properly conducted her corporate business under normal corporate routines. Thus, if others are bound to acknowledge the corporate presence, so too is Flemming (D). Flemming (D), however, is not unjustified in making an objective reappraisal of Stark's (P) salary to determine whether it was reasonable, considering, for example, competitive salaries paid by commercial farm agencies and residential rental agencies in her area. Because Flemming (D) did not entertain this inquiry, the matter must be remanded. Stark's (P) social security benefits can then be properly determined based on a reasonable salary. Reversed and remanded.

Analysis:

As intimated by the dispute, corporations are formed under the laws of a particular state and as such owe their entire existence to state laws. When federal laws are implicated concerning the business operation of a corporation, issues of federal supremacy often arise. While generally federal law prevails when state law conflicts with federal requirements, federal law also owes some deference to state sovereignty.

Roccograndi v. Unemployment Comp. Bd. of Review

(Laid-Off Corporate Officers of Family Business) v. *(Unemployment Agency)*

197 Pa.Super. 372, 178 A.2d 786 (1962)

A CORPORATE EXISTENCE MAY NOT BE USED TO DEFEAT PUBLIC POLICY

■ **INSTANT FACTS** Corporate officers of family wrecking business who were systematically laid off when it was their turn sought unemployment benefits as employees of corporation.

■ **BLACK LETTER RULE** Corporate status will be disregarded if corporate officers asserted corporate status for a purpose used to defeat public policy.

■ **PROCEDURAL BASIS**

Appeal to Superior Court from decision of Board of Review in action concerning eligibility for unemployment benefits.

■ **FACTS**

Roccograndi (P) and two others are all members of a family who own shares in the family's incorporated wrecking business. Each owns 40 shares of the stock, and all are officers of the company. The officers of the company, in periods of business slow down, hold a meeting and by majority vote decide which members shall be "laid off." Roccograndi (P) and the two other officers were laid off, after majority vote, because it was their respective turns. They thereafter filed claims for unemployment compensation benefits, which were denied because they were self-employed. Upon appeal, the referee reversed the Bureau and held that Roccograndi (P) and the others were entitled to benefits. Upon appeal from that decision, the Board of Review reversed the referee's decision, holding that Roccograndi (P) and the others had sufficient control to lay themselves off and that they did just that. Appeal was taken by Roccograndi (P) and the others to the State Superior Court.

■ **ISSUE**

Will corporate status be disregarded if corporate officers asserted corporate status for a purpose used to defeat public policy?

■ **DECISION AND RATIONALE**

(Montgomery, J.) Yes. A company's corporate status will be disregarded to determine whether the corporate officers laid themselves off due to business slow down thus making them ineligible for unemployment benefits. As this court has ruled in a previous case, the corporate entity may be ignored in determining whether the claimants, in fact, were "unemployed" under the unemployment insurance act, or were self-employed persons whose business merely proved to be unremunerative during the period for which the claims for benefits was made. Affirmed.

Analysis:

This case is an example of a different type of situation justifying disregard of the corporate entity. If the corporate entity is used to defeat a public policy, the corporate status will be disregarded. The court determined here that the corporate status was being used for a purpose that defeated public policy, i.e., to qualify for benefits that one would not otherwise be entitled to if not incorporated. In this situation, unemployment benefits are not intended for those who are self-employed or owners of a business. Thus, the corporate status was being used for an improper purpose. Note that if the corporate status had been used in order to improve one's entitlement to social security benefits, the result would be different, because the purpose of the social security system is to assure an adequate retirement income, and if incorporating one's business and becoming an employee thereof improves the earnings entitlement, that is not an improper use of the corporation.

Cargill, Inc. v. Hedge

(Creditor) v. *(Debtor)*
375 N.W.2d 477 (Minn. 1985)

THE CORPORATE VEIL CAN BE PIERCED FROM EITHER DIRECTION

■ **INSTANT FACTS** Hedge (D) tried to claim a homestead exemption for corporate-owned farm property to save it from an execution sale.

■ **BLACK LETTER RULE** When a corporation acts as the alter ego of its shareholders, the corporate veil may be reverse pierced to further strong public policy interests.

■ PROCEDURAL BASIS

On appeal to review a decision of the court of appeals affirming a district court injunction.

■ FACTS

Hedge (D) purchased about $17,000 worth of farming supplies from Cargill, Inc. (P), over a four-year period. When Hedge (D) defaulted on the outstanding indebtedness, Cargill (P) initiated suit and learned that Hedge (D) operated his farm as a family farm corporation authorized by state law. Cargill (D) took a confession of judgment against Hedge (D) and the corporation and sought to enforce the judgment against Hedge's (D) farm. After an execution sale in which Cargill (P) was the successful bidder, the district court granted Hedge's (D) motion to enjoin further execution and allow his wife, Annette, to intervene. The court determined that Annette could intervene because, as sole shareholder of the corporation, she had an equitable interest in the corporate property. The homestead exemption was allowed, thus saving eighty acres of the farm. The court of appeals affirmed.

■ ISSUE

Do the owner-occupants of a farm, by placing their land in a family farm corporation, lose their homestead exemption?

■ DECISION AND RATIONALE

(Simonnet, J.) No. When a corporation acts as the alter ego of its shareholders, the corporate veil may be reverse pierced to further strong public policy interests. Whether Annette possessed an equitable interest in the homestead is immaterial, because she is not a judgment debtor against whose property the judgment may be enforced. However, the exemption is available through a reverse pierce of the corporate veil. A reverse pierce is available to disregard the corporate entity when the corporation operates as the alter ego of the individual and where third parties would be harmed by operation of corporate protection. Here, the Hedges (D) and the corporation were virtually the same identity. The Hedges (D) maintained some corporate formalities, such as keeping minutes, filing corporate tax returns, and dealing with some parties as a corporation, but they operated the farm as their own. The farmhouse was their home and the directors were all family members. None received salaries from the corporation. Although debtors should not be entitled to raise the corporate shield to limit personal liability while lowering it when it is most advantageous, the strong policy of promoting the homestead exemption demands reverse piercing under these circumstances. Affirmed.

Analysis:

Consider the mirror image of this case. If Hedge (D) had confessed judgment to Cargill (P) individually, and Hedge (D) sought to escape an execution sale on the farm because its title was held by his corporation, Cargill (P) would have certainly claimed the farm was merely Hedge's (D) alter ego and sought to pierce the corporate veil. This remedy is designed to prevent interference with the de facto legal relationship between debtor and creditor by superficial legal barriers. Reverse piercing serves the same purpose when the creditor seeks to use the corporate veil to its advantage.

■ CASE VOCABULARY

ALTER EGO: A corporation used by an individual in conducting personal business, the result being that a court may impose liability on the individual by piercing the corporate veil when fraud has been perpetrated on someone dealing with the corporation.

CORPORATE VEIL: The legal assumption that the acts of a corporation are not the actions of its stockholders, so that the stockholders are exempt from liability for the corporation's actions.

EXECUTION: A court order directing a sheriff or other officer to enforce a judgment, usually by seizing and selling the judgment debtor's property.

HOMESTEAD LAW: A statute exempting a homestead from execution or judicial sale for debt, unless all owners, usually a husband and wife, have jointly mortgaged the property or otherwise subjected it to creditors' claims.

PIERCING THE CORPORATE VEIL: The judicial act of imposing personal liability on otherwise immune corporate officers, directors, and stockholders for the corporation's wrongful acts.

Pepper v. Litton

(Creditor) v. (Shareholder of Bankrupt Corporation)

308 U.S. 295, 60 S.Ct. 238, 84 L.Ed. 281 (1939)

THE BANKRUPTCY COURT HAS THE POWER TO DISALLOW OR SUBORDINATE AN INEQUITABLE CLAIM OF AN OWNER/SHAREHOLDER TO THE CLAIMS OF OTHER CREDITORS

■ **INSTANT FACTS** Bankruptcy court disallowed the claim of owner shareholder of corporation for back salary to prevent fraud and unfairness to the other creditors.

■ **BLACK LETTER RULE** Bankruptcy court may use its equitable powers to disallow either as a secured or as a general or unsecured claim a judgment obtained by the dominant and controlling stockholder of the bankrupt corporation.

■ FACTS

Pepper (P) sued Dixie Splint Coal Company (Dixie) for an accounting of royalties due it. While the case was pending [and realizing that the financially troubled Dixie may have to pay out money to Pepper (P)], Litton (D), the sole shareholder of Dixie, caused Dixie to confess a judgment in favor of Litton (D) for [long ago due] back salary. [In other words, Litton (D) obtained a judgment in his favor against his own corporation.] Pepper (P) obtained a judgment against Dixie, and Litton (D) [wanting to be the first to get to the assets] executed on his own judgment against Dixie by purchasing the corporate assets at the execution sale, and then caused Dixie to file for bankruptcy. The trustee in bankruptcy sued in state court to have Litton's (D) judgment set aside and the execution sale quashed, but lost. Litton (D) filed a claim in bankruptcy court to obtain a portion of the judgment not satisfied from the proceeds of the execution sale. The district court disallowed Litton's (D) claim and directed that the trustee should recover the property purchased by Litton (D) at the execution sale for the benefit of the bankruptcy estate. Litton (D) appealed and the court of appeals reversed on the ground that the state court decision was res judicata.

■ ISSUE

May the bankruptcy court use its equitable powers to disallow either as a secured or as a general or unsecured claim a judgment obtained by the dominant and controlling stockholder of a bankrupt corporation?

■ DECISION AND RATIONALE

(Douglas, J.) Yes. We hold that the bankruptcy court may use its equitable powers to disallow either as a secured or as a general or unsecured claim a judgment obtained by the dominant and controlling stockholder of the bankrupt corporation. The evidence in this case reveals a scheme to defraud creditors by use of a so-called "one-man" or family corporation. We do not agree that res judicata prevented the district court from hearing the matter. Even if the salary claim on which the Litton (D) judgment was based actually existed, we believe that the district court properly disallowed or subordinated the claim. Courts of bankruptcy are essentially courts of equity and their equitable power allows passing on claims presented by an officer, director, or stockholder in the bankruptcy proceedings of his corporation. The mere fact that he has a claim against his own bankrupt corporation or has reduced it to a judgment does not mean that the bankruptcy court must honor it. Disallowance or subordination of claims may be necessitated by certain cardinal principles of equity jurisprudence, such as where the transaction does not reflect an arm's length bargain. [And that's what happened here.] At times equity has ordered the disallowance or subordination of these claims by disregarding the corporate entity. In other words, it has treated the debtor-corporation as a part of the stockholder's own enterprise where there is a violation of rules of fair play and good conscience by the claimant, or a breach of the fiduciary standards of conduct which he owes the corporation, its stockholders and creditors. Using this test, the district court was clearly correct in disallowing or subordinating Litton's (D) claim. Litton (D) allowed his salary claims to lie dormant for years and sought to enforce them only when his debtor corporation was in financial difficulty. By asserting the claims, the rights of another creditor were impaired. This coupled with the existence of a planned and fraudulent scheme necessitates the exercise of the court's equitable powers. Judgment of the court of appeals is reversed and that of the district court is affirmed. Reversed.

Analysis:

Although the phrase is not used in the opinion, this case applies the "deep rock" doctrine (derived from the name of a corporation involved in an early case), which provides that the bankruptcy court has the power to subordinate inequitable claims of dominant and controlling shareholders. After the Supreme Court rendered its decision in this case, the holding was codified in the Bankruptcy. Act of 1978, § 510(c). Instead of piercing the corporate veil, the court may use subordination to change the order of payment so that other creditors' claims may be satisfied before the inequitable claim of the shareholder. The Court determined the claim of Litton (D) to be inequitable because he had let his salary claims lie dormant for years and only sought to pursue them when his corporation was having financial difficulty and after Pepper (P) had filed suit against the corporation. It was clear that Litton (D) acted in a manner to obtain the assets of his corporation before Pepper (P) could reach them.

■ CASE VOCABULARY

CLAIM: As used in the context of a bankruptcy proceeding, a claim is a formal request by a creditor to be paid what it is owed by the debtor in bankruptcy.

PARI PASSU: Latin for "By an equal progress"; where creditors receive debtor's assets without any priority over one another.

QUASHED: To annul or vacate something.

RES JUDICATA: Where a matter has already been finally decided by the court by way of judgment so as to bar a subsequent action involving the same claim.

Nissen Corp. v. Miller

(Successor Corporation) v. *(Treadmill Buyer)*

323 Md. 613, 594 A.2d 564 (Ct. App. 1991)

THE TRADITIONAL RULE OF SUCCESSOR LIABILITY DOES NOT INCLUDE A "CONTINUITY OF ENTERPRISE"

■ **INSTANT FACTS** Brandt purchased a treadmill marketed by American Tredex Corporation, which then sold its assets to Nissen Corporation. Subsequently, Brandt was injured by an alleged defect in the treadmill and now seeks to sue Nissen Corp., as successor in interest to American Tredex.

■ **BLACK LETTER RULE** A corporation acquiring all or a portion of the assets of another corporation does not also acquire that corporation's liabilities and debt except where: (1) such is expressed or implied in the agreement; (2) the acquisition actually amounts to a merger or consolidation; (3) the successor corporation is actually a continuation of the predecessor corporation or entity; or (4) the agreement was fraudulent, lacked good faith, or was made with inadequate consideration.

■ **PROCEDURAL BASIS**

Appeal to the State Court of Appeals from a reversal of the trial court's grant of summary judgment to Nissen Corp. by the Court of Special Appeals.

■ **FACTS**

In January 1981 Brandt (R1) purchased a treadmill from Atlantic Fitness Products (Atlantic)(R2). This treadmill was designed, manufactured and marketed by American Tredex Corporation (Tredex). Later in 1981, Nissen Corporation (Nissen) (P) entered into a agreement to purchase the trade name, patents, inventory and other assets of Tredex. This contract expressly excluded assumption by Nissen (P) of Tredex's liability arising from any product previously sold by Tredex. The contract did provide for the continuation of Tredex for five years during which it would be known as AT Corporation. More than five years later, Brandt (R1) was injured while attempting to adjust the tread while it was running. Little more than one year later, Tredex was administratively dissolved. A short time later, Brandt (R1) and his wife filed suit against Tredex, AT Corporation, Nissen (P) and Atlantic (R2), claiming damages for negligence, strict liability, breach of express and implied warranties, and loss of consortium. Nissen's (P) motion for summary judgment was granted. The Court of Special Appeals reversed. Nissen's (P) petition for writ of certiorari was granted.

■ **ISSUE**

Should the general rule of nonliability of successor corporations, with its four recognized exceptions, have a fifth exception added to cover continuity of enterprise?

■ **DECISION AND RATIONALE**

(Chasanow, J.) No. The general rule is that a corporation acquiring all or a portion of the assets of another corporation does not acquire that corporation's liabilities and debt as well except where: (1) such is expressed or implied in the agreement; (2) the acquisition actually amounts to a merger or consolidation; (3) the successor corporation is actually a continuation of the predecessor corporation or entity; or (4) the agreement was fraudulent, lacked good faith, or was made with inadequate consideration. It is agreed by all parties that this rule, with its four exceptions, should be adopted. Brandt (R1) and Atlantic (R2) ask the Court to also adopt the "continuity of enterprise" as a fifth exception in product liability cases. This exception is distinguished from the continuity of entity exception, which applies where there is a continuation of directors, management, shareholder's interest and, sometimes, inadequate consideration. In contrast, the continuity of enterprise theory focuses on continuation of the business enterprise or operation where there is no continuation in ownership. It is clear that only if we expand the traditional exceptions to include a "continuity of enterprise" exception would Brandt (R1) be entitled to proceed against Nissen (P). Brandt (R1) contends that we should not allow a major corporation to purchase only the benefits in an asset purchase transaction, while denying any liability to the consuming public. Further, that the general rule evolved to protect the rights of creditors and shareholders in the corporate context and is thus inapplicable in the case of products liability plaintiffs. Finally, Brandt (R1) argues that Nissen (P) should not be able to benefit by effectively continuing Tredex's business, selling replacement parts, performing some contracts, honoring existing 90-day warranties, and servicing customer accounts without also bearing the liability for defective products. Nissen (P) counters that it was not part of the manufacturing and selling chain; it merely purchased Tredex's assets, with the agreement providing for no assumption of potential liability for defective products previously sold, and that the price reflected this agreement. Nissen (P) also argues that the general rule with its four exceptions should be kept intact because they have worked well to balance the rights of creditors and successor corporations by preserving traditional principles of corporate law and promoting free alienability of business assets. This while adequately protecting consumers and creditors from fraudulent and unjust corporate transactions. Finally, Nissen (P) asserts adoption of the fifth exception could harm smaller businesses who purchase assets and carry on a business, even while abandoning it predecessor's defective, injury-causing products. In response, Brandt (R1) and Atlantic (R2) assert that some of the same rationales behind strict products liability counsel in favor of adopting the fifth exception. However, inherent in our recognition of strict products liability is the concept that when a company places dangerously defective products on the market, they should be liable when those products cause injury. A corporate successor is not a seller and bears no blame for such products. It thus seems patently unfair to hold such a party liable for harm caused by products with which had nothing to do as far as manufacturing and marketing are concerned. Moreover, were we to adopt continuity of enterprise, not only would liability be imposed upon major corporations, but also upon the small business operation which may be unable to spread the risk or insure against it. For these reasons, we reject the continuity of enterprise theory of successor corporate liability. Rather, we adhere to the general rule with its for well-recognized exceptions.

■ DISSENT

(Eldridge, J. & Hinkel, J.) We agree with the adoption of the general rule with its four exceptions. We would, however, adopt the fifth exception for continuity of enterprise with regard to defective products. Therefore, we dissent.

Analysis:

This case sets forth some very basic, if not obvious, arguments for and against the adoption of a new continuity of enterprise exception to the general rule against successor liability. Nissen (P) argues, quite simply, that the contract by which it acquired the assets of Tredex foreclosed any prospect of liability for product defects, that the contract price did not contemplate any such liability, and that adopting the new exception would decrease the alienability of corporations in the future. On the other hand, Brandt (R1) stresses that when a defective product harms a consumer, it is only fair that the consumer be adequately compensated, whether by the original producer or its successor in interest. This is especially so where the successor has continued to benefit from the products, as was the case here where Nissen (P) continued to service the products. In the end, what seemed to matter to the court most is that Nissen (P) had no direct connection to the product; it did not produce it, market it, service it, guarantee it, or benefit from it.

■ CASE VOCABULARY

SUCCESSOR IN INTEREST: A party that follows another party in control or ownership of some property.

CHAPTER EIGHT

Financial Matters and the Corporation

Hanewald v. Bryan's Inc.

Instant Facts: Individual shareholders who did not pay for initial stock were liable to creditor for corporation's debts.

Black Letter Rule: Shareholders who do not pay for their stock will be statutorily liable to the corporation's creditors, to the extent their stock has not been paid for, and the creditors may sue shareholders directly.

Torres v. Speiser

Instant Facts: Torres (P) sought to invalidate sale of stock because the price was less than par value.

Black Letter Rule: Liability for issuance of stock for less than par value arises only in connection with the original issuance of shares.

S.E.C. v. Ralston Purina Co.

Instant Facts: Ralston (D) sold stock to employees without registration, claiming a private offering exemption to the registration requirement of the Securities Act of 1933.

Black Letter Rule: An offering to those shown to not need the protection of the Act is a transaction "not involving any public offering," and thus, is exempt from the registration requirements.

Smith v. Gross

Instant Facts: Earthworm buyers sued for violation of federal securities laws alleging that an investment contract existed and it was an illegal transaction.

Black Letter Rule: An investment contract constituting a "security" exists if there is a scheme involving an investment of money, in a common enterprise, and with profits to come solely from the efforts of others.

Stokes v. Continental Trust Co. of City of New York

Instant Facts: Shareholder sued for the right to purchase a proportionate share of new stock issued by the corporation.

Black Letter Rule: A stockholder has the right to purchase a proportionate amount of shares of new stock issued for money.

Katzowitz v. Sidler

Instant Facts: Shareholder sued to prevent other shareholders from reaping disproportionate distributions at dissolution because his equity had been diluted when he declined to buy unreasonably low priced shares.

Black Letter Rule: Directors breach their fiduciary duty if they offer stock for sale at a price substantially below book value and from which they benefit without showing valid business reasons for such a low price.

Lacos Land Company v. Arden Group, Inc.

Instant Facts: A majority of a corporation's shareholders voted to approve a new class of common stock following statements by a corporation's largest shareholder to the effect that, absent shareholder approval of a new class of common stock, he might use his position as the corporation's chief executive adversely to the corporation's interests.

Black Letter Rule: Shareholder vote to authorize a new class of shares is invalid where threats of adverse action by a shareholder/officer seeking such authorization act to subvert the will of the shareholders.

Gottfried v. Gottfried

Instant Facts: Minority shareholders of family owned corporation sued corporation and board to have dividends declared.

Black Letter Rule: If an adequate corporate surplus is available for the purpose, directors may not withhold the declaration of dividends in bad faith.

Dodge v. Ford Motor Co.

Instant Facts: Minority shareholders sued Ford Motor Company (D) to declare dividends after board, influenced by president Henry Ford, adopted plan to not pay dividends.

Black Letter Rule: A corporation's board of directors has discretion to decide whether to pay dividends, but that discretion is abused when there is a large accumulation of surplus cash that is not needed for corporate business.

Wilderman v. Wilderman

Instant Facts: Ex-wife, 50% shareholder in family corporation, sued her ex-husband to have him return excessive compensation to the corporation so that she could receive profits.

Black Letter Rule: Where an officer of a corporation determines his own compensation, upon challenge by other shareholders, the officer has the burden of proving the reasonableness of the compensation.

Donahue v. Rodd Electrotype Co.

Instant Facts: A minority shareholder of a closely-held corporation seeks to rescind the corporation's purchase of the controlling shareholder's stock.

Black Letter Rule: Stockholders in a close corporation owe each other a fiduciary duty of the utmost good faith and loyalty, similar to the duty that partners in a partnership owe to each other.

Hanewald v. Bryan's Inc.

(Creditor) v. *(Debtor)*

429 N.W.2d 414 (N.D. 1988)

WATERED STOCK RESULTS IN INDIVIDUAL SHAREHOLDER LIABILITY FOR CORPORATE DEBTS

■ **INSTANT FACTS** Individual shareholders who did not pay for initial stock were liable to creditor for corporation's debts.

■ **BLACK LETTER RULE** Shareholders who do not pay for their stock will be statutorily liable to the corporation's creditors, to the extent their stock has not been paid for, and the creditors may sue shareholders directly.

■ PROCEDURAL BASIS

Appeal to State Supreme Court from judgment following trial in action for breach of lease and promissory note seeking damages.

■ FACTS

Bryan's, Inc. (D) was incorporated by Keith and Joan Bryan for the purpose of operating a retail store. The first board of directors meeting elected Keith as president and Joan as secretary-treasurer. George Bryan was elected vice president, appointed registered agent, and designated manager of the prospective business. Bryan's, Inc. (D) issued 50 shares of common stock with a par value of $1,000 per share to Keith and 50 shares to Joan. Hanewald (P) sold his store to Bryan's, Inc. (D) for $60,000, payable $55,000 cash and a promissory note for $5,000 due in the future. In addition, Bryans, Inc. (D) agreed to lease the building for five years. The $55,000 cash payment was made from a loan from the bank to Bryan's, Inc. (D), personally guaranteed by Keith and Joan. The business only lasted four months with an operating loss before Keith and Joan decided to close the store. Bryan's, Inc. (D) sent a notice of rescission to Hanewald (P) in an attempt to avoid the lease. Bryan's, Inc. (D) did not pay the $5,000 promissory note to Hanewald (P) but paid off the rest of its creditors, including the $55,000 loan from the bank and a $10,000 loan from Keith and Joan. Hanewald (P) [was not pleased with being the only one not paid and] sued Bryan's, Inc. (D) and Keith, Joan and George for breach of the lease and the promissory note, seeking to hold the individual Bryans personally liable. After trial, the trial court entered judgment against Bryan's, Inc. (D), but refused to pierce the corporate veil in order to hold the individual defendants personally liable for the judgment against Bryan's, Inc. (D). The court found that Bryan's, Inc. (D) did not receive any payment, either in labor, services, money, or property, for the stock which was issued. Hanewald (P) appealed from the refusal to hold the individual defendants personally liable.

■ ISSUE

Are shareholders who do not pay for their stock liable to the corporation's creditors?

■ DECISION AND RATIONALE

(Meschke, J.) Yes. Shareholders who do not pay for their stock will be statutorily liable to the corporation's creditors, to the extent their stock has not been paid for. Moreover, we hold that the creditors may sue the shareholders directly on the debt. The shareholders' initial capital investment is what protects their personal assets from further liability in the corporate enterprise. This protection for

---

corporate shareholders is codified in the Model Business Corporation Act (MBCA) § 25, which obligates shareholders to pay for their shares as a prerequisite for their limited personal liability. The State Constitution says, "no corporation shall issue stock or bonds except for money, labor done, or money or property actually received; and all fictitious increase of stock or indebtedness shall be void." In this case, Bryans, Inc. (D) was authorized to issue 100 shares of stock each having a par value of $1,000. Keith and Joan were each issued 50 shares but Bryan's, Inc. (D) did not receive any payment, either in labor, services, money or property, for the stock which was issued. Because the individual defendants had a statutory duty to pay for shares that were issued to them by Bryan's, Inc. (D), we hold that the individuals' failure to pay for their shares of stock makes them personally liable under MBCA § 25 for the corporation's debt to Hanewald (P). The shareholder liability created by this statute may be enforced in a direct action by a creditor of the corporation. This conclusion derives from the common law that a shareholder is liable to corporate creditors to the extent his stock has not been paid for. The shareholder is liable to the extent of the difference between the par value and the amount actually paid, and to such an extent only as may be necessary for the satisfaction of the creditor's claim. The $10,000 loan from Keith and Joan to Bryan's, Inc. (D) is a debt, not an asset, to the corporation. Where a loan is repaid by the corporation to the shareholders before its operations are abandoned, the loan cannot be considered a capital contribution. [There went Keith and Joan's defense.] Thus, having not paid for their stock, the trial court erred in refusing to hold Keith and Joan personally liable for the corporation's debt to Hanewald (P). The debt does not exceed the difference between the par value of their stock and the amount they actually paid. Therefore, we reverse in part to remand for entry of judgment holding Keith and Joan jointly and severally liable for the entire Hanewald (P) debt. The judgment is otherwise affirmed.

Analysis:

This case involves the concept of "watered stock," involving shares issued for improper consideration. When the business is a failure, as Bryan's, Inc. was in this case, the creditors of the corporation can impose personal liability upon the individuals who received the stock. Note that in most states, watered stock liability arises only in connection with the original issuance of shares. The historical explanation for watered stock liability was that the corporation's capital is a trust fund for creditors who rely upon it when extending credit. This is really a fiction, since the capital of a corporation may be lost if it does not succeed. The liability has also been explained on a fraud theory, in that the shareholders who received watered stock were involved in a misrepresentation to the public, who viewed the par value of issued shares as the amount of equity capital received by the corporation. This case used the statutory liability under MBCA § 25 as a basis for holding the shareholders liable.

■ CASE VOCABULARY

COMMON STOCK: A class of shares of stock that carry the right to vote and receive dividends.

JOINTLY AND SEVERALLY LIABLE: A form of liability where the injured party may sue one or more wrongdoers separately, or all together, and enforce the judgment obtained against one or all.

PAR VALUE: The price of the stock as set forth in the articles of incorporation and on the face of stock certificates.

WATERED STOCK: Shares in a corporation that have been issued to stockholders but have not been paid for in full by the stockholders.

Torres v. Speiser

(Seller of Stock) v. *(Buyer of Stock)*

268 A.D.2d 253, 701 N.Y.S.2d 360 (App. Div. 2000)

LIABILITY FOR WATERED STOCK ONLY APPLIES TO INITIAL ISSUANCE OF SHARES

■ **INSTANT FACTS** Torres (P) sought to invalidate sale of stock because the price was less than par value.

■ **BLACK LETTER RULE** Liability for issuance of stock for less than par value arises only in connection with the original issuance of shares.

■ **PROCEDURAL BASIS**

Appeal from order denying partial summary judgment in action to invalidate sale of interest in corporation.

■ **FACTS**

Torres (P) contends that the subsequent re-sale of his minority interest of stock in the defendant corporation (D1) to the individual defendant (D2) is invalid because the price of the stock was less than its par value. [Is this seller's remorse?] He brought a motion for partial summary judgment and the trial court denied the motion. Torres (P) appealed.

■ **ISSUE**

Can there be liability for issuance of stock for less than par value in connection with transactions subsequent to the original issuance of shares?

■ **DECISION AND RATIONALE**

(Memorandum Decision) No. Liability for issuance of stock for less than par value arises only in connection with the original issuance of shares. Business Corporation Law § 504 prohibits an initial issuance of stock in a new corporation for less than par value or before the full purchase price is paid. However, it has no bearing on a re-sale of issued shares among shareholders. Nor can summary judgment be granted to Torres (P) on the ground that the individual defendant's (D2) promises to assist him in establishing a business that he was to manage, and to establish a corporation to own that business the stock of which was to be divided between himself and defendant (D2) in a mutually acceptable manner, were material terms of his agreement to retransfer his stock that are so indefinite as not to be susceptible to enforcement, and that the entire transaction therefore was nothing more than an unenforceable agreement to agree. There are issues of fact and the motion must be denied.

Analysis:

This case demonstrates that liability for watered stock arises only in connection with the original issuance of shares. Thereafter, any subsequent re-sale of the stock is not governed by the par value. The stock may be sold for less than the par value and liability will not result. Torres (P) incorrectly attempted to apply the statutory law that prohibited an initial issuance of stock in a new corporation for less than par value to his subsequent sales transaction.   Thus, par value plays a very narrow role in modern day corporate law.

■ **CASE VOCABULARY**

MEMORANDUM DECISION: Where the court gives a ruling on a matter, but does not express its reasons for the rulings.

S.E.C. v. Ralston Purina Co.

(*Government Agency*) v. (*Stock Selling Company*)

346 U.S. 119, 73 S.Ct. 981, 97 L.Ed. 1494 (1953)

STOCK SALE TRANSACTIONS NOT INVOLVING ANY PUBLIC OFFERING ARE EXEMPT FROM THE REGISTRATION REQUIREMENTS OF THE SECURITIES ACT OF 1933

■ **INSTANT FACTS** Ralston (D) sold stock to employees without registration, claiming a private offering exemption to the registration requirement of the Securities Act of 1933.

■ **BLACK LETTER RULE** An offering to those shown to not need the protection of the Act is a transaction "not involving any public offering," and thus, is exempt from the registration requirements.

■ **PROCEDURAL BASIS**

Certiorari granted in response to the Court of Appeals' affirmance of the District Court's dismissal of the complaint.

■ **FACTS**

Ralston Purina (D) has processing and distribution facilities scattered throughout the United States and Canada, staffed by about 7,000 employees [including cats and dogs]. The company has a policy of encouraging stock ownership among its employees, and has made authorized but unissued common shares available to some of them. During the period covered by the record in this case, Ralston Purina (D) sold nearly $2 million of stock to employees without registration and in so doing made use of the mails. In each of these years, a corporate resolution authorized the sale of common stock to employees who, without any solicitation by the company, inquire as to how to purchase stock in the company. A memorandum was issued to branch and store managers after the resolution was adopted, advising that the only employees to whom the stock would be available were those who took the initiative and are interested in buying stock at present market prices. The S.E.C. (P) brought a complaint under the Securities Act of 1933 seeking to enjoin Ralston Purina's (D) unregistered offerings. Ralston Purina (D) claims the offerings were exempt from registration, as the transactions did not involve any "public offering." The company bottoms its exemption claim on the classification of all offerees as "key employees" in its organization, thus it is a private offering. The District Court agreed with Ralston Purina (D), held the exemption applicable and dismissed the suit. The Court of Appeals affirmed. The question has arisen many times since the Act was passed, and an apparent need to define the scope of the private offering exemption prompted certiorari.

■ **ISSUE**

Are a corporation's offerings of treasury stock to its "key employees" within the exemption from the registration requirements of the Securities Act of 1933?

■ **DECISION AND RATIONALE**

(Clark, J.) No. Section 4(1) of the Securities Act of 1933 exempts "transactions by an issuer not involving any public offering" from the registration requirements of Section 5 of the Act. We must decide whether Ralston Purina's (D) offerings of treasury stock to its "key employees" are within this

---

exemption. The problem was first dealt with in Section 4(1) of the House Bill, H.R. 5480, which exempted "transactions by an issuer not with or through an underwriter." The bill, as reported by the House Committee, added "and not involving any public offering." This was thought to be one of those transactions "where there is no practical need for the bill's application or where the public benefits are too remote." The exemption as thus delimited became law. It assumed its present shape with the deletion of "not with or through an underwriter" by Section 203(a) of the Securities Exchange Act of 1934, a change regarded as superfluous language. Decisions under comparable exemptions in the English Companies Acts and state "blue sky" laws, the statutory antecedents of federal securities legislation, have made one thing clear—to be public, an offer need not be open to the whole world. Therefore, we conclude that an offering to those shown to not need the protection of the Act is a transaction "not involving any public offering," and thus, is exempt from the registration requirements. To determine the distinction between "public" and "private" in any particular context, it is essential to examine the circumstances under which the distinction is sought to be established and to consider the purposes sought to be achieved by such distinction. The purpose of the statute is to protect investors. The participants in employee stock investment plans may be in as great a need of the protection afforded by availability of information concerning the issuer for which they work as are most other members of the public. Once it is seen that the exemption question turns on the knowledge of the offerees, the focus of the inquiry should be on the need of the offerees for the protections afforded by registration. The employees here were not shown to have access to the kind of information which registration would disclose. The obvious opportunities for pressure and imposition make it advisable that they be entitled to compliance with Section 5 of the Securities Act. Reversed.

Analysis:

Exemption from the registration requirements of the Securities Act is the question presented in this case. The Securities Act nowhere defines the scope of § 4(1)'s private offering exemption. Nor is the legislative history of much help in staking out its boundaries. The design of the statute is to protect investors by promoting full disclosure of information thought necessary to informed investment decisions. The natural way to interpret the private offering exemption is in light of the statutory purpose. Since exempt transactions are those as to which there is no practical need for the bill's application, the applicability of the Securities Act should turn on whether the particular class of persons affected needs the protection of the Act. This is why the Court correctly concluded that an offering to those who are shown to be able to fend for themselves is a transaction "not involving any public offering." Keeping in mind the broadly remedial purposes of federal securities legislation, it seems fair and reasonable that the burden of proof be on an issuer who would plead the exemption.

■ CASE VOCABULARY

"BLUE SKY" LAWS: Regulate the sales of corporate securities through investment companies.

ENJOIN: To suspend or refrain another from doing a certain act.

PRIVATE OFFERING: Any sale of securities in a corporation not subject to registration requirements.

REGISTRATION: Document describing the securities offered which must disclose, in detail, information on the nature of the business, accounting statements, identity of management and key stockholders, and the purpose of the offering, including the use to be made of profits.

TREASURY STOCK: Common or preferred stock issued by a company and later reacquired by it; earns no dividends and has no vote in company affairs.

Smith v. Gross

(Earthworm Buyers) v. *(Seller)*
604 F.2d 639 (9th Cir. 1979)

THE SECURITIES LAWS MAY BE USED TO ATTACK ILLEGAL INVESTMENT SCHEMES

■ **INSTANT FACTS** Earthworm buyers sued for violation of federal securities laws alleging that an investment contract existed and it was an illegal transaction.

■ **BLACK LETTER RULE** An investment contract constituting a "security" exists if there is a scheme involving an investment of money, in a common enterprise, and with profits to come solely from the efforts of others.

■ **FACTS**

Gerald and Mary Smith (P) sued Gross (D) and two others for violation of federal securities laws. In newsletters, Gross (D) solicited buyer-investors to raise earthworms and promised that the seller's growing instructions would enable the buyers to profit, that the quantity of earthworms would double every 60 days, and that the seller would buy back all the bait size worms at $2.25 per pound. The Smiths (P) responded to the newsletter and were told by Gross (D) that very little work was required, that success was guaranteed because of the repurchase agreement, and that Gross (D) needed the Smiths (P) help in supplying the worms to the bait industry. The Smiths (P) allege that they would not have purchased the worms without Gross' (D) promise to repurchase at $2.25 per pound. The worms did not multiply as represented, and they could not make a profit. They also alleged that $2.25 is greater than the market price and that Gross (D) could pay that price only by selling the worms to new worm farmers [i.e., suckers] at inflated prices. The Smiths (P) assert that the transaction between the parties involved an investment contract type of security. If this is true, the Smiths (P) are entitled to rescind the transaction. The district court dismissed the suit for lack of subject matter jurisdiction on the ground that there was no security involved in the transactions between the parties. The Smiths (P) appealed.

■ **ISSUE**

Does an investment contract constituting a "security" exist if there is a scheme involving an investment of money, in a common enterprise, and with profits to come solely from the efforts of others?

■ **DECISION AND RATIONALE**

(Per Curiam) Yes. The Supreme Court has held that in order to determine whether an investment contract exists there must be a scheme involving an investment of money, in a common enterprise, and with profits to come solely from the efforts of others. Our court has further held that the use of the word "solely" by the Supreme Court is interpreted to mean, "whether the efforts made by those other than the investor are the undeniably significant ones, those essential managerial efforts which affect the failure or success of the enterprise." In order for the Smiths (P) to be able to rescind the earthworm purchase agreement with Gross (D), they must establish that the transaction involved a "security." Since the Securities Act's defines "security" to include an "investment contract," the issue thus becomes whether an investment contract existed. In another case involving chinchillas, the defendant sellers entered into contracts to sell the animals to the plaintiffs with the promise to repurchase the offspring. The buyers were told that breeding was simple and the venture would be highly profitable. The opposite was true, and the profits could be had only if the sellers repurchased the offspring and sold them to other prospective buyers at inflated prices. The chinchilla case is virtually identical to the

---

case before us [and all other cases where a pot of gold is promised]. The court found an investment contract existed because 1) the sellers persuaded the buyers to invest by representing that the efforts required would be minimal, and 2) that if the buyers diligently exerted themselves, they still would not gain the profits because they could only be achieved if the sellers obtained additional investor buyers at inflated prices. In this case, the Smiths (P) allege that they were promised that the effort to raise the worms was minimal and that they could not receive the promised income unless Gross (D) repurchased the worms. We hold that if these facts are proved true, an investment contract can be established. Reversed.

Analysis:

This case demonstrates how the securities laws may be used to protect the public from fraudulent or misrepresented investment schemes, even though they may not involve traditional securities. "Securities" may include "investment contracts," and this case looks at the issue of whether or not an investment contract existed. Generally, any transaction involving the investing of money in a common enterprise and an expectation of profits solely from the efforts of others will be considered an investment contract. As the court noted, "solely" has not been construed literally, and thus it may be found even where the investor is required to make a small amount of individual effort. The only way for the Smiths (P) to make the promised profits was if Gross (D) repurchased above market price, and this could only be done if Gross (D) obtained additional investors at inflated prices. Thus, the profits had to come solely from the efforts and success of Gross (D).

■ CASE VOCABULARY

PER CURIAM: An opinion by the whole court, rather than one judge.

WITHOUT PREJUDICE: Dismissal of an action with the right to re-file a complaint.

Stokes v. Continental Trust Co. of City of New York

(Shareholder) v. *(Corporation)*

186 N.Y. 285, 78 N.E. 1090 (Ct. App. 1906)

EXISTING SHAREHOLDERS HAVE RIGHTS TO ACQUIRE NEWLY ISSUED STOCK

■ **INSTANT FACTS** Shareholder sued for the right to purchase a proportionate share of new stock issued by the corporation.

■ **BLACK LETTER RULE** A stockholder has the right to purchase a proportionate amount of shares of new stock issued for money.

■ **PROCEDURAL BASIS**

Appeal to State Supreme Court from judgment after trial in action seeking right to purchase securities.

■ **FACTS**

Mr. Stokes (P), an original stockholder, sued his corporation, Continental Trust Co. of City of New York (Continental) (D) to compel it to issue him at par a proportionate number of the newly issued stock as held by him before the increase of issued shares. Stokes (P) owned the original stock issued to him on the date of Continental's (D) organization, plus more acquired since then for a total 221 shares. Blair & Co., a firm of private bankers, proposed to Continental (D) that if the stockholders voted to increase the capital stock from $500,000 to $1,000,000, it would purchase the additional stock at $450 per share ($100 par value). On the date of the shareholders meeting to vote on the proposal, Continental (D) had a surplus of funds, which made the book value of the stock $309.69 per share. After the special meeting occurred, a resolution was adopted to increase the stock. Stokes (P) demanded from Continental (D) the right to subscribe for 221 shares of the new stock at par, but the demand was refused. A resolution was adopted directing a sale to Blair & Co. at $450 a share. Stokes (P) voted for the increase in stock but against the sale to Blair & Co. He again demanded the right to subscribe and pay for the stock, but he was again refused. The stock was thereafter increased and sold to Blair & Co. at $450 a share. Over the following months and years, the stock increased up to $700 per share by the time of trial. The trial court entered judgment in favor of Stokes (P) and held that he had the right to subscribe for such proportion of the increase, as his holdings bore to all the stock before the increase was made; that Continental (D) had no power to deprive him of that right, and that he was entitled to recover the difference between the market value of 221 shares on the date of the sale and the par value thereof. The appellate division reversed and Stokes (P) appealed to the State Supreme Court.

■ **ISSUE**

Does a stockholder have the right to subscribe and take at par value the same number of shares of new stock that he held of the old?

■ **DECISION AND RATIONALE**

(Vann, J.) Yes. A stockholder has the right to purchase a proportionate amount of shares of new stock issued for money. To reach this holding, we must determine whether Stokes (P) had a right of property belonging to him as stockholder, for which he could not be deprived of by other stockholders and the corporation. As a stockholder, he has an inherent right to his proportionate share of any dividend declared, or of any surplus arising upon dissolution, he can prevent waste or misappropriation of the

---

corporation's property by those in control, and he also has the right to vote. The right to vote for directors and upon propositions to increase the stock or mortgage the assets is about all the power a stockholder has. The power to manage resides with the directors who are elected by the stockholders. Hence, the power of the stockholder to vote his proportion to the number of his shares is vital, and cannot be cutoff or curtailed by others. In this case, by the increase of stock, the voting power of Stokes (P) was reduced one-half, and although he consented to the increase of new stock, he did not consent to selling it to Blair & Co. at less than its market value. The action taken by the majority, against Stokes' (P) will and protest, causes him to have only one-half the voting power that he had before, because the number of shares has been doubled while he still owns but 221. This action deprives him of a right of property. Blair & Co. acquires virtual control, while Stokes (P) lost it. We therefore hold that a stockholder has an inherent right to purchase a proportionate share of new stock issued for money only and not to purchase property for the purposes of the corporation or to effect a consolidation. Stokes' (P) damages should have been measured by the difference between the $450 sale price and the $550 market value of the shares rather than the difference between par value and market value of the shares. The order appealed from should be reversed and the judgment of the trial court modified by reducing the damages. The judgment of the trial court is affirmed.

■ DISSENT

(Haight, J.) I do not believe that Stokes (P) should be given as damages such increase in the market value of the stock, even though such value was based upon the understanding that Blair & Co. was to become a stockholder in the corporation, which the acceptance of Stokes' (P) offer to subscribe would have prevented. I favor an affirmance.

Analysis:

The case demonstrates the rights of existing shareholders when a corporation issues new shares. The existing shareholders are said to have "preemptive rights." Such rights are given to holders of outstanding shares of stock so that they may subscribe and pay for a proportionate part of any new issue of stock by the corporation. This common law right is not codified in state statutes. However, it is now generally agreed that the preemptive right is not an inherent aspect of the ownership of stock, but a right that may be granted or withheld pursuant to the articles of incorporation. The court in this case, however, termed the right as an inherent one.

■ CASE VOCABULARY

BOOK VALUE: The value of a thing as reflected on the balance sheet.

CAPITAL STOCK: Those shares of stock that the corporation issued and reflecting ownership of the company.

MARKET PRICE: The price the seller and buyer will actually pay and receive.

PREEMPTIVE RIGHTS: The right of a shareholder to purchase newly issued stock in a corporation in proportion to the number of shares already owned by the shareholder.

PROXY: One who is given authority by another to represent and act on behalf of the other person.

RESOLUTION: A writing that reflects the action taken by the board of directors of a corporation.

Katzowitz v. Sidler

(*Director-Shareholder*) v. (*Director-Shareholder*)

24 N.Y.2d 512, 301 N.Y.S.2d 470, 249 N.E.2d 359 (1969)

SHAREHOLDERS HAVE THE RIGHT TO AVOID DILUTION OF THEIR EQUITY BY PREVENTING A SALE OF STOCK AT A LEGALLY INADEQUATE PRICE

■ **INSTANT FACTS** Shareholder sued to prevent other shareholders from reaping disproportionate distributions at dissolution because his equity had been diluted when he declined to buy unreasonably low priced shares.

■ **BLACK LETTER RULE** Directors breach their fiduciary duty if they offer stock for sale at a price substantially below book value and from which they benefit without showing valid business reasons for such a low price.

■ **PROCEDURAL BASIS**

Appeal from an Appellate Division decision affirming a Special Term ruling that objection to the inequitable effects of an earlier stock sale was too late at the time of the corporation's dissolution.

■ **FACTS**

Katzowitz (P), Sidler (D) and Lasker (D) were the shareholders and directors of Sulburn Holding Corp. ["Sulburn"] (D), a propane gas supplier. These three men also owned three other companies and had had business dealings for 25 years. As in all of their previous ventures, the three men were equal investors in Sulburn (D). Each of the three invested $500 in Sulburn (D) and each received 5 shares of Sulburn (D) stock. As a result of inter-personal squabbling, the three men agreed that Katzowitz (P) would withdraw from all day-to-day management of any of the businesses, but would remain a director (along with Sider (D) and Lasker (D) or their designees) in each corporation. The three men also agreed that each would remain an equal shareholder in the corporations and that Katzowitz (P) would receive the same compensation and benefits as the other two. Although Sidler (D) and Lasker (D) complied with the agreement, they continued to want Katzowitz (P) out of the picture. In 1961, Sulburn owed each shareholder $2,500 for earnings. Sidler (D) and Lasker (D) proposed that, instead of distributing cash, Sulburn issue shares for the amount owed and loan the cash to another of the three men's ventures. Katzowitz (P) disagreed. The directors passed a resolution that Sulburn would pay each man $2,500. On December 1, 1961, Sidler (D) and Lasker (D) called a special directors meeting which only they attended. They approved issuance of 75 shares of common stock of Sulburn, offered at $100/share, a price just 1/18 of the book value of the stock. Notice was mailed to each of the shareholder's of the offer of 25 shares. Sidler (D) and Lasker (D) purchased their shares, but Katzowitz (P) did not. The newly purchased shares diluted the value of outstanding shares of Sulburn. Eight months later, Sulburn's truck (the corporation's main asset) was destroyed and all three directors voted to dissolve Sulburn. At dissolution, Sidler (D) and Lasker (D) each received over $18,000, while Katzowitz (P) got just over $3,000. Katzowitz (P) sued for his proportional interest in the corporation's liquidated assets minus the $5,000 that the other two shareholders had invested in 1961. The trial court found that the value of the shares offered in December 1961 was $1,800 each, but concluded that Katzowitz (P) waived his right to object to the stock sale because he did not exercise his pre-emptive right to purchase the shares or object at the time of the sale. The appellate court agreed, finding that the price-value disparity of the stock was insufficient to establish fraud on the part of Sidler (D) and Lasker (D).

■ ISSUE

Can a shareholder block a sale of stock at a price substantially below book value for which there is no valid business purpose if that shareholder declined to exercise the right to purchase shares at the low price?

■ DECISION AND RATIONALE

(Keating, Judge) Yes. It was unfair for Katzowitz (P) to suffer dilution of his equity in Sulburn as a result of his choice not to purchase the shares offered at a legally inadequate price in December 1961. The function of pre-emptive rights is to protect shareholders against dilution of their voting and their equity in the corporation. Directors' fiduciary duty to the corporation means that, when setting the price for newly issued shares, they must act in the interest of the corporations and with fairness toward all shareholders. In most cases, pre-emptive rights protect shareholders' equity because the shareholder can exercise the rights or sell them. In a close corporation like Sulburn, however, pre-emptive rights offer illusory protection if new shares are offered at significantly deflated prices. This is because, if shareholders (like Katzowitiz (P)) are unwilling or unable to make further investment, they "can have their equity interest in the corporation diluted to the vanishing point." Courts give directors broad discretion in setting the prices of new shares, but a shareholder can establish a case for judicial relief by showing (1) that the price of the new shares is "markedly below book value" and (2) that the other "shareholder-directors benefit from the issuance." Such a showing shifts the burden to the directors to show valid business reasons for issuing new shares at the low price. In this case, Sidler (D) and Lasker (D) argue simply that Katzowitz (P) cannot complain of unfairness because he had a chance to purchase a compliment of shares equal to theirs. This argument fails because shareholders also have the corollary right not to purchase shares without facing dilution of equity for which there is no valid business purpose. That right is threatened by stock offered at significantly low prices. To determine if an offering price is legally inadequate, courts are limited to asking whether, given the circumstances of the company (i.e., offer price versus book value of securities, need for capital, ability to sell pre-emptive rights), the directors established the price without "reference to financial considerations" as to the disposition of shares. In this case, the low price was "a tactic, whether conscious or unconscious" to force Katzowitiz (P) to purchase the new shares. Moreover, because of the agreement between the three shareholders, Katzowitz (P) continued to receive equal compensation from Sulburn, thus disguising the dilution of his equity at dissolution. Sidler (D) and Lasker (D), who stood to benefit from the infusion of capital generated by the sale, offered no valid business reasons for the low price. The $5,000 Sidler (D) and Lasker (D) invested in December 1961 should be returned to them and the remaining assets of Sulburn divided equally between the three shareholders. Reversed.

Analysis:

For most people without direct experience with closely held corporations, the problems in *Katzowitz* may seem somewhat obscure. The court does a very good job of explaining why Katzowitz's right to purchase the additional shares does not protect his equity in the company. Sidler and Lasker's argument seems intuitive at first, but then the court reminds us of the special problems facing shareholders in close corporations; if the shareholder chooses not to purchase the additional shares, there is no one to whom she can sell the right to purchase. Even with closely held corporations, the non-purchasing shareholder is protected if the shares are offered at or near their book value, because the non-purchasing shareholder's equity will be reduced only by the amount of the cash still in his bank account, which he can use to invest elsewhere if he so chooses. But, when the shares are offered at a price substantially below book value, the message to the shareholder is, "pony up the money for these new shares or become a disproportionately smaller owner of the corporation."

■ CASE VOCABULARY

BOOK VALUE: The actual amount that a share of a company is worth (regardless of its original price or whether anyone currently wants to buy); roughly, the value of the company divided by the number of outstanding shares.

Lacos Land Company v. Arden Group, Inc.

(Shareholder) v. *(Corporation)*

517 A.2d 271 (Ct. Ch. Del. 1986)

SHAREHOLDER VOTE TO RECAPITALIZE A CORPORATION IS INVALID IF PRINCIPAL SHAREHOLDER/OFFICER HAS THREATENED TO ACT AGAINST THE INTERESTS OF THE CORPORATION IF RECAPITALIZATION IS NOT APPROVED

■ **INSTANT FACTS** A majority of a corporation's shareholders voted to approve a new class of common stock following statements by a corporation's largest shareholder to the effect that, absent shareholder approval of a new class of common stock, he might use his position as the corporation's chief executive adversely to the corporation's interests.

■ **BLACK LETTER RULE** Shareholder vote to authorize a new class of shares is invalid where threats of adverse action by a shareholder/officer seeking such authorization act to subvert the will of the shareholders.

■ **PROCEDURAL BASIS**

Application to enjoin corporation from issuing a newly created class of common stock.

■ **FACTS**

On June 10, 1986, at their annual meeting, the shareholder's of Arden Group, Inc. [Arden] (D) voted to amend the corporation's Articles of Incorporation to create a new class of common stock—Class B— that would have 10 votes per share and would be entitled to elect three-quarters of Arden's (D) Board of Directors. The Class B shares would also have certain dividend privileges and restrictions on transferability. Class B shares were to be offered on a one-to-one exchange basis to current holders of Arden's Class A Common Stock. Being offered on an exchange basis, the new shares were not intended to raise capital but rather to consolidate shareholder control of Arden (D) in the person of a Mr. Briskin (D), Arden's (D) chief executive officer and primary shareholder. Thus, the voting privileges were the most important features of the new shares. Briskin (D) approached Arden's (D) Board of Directors with the idea of the new class of shares in November 1985. The Board created a committee to make a recommendation concerning the proposal. The committee recommended adopting a dual share structure at an April 1986 Board of Directors meeting. The Directors set the date of the annual shareholder's meeting for June 10, 1986 and prepared a proxy statement concerning the new share proposal. The proxy statement explicitly stated that Briskin (D), as CEO and principal shareholder, could and would use his positions of power within the corporation to block certain potential transactions that could benefit the corporation if the new Class B Common Shares were not approved to consolidate his position as principal shareholder. At the June 10 meeting, majorities of the shareholders of both common and preferred shares voted to adopt the new dual common share organization. Following the vote, Arden (D) prepared an Offering circular for exchange of Class A Common Shares for the new Class B shares. Minority shareholders, Lacos Land Company (P) applied to the Court of Chancery for a preliminary injunction against the issuance of the new Class B Common Stock.

■ **ISSUE**

Did Arden (D) shareholders effectively exercise their will to amend the corporation's Articles to authorize a new common stock structure?

■ DECISION AND RATIONALE

(Allen, Chancellor) No.   Statements by Arden's (D) chief executive officer Briskin (D) inappropriately influenced shareholders and thereby flawed the shareholders' vote to approve the new Class B common stock.   Because Briskin (D) was a director and officer of Arden (D), he had a fiduciary duty to act in the interests of the corporation.   Briskin (D) therefore had no right to make the statements, reported in the proxy statement, that he would potentially act against the interests of all shareholders if the new stock structure were not approved.   Moreover, the proxy statement made it clear that Briskin (D) would use his powers *as an officer and director* (as opposed to just his power as a shareholder) to prevent the types of transactions that could benefit the corporation but dilute his shareholder status.   It is not necessary for the plaintiffs to show that Briskin's (D) actions were selfishly motivated.   The fact that shareholders were told that if they failed to adopt the new Class B Common Shares, Briskin (D) would act to block possible favorable transactions was sufficient to undermine shareholder consent to the amendments as required by statute.   Delaware law provides for great flexibility for shareholders to design the capital structures of firms.   The differential voting rights, restrictions on transfer and provisions allowing holders of Class B shares to vote for a majority of the corporation's directors are all legal provided that the shareholders validly adopt the new class of shares.   Briskin's (D) threats of adverse action, however, invalidated the vote of Arden's (D) shareholders in this instance.   The injunction against issuance of the Class B Common Shares is granted.

Analysis:

At first blush, it might seem like the Chancellor's decision to grant the injunction in *Lacos* is designed to punish Briskin (D) for some kind of devious self-interested dealings.   Closer reading, however, indicates that the court does not really think that Briskin (D) is motivated by bad intentions toward the company or the other shareholders.   In fact, the court noted that the company had done quite well under Briskin's stewardship and went on to state that, although suspicious, Briskin's (D) intention to preserve his control of Arden (D) through the new share structure was not a legal wrong.   The problem in *Lacos* was not the share proposal, but Briskin's ... over the shareholders' collective will.   Two questions are interesting to consider in light of the case.   First, what if the only adverse actions threatened by Briskin (D) had been actions that he could take as a shareholder, not as an executive or director of the corporation?   Would his influence on the other shareholders still have been considered inappropriate?   Second, what if Briskin's (D) comments had not been printed in the proxy statement prepared for the shareholder meeting?   Could Lacos (P) have presented evidence of Briskin's (D) inappropriate influence?

■ CASE VOCABULARY

PROXY: A person authorized to vote another person's shares at a corporation's shareholder meeting.

PROXY STATEMENT: A document prepared by a corporation to explain the purposes behind a proposed corporate action to shareholders who will be voting to approve the action.

Gottfried v. Gottfried

(Minority Shareholders) v. *(Corporation)*

73 N.Y.S.2d 692 (1947)

COURT WILL NOT INTERVENE TO FORCE CORPORATION TO DECLARE DIVIDENDS UNLESS THERE IS BAD FAITH

■ **INSTANT FACTS** Minority shareholders of family owned corporation sued corporation and board to have dividends declared.

■ **BLACK LETTER RULE** If an adequate corporate surplus is available for the purpose, directors may not withhold the declaration of dividends in bad faith.

■ **PROCEDURAL BASIS**

Proceeding in trial court to dismiss complaint and enter judgment in action to compel corporation to declare dividends.

■ **FACTS**

The Gottfrieds (Gottfrieds) (P) are minority stockholders of Gottfried Baking Corporation (Corporation) (D), a closely held family corporation engaged in the manufacture and sale of bakery products, along with its wholly owned subsidiary, Hansom. The Gottfrieds (P) sued the Corporation (D), its directors and Hansom to compel the Board of Directors of the Corporation (D) to declare dividends on its common stock. For approximately 13 years prior to the action being brought in 1945, no dividends had been paid upon the common stock, although dividends had been paid regularly upon the outstanding preferred stock and intermittently upon the "A" stock. The Gottfrieds (P) contend that the Board's policy with respect to declaring dividends is based upon considerations not in the best welfare of the corporation (D) or the stockholders, and is in fact based upon the Board's bitter animosity against The Gottfrieds (P). The Gottfrieds (P) contend that the Board has eliminated the need of dividends by paying themselves excessive salaries, bonuses and corporate loans.

■ **ISSUE**

May corporate directors refuse to declare dividends in bad faith when there are adequate funds to do so?

■ **DECISION AND RATIONALE**

(Corcoran, J.) No. The law is clear that if an adequate corporate surplus is available for the purpose, directors may not withhold the declaration of dividends in bad faith. However, the mere existence of an adequate corporate surplus is not sufficient to compel payment of dividends. There must be bad faith on the part of the directors. The test of bad faith is whether the policy of the directors is dictated by their personal interests rather than the corporate welfare. The evidence in this case does not establish the requisite bad faith. Although there was intense hostility between the majority and minority stockholders, and the majority was paid high salaries, bonuses and loans, there must be bad faith by showing that their actions were dictated by their personal interests. The loans were not made with a view to the dividend policy of the corporation. They were incurred, in large part, long before any dispute arose regarding dividends. With respect to the retirement of the outstanding preferred stocks in the sum of $165,000, the Gottfrieds (P) were in at least as good a position as a result of this preferred stock retirement as though dividends had been paid upon the common stock in the sum of $165,000. With respect to the payments of dividends on preferred stock of both corporations and the dividends of the "A" stock, the Gottfrieds (P) were pro rata beneficiaries. It cannot be said that the directors' policy regarding common stock dividends was unduly conservative, and it clearly does not appear to have been inspired by bad faith. The complaint is dismissed and judgment directed for the corporation (D) and other defendants.

Analysis:

This case is an example of what can occur when an internal family dispute arises because of the payment of salaries, bonuses, and loans to some shareholders to the exclusion of others. The underlying contention of the Gottfrieds (P) was that the majority was taking the actions alleged in an effort to persuade them to sell their shares. It is not unusual to have litigation when this occurs. However, courts are reluctant to compel the payment of dividends unless there is a clear showing of bad faith, and that bad faith must be tied to the corporate policy concerning the dividends. Although in certain cases the payments of excessive salaries and bonuses may raise the bad faith flag, the court in this case determined that the actions of the majority were justified and did not reflect bad faith. The court relied upon the timing of when the loans were incurred as well as finding that the Gottfrieds (P) were in as good a position after the payments of the preferred stock dividends had dividends been paid on the common stock and "A" stock.

■ CASE VOCABULARY

DIVIDEND: Payment of corporation's accumulated earnings to shareholders

PREFERRED STOCK: Those shares of stock that have a preference over common shares so that they are entitled to the payment of dividends or liquidation first.

Dodge v. Ford Motor Co.

(Minority Shareholders) v. *(Henry Ford's Company)*

204 Mich. 459, 170 N.W. 668 (1919)

ACCUMULATION BY CORPORATION OF VERY LARGE SURPLUS MAY DICTATE THE PAYMENT OF DIVIDENDS

■ **INSTANT FACTS** Minority shareholders sued Ford Motor Company (D) to declare dividends after board, influenced by president Henry Ford, adopted plan to not pay dividends.

■ **BLACK LETTER RULE** A corporation's board of directors has discretion to decide whether to pay dividends, but that discretion is abused when there is a large accumulation of surplus cash that is not needed for corporate business.

■ **PROCEDURAL BASIS**

Appeal from decree in action to compel payment of corporate dividends.

■ **FACTS**

Dodge (P) and others are minority shareholders in the Ford Motor Company (D), with [the famous] Henry Ford as president and owner of 58 percent of the outstanding capital stock. Ford Motor (D) was prospering and had profits, assets, a surplus of almost 112 million, cash, and municipal bonds. However, the corporation declared no special dividends during the business year, although it had been the practice to declare dividends. The directors of Ford Motor (D) had developed a general plan wherein it was determined that the company would not continue to reduce the selling price of the cars, but would maintain the price and accumulate a large surplus to pay for the proposed expansion of plant and equipment, and perhaps to build a plant for smelting ore. Thereafter, the selling price of the cars would be reduced. The plan did not call for and was not intended to produce immediately a more profitable business. Rather, a less profitable plan was created. Dodge (P) contended that the effect of the plan would result in the corporation being a semi-charitable institution rather than a business institution. [Dodge was part of the Dodge brothers who later developed their own auto company.] The immediate effect of the plan diminishes the value of shares and the returns to the shareholders. The evidence established that Henry Ford had a large influence in determining Ford Motor's (D) policy. Ford Motor (D) refused to declare dividends and Dodge (P) and the other minority shareholders sued for further dividends. The trial court entered a decree fixing and determining the specific amount to be distributed to the stockholders. Ford Motor (D) appealed.

■ **ISSUE**

Is the discretion of a corporation's board of directors as to whether to pay dividends abused if there is a large accumulation of surplus cash that is not needed for corporate business?

■ **DECISION AND RATIONALE**

(Ostrander, J.) Yes. We hold that a corporation's board of directors has discretion to decide whether to pay dividends, but that discretion is abused when there is a large accumulation of surplus cash that is not needed for corporate business. A business corporation is organized and carried on primarily for the profit of the stockholders. The discretion of directors is to be exercised in the choice of means to attain that end, and does not extend to a change in the end itself, to the reduction of profits, or to the nondistribution of profits among stockholders in order to devote them to other purposes. We are not persuaded that we should interfere with the proposed expansion of the business of Ford Motor (D). The judges are not business experts, and plans often are made for a long future, for expected competition, and for a continuing as well as an immediately profitable venture. Ford Motor (D) has demonstrated capable management of its affairs. [That's an understatement.] However, assuming the plan and policy were for the best interest of the company and its shareholders, we must look at the justification for refusal to pay a dividend. We note that the contemplated expenditures were not to be immediately made, and the large sum for the smelter plant was payable over time. It appears that the directors had a duty to distribute a very large sum of money to the stockholders. Affirmed.

■ DISSENT

(Moore, J.) I do not agree with all that is said in the majority opinion but I do agree with the conclusion.

Analysis:

This is considered to be a very famous case, and its holding is significant. In this case, the court upheld the order compelling payment of dividends because of the huge excess surplus and the apparent lack of need therefor. Generally speaking, the courts are reluctant to interfere with businesses and will not order payment of a dividend absent a showing of bad faith. Apparently, the court in this case believed that the board abused its discretion because there was no specific plan to spend the vast amount of earnings, the expansion expenditures were not immediate, and building the potential smelting plant could be paid for over time.

■ CASE VOCABULARY

DECREE: Equivalent to a judgment in a court of law, but rendered in a court of equity.

Wilderman v. Wilderman

(Ex-Wife Shareholder) v. *(Ex-Husband President)*

315 A.2d 610 (Del. Ch. 1974)

A CLOSELY HELD CORPORATION MAY AVOID DOUBLE TAXATION BY PAYING OUT ALL PROFITS IN THE FORM OF COMPENSATION, RATHER THAN DIVIDENDS

■ **INSTANT FACTS** Ex-wife, 50% shareholder in family corporation, sued her ex-husband to have him return excessive compensation to the corporation so that she could receive profits.

■ **BLACK LETTER RULE** Where an officer of a corporation determines his own compensation, upon challenge by other shareholders, the officer has the burden of proving the reasonableness of the compensation.

■ **FACTS**

Mrs. Wilderman (P), the ex-wife of Mr. Wilderman (D1) sued to have the alleged unearned and unauthorized salary and bonuses, which Mr. Wilderman (D1) paid to himself, returned to Marble Craft Company (D2). After Mr. and Mrs. Wilderman divorced, Mrs. Wilderman (P) sued in her own right and in her capacity as a 50% stockholder of Marble Craft (D2) in order to open the way for her to share in the net corporate profits. She also sought the appropriate adjustments to Marble Craft's (D2) pension plan to reflect the returned sums, plus various other injunctive requests. Marble Craft (D2) is a family owned ceramic tile and marble business, operating for fifteen years. Mr. Wilderman (D1) is the president, and Mrs. Wilderman (P) is primarily a bookkeeper although she is well versed in the tile business since her father started such a business years earlier. The controversy surrounds the compensation Mr. Wilderman (D1) paid compensation to himself for the fiscal years 1971 through 1973. For year 1970, his salary in the sum of $60,000 was not questioned. In 1971, he made himself a bonus exceeding $71,000 in addition to a flat salary of $20,800. In 1972, he paid himself $35,000, and in 1973, he paid himself a total compensation of over $86,000. For years, the corporation did not pay dividends because net corporate profits were paid out in the form of executive compensation, thereby avoiding a corporate tax. [Mrs. Wilderman (P) had no complaints then.] Following the Wildermans' divorce, Mrs. Wilderman (P) was excluded from benefiting from the large amounts of compensation Mr. Wilderman (D1) paid to himself.

■ **ISSUE**

Where an officer of a corporation determines his own compensation, may it be challenged by other shareholders who claim a right to the profits?

■ **DECISION AND RATIONALE**

(Marvel, J.) Yes. Where an officer of a corporation determines his own compensation, upon challenge by other shareholders, the officer has the burden of proving the reasonableness of the compensation. The authority to compensate corporate officers is normally vested in the board of directors, and the compensating of corporate officers is usually a matter of contract. However, the owner-managers were in complete disagreement as to the amount of compensation to be paid to Mr. Wilderman (D1), and the only amount agreed upon by the board was the rate of $20,800 per year.] Additional compensation received by him for the years in question must be authorized based upon the reasonable value of services rendered. Mrs. Wilderman (P) argues that the amount paid was unreasonable. Since Mr.

Wilderman's (D1) vote was necessary to fix the amount of his compensation, the burden of showing the reasonableness of such compensation is upon him. An expert testified that a reasonable compensation would range between $25,000 and $35,000. The IRS permitted Marble Craft (D2) to deduct $52,000 of the $92,538 compensation paid. I am not convinced that Mr. Wilderman (D1) has met his burden as to the reasonableness of the amounts he has drawn. I am of the opinion that he is entitled to $45,000 for 1971 and the same amount for 1973. His compensation of $35,000 for 1972 will not be disturbed. Thus, Mr. Wilderman (D1) is ordered to return the excess compensation to the corporate treasury, with interest, plus repayment to the company of the excessive payments to the pension fund.

Analysis:

There are a number of points that should be highlighted from the holding of this case. It primarily demonstrates that the court may order a shareholder who fixes his own compensation to return some of that compensation to the corporation if the shareholder cannot meet his burden of proof with respect to its reasonableness. Note that there was no dispute as to the amount of salaries paid out prior to the divorce. Although Mrs. Wilderman (P) presumably benefited to some degree from the compensation paid to her husband during marriage, the reason for paying out all of the corporation's net profit in the form of executive compensation was to avoid having to pay double taxation. If the corporation retained profits, it would have to pay the corporate tax on them, as would also be the case if the corporation paid out dividends to the shareholders. Instead, the corporation paid out executive compensation in an amount proportionate to the net profit, which was deductible by the corporation, and thus, the only tax paid was by the individual recipient of the compensation. However, once they were divorced, Mrs. Wilderman (P) no longer gained any benefit from Mr. Wilderman's (D1) salary. Accordingly, she sought to have the excessive compensation returned to the corporation so that a dividend could be paid from the profits. Ultimately, the court agreed and ordered Mr. Wilderman (D1) to return a portion of his compensation received over the 3-year period.

■ CASE VOCABULARY

CUSTODIAN: A third person in charge of the property and affairs, such as a receiver or trustee.

QUANTUM MERUIT: Reasonable value of services rendered.

VICE CHANCELLOR: A judge in the court of chancery.

Donahue v. Rodd Electrotype Co.

(Minority Stockholder) v. *(Closely-held Corporation)*
367 Mass. 578, 328 N.E.2d 505 (1975)

A SPECIAL DUTY OF THE UTMOST GOOD FAITH AND LOYALTY EXISTS AMONG SHAREHOLDERS
OF A CLOSELY HELD CORPORATION

■ **INSTANT FACTS** A minority shareholder of a closely-held corporation seeks to rescind the corporation's purchase of the controlling shareholder's stock.

■ **BLACK LETTER RULE** Stockholders in a close corporation owe each other a fiduciary duty of the utmost good faith and loyalty, similar to the duty that partners in a partnership owe to each other.

■ **PROCEDURAL BASIS**

Appeal from the Massachusetts Superior Court's dismissal of a suit in equity for recision of a stock purchase agreement.

■ **FACTS**

Euphemia Donahue ("Donahue") (P) was a minority shareholder in Rodd Electrotype Co. of New England, Inc. ("Rodd Co.") (D1), a small corporation. Donahue had inherited her shares from her husband, a former employee of the company. Harry Rodd ("Harry") (D2), the former president and general manager of the company was the controlling shareholder in Rodd Co. (D1). The Rodd Co. (D1) board of directors consisted of Harry's two sons and a lawyer. At a special meeting, the Board of Directors voted to purchase most of Harry's (D2) shares at $800 a share. On hearing these terms, Donahue (P) offered her shares to Rodd Co. (D1) for the same share price. Rodd Co. (D1) refused to buy at $800 a share and offered Donahue (P) a much lower price. Donahue (P) then sued Rodd Co. (D1) and Harry (D2), seeking to rescind the purchase of Harry's (D2) shares as a violation of the fiduciary duty owed to her as a minority shareholder. The trial court dismissed Donahue's (P) suit, finding that the stock purchase had been carried out in good faith. The appeals court affirmed the trial court and Donahue (P) appealed to the Supreme Judicial Court of Massachusetts.

■ **ISSUE**

Do stockholders in a close corporation owe each other a fiduciary duty of the utmost good faith and loyalty, similar to the duty that partners in a partnership owe to each other?

■ **DECISION AND RATIONALE**

(Tauro, C.J.) Yes. A close corporation is typified by: (1) a small number of shareholders; (2) no ready market for the corporate stock; and (3) substantial majority stockholder participation in the management, direction, and operations of the corporation. These features make a close corporation resemble a partnership, where, in order for the entity to succeed, the relationship among the owners must be one of trust and absolute loyalty. In general, minority shareholders are vulnerable to oppressive actions by the majority known as "freeze-outs," which can include the refusal to declare dividends, a draining of corporate earnings through exorbitant salaries and bonuses to majority shareholders, and the exclusion of the minority from corporate offices and employment. While the minority can file suit against the majority and the corporate directors under such circumstances, such suits are often difficult to win because corporate directors generally have wide latitude on matters such as dividends and employment. The minority is then left trapped in a disadvantageous situation or is forced to sell out to the majority at less than fair market value. Because of the resemblance of a close corporation to a partnership, we hold that the stockholders of a close corporation owe each other a duty of the utmost good faith and loyalty, similar to the duty that partners in a partnership owe to each other. Under this standard, if a controlling stockholder causes the corporation to purchase his shares, the controlling stockholder must also cause the corporation to offer every other stockholder the chance to sell a ratable number of shares to the corporation at an identical price. Otherwise, the controlling stockholder unfairly benefits from the creation of a market for company shares and from the preferential distribution of company assets. Here, Rodd Co. (D1) is a close corporation and Harry's (D2) family constituted a "controlling group." Since Donahue (P) was not given an equal opportunity to sell her shares, the controlling group breached its fiduciary duty to her. On remand, the trial court is to enter an order to either rescind the purchase of Harry's (D2) shares or compel Rodd Co. (D1) to buy all of Donahue's (P) shares at the same price paid for Harry's (D2) shares. Reversed and remanded.

■ CONCURRENCE

(Wilkins, J.) The rule concerning the purchase of a controlling stockholder's shares does not necessarily apply to all operations of the corporation as they affect minority shareholders. The majority's comments regarding dividend and salary policy involve matters not directly in issue in this case and the partnership analogy might not hold in a future case concerning such items.

Analysis:

As their very name suggests, close corporations can involve small, intimate, and personal relationships. In many cases, the shareholders of a closely-held corporation have a large portion of their personal wealth tied up in that corporation. The same people will often be the shareholders, management, and employees of the company. In publicly-held corporations, entity ownership and management are separate. Having the same people own and manage a business can create difficulties for the business when those people disagree over management policies. This court recognizes the special problems confronting closely held shareholders and rightfully likens their situation to the situation faced by partners in a partnership. The court imposes a very strict duty of good faith and loyalty on the shareholders of a closely-held corporation, analogous to the duty held by partners in a partnership and much more demanding than the duty required of shareholders and management of publicly-held companies.

■ CASE VOCABULARY

CLOSE CORPORATION: A corporation with a small number of stockholders who lack a ready market for their stock and in which there is substantial majority stockholder participation in the management, direction, and operations of the company.

FIDUCIARY DUTY: A special duty imposed by law on various business relationships, requiring a high standard of loyalty and trust, even at some personal cost.

FREEZE-OUT: An attempt by the majority shareholder of a corporation to exclude the minority shareholders from the economic benefits of corporate ownership or participation in corporate policy decisions.

CHAPTER NINE

Management and Control of Corporation

McQuade v. Stoneham

Instant Facts: After being voted off the board of directors and removed as an officer of a closely-held corporation, a minority shareholder sued to enforce an agreement requiring the controlling shareholders to use their best efforts to keep him in office.

Black Letter Rule: An agreement among shareholders of a corporation to restrict their discretion as directors of the corporation is invalid and unenforceable as against public policy.

Galler v. Galler

Instant Facts: The widow of one of two principal shareholders of a closely-held corporation sued the other principal shareholder seeking to enforce an agreement prescribing how the shareholders would vote for corporate offices and requiring the declaration of annual dividends and the payment of a widow's pension.

Black Letter Rule: A shareholder agreement limiting the discretion of the board of directors of a close corporation will be upheld where no minority shareholder is prejudiced, neither the corporate creditors nor the public are injured, and no clearly prohibitory statutory language is violated by its enforcement.

Zion v. Kurtz

Instant Facts: The founding shareholders of a closely held corporation agreed between themselves that the corporation would not do any business that was not approved by the minority shareholder.

Black Letter Rule: An agreement among shareholders to limit the power of the directors is, as between the shareholders, enforceable as a matter of public policy.

Matter of Auer v. Dressel

Instant Facts: Pursuant to the corporation's bylaws, Class A shareholders demanded the President to call a shareholders' meeting for the purpose of affecting certain changes in the corporation's leadership structure.

Black Letter Rule: If the corporate certificate and bylaws permit, shareholders are entitled to remove directors for cause, amend the bylaws, and elect successor directors.

Salgo v. Matthews

Instant Facts: At a shareholders' election, election inspector refused to accept a proxy from the record owner of the stock, instead arguing that the beneficial owner was entitled to vote those shares.

Black Letter Rule: At a shareholders' election, the record owner of shares of stock gets to vote the shares.

Humphrys v. Winous Co.

Instant Facts: The majority shareholders of a corporation changed the method of electing directors, from electing all three at once to electing one at a time, which effectively nullified the minority's cumulative voting strength.

Black Letter Rule: The statutory right to cumulative voting only guarantees the right to cumulate votes, not the right to representation on the board of directors.

Ringling Bros.-Barnum & Bailey Combined Shows v. Ringling

Instant Facts: A shareholder of a closely-held corporation operating a circus sued to enforce the terms of a vote-pooling agreement entered into with another shareholder who had refused to vote according to the terms of the agreement.

Black Letter Rule: In general, shareholders may enter into an agreement to vote their shares jointly.

Brown v. Mclanahan

Instant Facts: Trustees of a voting trust voted to amend the corporate charter in such a way that they diluted the voting power of the shareholders to the benefit of the debenture holders, who were mainly the trustees themselves.

Black Letter Rule: The trustees of a voting trust are under a duty to act in the best interest of the shareholders that they represent.

Lehrman v. Cohen

Instant Facts: To resolve a dispute over control of a corporation, shareholders agreed to create a new class of stock, the sole purpose of which was to elect a director to break ties of the board of directors.

Black Letter Rule: A class of stock that has no rights other than to elect a director is not a voting trust simply because it dilutes the voting power of the other voting shares.

Ling and Co. v. Trinity Sav. and Loan Ass'n

Instant Facts: A bank wanted to sell some stock that had been pledged as security for a loan that was in default, but the corporation that issued the stock objected because there were restrictions on the transfer of its stock.

Black Letter Rule: In order to be valid, restrictions on the transfer of stock must be reasonable and must be conspicuously referenced on the front of the stock certificate.

Gearing v. Kelly

Instant Facts: Two directors voted to fill the vacancy left by the resignation of a third director in a board comprised of four directors, even though the two directors did not constitute a quorum under corporate bylaws and thus could not conduct business.

Black Letter Rule: A director that is intentionally absent from a board meeting for the purpose of preventing a quorum may not later complain that the board transacted business in the absence of a quorum.

In Re Radom & Neidorff, Inc.

Instant Facts: Because the two shareholders in a corporation did not like each other, one shareholder petitioned the court for dissolution of the corporation.

Black Letter Rule: Dissolution is an extreme remedy that will only be granted if the corporation is no longer able to function because of shareholder disagreement.

Davis v. Sheerin

Instant Facts: The court ordered a buy-out of a minority shareholder's shares after a jury found that the majority shareholders acted oppressively toward a minority shareholder.

Black Letter Rule: The court is warranted in using its equitable power to order a buy-out if the majority shareholders in a closely held corporation engage in oppressive conduct toward a minority shareholder.

Abreu v. Unica Indus. Sales, Inc.

Instant Facts: After one director on a three-director board was removed for self-dealing and usurping a corporate opportunity, the court appointed a provisional director with the limited function of overseeing the board of directors and breaking any deadlocks of the directors.

Black Letter Rule: The court may appoint a provisional director if it is in the best interests of the corporation.

In the Matter of Drive–In Dev. Corp.

Instant Facts: The corporation's secretary certified to a bank that the board of directors had resolved to guarantee a loan and the bank lent money based on that certification, but the corporation now wishes to deny that it made any such resolution.

Black Letter Rule: Statements made by a corporate officer in the course of a transaction in which the corporation is engaged and that relate to a matter within the scope of the officer's authority are binding upon the corporation.

Lee v. Jenkins Bros.

Instant Facts: An employee was induced to switch employers by the corporation's president's promise of a pension at retirement age, but then the company fired him prior to reaching retirement and did not pay him the pension.

Black Letter Rule: Promising a pension is one part of the president's ordinary and usual duty of hiring and firing employees, and therefore such a promise by the president is binding on the corporation.

Debaun v. First Western Bank and Trust Co.

Instant Facts: Majority shareholder of a corporation breached its duty of due care by selling its shares to an entity which looted and destroyed the corporation.

Black Letter Rule: A majority shareholder who intends to sell the shares he holds, when possessed of facts establishing a reasonable likelihood that the purchaser intends to exercise the control to be acquired by him to loot the corporation of its assets, owes a duty of reasonable investigation and due care to the corporation.

Perlman v. Feldmann

Instant Facts: A steel company's minority stockholders brought a derivative action against the corporation's former controlling stockholder for selling his controlling bloc at a premium to a group of buyers who were solely interested in using the corporation's supply of steel during a tight market.

Black Letter Rule: Where a call on a corporation's product commands an unusually large premium, a fiduciary may not appropriate to himself the value of this premium.

McQuade v. Stoneham

(Minority Stockholder) v. *(Majority Stockholder)*

263 N.Y. 323, 189 N.E. 234 (1934)

NEW YORK COURT OF APPEALS HOLDS THAT A SHAREHOLDER AGREEMENT PURPORTING TO RESTRICT THE SHAREHOLDERS' POWERS AS DIRECTORS IS UNENFORCEABLE, EVEN IN A CLOSE CORPORATION

■ **INSTANT FACTS** After being voted off the board of directors and removed as an officer of a closely-held corporation, a minority shareholder sued to enforce an agreement requiring the controlling shareholders to use their best efforts to keep him in office.

■ **BLACK LETTER RULE** An agreement among shareholders of a corporation to restrict their discretion as directors of the corporation is invalid and unenforceable as against public policy.

■ **PROCEDURAL BASIS**

Appeal from a judgment of an appellate court affirming a trial court judgment awarding damages for wrongful discharge.

■ **FACTS**

Charles A. Stoneham ("Stoneham") (D1) was the majority shareholder of the close corporation operating the New York Giants baseball franchise. Stoneham sold a minority stake in the franchise to John J. McGraw ("McGraw") (D2), the team manager, and Francis X. McQuade ("McQuade") (P), a New York City magistrate. As part of the stock sale, the three men entered into an agreement that they would each use their best efforts to maintain each other as directors and officers of the corporation. For six years, all three men served on the board of directors and as paid corporate officers. After a disagreement between McQuade (P) and Stoneham (D1), Stoneham (D1) and McGraw (D2) refused to vote for McQuade's (P) re-election as a corporate officer and McQuade (P) was not elected. He was later dropped from the board of directors, as well. McQuade (P) sued for breach of contract, seeking reinstatement as an officer and a director. The trial court and the appellate court both refused the reinstatement remedy, but gave McQuade (P) damages for wrongful discharge. Stoneham (D1) and McGraw (D2) appealed.

■ **ISSUE**

Is an agreement among shareholders of a corporation to restrict their discretion as directors of the corporation valid and enforceable?

■ **DECISION AND RATIONALE**

(Pound, C.J.) No. Directors are the exclusive executive representatives of a corporation and are charged with the management and administration of its assets. Directors have a legal duty to act for the corporation. Past cases have held that an agreement among shareholders that attempts to prevent a board of directors from firing an unfaithful employee is illegal as against public policy. We now find that shareholders may not, by agreement, among themselves, control the power of a board of directors to elect officers or fix salaries. The directors must be free to exercise their independent business judgment. While shareholders can unite to elect directors, they cannot unite to limit the power of elected directors to manage the business according to their best judgment. Here, Stoneham (D1) and McGraw (D2) were not trustees for McQuade (P) as an individual. Their duty as directors was to exercise their lawful judgment for the benefit of the corporation and all of its stockholders. To the extent it attempts to restrict a board of directors from changing officers, salaries, or other corporate policies, a contract violates public policy and is illegal. This result is preferable to a judicial inquiry into the motives of directors in the exercise of their business judgment. Reversed.

Analysis:

In rejecting, outright, any shareholder agreement seeking to bind the voting discretion of corporate directors, this court takes an older view, rejected by most courts today. This court finds that the traditional notion that a corporate director owes a fiduciary duty of undivided loyalty to the corporation should apply in all circumstances, even in the special context of a closely held corporation, to prevent any shareholder agreement attempting to limit a shareholder's discretion *as a director.* The rationale for this result appears to have been a concern that such agreements could do harm to other shareholders who were not parties to the agreement. More recent decisions, however, have been willing to enforce voluntary agreements among investors in closely held corporations under certain circumstances. The modern trend recognizes that in the context of a closely held corporation, these contracts limiting the discretion of the board can play an important role in helping to protect minority shareholders from the tyranny of the majority. Several states also now have laws making such agreements enforceable.

■ **CASE VOCABULARY**

BOARD OF DIRECTORS: The governing body of a corporation, elected by the corporation's shareholders and charged with the power to elect or appoint corporate officers and set corporate policy.

Galler v. Galler

(Widow) v. *(Controlling Shareholder)*

32 Ill.2d 16, 203 N.E.2d 577 (1964)

ILLINOIS SUPREME COURT ADOPTS MODERN VIEW AND UPHOLDS SHAREHOLDER AGREEMENT
LIMITING DIRECTOR DISCRETION

■ **INSTANT FACTS** The widow of one of two principal shareholders of a closely-held corporation sued the other principal shareholder seeking to enforce an agreement prescribing how the shareholders would vote for corporate offices and requiring the declaration of annual dividends and the payment of a widow's pension.

■ **BLACK LETTER RULE** A shareholder agreement limiting the discretion of the board of directors of a close corporation will be upheld where no minority shareholder is prejudiced, neither the corporate creditors nor the public are injured, and no clearly prohibitory statutory language is violated by its enforcement.

■ **PROCEDURAL BASIS**

Appeal from an order of the First District Appellate Court reversing a Superior Court decree in equity for specific performance of a shareholder agreement.

■ **FACTS**

Emma Galler ("Emma") (P) was the widow of Benjamin Galler, one of two founding shareholders of Galler Drug Co., a wholesale drug business. The other founding shareholder of the company was Benjamin's brother, Isadore Galler ("Isadore") (D). Benjamin and Isadore (D) each owned approximately one half of the shares of the company. In order to assure their families equal control of the business in the event either brother died, the brothers signed a shareholders' agreement which, among other things, prescribed how the parties would vote for corporate directors and officers, required certain dividends to be paid by the corporation each year and, in the event of the death of either brother, established a pension to be paid to his widow. After Benjamin's death, Isadore (D) refused to honor the agreement and Emma (P) brought a suit in equity for specific performance and an accounting. The trial court ruled in favor of Emma (P), but on appeal, the First District Appellate Court of Illinois reversed that ruling. Emma (P) appealed to the Illinois Supreme Court.

■ **ISSUE**

Are there circumstances where a shareholder agreement limiting the discretion of the board of directors of a close corporation will be upheld?

■ **DECISION AND RATIONALE**

(Underwood, J.) Yes. We think that special rules, not applicable to a publicly-held corporations, should apply to shareholder agreements in a close corporation context. A shareholder of a publicly-held corporation generally has a ready market for his shares and can sell them if he disagrees with the way management is operating the business. A minority shareholder in a close corporation, however, has no ready market for his shares, and may find himself at the mercy of an oppressive or unknowledgeable majority, if he cannot rely on a shareholder agreement to protect his interest. As in this case, the shareholders of a close corporation are often also the directors and officers of the

---

company. Thus, unlike a publicly-held corporation, in a close corporation, with the directors and officers often having a major financial interest in the company, it is often impossible to obtain a truly neutral, independent judgment of the board of directors. In our view, these conceptual differences between a close corporation and a publicly-held corporation justify permitting the shareholders of a close corporation to reach agreements concerning its management. We will uphold such agreements where no minority shareholder is prejudiced, there is no fraud or injury to a corporate creditor or the public, and no clearly prohibitory statutory language is violated by their enforcement. Here, those conditions are met. No shareholder who was not a party to the agreement has claimed injury as a result of the proposed enforcement of the agreement. We disagree with the Appellate Court that the public policy of this state demands a voiding of this shareholder agreement and will uphold the agreement under these circumstances. Reversed.

Analysis:

The Illinois Supreme Court adopts the modern view that close corporations are special entities requiring special rules that may differ from the regular rules applicable to a publicly held corporation. Public investors typically expect that the board they elect will exercise its best independent business judgment. Shareholders in a close corporation generally recognize that there will be a blurring of the lines between the shareholders, the board, and the corporate officers. Understanding that close corporations usually involve ''close,'' personal relationships and that the shareholders of such companies often have their blood, sweat, and tears wrapped up in the business, this court goes out of its way to offer some protection to such shareholders from a potentially oppressive majority. In the absence of a state statutory scheme protecting such shareholders, this court gives the minority shareholder in a close corporation a chance to protect himself, by developing judicial rules that will uphold certain protective agreements where they can be negotiated by the shareholders and no other minority shareholder is prejudiced by their enforcement. Most courts today would agree with this view. More significantly, most states have adopted comprehensive statutory schemes that specifically govern close corporations and approve the kinds of protective agreements at issue in this case.

■ CASE VOCABULARY

ACCOUNTING: An equitable remedy to determine the earnings and profits of a company and recover any profits taken by a party in breach of a fiduciary duty to another party.

PUBLICLY-HELD CORPORATION: A corporation with stock held by and available for sale to the public at large, usually through a government-regulated stock exchange. In general, the corporation's management is separated from stock ownership.

Zion v. Kurtz

(Shareholder) v. *(Shareholder)*

50 N.Y.2d 92, 428 N.Y.S.2d 199, 405 N.E.2d 681 (Ct. App. 1980)

SHAREHOLDER AGREEMENTS THAT LIMIT THE DISCRETION OF THE DIRECTORS ARE VALID

■ **INSTANT FACTS** The founding shareholders of a closely held corporation agreed between themselves that the corporation would not do any business that was not approved by the minority shareholder.

■ **BLACK LETTER RULE** An agreement among shareholders to limit the power of the directors is, as between the shareholders, enforceable as a matter of public policy.

■ **PROCEDURAL BASIS**

Appeal from judgment that shareholder agreement was unenforceable as against public policy.

■ **FACTS**

Harold Kurtz (D) formed a Delaware corporation known as the Lombard-Wall Group, Inc. Abraham Zion (P), as part of the initial funding for the corporation, acquired all of its Class A stock. Kurtz (D) held all of the Class B stock. Zion (P) and Kurtz (D) executed a shareholders' agreement that provided that the corporation could not do any business without the consent of the holders of the Class A stock. The corporation's articles of incorporation do not refer to this veto power. The corporation's board of directors approved two agreements over the objection of Zion (P). Zion (P) brought suit to cancel the agreements as violating the shareholders' consent agreement.

■ **ISSUE**

Is a shareholders' agreement void as against public policy if it takes management decisions out of the hands of the directors and puts them into the hands of the shareholders?

■ **DECISION AND RATIONALE**

(Meyer, J.) No. The agreement relates to the internal affairs of the corporation, and therefore the law of the forum of incorporation (in this case Delaware) must by applied. The General Corporation Law of Delaware provides that ordinarily the business and affairs of a corporation are managed by the board of directors. However, there are two exceptions to this general rule. First, the law provides an exception if the certificate of incorporation provides otherwise. Second, the law provides that a shareholders' agreement between the majority of the shareholders in a close corporation "is not invalid, as between the parties to the agreement, on the ground that it so relates to the conduct of the business and affairs of the corporation as to restrict or interfere with the discretion or powers of the board of directors." § 350. From this section, we conclude that the public policy of Delaware does not prohibit shareholder agreements like the one between Kurtz (D) and Zion (P). Kurtz (D) argues that the agreement is invalid because the corporation was not incorporated as a close corporation under Delaware law and because the shareholders' agreement was not in the certificate of incorporation. However, a corporation in Delaware can become a close corporation by filing an appropriate certificate of amendment. In addition, the certificate of incorporation could be amended to incorporate the shareholders' agreement. In executing the shareholders' agreement, Kurtz (D) promised to take all steps necessary to give effect to the provisions, intent, and purpose of the agreement. Thus, it is within this court's equitable power to order the certificate of incorporation to be reformed, and, in any event, Kurtz (D) is now estopped from relying on the absence of the amendments to the corporate charter when he should have made such amendments in order to comply with the shareholders' agreement. An examination of the authorities of this jurisdiction convinces us that there is no public policy in this jurisdiction against our application of the Delaware law referred to above. Reversed.

■ DISSENT

(Gabrielli, J.) I conclude that under the public policy of both this state and Delaware, the shareholders' agreement was an illegal attempt by shareholders to deprive the board of directors of its inherent authority to exercise its discretion in managing the affairs of the corporation. It is true that a shareholders' agreement may limit slightly the board's authority. However, neither the courts of our State nor the courts of Delaware have gone so far as to hold that an agreement among shareholders such as the agreement in this case, to "sterilize" the board of directors by completely depriving it of its discretionary authority. The statutory provisions referred to by the majority permit deviations from the norm only under certain controlled conditions. In order to protect potential creditors and future purchasers of shares, such agreements that restrict the authority of the board of directors must be included in the certificate of incorporation. Since the statutory requirements are prophylactic in nature, they cannot be excused merely because in fact no third party was injured. Thus, I dissent from the majority's holding in this case and I would order the agreement between Kurtz (D) and Zion (P) to be void and unenforceable.

Analysis:

Courts have struggled with the validity of shareholder agreements. Such agreements, which would be an undesirable limitation on the management of a large, publicly held corporation, were a useful means of encouraging investment in a small, closely held corporation. In publicly held corporations, shareholders do not need the kind of protection that shareholders' agreements offer—unlike the shareholder of a closely held corporation, the shareholder of a large corporation can always sell his shares if he does not like the way the corporation is being managed. In an effort to clarify matters, many legislatures have enacted statutes addressing the validity of shareholder agreements. It is this type of statute that is at issue in the present case. Note that the New York Court is applying a Delaware Statute. The majority opinion reflects the broad remedial purposes that the statute was meant to serve. It recognizes that the statute meant to give effect to the agreements between shareholders in a closely held corporation and reflects the reality that closely held corporations are different than their publicly held cousins. The dissent reflects a narrow and literal interpretation of the statute, requiring strict compliance.

■ CASE VOCABULARY

CLOSELY HELD CORPORATION: Sometimes also called a close corporation, a small corporation that has few shareholders and seems more like a partnership because the owners are usually also employees and managers. There are often special statutory rules designed to reflect the reality of a corporate form that does not recognize a separation between ownership and management.

SHAREHOLDERS' AGREEMENT: An agreement between shareholders in a closely held corporation to act or refrain from acting in a certain way. Such agreements are one way to give investors the incentive they need to invest in small corporations with no market for their stock—it gives them the means to protect their investment.

Matter of Auer v. Dressel

(Ex-President) v. *(Current President)*

306 N.Y. 427, 118 N.E.2d 590 (1954)

SHAREHOLDERS ARE IN CONTROL OF THE ELECTION OF DIRECTORS AND MAY REMOVE A DIRECTOR FOR CAUSE

■ **INSTANT FACTS** Pursuant to the corporation's bylaws, Class A shareholders demanded the President to call a shareholders' meeting for the purpose of affecting certain changes in the corporation's leadership structure.

■ **BLACK LETTER RULE** If the corporate certificate and bylaws permit, shareholders are entitled to remove directors for cause, amend the bylaws, and elect successor directors.

■ **PROCEDURAL BASIS**

Appeal from judgment enforcing a provision in the corporate bylaws.

■ **FACTS**

The class A stockholders (P) of a corporation, R. Hoe & Co., Inc. (D), petitioned the corporation's current President (D) to hold a special meeting pursuant to the corporation's bylaws. The bylaws vest no discretion in the President (D)—if a meeting is properly called, then it must be held. The meeting is properly called if demanded by stockholders owning a majority of the shares that would be entitled to vote at the meeting. The class A shareholders (P) submitted a written request to the President (D) for such a meeting. The request was signed by the holders of slightly more than 55% of the holders of record of the corporation's class A stock. The stockholders (P) stated four purposes for which they wished the special meeting to be held: (A) to vote upon a resolution calling for the endorsement and reinstatement of the corporation's former president; (B) to vote on a proposal to amend the charter and bylaws to provide that vacancies on the board of directors arising from a removal or resignation of a director could be filled only by the holders of the class of stock represented by that director; (C) to hear charges against four of the current directors, vote upon their removal, and elect their successors; (D) to vote on a proposal to amend the bylaws as to the definition of what constitutes a quorum of directors. The President (D) did not call a special meeting as demanded, and the class A shareholders (P) initiated this suit to force the President (D) to call the meeting. The President (D) opposes, claiming that none of these stated items are properly conducted at a class A shareholders' meeting.

■ **ISSUE**

Are stockholders allowed to remove directors and appoint successor directors?

■ **DECISION AND RATIONALE**

(Desmond, J.) Yes. We see no reason why the class A shareholders (P) should not be allowed to vote on any or all of the four proposals. Regarding purpose (A), there is nothing invalid about the class A shareholders (P) expressing their opinion to the directors, who will stand for election at the annual meeting. As for purpose (B), it seems to be settled law that the stockholders who are empowered to elect directors also have the inherent power to remove them for cause—as long as the affected directors get served with specific charges, adequate notice, and have a full opportunity to be heard.

There is no showing that any of these requirements is missing here. Since the class A shareholders (P) have the power to remove directors for cause, they may amend the bylaws to provide that only the shareholders themselves may fill vacancies by resignation or removal. Such a change would not affect the rights of the common stockholders, who select the two directors that are not elected by the class A shareholders (P). As for purpose (C), it has been argued that it is impractical and unfair to allow the shareholders to gather a tribunal to hear and decide upon charges that the shareholders themselves have brought. However, this question is really not before us on this appeal. Any director who feels himself to have been illegally removed can have his remedy in the courts. Affirmed.

■ DISSENT

(Van Voorhis, J.) An examination of the request for a special meeting by these stockholders (P) indicates that none of the proposals could be voted upon legally at the projected meeting. Regarding purpose (A), it would be an idle gesture for the stockholders to vote to endorse the administration of the former president and demand his immediate reinstatement. It is the directors, not the shareholders, who appoint the officers of the corporation. Next, purpose (B), giving class A shareholders the exclusive right to fill vacancies of class A directors, must be read in context: The certificate of incorporation provides for eleven directors—two elected by the common shareholders and nine elected by the class A shareholders (P). The common shareholders are entitled to participate directly in the election of two directors, who, in turn, are authorized to participate in filling vacancies occurring among the directors elected by the class A shareholders. Purpose (B) would deprive the directors elected by the common shareholders of the power to participate in filling the vacancies of retired or removed directors, thereby impairing the rights of the common shareholders. Since the common shareholders would be excluded from the class A shareholders' (P) meeting, purpose (B) could not be legally adopted. Purpose (C), whereby the class A shareholders (P) propose to hear charges against four of the directors, vote upon their removal, and then fill the vacancies caused by the removals, is likewise not something that the shareholders (P) can legally do. In essence, the class A shareholders (P) are attempting to do indirectly what they cannot do directly; namely, they are attempting to oust the directors that are friendly to the new president and elect directors who will reappoint the ex-president (P). However, nothing in the corporation law or the corporation's certificate or bylaws allows shareholders to remove directors before their term has expired in order to change the policy of the corporation. Under corporate law, stockholders must follow certain procedures and must show that the director whose removal is sought has committed fraud or breach of fiduciary duty. Here, the class A stockholders (P) propose to follow an improper procedure. First, they do not adequately give notice of the charges against the directors, and what little notice has been given charges the directors with behavior that does not amount to fraud or breach of fiduciary duty. Second, the class A shareholders (P) will not all be allowed to give a full hearing to the accused directors. Rather, a few select shareholders (who have already prejudged the directors) will vote the proxies for the rest of the shares. In essence, the class A shareholders (P) propose to judge these directors guilty of fraud or breach of faith in absentia by shareholders who have neither heard nor ever will hear the evidence against them or in their behalf. This procedure does not comport with the requirements of our law or of the corporation's certificate of incorporation. For the foregoing reasons, we conclude that none of the business for which the special meeting is proposed to be called could legally be transacted, and thus this proceeding should be dismissed.

Analysis:

Holding stock in a corporation carries with it certain rights. Chief among these is the right to vote at annual shareholders meetings (to elect corporate directors) and any special meetings that may be called. At special meetings shareholders may vote on significant events in the life of the corporation, such as amendment of the articles, mergers, sale of all of the corporate assets, or dissolving the corporation. The shareholders do not have any positive power to make decisions for the corporation or to command action by the board of directors. Rather, they vote yes or no on decisions made by the board. Shareholders are entitled to notice of special meetings, which tells them when and where the meeting will take place and what the meeting will be about. As in the present case, corporate bylaws or the articles of incorporation usually provide for how a special meeting may be called. In some cases, statutes mandate that a special meeting must be held if a certain percentage of shares call for the meeting. The court here affirms the rule that part of the power to elect directors is the implied power to remove directors for cause.

■ CASE VOCABULARY

DIRECTOR'S FIDUCIARY DUTIES: Directors are fiduciaries of the corporation, and owe a certain duties to the corporation in managing its affairs. Specifically, directors owe the corporation a duty of care (to manage the corporation in the same way that a prudent person would manage his or her own business) and a duty of loyalty (to act in good faith and with the reasonable belief that what he or she does is in the corporation's best interest).

PROXY: Written permission given by one shareholder to another, allowing the second shareholder the vote the shares of the first at a shareholders' meeting.

REMOVAL FOR CAUSE: Normally a director cannot be removed until he or she stands for election at the annual meeting. However, a director who has committed fraud upon the corporation or has breached a fiduciary duty may be removed for cause.

SPECIAL MEETING: Any meeting of the shareholders other than the annual meeting. The procedure for calling a special meeting may be prescribed by statute or provided for by the bylaws or articles of incorporation.

Salgo v. Matthews

(Shareholders) v. *(Corporation President)*
497 S.W.2d 620 (Tex. Civ. App. 1973)

DIRECTORS ARE ELECTED BY THE SHAREHOLDERS OF RECORD

■ **INSTANT FACTS** At a shareholders' election, election inspector refused to accept a proxy from the record owner of the stock, instead arguing that the beneficial owner was entitled to vote those shares.

■ **BLACK LETTER RULE** At a shareholders' election, the record owner of shares of stock gets to vote the shares.

■ **PROCEDURAL BASIS**

Appeal from grant of injunction in corporate election dispute.

■ **FACTS**

This was an action brought by two shareholders (P) representing a faction opposed to the current management of the corporation. The dispute arises from the election of directors at a shareholders' meeting. The current president (D1) was acting as chair of the shareholders' meeting and appointed a well-known attorney as election inspector (D2). At the meeting the shareholders (P) presented to the election inspectors proxies purporting to have been executed in their favor on behalf of Pioneer Casualty Company ("Pioneer"). Pioneer is the record owner of 29,934 shares of stock. Beneficial title in the shares had been transferred to Don Shepherd, an individual who was in bankruptcy. Pioneer was in receivership. The shareholders (P) presented the election inspector (D2) with a court order that directed Pioneer's receiver to give the shareholders (P) a proxy to vote those shares. The election inspector (D2) refused to accept the proxies. The shareholders (P) brought this action to require the corporation's president (D1) and the election inspector (D2) to accept the shareholders' (P) proxies and declare that their candidates had been elected as directors of the corporation.

■ **ISSUE**

May the corporation look beyond the corporate records of stock ownership in order to determine the identity of stockholders who are allowed to vote?

■ **DECISION AND RATIONALE**

(Guittard, J.) No. The election inspector (D2) did have the discretion to make a preliminary determination of the validity of the proxies for the purpose of tabulating them, counting the votes, and certifying the result. However, the correctness of his decision is subject to review after the election by proceeding in *quo warranto*. The election inspector (D2) may not go beyond the corporate records in determining the identity of stockholders entitled to vote. The president (D) and election inspector (D) argue that, as the beneficial owner, it was the bankruptcy trustee of Don Shepherd who had the right to vote. We disagree. Beneficial ownership does not carry with it the right to vote without having the shares transferred on the books of the corporation. There are several reasons that corporations and their stockholders have an interest in determining stock ownership quickly by reference to the corporate records. First, Where beneficial title is in dispute, that dispute cannot properly be resolved by an election inspector. Second, losing factions should not be able to go into court to invalidate elections

---

on the ground that true ownership of certain shares was not correctly shown by the corporate records. Additionally, an election should not be interrupted or suspended while complicated questions of title to stock are litigated to a final judgment. Eligibility to vote at corporate elections is determined by the corporate records rather than by the ultimate judicial decision of beneficial title of disputed shares. Such a rule does not leave a beneficial owner without remedy. If a beneficial owner wants to vote his shares, he has the ability to require a transfer on the books or to demand a proxy from the record owner. The courts will enforce such a demand. In this case, the stockholder of record was Pioneer, and the receiver was authorized by court order to act for Pioneer. The election inspector (D2) should have determined from the corporate records that that Pioneer had the right to vote the shares and accepted the proxies given to the shareholders (P) as valid. The election inspector (D2) was bound by the stock book to consider Pioneer the legal owner for the purpose of the election, and to determine who could act for that owner. He could not, however, look any further to determine to determine beneficial ownership. Reversed.

Analysis:

As this case illustrates, determining who has the right to vote is important, especially in heavily contested elections. Thus, prior to the election the corporation needs to compile a quick and convenient list of who is allowed to vote at that election. As the court points out in the present case, since an election would soon grind to a halt if every ownership dispute that arose in the course of an election had to be litigated prior to the corporation determining who gets to vote, the law allows corporations to rely upon the corporate records of who owns how many shares. If a record owner holds shares for a beneficial owner, it is up to the beneficial owner to demand a change on the corporate books if he wants to vote his shares. This is a sensible way to shift the burden of producing this information, since the corporation can easily find out who it sells the shares to in the first instance, but has no control over where they may go after that and no practical way of finding out. This case is also concerned with another issue raised by the question of who may vote—that of proxy. The list of eligible voters at any given election is also important because voting by proxy is very common. If it weren't for proxy voting, many shareholders would not vote at all. The corporation is allowed to determine who has a valid proxy by using the list of record owners as of the record date.

■ CASE VOCABULARY

BENEFICIAL OWNER: A person who owns shares in a corporation, but those shares are listed in the corporation's records under someone else's name.

QUO WARRANTO: A court proceeding to determine whether the corporation has the power to take certain actions.

RECEIVERSHIP: A court may place an insolvent business into receivership, whereby a neutral person (called a receiver) is given control over the assets of the business in order to protect the assets and preserve them for creditors that have claims against the business.

RECORD OWNER: A person who is listed in the corporation's books as the owner of shares, but is not necessarily the person who actually owns the shares.

STREET NAME: When one person or entity (the record owner) is listed in the corporate books as holding stock that is really owned by another person (the beneficial owner), the record owner is said the be holding the stock in street name.

Humphrys v. Winous Co.

(Not Stated) v. *(Not Stated)*
165 Ohio St. 45, 133 N.E.2d 780 (1956)

CUMULATIVE VOTING DOES NOT GUARANTEE THE ELECTION OF A MINORITY DIRECTOR

■ **INSTANT FACTS** The majority shareholders of a corporation changed the method of electing directors, from electing all three at once to electing one at a time, which effectively nullified the minority's cumulative voting strength.

■ **BLACK LETTER RULE** The statutory right to cumulative voting only guarantees the right to cumulate votes, not the right to representation on the board of directors.

■ PROCEDURAL BASIS

Appeal from court's determination of corporate election law.

■ FACTS

The Winous Co. ("Winous") (D) had three directors. Winous (D) changed its management structure to allow for the election of each director for a three-year term, and each director was to be elected in a different year. The state had a statute permitting cumulative voting for all corporations.

■ ISSUE

Does a statutory guarantee of the right to cumulative voting also act to guarantee the effectiveness of cumulative voting to ensure minority representation on the board of directors?

■ DECISION AND RATIONALE

(Bell, J.) No. The classification of the three directors into three classes containing one director each effectively divests the minority shareholders of a measure of control that they formerly held over the corporation. Since only one director may be elected each year under the new classification scheme, such classification has divested the minority shareholders of their cumulative voting power. The question is whether this result may legally be accomplished by the majority shareholders. Our statutes provide that the directors of a corporation may be divided into classes upon the basis of the expiration the terms of their office, so long as no director is appointed for a period of longer than three years. *Revised Code § 1701.64.* Our statutes also provide that any shareholder may cumulate his voting power—giving to any one candidate as many votes as the number of directors multiplied by the number of his shares—provided that he gives 24 hours notice of his intention to do so, and further provided that "such right to vote cumulatively shall not be restricted or qualified by the articles or the code of regulations." *Revised Code § 1701.58.* Although there has long been an interest in this state in cumulative voting and the power that such voting gives to minority interests so that they may have a say in the management of the corporation, there has been almost no discussion in our cases on the effect of classification of directors on cumulative voting. The Illinois Supreme Court has recently discussed a problem similar to the one at present. That court found that a statutory provision authorizing the classification of directors, and then staggering their election (so that only one director could be elected each year) directly conflicted with the Illinois constitution's right of shareholders to cumulate their votes. *Wolfson v. Avery.* In this case, however, the right to cumulative voting is statutory, not constitutional.

We do not think that the legislative intent in enacting the cumulative voting provisions was to limit the classification provisions. To give effect to both provisions of our statutes, the cumulative voting provisions must be construed as granting a right that may not be restricted or qualified. However, it does not insure minority representation on the board of directors. To hold otherwise would require a complete annihilation of the provision for classification because any classification would necessarily be a restriction or qualification on the effectiveness of cumulative voting. We also note that the General Assembly has, subsequent to the actions complained of in this case, revised our statutes to require that each class of directors must consist of not less than three directors each. The legislative committee that recommended the change made the following comment: "Under the present law the majority shareholders may fix the number of directors at three, each director to be in a separate class so that at each annual meeting only one director is to be elected. This devise would prevent the minority, even though holding 49 per cent of the shares, from electing a single director." Thus, the General Assembly obviated the possibility of a recurrence of the action taken by Winous (D). Reversed.

■ DISSENT

(Weygandt, J.) When the minimum number of three directors is provided for, and their terms of office are for three years, one to be elected each year, the right to cumulative voting is, in such case, *completely nullified.* This is a result that could hardly have been contemplated by the emphatic language of the General Assembly in its attempt to strengthen the right by adding to then-existing law the provision that a corporation cannot restrict cumulative voting by its articles or code of regulations.

Analysis:

In closely held corporations, cumulative voting is a way that minority shareholders may be able to protect their investment by having a say in the management of the corporation. The policy behind cumulative voting is that large minority shareholders are entitled to representation on the board to keep an eye on the majority directors. However, against cumulative voting it is argued that it leads to dissention on the board and to the election of some directors who look out for the interests of one shareholder, rather than the overall good of the corporation. There are a number of ways for majority shareholders to curtail or eliminate the power of cumulative voting. For example, in the present case, the majority of the shareholders simply staggered the voting of the directors—so that only one director at a time was to be elected. In essence, this brings back straight voting. Staggering the election of the directors was one strategy used by corporations in the 1980s to prevent hostile takeovers. Even if a hostile investor purchased a majority of the shares, he would not be able to gain control of the board for several years, which severely reduced the attractiveness of a corporation. A provision in the corporate charter to allow the removal of minority directors without cause will also circumvent cumulative voting power. A third method is to simply to reduce the number of directors. As the number of directors is reduced, the cumulative voting power of the minority shareholder is progressively weakened, until he is no longer able to elect any members of the board.

■ CASE VOCABULARY

CLASSIFICATION OF DIRECTORS: Corporations sometimes divide their directors into separate classes for various purposes, for example, for the purpose of staggering the election of directors.

CUMULATIVE VOTING: A mechanism in the shareholders' election of directors to insure that minority shareholders can have some say in the management of the corporation; the shareholder multiplies the number of shares that he owns by the number of directors to be elected—the shareholder can then cast that many votes for any one candidate.

STAGGERED VOTING: Where less than the full board of directors is elected at any given annual meeting, and each is elected to a term of more than one year. For example Class A directors are elected in year 1, Class B directors in year 2, Class C directors in year 3, Class A directors again in year 4, and so forth.

STRAIGHT VOTING: The shareholder votes all of his shares for one candidate. In other words, if the shareholder had 100 shares and was electing 5 directors, he can give 100 votes to each of 5 candidates, but no more than 100 to any particular candidate. Compare this to cumulative voting, where the shareholder could give as many as 500 votes to one candidate or one vote to each of 500 candidates.

Ringling Bros.–Barnum & Bailey Combined Shows v. Ringling

(Circus Corporation) v. *(Shareholder)*
29 Del.Ch. 610, 53 A.2d 441 (Supr. Ct. 1947)

SHAREHOLDER VOTE-POOLING AGREEMENTS ARE NOT AUTOMATICALLY UNLAWFUL

■ **INSTANT FACTS** A shareholder of a closely-held corporation operating a circus sued to enforce the terms of a vote-pooling agreement entered into with another shareholder who had refused to vote according to the terms of the agreement.

■ **BLACK LETTER RULE** In general, shareholders may enter into an agreement to vote their shares jointly.

■ **PROCEDURAL BASIS**

Appeal from an order of the Delaware Chancery Court enforcing the terms of a shareholder voting agreement.

■ **FACTS**

The outstanding shares of the stock of Ringling Bros.-Bamum & Bailey Combined Shows, Inc. ("Circus Co.") (D1) were divided among three shareholders as follows: Edith Conway Ringling ("Mrs. Ringling") (P) held 315 shares; Aubrey B. Ringling Haley ("Mrs. Haley") (D2) held 315 shares; and John Ringling North ("Mr. North") (D3) held 370 shares. Mrs. Ringling (P) and Mrs. Haley (D2) had entered into a contract under which each agreed, among other things, to consult and confer with the other and act jointly in exercising corporate voting rights. If the two women could not agree about a matter, they agreed to submit the issue to an arbitrator. For three years, the women voted their shares in accordance with their mutual agreement, each year jointly voting in a way that would let them name five of the seven directors of Circus Co. (D1). Just before the 1946 annual stockholders' meeting, Mrs. Ringling (P) and Mrs. Haley (D2) could not agree on who should be named the fifth director for that year. Mrs. Haley (D2) refused a sixty-day delay of the stockholders' meeting to try to work out an agreement on the issue. Mrs. Ringling (P) then took the matter to the arbitrator. The arbitrator directed that the stock of both women be voted to delay the meeting for sixty days. Mrs. Ringling (P) voted to delay the meeting. Mrs. Haley (D2) and Mr. North (D3) voted against a delay. Although the corporate chairman ruled that Mrs. Haley's stock could not be voted other than in accordance with the arbitrator's ruling, the meeting nevertheless proceeded to the election of directors. Mrs. Ringling voted for one set of directors and the arbitrator directed Mrs. Haley (D2) to vote in a way that would elect those directors. Instead, Mrs. Haley (D2) attempted to vote in a way that would benefit Mr. North's (D3) state of directors. Even though the corporate chairman ruled that Mrs. Ringling's (P) slate should be seated as the directors of the corporation, the other set of directors tried to participate in voting for corporate officers. Mrs. Ringling (P) then filed a complaint in equity with the Delaware Chancery Court to determine the validity of the election and which set of directors could sit on the Circus Co. (D1) board. The Chancery Court ruled that the "stock pooling agreement" between Mrs. Ringling (P) and Mrs. Haley (D2) gave their arbitrator an implied and irrevocable proxy to vote their shares as he determined. It ordered a new election where Mrs. Haley (D2) would be required to vote according to the direction of the arbitrator. Contending that the vote-pooling agreement was invalid, Mrs. Haley (D2) appealed.

■ ISSUE

Is a vote-pooling agreement among shareholders automatically unlawful?

■ DECISION AND RATIONALE

(Pearson, J.) No. Mrs. Haley (D2) contends that the voting agreement in this case is really a disguised voting trust which must meet certain Delaware statutory requirements in order to be enforced, such as the actual conveyance of legal title to the shares to the voting trustee. Mrs. Haley argues that the agreement she signed does not meet those statutory requirements and therefore cannot be enforced. We think that the voting trust statute does not apply and that, in general, a vote-pooling agreement among shareholders is not unlawful. Traditionally, shareholders have been permitted to exercise wide discretion in corporate voting. It is not legally objectionable if the shareholder's motives in casting a vote are for personal profit or based purely on whim, so long as the shareholder is not violating any duty owed to the other shareholders of the company. In fact, there is no requirement that a shareholder vote at all. A group of shareholders, then, can properly vote their shares so as to obtain the advantage of joint action. They can lawfully contract with each other to vote in the future in such a way as they or a majority of their group determine is appropriate. Moreover, the group can provide for deadlock-breaking measures like the arbitrator used in this case. Legal consideration for such an agreement is found in the mutual promises of the shareholders in the group. Here, the agreement to act according to the decision of the arbitrator is valid. The arbitrator's good faith has not been challenged and the record indicates he acted in good faith. Mrs. Haley (D2) breached the contract by not voting in accordance with the arbitrator's direction. We do not, however, agree with the Chancery Court that the election should be held again. The agreement here did not create an implied and irrevocable proxy permitting the arbitrator to cast any votes. Mr. North (D3) was not a party to the vote-pooling agreement and did not do anything wrong at the shareholders' meeting. Instead of a new election, we hold that Mrs. Haley's (D2) votes should not be counted. Reversed.

Analysis:

Shareholders in a closely held corporation often seek to protect their interests through various planning devices designed to create a stable corporate structure and assure control of corporate policies. These planning devices can include measures like voting trusts, irrevocable proxies, and the planning device at issue in this case, a vote-pooling agreement. As this case shows, under modern law, vote-pooling agreements among shareholders requiring them to vote their shares together as a unit are generally considered valid contracts. Courts around the country, however, have split over whether such vote-pooling agreements will be specifically enforced when breached. Here, the Delaware Supreme Court refused to grant specific performance of the vote-pooling agreement at issue in this case, overturning the relief entered by the lower court, which would have allowed the arbitrator to cast Mrs. Haley's (D2) vote. In response to the result in this case, the Delaware legislature and the legislatures of many other states have passed laws making vote-pooling agreements specifically enforceable.

■ CASE VOCABULARY

ARBITRATOR: A neutral person chosen by parties disputing an issue to hear and decide the dispute.

PROXY: A power to vote a shareholder's stock given by the shareholder to an agent. A proxy is generally revocable, but may be made irrevocable when "coupled with an interest" (i.e., when the proxy holder has an independent interest in the shares being voted; as where the shares have been pledged to the proxy).

VOTE-POOLING AGREEMENT: A contract in which two or more shareholders of a corporation agree to vote their stock together as a unit on one or more corporate issues.

VOTING TRUST: A legal device in which corporate shareholders transfer legal title and voting rights to a voting trustee who is authorized to vote on their behalf, but still retain the beneficial right to corporate distributions and stock appreciation.

Brown v. McLanahan

(Shareholder) v. *(Voting Trustee)*

148 F.2d 703 (4th Cir. 1945)

VOTING TRUSTEES MUST BE LOYAL TO THE SHAREHOLDERS WHOM THEY REPRESENT

■ **INSTANT FACTS** Trustees of a voting trust voted to amend the corporate charter in such a way that they diluted the voting power of the shareholders to the benefit of the debenture holders, who were mainly the trustees themselves.

■ **BLACK LETTER RULE** The trustees of a voting trust are under a duty to act in the best interest of the shareholders that they represent.

■ **PROCEDURAL BASIS**

Appeal from an order dismissing a suit challenging the actions of the trustees of a voting trust.

■ **FACTS**

Dorothy K. Brown (P) held a voting trust certificate for shares of preferred stock in the Baltimore Transit Company, which had been reorganized under the bankruptcy laws. The reorganization plan provided for the establishment of a voting trust on all of the stock of the reorganized company for a period of 10 years, which was to terminate on July 1, 1945. On termination of the trust, the voting rights were to revert back to the shareholders. Holders of preferred stock (P) were entitled to one vote per share, and holders of common stock were entitled to one vote per three shares. The reorganized company issued 233,427 shares of preferred stock and 169,112 shares of common stock. As long as dividends to the preferred shareholders (P) remained in arrears, they had the exclusive right to vote for the election of all but one director; that director was to be elected by the common shareholders. Under the voting trust, there were eight voting trustees (D). The eight trustees (D) were also a majority of the directors, elected as such by their own vote as trustees. On June 21, 1944 (approximately one year before the voting trust was to expire) and without giving notice to any of the shareholders, the voting trustees (D) voted to amend the company's charter. The amendment eliminated the arrearage clause, which had provided for the exclusive voting rights in the preferred stock. It also granted voting rights to debenture holders, creating approximately 221,000 new votes eligible to be cast in all corporate elections. These new votes substantially dilute the votes of the shareholders and deprive the shareholders of their right to control the management of the company. Finally, the common stockholders were deprived of their right to elect one director. It is also alleged that the voting trustees (D) hold substantial amounts of debentures, either in their own right or as officers of various banks. Brown (P), with the approval of 45,000 shares of preferred stock, brought this action, alleging that the voting trustees (D) had abused their position, voting for the amendment so that they were guaranteed to remain in control of the company even after the reorganization plan expired.

■ **ISSUE**

Can voting trustees amend the corporate charter so as to dilute the shareholders' votes?

■ **DECISION AND RATIONALE**

(Dobie, J.) No. We think it perfectly clear that the voting trust agreement was not intended to vest the trustees (D) with power either to impair the voting power of the preferred stock, which they held in trust, or to use the power for the benefit of the debenture holders and to the detriment of the holders of preferred stock (P). Even though the trustees (D) did have the power to amend the corporate charter, they could not do so in such a way as to take from the shareholders part of the very power that had been conferred upon the trustees to be held for the shareholders' benefit. It is elementary that a trustee may not exercise his powers in a way that is detrimental to the beneficiary of the trust. Furthermore, one who is trustee for different classes may not favor one class at the expense of another. The voting trustees (D) argue that the true beneficiaries in this case are the debenture holders because it is the existence of a voting trust, in many cases restricting the powers of the shareholder, that attracts lending by bondholders. Even assuming this contention to be true, that was clearly not the situation here, where the debenture holders invested in the company before the voting trust was imposed as the result of a reorganization in bankruptcy. The action taken by these trustees was beyond the limit of their authority. Reversed.

Analysis:

A voting trust occurs when shareholders transfer legal title of their shares to another person, who holds them in trust. The trustees of a voting trust, like with all other trusts, have a fiduciary duty to look after the best interest of the shareholders by adhering to the terms of the voting trust agreement. The trust agreement also creates contractual duties. As this case demonstrates, courts can use their equitable power to insure that the trustees are not doing anything to prejudice the interests of the beneficial shareholders. Under the voting trust, the beneficial owners of the shares retain all other incidents of stock ownership, including the right to receive dividends. Voting trusts are another way in which minority shareholders can buy or otherwise obtain enough votes to secure a position on the board of directors. In addition, such agreements can be used to induce creditors to invest in a corporation by assuring them that the corporation will be controlled by acceptable management. They can also be used where one person wants to remain active in the corporation, but another wants the beneficial ownership of the stock. As these examples illustrate, voting trusts are most useful where the owners also want some active involvement in the management of the corporation. Thus, they are of limited use in a publicly held corporation.

■ CASE VOCABULARY

DEBENTURE: A loan to the company that is not secured by any specific property, but is usually made on the good credit and earnings history of the company. Think of a debenture as an unsecured bond.

PREFERRED STOCK: Stock that is somehow different from common stock - usually in that preferred stock has superior rights to dividends or distribution upon liquidation.

VOTING TRUST CERTIFICATE: As evidence of their beneficial ownership of stock placed in a voting trust (which is important for receiving dividends and voting rights after the voting trust expires), the beneficial owners of the stock (who gave legal title to the stock to the trust) receive a certificate from the trust verifying the number of shares that came from each owner.

Lehrman v. Cohen

(Shareholder) v. *(Shareholder)*

43 Del.Ch. 222, 222 A.2d 800 (Supr. Ct. 1966)

A VOTING TRUST IS CREATED WHEN THE EXISTING RIGHT TO VOTE IS DIVESTED AND SEPARATED FROM THE OTHER ASPECTS OF STOCK OWNERSHIP

■ **INSTANT FACTS** To resolve a dispute over control of a corporation, shareholders agreed to create a new class of stock, the sole purpose of which was to elect a director to break ties of the board of directors.

■ **BLACK LETTER RULE** A class of stock that has no rights other than to elect a director is not a voting trust simply because it dilutes the voting power of the other voting shares.

■ **PROCEDURAL BASIS**

Appeal from summary judgment.

■ **FACTS**

N.M. Cohen (D) and Samuel Lehrman founded Food Giant, Inc. in 1935. The company was run by the two families, each of which possessed equal shares of voting stock, designated as Class AC (Cohen family) and Class AL (Lehrman family) common stock. Each class of stock was entitled to elect two directors of the company's four-member board of directors. On the death of Samuel Lehrman in 1949, a dispute arose in the Lehrman family regarding the distribution of his stock in the company. To resolve the dispute, an agreement was worked out where Samuel Lehrman's son (P) was permitted to obtain all of the outstanding Class AL stock and other arrangements were made so that the junior Lehrman (P) would have voting power equal to that of the Cohen family (D). An essential part of the arrangement, upon the insistence of the Cohen family (D), was the establishment of a fifth directorship for the sole purpose of breaking any deadlocks resulting from the equal division between AC stock and AL stock. To that end, the company issued one share of Class AD common stock, having a nominal par value ($10), with no rights except the right to elect one director to the board. The share was sold to Joseph B. Danzansky (D), who had served as counsel to the corporation since 1944. Danzansky (D) voted his share to elect himself as the company's fifth director and thereafter was active on the company's board of directors, but he did not have to break any ties until 1964. The company went public in 1959. The prospectus published in connection with the public issue stated that the sole purpose of the AD stock was to prevent a deadlock in case the AC and AL directors could not reach an agreement on an issue. On October 1, 1964, N.M. Cohen (D) resigned as president of the company, and the board of directors elected Danzansky (D) as president by a vote of 3 to 2. The AC and AD stock voted for Danzansky (D) as president, the AL stock voted against. This was the first time that Danzansky (D) had been called upon to break a tie. Danzansky (D) resigned as director and voted his share of AD stock to elect a new director. The new board ratified the election of Danzansky (D) as president. Lehrman (P) brought this action challenging the election of Danzansky (D) as president on two grounds: (1) that the share of AD stock constituted an illegal voting trust; and (2) that the election of Danzansky (D) as president violated the terms of the deadlock-breaking agreement under which the AD stock was issued.

■ ISSUE

Does the creation of a new class of voting stock, which will dilute the voting power of the other classes, constitute a voting trust or pooling arrangement?

■ DECISION AND RATIONALE

(Herrmann, J.) No. Lehrman's (P) primary contention is that the Class AD stock arrangement is in substance and effect a voting trust and is therefore illegal because it is not limited to a ten-year period as required by the Voting Trust Statute. In order for a voting trust to exist, the following three elements must be present: (1) the voting rights of the stock are separated from the other attributes of ownership; (2) the voting rights granted are intended to be irrevocable for a definite period of time; and (3) the principal purpose of the grant of voting rights is to acquire voting control of the corporation. *Abercrombie v. Davies.* Lehrman (P) argues that the Class AD stock, which carries no rights other than to elect a director who can break deadlocks, is in effect nothing more than a pooling by the AC and AL stockholders of a portion of their voting rights, which are given to a trustee (the AD stockholder) to vote for a fifth director. We cannot agree with this contention. The Class AD arrangement did not separate the voting rights of the AC or AL stock from the other attributes of ownership of those classes of stock. Each holder of Class AC and AL stock retains the right to vote his stock as he sees fit and retains the right to elect two directors for each class. It is true that the creation of the Class AD stock diluted the voting power of AC and AL stock. However, this is the usual consequence of creating additional voting stock. The key to this case is that the creation of the Class AD stock did not divest and separate the voting power from the Class AC and AL shares. Since the first *Abercrombie* test is not met, there was no voting trust established here - the crucial element of a divestiture of the voting rights of Class AC and AL stock is entirely absent. Lehrman's (P) argument also fails to take into account the main purpose of a voting trust: to avoid secret, uncontrolled combinations of stockholders formed to acquire voting control of the corporation to the possible detriment of non-participating shareholders. The AD stock arrangement, which all shareholders here acquiesced in, does not contravene that purpose. In short, there is nothing illegitimate about the creation of the Class AD shares. The arrangement was created by the unanimous action of the stockholders of the company by amendment to the certificate of incorporation. The stockholders thereby provided how the business of the corporation is to be managed, as is their privilege and right. We conclude that the AD stock arrangement is valid. Affirmed.

Analysis:

The premise of the plaintiff's argument in this case is that voting trusts, like other trusts, may be found without the adherence to any formalities. For a regular trust, involving money or property, there are no specific formalities required, just the intent to leave property in the hands of one person for the benefit of another. It is not surprising that the court, which dislikes voting trusts to begin with, would not go out of its way to find a voting trust here. In addition, the case would probably turn out the same way in a jurisdiction with a modern voting trust statute, because not all of the statutory requirements (especially the 10–year duration and writing requirements) were complied with.

■ CASE VOCABULARY

CLASSIFICATION OF STOCK: Where stock in a corporation is placed into different classes, each class of stock having slightly different characteristics. For example, Class A stock has no voting rights but greater rights to dividends, Class B stock has voting rights but fewer rights to dividends, and Class C stock has voting rights the same as Class A and the dividend rights the same as Class B.

Ling and Co. v. Trinity Sav. and Loan Ass'n

(Security Issuer) v. *(Secured Party)*

482 S.W.2d 841 (Tex. 1972)

REASONABLE AND CONSPICUOUS RESTRICTIONS ON THE TRANSFER OF STOCK ARE ENFORCE-
ABLE

■ **INSTANT FACTS** A bank wanted to sell some stock that had been pledged as security for a loan that was in default, but the corporation that issued the stock objected because there were restrictions on the transfer of its stock.

■ **BLACK LETTER RULE** In order to be valid, restrictions on the transfer of stock must be reasonable and must be conspicuously referenced on the front of the stock certificate.

■ **PROCEDURAL BASIS**

Appeal from grant of summary judgment invalidating restrictions on the sale of stock.

■ **FACTS**

Bruce W. Bowman (D) took out a loan with Trinity Savings and Loan Association (Trinity) (P), pledging stock in Ling & Company, Inc. (Ling) (D) as security for the loan. Bowman (D) did not pay back the loan, and Trinity (P) sued him for the balance of the loan and to foreclose on a certificate for 1500 shares of Class A Common Stock in Ling (D). Ling (D) was made party to this suit because it would not allow the sale of the its stock, claiming that there were restrictions on the transfer of the stock that had not been fulfilled. Ling's (D) articles of incorporation require shareholders to obtain written approval of the New York Stock Exchange if Ling (D) is a member corporation of the Exchange at the time of the sale. The articles also require that, before sale to an outsider, the shareholder must first give the corporation the opportunity to buy the stock, and, if the corporation does not wish to purchase it, then all of the other holders of the same class of stock must have the opportunity to purchase the stock. Trinity (P) argues that the restrictions on the transfer of any interest in the stock are invalid. The court of appeals struck down the restrictions because the stock certificate did not give conspicuous notice of them and because they were unreasonable.

■ **ISSUE**

May a corporation restrict the transferability of its stock?

■ **DECISION AND RATIONALE**

(Reavley, J.) Yes. Our statutes allow a corporation to impose restrictions on the transfer of its stock if such restrictions are expressly set forth in the articles of incorporation. The restrictions in the articles must be either copied in full, summarized, or incorporated by reference on the face of the stock certificate. Alternatively, the restrictions may be set out on the back of the stock certificate, but must then be referred to on the front of the stock certificate. In this case, the restrictions on the stock transfer were incorporated onto the back of the stock certificate by specific reference to the appropriate provisions in the articles of incorporation. Reference is made on the face of the certificate to the restrictions described on the back. Therefore, the content of the stock certificate complies with the requirements of the statute. However, as the court of appeals held, there are two additional requirements that must be met in order for the restrictions to be valid. The first, imposed by the Uniform Commercial Code, is that the restrictions must be conspicuously set out on the stock certificate. A conspicuous term is one that is written so that it would attract the attention of a reasonable person when he looks at the certificate. For example, it might be printed in all capitals, in larger type, in contrasting type, or in a different color. Here, the line of print on the face of the Ling (D) certificate that references the restrictions does not stand out and therefore cannot be considered conspicuous. Nonetheless, Trinity (P) is still not entitled to summary judgment on this record. A restriction, even though not conspicuous, is still valid as against someone with *actual knowledge* of it. This record does not establish that Trinity (P) lacked actual knowledge. The second statutory requirement is that the restrictions must not unreasonably restrain or prohibit transferability. Examining the restrictions themselves, we find nothing unreasonable about them. The requirement of approval from the New York Stock Exchange is a rule imposed by the Exchange on all companies that are members of the exchange. Additionally, requiring a holder of Class A Common Stock to give a first option of purchase to other holders of Class A Common Stock is neither unusual nor oppressive per se. Conceivably, the number of such stockholders might be so great as to create an unreasonable burden on the stockholder who wishes to sell. However, there is nothing in the record to indicate that such is the case here. The record does not justify summary judgment in this matter. Reversed.

Analysis:

Restrictions on the transfer of shares is yet another way that shareholders can control the management of the corporation. By limiting who can purchase and sell a corporation's shares, the owners of the small corporation can insure the continuing and harmonious relationship of corporate management. They also prevent a sudden shift in the balance of power in corporate management that would be caused if one shareholder suddenly bought large numbers of shares from other shareholders. There are two types of restraints on transferability. The first is known as a consent restraint—which prohibits the shareholder from transferring shares without the consent of a corporation. The second type is a buy-out restraints—which controls who can purchase the shares and for how much. Such restraints include the first refusal (the selling shareholder must get an offer for the shares from an outsider and then offer the shares at the same price to the corporation or other shareholders before selling to the outsider), the first option (the selling shareholder must offer the shares to the corporation or other shareholders for a specified price—usually the book value of the shares—before looking for an outside buyer), and buy-sell agreements (where the shareholder must sell and the corporation must buy the shares on the happening of some triggering event—commonly the triggering event is the death of the shareholder).

■ CASE VOCABULARY

BOOK VALUE: The book value of a corporation is the sum of all of the corporate assets. This number would be divided by the number of outstanding shares to determine how much each share is worth if a corporation must purchase a shareholder's stock under a transfer restriction agreement.

Gearing v. Kelly

(*Shareholder*) v. (*Director*)

11 N.Y.2d 201, 227 N.Y.S.2d 897, 182 N.E.2d 391 (Ct. App. 1962)

AN EVEN SPLIT IN CONTROL OF A CORPORATION HAS THE POTENTIAL FOR DEADLOCK

■ **INSTANT FACTS** Two directors voted to fill the vacancy left by the resignation of a third director in a board comprised of four directors, even though the two directors did not constitute a quorum under corporate bylaws and thus could not conduct business.

■ **BLACK LETTER RULE** A director that is intentionally absent from a board meeting for the purpose of preventing a quorum may not later complain that the board transacted business in the absence of a quorum.

■ **PROCEDURAL BASIS**

Appeal from refusal of the court to set aside a corporate election.

■ **FACTS**

The bylaws of Radium Chemical Company (Radium) provided for a board of four directors. The bylaws also provided that a majority of the four directors was necessary to constitute a quorum for the transaction of business. There are two factions vying for control of Radium (the Kellys (D) and the Gearings (P)), each of which owns 50% of Radium's stock and each of which was represented by two directors on the board. In 1961, Margaret E. Lee, who was a director for the Gearing faction (P), offered her resignation. The resignation was accepted at a meeting of the board of directors in which Lee and the two Kelly faction (D) directors were present. Mrs. Meacham, the other Gearing faction (P) director, was absent from the meeting. After accepting Lee's resignation, the two Kelly (D) directors elected Julian Hemphill, a son-in-law in the Kelly family (D), to replace her. This gave the Kelly family (D) three out of the four directorships—in essence, control of the corporation. The Gearing faction shareholders (P) now petition this court to set aside that election on the ground that it was not valid because a quorum was not present.

■ **ISSUE**

Was the action of the board of directors valid, even though a quorum was not present?

■ **DECISION AND RATIONALE**

(Per Curiam) Yes. In this case the court sits as a court of equity, and we may order a new election *as justice may require.* We conclude that the Gearings (P) have not established that justice requires a new election in this case. Mrs. Meacham's absence from the board meeting was intentional and deliberate for the sole purpose of preventing a quorum. It is equally clear that Meacham, who is the daughter of shareholder Gearing (P), was actively encouraged by Gearing (P) not to attend the meeting. Therefore, the irregularity in the election is one that was caused by the Gearings (P) themselves. Furthermore, ordering a new election would be futile in this case—Meacham would be required to attend, and the Kelly (D) directors would elect Hemphill by a vote of 2–1. Meacham's failure to attend the meeting bars the Gearings (P) from invoking the equitable powers of the court in this case. Affirmed.

■ DISSENT

(Froessel, J.) Two members of the board did not constitute a quorum in this case, and therefore the election of Hemphill by the two Kelly (D) directors, acting without a third director present, is wholly void and must be set aside. Our statutes grant us two alternatives in a case such as this one: (1) to confirm the election; or (2) to order a new election as justice may require. The clause "as justice may require" does not enlarge the court's power or authorize it to grant different relief from that specified in the statute. There is no basis for the majority's application of the doctrine of estoppel. The court should not assist either side in a contest for control of a corporation. Here, Meacham was willing to attend meetings for the purpose of transacting necessary business, but not for the purpose of stripping the Gearings (P) of every vestige of control. The statute mandates a new election, and that is what should be ordered. It is not the court's place to help one side or the other in this struggle for control of the corporation.

Analysis:

This case provides an example of a deadlock by shareholders, though it is not obvious from the face of the opinion. Deadlocks occur most commonly in corporations where two factions each own 50% of the corporation, or where there is an even number of directors and each of two factions may elect the same number. In this case, the shareholders' deadlock will block effective shareholder action and preserve the status quo, thus allowing the Kelly (D) faction to control the corporation. To see why, we must first understand the general rule that directors serve until their successors are qualified. If there is a deadlock in the election, those who are in office remain in office indefinitely until something happens to break the deadlock. This is an example of a case where preventative lawyering when the corporation was formed would have saved a big headache for both parties and the court. A proactive approach would have been for the parties to agree in advance what should be done in case of a deadlock. For example, the parties could have agreed that if one faction loses control of the board, that faction may demand that the other faction buy it out, or vice-versa (the losing faction would have the right to buy-out the winning faction—if the winning faction could be bought out by the losing faction, this would give each faction an incentive to keep the board split 50–50). Aside from agreeing on who buys out whom and when, the agreement would also have to set a price for the shares and decide whether a non-competition agreement from the bought-out party would be appropriate.

■ CASE VOCABULARY

DEADLOCK: Control arrangements that effectively prevent the board or shareholders from taking action.

ESTOPPEL: Out of considerations of fairness, a court has the equitable power to prevent a party which has affirmatively acted from later claiming that it has been prejudiced by that action.

QUORUM: The minimum number of people who are entitled to vote that must be present at a meeting in order for the meeting to legitimately conduct business.

In re Radom & Neidorff, Inc.

(Shareholder) v. *(Shareholder)*

307 N.Y. 1, 119 N.E.2d 563 (Ct. App. 1954)

AS LONG AS A CORPORATION CAN FUNCTION, THE COURT WILL NOT DISSOLVE IT

■ **INSTANT FACTS** Because the two shareholders in a corporation did not like each other, one shareholder petitioned the court for dissolution of the corporation.

■ **BLACK LETTER RULE** Dissolution is an extreme remedy that will only be granted if the corporation is no longer able to function because of shareholder disagreement.

■ PROCEDURAL BASIS

Appeal from the denial of a petition to dissolve a corporation.

■ FACTS

Henry Neidorff and David Radom (P), who were brothers-in-law, for thirty years ran with great success a company in the business of lithographing or printing musical compositions. Henry Neidorff and Radom (P) were the corporation's only shareholders, holding 80 shares each. Upon his death, Henry Neidorff left his shares to his wife, Anna Neidorff (D), who is Radom's (P) sister. Radom (P) and Neidorff (D), although brother and sister, do not get along with each other. From the papers of the two parties, we have determined that the following facts are undisputed. Radom (P) has continued for the past three years (since the death of Henry Neidorff) as president of the corporation. The corporation is solvent and its operations are successful, having shown a large profit in each of the last three years. The corporation appears to be financially stable and healthy. Neidorff (D), however, refuses to sign Radom's (P) salary checks. Therefore, Radom (P) has gone without salary for the past three years. Neidorff (D) claims that she has declined to sign Radom's (P) salary checks because of a stockholder's suit that she brought against Radom (P), alleging that he has enriched himself at the corporation's expense. Radom (P) has offered to buy-out Neidorff's (D) stock, but Neidorff (D) has refused to sell. Five months after the death of Henry Neidorff, Radom (P) petitioned the court to dissolve the corporation. Because of a will contest to determine the ownership on Henry Neidorff's stock (which has now been concluded), the petition was not answered for three years.

■ ISSUE

Will the acrimonious relationship between the corporation's major shareholders be enough for the court to order dissolution of the corporation?

■ DECISION AND RATIONALE

(Desmond, J.) No. Radom (P) brings this petition for dissolution under § 103 of the General Corporation Law, which provides as follows: *"Petition in Case of Deadlock.* Unless otherwise provided in the certificate of incorporation, if a corporation has an even number of directors who are equally divided respecting the management of its affairs, or if the votes of its stockholders are so divided that they cannot elect a board of directors, the holders of one-half of the stock entitled to vote at an election of directors may [petition the court for dissolution of the corporation.]" This statute provides for the situation under which dissolution may be petitioned for, but it does not mandate granting dissolution in every such case. From the facts presented to the court, we conclude that, despite the feuding and backbiting of Radom (P) and Neidorff (D), there is no stalemate or impasse as to the management of corporate affairs, and indeed the corporation is thriving. Dissolution is not necessary for either the corporation or the stockholders. Although Radom (P) is in a disagreeable position (one for which he himself may be partially to blame) he has no grievance that is cognizable by a court, except as to the non-payment of his salary, which is hardly a ground for dissolving a corporation. There is no absolute right to dissolution; the order is granted only when the competing interests are so discordant as to prevent efficient management and the object of its corporate existence cannot be maintained. Here, as the appellate court pointed out, the corporation's activities have not been paralyzed—quite the opposite, profits have increased and assets have trebled during the three years that this action was pending. There was nothing that frustrated the corporate business, and Radom's (P) failure to receive his salary is remediable by means other than dissolution. The prime inquiry in deciding dissolution is whether judicially imposed death will be beneficial to the stockholders or members and not injurious to the public. This is not such a case. Affirmed.

■ DISSENT

(Fuld, J.) Our statutes permit a petition for dissolution of a corporation by the holders of one half of the shares of stock entitled to vote for directors " if the votes of its stockholders are so divided that they cannot elect a board of directors." *§ 103*. That is precisely the case here. While the last 30 years have been profitable and harmonious for the corporation, since Henry Neidorff's death, all has been discord and conflict. The two shareholders have been unable to elect a board of directors. Dividends have been neither declared nor distributed, even though the corporation has earned profits. Debts of the corporation have gone unpaid, even though the corporation is solvent. Radom (P), who has been the sole manager of the business since Henry Neidorff's death, has not received a penny of his salary for the last three years because Neidorff (D) refuses to sign a check to his name. Radom's (P) integrity, which was never before questioned, has been directly attacked by Neidorff (D) by instituting a shareholder's derivative suit against him. Negotiations for a buy-out of one shareholder by the other were begun, but failed. We agree with Radom's (P) assertion that such a business cannot long continue to run. Neidorff (D) suggests that, in view of the fact that Radom (P) is managing the business profitably, he should continue to do so, defend against the derivative suit that she brought against him attacking his honor and integrity, and himself start an action for the compensation denied him for more than three years. However, it seems to me self-evident that more litigation would do nothing but exacerbate the underlying deadlock of which petitioner complains. Although the corporation is now solvent and running at a profit, if Radom (P) carries out his plan to resign as president, there may be irreparable loss to both the corporation's shareholders and the corporation's creditors. However, the sole issue in the present case is whether there is a deadlock as to the management of the corporation, not whether the business is operating at a profit or a loss. Nothing in the statute or legislative history suggests that a "Petition in Case of Deadlock" must wait until the corporation's profits have dried up and financial reverses set in.

Analysis:

Corporations are entities that can have perpetual life. Thus, an involuntary dissolution was traditionally viewed by the court as an extreme remedy—one to be exercised only where continuing the corporation would be worse for the shareholders and creditors than breaking it up. This reluctance may have been due to a presumption that ordering dissolution means destroying the business, which would put employees out of work and be bad for the economy generally. However, this presumption ignores the reality of what happens after dissolution is ordered. In most cases after dissolution was ordered, one shareholder simply bought out the other. Generally, dissolution may be granted for illegal or oppressive conduct, irreparable injury to the corporation that prevents it from conducting business, the failure to elect directors, and misapplication or waste of corporate assets. The remedy of dissolution is normally discretionary in the court.

CASE VOCABULARY

INVOLUNTARY DISSOLUTION: Where the court orders that a corporation be ended, its assets sold, its creditors paid off, and any remaining profits given to the stockholders. As opposed to a voluntary dissolution, where the shareholders agree that they no longer want to keep going, an involuntary dissolution closes down the corporation even if some or all of the shareholders would like to continue.

Davis v. Sheerin

(Minority Shareholder) v. *(Majority Shareholder)*

754 S.W.2d 375(Tex. Ct. App. 1988)

AN ALTERNATIVE REMEDY FOR OPPRESSION IS BUY-OUT

■ **INSTANT FACTS** The court ordered a buy-out of a minority shareholder's shares after a jury found that the majority shareholders acted oppressively toward a minority shareholder.

■ **BLACK LETTER RULE** The court is warranted in using its equitable power to order a buy-out if the majority shareholders in a closely held corporation engage in oppressive conduct toward a minority shareholder.

■ **PROCEDURAL BASIS**

Appeal from the trial court's order of a buy-out of the minority shareholder.

■ **FACTS**

In 1955, Sheerin (P) and Davis (D) incorporated a business that had previously been started by Davis (D). Davis (D) owned 55% and Sheerin (P) owned 45% of the stock. Both Sheerin (P) and Davis (D) were officers and directors of the corporation. Davis (D) was the president and ran the day-to-day operations of the business. In 1985, Davis (D) refused to allow Sheerin (P) to inspect the corporate books. Davis (D) claimed that Sheerin (P) had gifted his 45% interest in the corporation to Davis (D). After a six-week trial to a jury, the court declared that Sheerin (P) owned a 45% interest in the corporation and ordered Davis (D) to buy out Sheerin's (P) 45% for $550,000, the fair market value as determined by the jury. Davis appeals from that order, arguing that a buy-out remedy is not available to a minority shareholder under Texas law and that, even if it were available, a buy-out is not appropriate in this case.

■ **ISSUE**

Was the majority shareholder's conduct oppressive enough so that the court may force him to buy-out the minority shareholder?

■ **DECISION AND RATIONALE**

(Dunn, J.) Yes. The Texas Business Corporation Act does not expressly provide for the remedy of a buy-out for an aggrieved shareholder. However, our statutes do provide for liquidation in extreme circumstances. We cannot find any Texas case where the remedy of a buy-out has been ordered unless such a remedy was provided for by contract between the parties. However, other jurisdictions have recognized a buy-out as an appropriate remedy even absent express statutory or contractual authority. These jurisdictions, which all have statutes providing only for the dissolution of corporations due to oppressive behavior, allow a buy-out as a less harsh alternative remedy. We conclude that Texas courts have the equitable power to order a buy-out in an appropriate case. Oppressive conduct is the most common reason that a court may order a buy-out. A buy-out is especially appropriate where the oppressive acts of a majority are an attempt to squeeze out the minority in a closely held corporation. Minority shareholders do not have a ready market for the corporation's shares and are thus at the mercy of the majority. Oppressive conduct is an expansive term used to cover a multitude of terms dealing with improper conduct. Oppressive conduct should be determined according to the facts of each case whether the acts of the majority serve to frustrate the legitimate expectations of minority shareholders, or whether they are so severe as to warrant the requested relief. The jury here found that the majority shareholders conspired to deprive Sheerin (P) of his interest in the corporation and that Davis (D) willfully breached his fiduciary duty to Sheerin (P). Combined with the undisputed evidence that Sheerin (P) would be denied any future voice in the corporation, the jury's findings are sufficient to support the trial court's conclusion of oppressive conduct. We therefore find that buy-out was an appropriate remedy. Affirmed.

Analysis:

Some states have statutes that expressly allow for a buy-out in the case of oppression. Others, like the Texas statute in this case, only authorize dissolution. Corporations are creatures conceived and born of statute. They did not exist at common law. Therefore, it may be difficult to understand how a court can exercise its common-law powers to go beyond the statute and proclaim that disputes such this can be resolved by ordering a buy-out—especially if the state's statute specifically mentions dissolution as a remedy, but omits buy-out. Indeed, some courts have refused to judicially modify their corporation statutes to include a buy-out remedy where such a remedy is not written into the statute. As the court here indicates, many courts may see a court-ordered buy-out as a less harsh way of getting the shareholders "unstuck" from each other. As a practical matter, most judicially ordered dissolutions end in buy-outs anyway. In essence, it seems that the explicit buy-out remedy is merely a recognition of what goes on in practice.

■ CASE VOCABULARY

BUY-OUT: Where the majority shareholder has acted oppressively to the minority shareholder, the court may order that the majority shareholder buy all of the stock held by the minority shareholder.

INSPECTION RIGHT: Shareholders, as owners of the corporation, have the right to inspect the corporate books to make sure it is being managed properly.

SHAREHOLDER'S FIDUCIARY DUTY: Courts and statutes often treat the shareholders in closely held corporations in the same manner as partners in a partnership, and impose upon the shareholders the same fiduciary duties (e.g., loyalty, fair dealing, candor, accounting) towards each other that the law imposes upon partners in a partnership.

Abreu v. Unica Indus. Sales, Inc.

(Shareholder) v. *(Shareholder)*

224 Ill.App.3d 439, 166 Ill.Dec. 703, 586 N.E.2d 661 (1991)

THE COURT MAY APPOINT A PROVISIONAL DIRECTOR AS AN ALTERNATIVE TO DISSOLUTION

■ **INSTANT FACTS** After one director on a three-director board was removed for self-dealing and usurping a corporate opportunity, the court appointed a provisional director with the limited function of overseeing the board of directors and breaking any deadlocks of the directors.

■ **BLACK LETTER RULE** The court may appoint a provisional director if it is in the best interests of the corporation.

■ **PROCEDURAL BASIS**

Appeal from trial court's appointment of a provisional director (even one that favors one faction over another) to oversee the board and break deadlocks.

■ **FACTS**

Zenaida Abreu (P) owns 50% of the corporation Ebro Foods, Inc. La Preferida, Inc. (D) owns the other 50% of Ebro Foods. La Preferida (D), in turn, is owned by Ralph and William Steinbarth (D). At all relevant times prior to the filing of this suit, there were three directors on Ebro Foods: Abreu (P), Ralph Steinbarth (D), and Emil Smider (a director who was friendly to the Steinbarth faction). The trial court below found that Ralph Steinbarth (D) created a company and named it Ebro Industrial Sales, Inc. (later renamed Unica Industrial Sales, Inc. (D)) for the purpose of directly competing with Ebro Foods in securing a large contract with Kraft Foods. The court awarded damages to Ebro Foods for the lost Kraft contract. The court also found that Unica (D) and Steinbarth (D) repeatedly tried to obtain formulas for Ebro Foods' products in order that Unica (D) could produce and sell the products in competition with Ebro Foods. The court determined that Ebro Foods owned the formulas and enjoined all shareholders from disclosing the formulas or other data from which the formulas may be ascertained. The court also removed Ralph Steinbarth (D) as director of Ebro Foods for his oppressive and fraudulent self-dealing conduct that threatened the viability of Ebro Foods as a solvent corporation. The court then appointed a provisional director to replace Steinbarth (D). The court appointed Silvio Vega, son-in-law of Abreu (P). The court assigned Vega a limited role in the corporation, instructing him to vote only upon deadlocked matters. La Preferida (D) appeals the appointment of Vega as director and contend that Vega should now be removed because he has acted inappropriately.

■ **ISSUE**

Must the trial court appoint a completely neutral and independent third party to act as a provisional director of a corporation?

■ **DECISION AND RATIONALE**

(Greiman, J.) No. La Preferida (D) contends that the Illinois Business Corporation Act (the Act) implicitly requires a provisional director to be an impartial third party and that Vega could not possibly be impartial because he is Abreu's (P) son-in-law. We disagree. A provisional director is appointed as an alternative remedy to judicial dissolution in times of corporate strife to help guide the company through crisis toward the goal of stabilization and prosperity. When appointing a provisional director, the trial court considers only the best interests of the corporation. If the trial court finds that here is no traditionally independent third party with the required knowledge and skill, it may use its discretion to appoint a provisional director who may be aligned with a particular group of shareholders if this is in the best interest of the corporation. Given the situation at hand, we find that Vega's appointment was in the best interest of Ebro Foods. Vega has worked for Ebro Foods for over 17 years and is familiar with every aspect of the corporation; he holds a CPA degree and understands the financial complexities of business; and he has complete knowledge of the history and nature of the relationship between Ebro Foods, the Steinbarths (D), and La Preferida (D). La Preferida (D) argues that the appointment of Vega deprives it of a voice in the management of the corporation because the appointment gave Abreu (P) a majority on the board. This argument is unconvincing. Corporation law does not guarantee share-holders the outcome of a vote, only the right to vote. La Preferida (D) also argues that several of Vega's actions as director were inappropriate. We agree with La Preferida (D) on two of those points. First, Vega unilaterally hired a new auditor to prepare a certified audit for 1990 without the approval of the board of directors. It is improper for management of a corporation to directly hire the auditors to evaluate management's performance. Here, since Vega is General Manger of Operations at Ebro Foods as well as provisional director, the appointment was inappropriate—it should have been made by the full board of directors. Second, it was improper for Vega to vote on the question of whether the corporation should reimburse Abreu's (P) attorneys' fees. There was no deadlock. Director Smider simply asked for more time to study the proposal, which is a request that we find reasonable under the circumstances. Since Vega was instructed by the court to vote only on deadlocked issues, his vote on this matter was inappropriate. Affirmed in part, Reversed in part.

Analysis:

The provisional directorship is yet another alternative that some courts employ to keep from ordering dissolution of what they see as a thriving business concern. The provisional director is usually an outsider (though not necessarily, as in the current case) who is appointed when the board is in such a state of strife and deadlock that it cannot get business done. The provisional director does not actually run the corporation, but only has the power to suggest courses of action and break deadlocks—essentially to choose which of two competing alternatives proposed by the board will be the best for the corporation. Another option that some courts exercise is to appoint a custodian. Unlike a provisional director, who works with the board, a custodian is an outsider who is appointed to take control of the corporation and temporarily guide it. The custodian is there to get past whatever problems the directors were having, and then see if the corporation is strong enough to be managed again by the board. More drastic than a custodian is a receiver, whose job it is to take over the corporation, preserve its assets, and prepare it for dissolution.

■ CASE VOCABULARY

CORPORATE OPPORTUNITY: The director of a corporation, as part of the fiduciary duty of loyalty, may not compete directly with the corporation and steal business opportunities away from the corporation unless he notifies the corporation of the opportunity and the corporation turns it down.

PROVISIONAL DIRECTOR: A person appointed by the court to temporarily sit on the board of directors and break deadlocks if the court finds that the board is so divided that it can no longer act in the best interest of the corporation and anticipates that the board will soon be able to run without the provisional director.

SELF-DEALING: The director of a corporation, as part of the fiduciary of loyalty, may not make his own personal deals with the corporation unless they are approved by disinterested members on the board or by the shareholders, and even then it's risky.

In the Matter of Drive-In Dev. Corp.

(Creditor) v. *(Loan Guarantor)*

371 F.2d 215 (7th Cir. 1966)

OFFICERS ACTING WITHIN THE SCOPE OF THEIR AUTHORITY CAN BIND THE CORPORATION WITH THEIR ACTIONS

■ **INSTANT FACTS** The corporation's secretary certified to a bank that the board of directors had resolved to guarantee a loan and the bank lent money based on that certification, but the corporation now wishes to deny that it made any such resolution.

■ **BLACK LETTER RULE** Statements made by a corporate officer in the course of a transaction in which the corporation is engaged and that relate to a matter within the scope of the officer's authority are binding upon the corporation.

■ **PROCEDURAL BASIS**

Appeal from disallowance of a creditor's claim against a debtor in bankruptcy proceedings.

■ **FACTS**

Drive In Development Corporation (Drive In) (D) is a subsidiary of Tastee Freez Industries, Inc., which is strictly a holding corporation. The officers of Drive in (D) induced National Boulevard Bank (Bank) (P) to make a loan to Tastee Freez by executing documents whereby Drive in (D) guaranteed the loan. Bank (P) requested a copy of the resolution that authorized the guarantee. A document purporting to be a copy of the resolution, which was certified by Drive In's (D) corporate secretary, was delivered to Bank (P). It is uncertain whether the board of Drive In (D) in fact ever passed such a resolution. There is no record of such resolution in the corporate books. Bank (P) loaned substantial sums to Tastee Freez in reliance on the guarantee. Drive in (D) subsequently filed for bankruptcy and Bank (P) filed a claim against the bankruptcy estate based on the guarantee. Bank's (P) claim was disallowed. Bank (P) contends that the resolution binds Drive in (D) even if not formally noted upon by the board.

■ **ISSUE**

Does the secretary of a corporation have the authority to bind the corporation by the secretary's representations?

■ **DECISION AND RATIONALE**

(Swygert, J.) Yes. Drive in (D) cannot deny that its officers' had authority to sign the guarantee. Drive in (D) produced to Bank (P) a copy of a resolution by the board of directors purporting to grant such authority. The copy of the resolution was certified by the secretary of the corporation. Generally it is the duty of the secretary to keep the corporate records and to make proper entries of the actions and resolutions of the directors. Therefore, the secretary here had the authority to certify the resolution that was presented to Bank (P). Statements made by an officer or agent in the course of a transaction in which the corporation is engaged and which are within the scope of his authority are binding upon the corporation. Drive in (D) cannot now deny the representation made by its secretary in the document forwarded to Bank (P), unless Bank (P) had actual or constructive knowledge that the representation was untrue. There was no actual or constructive knowledge in this case. The realities of modern corporate business practices do not contemplate that those who deal with officers or agents acting for a corporation should be required to go behind the representations of those with authority to speak for the corporation in order to verify that authority. Reversed.

Analysis:

An officer is an agent of the corporation and, as such, can bind the corporation only if he has the authority to do so. Since the board of directors is ostensibly the only entity entitled to make decisions for the corporation, the traditional view was that officers only had the authority that was explicitly granted to them by the board. Furthermore, anyone who dealt with the corporate officer was charged with knowledge of this legal principal and, like the Bank (P) in this case, had the duty to confirm that the officers had the authority to do what they purported to do. Courts will sometimes reverse the traditional presumption—finding that, unless there is specific knowledge to the contrary, a third party may presume that officers have the authority to do all the things that are normal and customary for officers in that business community. Courts may also allow third parties to rely on the authority of officers to engage in transactions that arise in the usual and regular course of business, and then make very broad findings about what is "usual and regular" in the course of a particular business.

■ CASE VOCABULARY

CONSTRUCTIVE KNOWLEDGE: A party will be charged with knowledge of a fact if that party could have found out the fact had it made reasonable efforts to search. For example, mortgage lenders are charged with the knowledge of any previous encumbrance on property that is recorded in the public records.

HOLDING CORPORATION: A corporation that exists only to hold stock in other corporations and does no business of its own.

Lee v. Jenkins Bros.

(Employee) v. *(Employer)*
268 F.2d 357 (2nd Cir. 1959)

THE CORPORATION IS RESPONSIBLE FOR THE ACTS OF OFFICERS THAT ARE TAKEN IN THE USUAL AND ORDINARY COURSE OF BUSINESS

■ **INSTANT FACTS** An employee was induced to switch employers by the corporation's president's promise of a pension at retirement age, but then the company fired him prior to reaching retirement and did not pay him the pension.

■ **BLACK LETTER RULE** Promising a pension is one part of the president's ordinary and usual duty of hiring and firing employees, and therefore such a promise by the president is binding on the corporation.

■ **PROCEDURAL BASIS**

Appeal from judgment regarding the corporate president's scope of authority.

■ **FACTS**

Lee (P) was the business manager at Crane Company (Crane). Jenkins Brothers (Jenkins) (D) bought Crane's Bridgeport, Connecticut plant. In order to secure competent personnel, Yardley, president and substantial shareholder at Jenkins (D), met with Lee (P) to discuss employment by Lee (P) to Jenkins (D). In considering whether to switch employment, Lee (P) and Yardley met with a vice president and his wife. They discussed the matter of Lee's (P) pension. Lee (P) testified about the meeting as follows: Yardley promised him a pension, a maximum of $1500 per year, when he reached the age of 60. In determining the amount, Lee (P) would receive credit for the 13 years that he had worked at Crane. Lee (P) was promised that he would receive the pension regardless of what happened, even if he was not employed by Jenkins (D) at the time he reached 60. Yardley personally guaranteed payment of the pension if Jenkins (D) would not pay. The agreement was never reduced to writing, and Yardley had died by the time this action commenced. Over the next 25 years, Lee (P) became vice president, general manager in charge of manufacturing, and a director of Jenkins (D). Jenkins (D) fired Lee (P) when he turned 55 and refused to pay any pension when Lee (P) turned 60.

■ **ISSUE**

Does the president of a corporation have the authority to agree to a pension plan in hiring an employee?

■ **DECISION AND RATIONALE**

(Medina, J.) Yes. We assume *arguendo* that there was sufficient evidence to support the facts as Lee (P) testified. The question here is that of Yardley's authority. There was no evidence to support the contention that the corporation gave Yardley the express authority to promise such a pension. There is also no evidence of any course of conduct between the corporation and Yardley that would allow a reasonable onlooker to assume that Yardley had such power. Specifically, the question here is whether, as a matter of law, Yardley, as president, chairman of the board, substantial stockholder and trustee and son-in-law of the estate of the major stockholder, had no power in the presence of the company's most interested vice president to secure for a reasonable length of time badly needed key personnel by promising an experienced local executive a life pension to commence in 30 years at a maximum of $1500 per year. The general rule is that the president has the authority to bind the corporation by acts arising in the usual and regular course of business, but not for contracts of an extraordinary nature. This rule recognizes the realities of modem corporate life, where the pace of business is too swift to insist on the approval by the board of directors of every transaction. Many courts have also noted the injustice caused by the practice of permitting corporations to act commonly through their executives and then allowing them to disclaim an agreement as beyond the authority of the contracting officer when the contract no longer suited corporate convenience. Therefore, the question becomes what constitutes an "extraordinary" agreement. It is generally recognized that the president as part of the regular course of business has the authority to hire and fire employees and fix their compensation. However, lifetime employment contracts are considered "extraordinary" and therefore beyond the authority of a corporate officer. Here, Jenkins (D) tries to analogize the promise to pay a pension with a lifetime employment contract. However, we believe that the analogy is inapt. It is true that pension agreements, like lifetime employment contracts, run for long and indefinite periods of time. However that is where the analogy ends. In pension agreements, unlike lifetime employment contracts, future director or shareholder control is not impeded, liability to the corporation is not disproportionate to potential benefit, the agreement here was beneficial and necessary to the corporation, and pensions are common fringe benefits in employment contracts. Unlike lifetime employment contracts, courts have gone out of their way to find pension promises binding. Apparent authority is essentially a question of fact. Whether the officer in any given case had such authority depends on all of the circumstances surrounding the contract. Some contracts may be so important that the only reasonable assumption is that only the board of directors can handle them. It is in this light that the ordinary course of business rule should be viewed. We find that reasonable people could differ as to whether or not Yardley had apparent authority to make the contract, and thus the trial court erred in determining the question as a matter of law. Reversed.

Analysis:

In this case, since the president of the corporation regularly engages employees in employment contracts, the doctrine of apparent authority was applied to save Lee's (P) pension. In addition, the president could be said to have had the inherent authority to make the employment contract that included a pension—since the president's job included managing the personnel of the corporation, he had the authority to do what was necessary to retain workers, including granting a pension. Additionally, although the court did not discuss it, the doctrine of ratification should also apply here. Although there are not specific facts before us, since Lee (P) eventually became a director and vice-president of the corporation, and since the president and vice-president who hired Lee (P) were also directors, it is very possible that the board at some point was aware of the pension arrangement. When the board has knowledge of a transaction entered into by an officer in excess of his authority and does not act to undo the transaction, the board is said to have ratified the transaction. The corporation is bound by a transaction that has been so ratified.

■ CASE VOCABULARY

INHERENT AUTHORITY: The grant of authority to an agent gives that agent the authority to do all of the incidental things that are necessary in carrying out his agency. For example, the supply officer for a corporation has the inherent authority to buy pens and paper for the corporation, even if the board did not explicitly tell him to purchase these things—contracts for the purchase of these items will not be set aside because they were not approved by the board.

DeBaun v. First Western Bank and Trust Co.

(Shareholder) v. *(Majority Shareholder in Trust)*

46 Cal.App.3d 686, 120 Cal.Rptr. 354 (1975)

SHAREHOLDERS OWE A DUTY OF REASONABLE INVESTIGATION AND DUE CARE TO THE CORPORATION WHEN INTENDING TO SELL THE SHARES TO A POTENTIAL LOOTER

■ **INSTANT FACTS** Majority shareholder of a corporation breached its duty of due care by selling its shares to an entity which looted and destroyed the corporation.

■ **BLACK LETTER RULE** A majority shareholder who intends to sell the shares he holds, when possessed of facts establishing a reasonable likelihood that the purchaser intends to exercise the control to be acquired by him to loot the corporation of its assets, owes a duty of reasonable investigation and due care to the corporation.

■ **PROCEDURAL BASIS**

Appeal from the trial court's ruling in favor of the plaintiffs in a shareholder's derivative action.

■ **FACTS**

Alfred S. Johnson Incorporated (Corporation) originally had 100 outstanding shares of stock owned by Johnson. Subsequently, Johnson sold 20 of his shares to James DeBaun (P), Corporation's primary salesman, and 10 shares to Walter Stephens(P), its production manager. Managerial control of Corporation was assumed by DeBaun (P), Stephens (P), and Hawkins, Corporation's estimator, after Johnson became seriously ill. Johnson subsequently died, and his will named First Western Bank and Trust Company (D) as executor and trustee of a trust created by the will. The 70 shares of Corporation owned by Johnson at the time of his death passed to the testamentary trust. While First Western (D) took no hand in the management of Corporation, leaving it to the existing management team, Furman, First Western's (D) employee and administrator of the trust, attended virtually all director's meetings and voted the 70 shares at stockholders' meetings. Under the guidance of DeBaun (P) and Stephens (P), the net after tax profit of Corporation increased dramatically. Twenty-two months after Johnson's death, First Western's (D) trust department decided to sell the 70 shares of Corporation. It also decided that no one connected with Corporation should be made aware of its decision to sell until a sale was firm; thus DeBaun (P) and Stephens (P) were not told of First Western's (D) plans. Almost eighteen months later, a competitor of Corporation showed DeBaun (P) a letter indicating Corporation was for sale. Subsequently, both DeBaun (P) and Stephens (P) were contacted by two potential buyers who sought to purchase their shares. They each refused, and DeBaun (P) then submitted an offer for the 70 shares held by First Western (D); the offer was rejected as inadequate. First Western (D) subsequently received successive offers for the 70 shares from Mattison, acting in the name S.O.F. Fund, an inter vivos revocable trust of which he was both settlor and trustee. The offers were rejected and, anticipating a further offer from Mattison and his trust, Furman, acting for First Western (D), ordered a Dun & Bradstreet report on Mattison and the fund.

The report noted pending litigation, bankruptcies, and tax liens against corporate entities in which Mattison had been a principal, and suggested that S.O.F. Fund no longer existed. The vice-president of First Western (D) had personal knowledge that: (1) there was a judgment against Mattison in favor of First Western's (D) predecessor in interest for compensatory and punitive damages as the result of Mattison's fraudulent misrepresentations and a fraudulent financial statement to obtain a loan; and (2) the judgment remained unsatisfied and was an asset of First Western (D) acquired from its predecessor in an acquisition of 65 branch banks. When Mattison submitted a third offer to purchase the 70 shares, representatives of First Western (D) met with Mattison and McCarrol, who was counsel for Mattison. Mattison attempted to explain away the Dun & Bradstreet report as not his fault. McCarrol also noted that all information regarding the status of the litigation was publicly available. First Western (D) did not pursue its investigation into the public records of Los Angeles County, where a mass of derogatory information lay. First Western (D) subsequently entered into an exchange agreement with S.O.F. Fund, and gave Mattison a proxy to vote the 70 shares of Corporation at a special shareholders meeting. DeBaun (P) and Stephens (P) relied upon Furman's statements and were misled by his failure to disclose material terms of the agreement. As such, DeBaun (P) and Stephens (P) approved the execution of the security agreement, and Mattison was elected president of Corporation [the beginning of the end]. At the moment of First Western's (D) sale of the controlling shares to Mattison, Corporation was an eminently successful going business with a bright future. Beginning with the date that he acquired control, Mattison implemented a systematic scheme to loot Corporation of its assets.

The business began to suffer, and DeBaun (P) decided to leave Corporation's employ as a result. Mattison continued to loot the corporation, although at a reduced pace by reason of its depleted assets. First Western (D) became aware of Mattison's misconduct, and although the conduct was a breach of the exchange agreement, First Western took no action [tsk, tsk]. At this time Stephens (P) also left Corporation's employ. First Western (D) took no action until four months later, when it filed an action in the superior court seeking the appointment of a receiver. Faced with resistance from Mattison, First Western (D) pursued neither its receivership nor its ouster of the board until it shut down the operations of Corporation. By that time, Corporation was hopelessly insolvent, and First Western, pursuant to the security agreement, sold all of Corporation's then remaining assets. After the sale, Corporation had no assets and owed $218,426 to creditors. DeBaun (P) and Stephens (P) filed two related actions against First Western. One asserted their right to recover, as shareholders, for damage caused by First Western (D). The other was a stockholder's derivative action brought on behalf of Corporation. The two cases were consolidated, and First Western (D) demurred to both complaints. In the demurrer to the first action, it contended that DeBaun (P) and Stephens (P), as shareholders, lacked capacity to pursue their claim.

In the demurrer to the second complaint, First Western (D) took the opposite tack, contending that its liability did not run to Corporation. The demurrer to the first complaint was sustained without leave to amend, and the demurrer to the second complaint was overruled. The case proceeded as a derivative action, and the trial court held for DeBaun (P) and Stephens (P), finding that First Western (D) had breached duties it owed as a majority controlling shareholder to the corporation it controlled. It assessed monetary damages in the amount of $473,836, computed by adding to $220,000, the net asset value of the corporation as of the date of transfer of the shares to Mattison, an amount equal to anticipated after-tax earnings of the corporation for the ensuing 10-year period, taking into account an 8% growth factor. The court additionally awarded Corporation an amount equal to the sum it would be required to pay and the cost of defending valid claims existing against it when it became defunct. The trial court also awarded attorney's fees, but it denied DeBaun (P) and Stephens' (P) claim for punitive damages. This appeal from the resulting judgment followed.

■ ISSUE

Does a majority shareholder owe a duty to the corporation whose shares he holds in selling the shares?

■ DECISION AND RATIONALE

(Thompson, A.J.) Yes. A majority shareholder who intends to sell the shares he holds, when possessed of facts establishing a reasonable likelihood that the purchaser intends to exercise the control to be acquired by him to loot the corporation of its assets, owes a duty of reasonable investigation and due care to the corporation. Here, First Western (D) was the controlling majority shareholder of Corporation. As it was negotiating with Mattison, it became directly aware of facts that would have alerted a prudent person that Mattison was likely to loot the corporation. First Western (D) knew from the Dun & Bradstreet report that Mattison's financial record was notable by the failure of entities controlled by him. First Western (D) knew that the only source of funds available to Mattison to pay it for the shares he was purchasing lay in the assets of the corporation. The after-tax net income from the date of the sale would not be sufficient to permit the payment of dividends to him which would permit the making of payments. An officer of First Western (D) possessed personal knowledge that Mattison, on at least one occasion, had been guilty of a fraud perpetrated on First Western's (D) predecessor in interest and had not satisfied a judgment First Western (D) held against him for damages flowing from that conduct. Armed with the knowledge of those facts, First Western (D) owed a duty to Corporation and its minority shareholders to act reasonably with respect to its dealings in the controlling shares with Mattison. It breached that duty. Knowing of McCarrol's refusal to express an opinion on litigation against Mattison and his entities, and that the information could be obtained from the public records, First Western (D) closed its eyes to that obvious source. Had First Western (D) investigated, as any prudent man would have done, it would have discovered from the public records the additional detail of Mattison's long, long trail of financial failure that would have precluded its dealings with him except under circumstances where his obligation was secured beyond question and his ability to loot Corporation precluded. Thus the record establishes the duty of First Western (D) and its breach. First Western (D) finally contends that the trial court improperly multiplied the measure of damages by adding to net asset value on the date of First Western's (D) tortious conduct an estimate for future net profit and an obligation that First Western (D) discharge the valid existing obligations of Corporation. The record refutes the contention. The trial judge arrived at a value of the corporation as a going concern at the time of First Western's (D) breach by adding to the value of Corporation's tangible assets a goodwill factor computed on the basis of future net income reasonably to be anticipated from the Corporation's past record. This the trial court was authorized to do in determining the amount which will compensate for all the detriment proximately caused by First Western's (D) breach of duty. The judgment is affirmed. The matter is, however, remanded to the trial court with directions to hold a hearing to determine the additional amount payable to DeBaun (P) and Stephens (P) from the fund recovered by them for the benefit of Corporation for counsel fees due for services on this appeal.

Analysis:

Early case law held that a controlling shareholder owed no duty to minority shareholders or to the controlled corporation in the sale of his stock. Decisional law, however, has since recognized that corporate control by ownership of a majority of shares may be misused. Thus the applicable proposition now is that in any transaction where the control of the corporation is material, the controlling majority shareholder must exercise good faith and fairness from the viewpoint of the corporation and those interested therein. That duty of good faith and fairness encompasses an obligation of the controlling shareholder, in possession of facts that should create suspicion and put a prudent man on his guard that a potential buyer of his shares may loot the corporation of its assets to pay for the shares purchased, to conduct a reasonable adequate investigation of the buyer. Since the derivative action is equitable in nature, the court properly framed part of its judgment in this case in terms of an obligation dependent upon future contingencies rather than at a fixed dollar amount.

■ CASE VOCABULARY

DEMURRER: A formal objection attacking the legal sufficiency of the opponent's pleadings.

INTER VIVOS REVOCABLE TRUST: A trust created during the grantor's lifetime which can be terminated at the grantor's discretion.

RECEIVER: A person appointed by the court to receive and preserve the property or fund that is the subject of the litigation.

SHAREHOLDER'S DERIVATIVE ACTION: An action based upon a primary right of a corporation, but asserted on its behalf by the stockholder.

TESTAMENTARY TRUST: A trust created under a will and which comes into existence after the grantor's death.

Perlman v. Feldmann

(Minority Shareholder) v. *(Controlling Shareholder)*

219 F.2d 173 (2d Cir. 1955)

A DOMINANT SHAREHOLDER MAY NOT RECEIVE A PREMIUM FOR THE CONTROL OVER CORPO-
RATE ASSETS OR BUSINESS OPPORTUNITIES

■ **INSTANT FACTS** A steel company's minority stockholders brought a derivative action against the corporation's former controlling stockholder for selling his controlling bloc at a premium to a group of buyers who were solely interested in using the corporation's supply of steel during a tight market.

■ **BLACK LETTER RULE** Where a call on a corporation's product commands an unusually large premium, a fiduciary may not appropriate to himself the value of this premium.

■ **PROCEDURAL BASIS**

Appeal in a diversity action to the Second Circuit Court of Appeals, challenging the district court's holding for the defendants.

■ **FACTS**

C. Russell Feldmann (D) was a director and the controlling shareholder in the Newport Steel Corporation. In order to combat the short supply of steel caused by the Korean War, the Wilport Company, a syndicate of end-users of steel, offered to purchase Feldmann's (D) controlling bloc at $20 per share. At the time of the purchase the market price for Newport's shares was under $12. Following the purchase minority shareholders filed suit, claiming that the premium paid was not for control of the corporation. Rather, they argued that a portion of the consideration was for the sale of a corporate asset, specifically the power to control the allocation of the steel in a time of short supply. The district court found that the sale involved only control rights, thus Feldmann (D) was entitled to act in his own interests. The court also held that Perlman (P) failed to prove that the sales price was not a fair price for the stock per se.

■ **ISSUE**

May a stockholder sell his controlling share at a premium in any manner he wishes, absent fraud or foreseeable looting?

■ **DECISION AND RATIONALE**

(Clark, C.J.) No. Where a call on a corporation's product commands an unusually large premium, a fiduciary may not appropriate to himself the value of this premium. It is well established that as a dominant stockholder, Feldmann (D) owed a duty to the minority shareholders. Feldmann's (D) siphoned off for personal gain corporate advantages deriving from a favorable market situation. This diversion of corporate opportunities represented a breach of his fiduciary duty. The corporate opportunities that were misappropriated need not have been certain for Feldmann (D) to be held liable. Since fiduciaries always have the burden of proof in establishing the fairness of their dealings with trust property, the burden was on Feldmann (D) to completely negate the possibility that Newport would benefit from its supply of steel in a tight market. This, he failed to do. We do not mean to suggest that a majority stockholder cannot dispose of his controlling bloc of stock to outsiders without having to account to his corporation for profits or even never do this with impunity when the buyer is an interested customer for the corporation's product. But when the sale necessarily results in a sacrifice of this element of corporate good will and consequent unusual profit to the fiduciary who has caused the sacrifice, he should account for his gains. Therefore, to the extent the price paid to Feldmann (D) represented a bonus, he is accountable to the corporation. The case is remanded for a determination as to the exact premium paid.

■ DISSENT

(Swan, J.) I agree with the general principles set out in the majority opinion as to the duties of fiduciaries. However, the opinion does not specify which fiduciary duty that Feldmann (D) violated or whether it was a duty imposed upon him in his capacity of dominant shareholder or as director. I believe that the opinion will be confusing to both the legal profession and the business world and neither will be guided by it or understand their duties under it. The shareholder of a controlling block of stock may sell his stock for whatever premium that the market will bear. As a shareholder, Feldmann (D) was absolutely privileged to get the best possible price that he could find, so long as he did not know or have reason to believe that the purchaser intended to exercise his control to the detriment of the corporation. Here, the district court judge found that Feldmann (D) had no reason to think that Wilport would use the power of management to injure Newport and there is no proof that it was ever so used. I disagree with the majority to the extent that it suggests that the ability to sell stock for a premium because the corporation has a valuable asset in short supply is a breach of a shareholder's duty. When market conditions are such as to induce the users of a corporation's product to buy a controlling block of stock in order to be able to purchase part of the corporation's output at market prices, I cannot agree that the shareholder is under a duty not to sell. If the majority is suggesting that the purchase price of Feldmann's (D) shares included a premium for voting to elect Wilport's directors to the Newport board, then Feldmann (D) would have breached his fiduciary duty as director. A director cannot accept outside payment for performing his duties. However, here there is nothing that would suggest that Feldmann (D) accepted anything in return for voting to fill the vacancies on Newport's board with Wilport's directors. I also cannot accept the proposition that the individual plaintiffs are entitled to recover in their own right. The theory that has been advanced from the outset is that the price of the stock that Feldmann (D) sold included compensation for the sale of a corporate asset. If indeed a corporate asset was sold, then the corporation (which is not a party to this action) should be the entity to recover.

Analysis:

The court here discusses one exception to the rule that a controlling stockholder has the right to sell his controlling bloc under any terms for any price. The exception prevents a controlling shareholder from selling control in such a manner that deprives the corporation of a business opportunity. The exception implies a fine distinction between the ability to control corporate affairs and the ability to control corporate assets. It is the former which may be sold at a premium. The ability to control corporate assets, however, belongs to the corporation.

CHAPTER TEN

Control and Management in the Publicly Held Corporation

Studebaker Corp. v. Gittlin

Instant Facts: When a dissident shareholder solicits other shareholders' authorization to view the corporation's shareholder list, the corporation contends he must comply with proxy solicitation rules.

Black Letter Rule: Requests for authorization to view the shareholder list must comply with Exchange Act § 14(a) proxy rules.

In the Matter of Caterpillar, Inc.

Instant Facts: A multinational corporation issues a consolidated annual report, without mentioning its profits were boosted by its Brazilian subsidiary's unusual, unsustainable profits.

Black Letter Rule: Corporate annual reports' MD & A must discuss (i) current unusual material conditions, and (ii) possible future events, if they are either reasonably likely to occur, or would have material effects should they occur.

J.I. Case Co. v. Borak

Instant Facts: When a shareholder sues a corporation for deceptive proxy solicitation, the corporation claims the proxy rules allow no private remedial relief.

Black Letter Rule: The Exchange Act § 14(a) proxy solicitation rules permit federal courts to grant remedial relief in private suits, including damages and/or rescission of transactions secured through misleading proxies.

TSC Indus., Inc. v. Northway, Inc.

Instant Facts: A shareholder sues a corporation for failing to disclose conflicts of interest in soliciting merger proxies, contending "material" facts are those which reasonable shareholders might consider important.

Black Letter Rule: Under § 14(a) proxy rules, an omitted fact is "material" if there is a substantial likelihood that a reasonable shareholder would consider it important in deciding how to vote, which is usually a question of fact.

Virginia Bankshares, Inc. v. Sandberg

Instant Facts: After a corporation asks minority shareholders to ratify a merger with proxy statements opining the buyout price is "high" and "fair," a dissenting shareholder sues under § 14(a), contending the opinion is misleading and actionable.

Black Letter Rule: False or misleading opinions, reasons, beliefs, or conclusory proxy statements are actionable under § 14(a) if (i) they are false or misleading, (ii) they are material, (iii) the plaintiff can produce extrinsic evidence of falsity, and (iv) either the plaintiff-shareholder was of a class whose vote was legally required to enact the transaction, or the misstatement deprived the plaintiff-shareholder of a remedy under state law.

Rauchman v. Mobil Corp.

Instant Facts: After an oil company elects a Saudi Arabian to its board, a shareholder proposes to amend the bylaws to bar citizens of OPEC nations to the board, but the company excludes the proposal.

Black Letter Rule: Corporations may exclude from their proxy statements any shareholder proposals which would prohibit the election/reelection of any current candidate/director.

Studebaker Corp. v. Gittlin

(Corporation and Management) v. *(Shareholder)*

360 F.2d 692 (2nd Cir. 1966)

PROXY SOLICITATION RULES APPLY TO PRE-SOLICITATION COMMUNICATIONS LEADING TO SOLICITATION

■ **INSTANT FACTS** When a dissident shareholder solicits other shareholders' authorization to view the corporation's shareholder list, the corporation contends he must comply with proxy solicitation rules.

■ **BLACK LETTER RULE** Requests for authorization to view the share-holder list must comply with *Exchange Act § 14(a)* proxy rules.

■ **PROCEDURAL BASIS**

In shareholder suit, appeal from order enjoining shareholder from using other shareholders' authorizations to view corporation's shareholder list until he complies with *Exchange Act* proxy rules.

■ **FACTS**

Gittlin (P) owned 5,000 shares of Studebaker Corp. (D). Gittlin (P) led dissatisfied shareholders demanding Studebaker's management (D) replace certain directors, but management (D) refused. Gittlin (P) obtained written authorization from other shareholders, representing 5%, to inspect the shareholder list, under New York corporate law [which says that shareholder(s) owning over 5% collectively may inspect the list on demand]. Studebaker (D) filed a separate suit against Gittlin (P), contending he violated *Exchange Act § 14(a)* by not filing proxy materials with the SEC before collecting the authorizations. *§ 14(a)* forbids any person "to solicit any proxy or consent or authorization" relating to securities "in contravention of [SEC] rules and regulations [which] the [SEC] may prescribe as necessary or appropriate in the public interest or for the protection of investors." Gittlin (P) defended, claiming *§ 14(a)* does not include authorizations for the limited purpose of qualifying under state statutes permitting inspection of the shareholder list. After trial, the district court enjoined Gittlin (P) from using the authorizations until he complied with *14(a)*'s proxy rules, holding *§ 14(a)* applies to solicitations to authorize viewing shareholder lists. Gittlin (P) appeals.

■ **ISSUE**

Must requests for authorization to view the shareholder list comply with proxy rules?

■ **DECISION AND RATIONALE**

(Friendly, J.) Yes. Requests for authorization to view the shareholder list must comply with *Exchange Act § 14(a)* proxy rules. *§ 14(a)* is worded broadly. We asked the SEC for its construction of *§ 14(a)*; its general counsel responded *§ 14(a)* should be construed literally, to include authorizations to inspect shareholder lists, even where this is not part of a plan to solicit proxies. However, we need not accept this broad interpretation. We previously held that letters which, though they did not request proxies, were part of "a continuous plan" intended to end in successful solicitation, were subject to the Proxy Rules. This rule is necessary, since holding otherwise would allow solicitors to spread misinformation in pre-solicitation literature, thus depriving the SEC of the power to protect shareholders. Moreover, the fact the shareholder list is a valuable instrument for gaining control is a good reason for ensuring shareholders have full information before aiding its procurement. Here, Gittlin's (P) request for authorization to view the list had this avowed purpose of eventually soliciting proxies, and requires § *14(a)* registration. Gittlin (P) claims Studebaker (D) has not made adequate showing of "irreparable injury," as required for injunction, but this objection is invalid. Plaintiffs seeking injunction need not show that rigor mortis will set in forthwith, but only that they will suffer harm which cannot be repaired, especially where the only consequence of an injunction is that the defendant must affect compliance after the fact. To be sure, time is of the essence in proxy contests, or at least the participants think so. But the district court could have decided the public interest in enforcing the Proxy Rules outweighed any inconvenience to Gittlin (P) in restarting. Such decision rested in the judge's sound discretion; we find no abuse. Injunction affirmed.

Analysis:

Here, Gittlin was faced with a corporate law that mandated that only shareholders (individually or collectively) owning over 5% of the corporation's stock may demand to see the shareholder list. Of course, this demand is usually a precursor to contacting major shareholders to solicit their votes or support, though it may have other purposes. Gittlin himself owned under 5%, so his solicitation was to other small shareholders to authorize him to pool their ownership with his to meet the 5% threshold. This case illustrates that the proxy solicitation rules are broad and interpreted to apply even to pre-proxy communications that do not explicitly ask for proxy voting power, as long as the eventual aim of the communication is to solicit proxy votes. The SEC had taken the position that the rules should apply to *all* requests for authorizations to inspect shareholder lists, even where no proxy solicitation is intended. However, the court here limits the rules' application to pre-solicitation requests.

In the Matter of Caterpillar, Inc.

(SEC) v. *(Corporation)*

Administrative Proceeding File No. 3–7692, SEC Rel. No. 34–30532 (Admin. Proceeding 1992)

FINANCIAL STATEMENTS MUST DISCUSS UNUSUAL OPERATIONS AT SUBSIDIARIES AND EXPECT-ED FUTURE RESULTS

■ **INSTANT FACTS** A multinational corporation issues a consolidated annual report, without mentioning its profits were boosted by its Brazilian subsidiary's unusual, unsustainable profits.

■ **BLACK LETTER RULE** Corporate annual reports' MD & A must discuss (i) current unusual material conditions, and (ii) possible future events, if they are either reasonably likely to occur, or would have material effects should they occur.

■ **PROCEDURAL BASIS**

In administrative proceeding, offer of settlement.

■ **FACTS**

Caterpillar, Inc. ("Caterpillar") (D) owned a Brazilian subsidiary, Caterpillar Brazil, S.A. ("CBSA"). In 1989, CBSA was exceptionally profitable, though much of that profit was due to Brazil's hyperinflation and more favorable exchange rates. Caterpillar (D) is highly integrated, and generally prepared internal financial documents on a consolidated basis. Caterpillar's (D) accountants realized CBSA's 1989 results were unique and impacted Caterpillar's (D) overall condition. However, its accountants also recognized CBSA's future performance was unpredictable, due to Brazil's pending elections and anticipated economic reforms. Caterpillar's (D) management advised the board it should explain its Brazilian operations in detail to shareholders. However, Caterpillar (D) presented CBSA's 1989 financials (Forms 10-K and 10-Q) consolidated with Caterpillar's (D) other divisions. A necessary component of an annual report is the "Management's Discussion and Analysis of Financial Condition and Results of Operations" ("MD & A"). The MD & A did not reveal management's concern or the extent to which CBSA's profits had affected/would affect Caterpillar's (D) bottom line in 1990. Later in 1990, Brazil's elections concluded, and the president-elect instituted monetary/economic reforms to combat hyperinflation. Caterpillar's (D) management concluded these reforms would cause CBSA losses, and lower Caterpillar's (D) overall profits. Caterpillar (D) issued a press release indicating its 1990 results would be lower than projected previously. The SEC launched an investigation, contending Caterpillar (D) violated *Exchange Act § 13a, Rule 13a-1,* and *Rule 13a-13* (MD & A requirements) by (i) failing, in its Form 10-K Annual Report, to provide adequate discussion of CBSA's 1989 operations' impact on Caterpillar's (D) overall financial statements, and (ii) failing, in its Form 10Q Quarterly Report, to adequately disclose known uncertainties on CBSA's future performance and its effects on Caterpillar (D). Caterpillar (D) settled with the SEC. This proceeding is a record of the SEC's findings.

■ **ISSUE**

Must annual reports' MD & A include discussion of unusual and unsustainable profits?

■ **DECISION AND RATIONALE**

(SEC) Yes. Corporate annual reports' MD & A must discuss (i) current unusual material conditions, and (ii) possible future events, if they are either reasonably likely to occur, or would have material effects should they occur. 10-K Reports must discuss the corporation's liquidity, capital, and operational results, and "provide such other information that the [corporation] believes to be necessary to an understanding of its financial condition …". *Form 10-K, Item 303(a).* Specifically, *303(a)* requires "where in the [corporation's] judgement a discussion of … information … of other subdivisions of [its] business would be appropriate to an understanding of such business, the discussion shall focus on each relevant, reportable … subdivision of the business and on the [corporation] as a whole." In discussing operational results, the corporation is to "describe any unusual or infrequent events or transactions … that materially affected the … reported income from continuing operations and in each case, indicate the extent to which income was so affected." *Item 303(a)(3)(i).* Also, the corporation is to discuss "any known trends or uncertainties that have had or [it] reasonably expects will have a material … impact on …. revenues … from continuing operations." *Item 303(a)(3)(ii).* "The discussion and analysis shall focus specifically on material events and uncertainties known to management that would cause reported financial information not to be necessarily indicative of future operating results." *Item 303(a), Instruction 3.* The instructions tell corporations to discuss both new matters and existing conditions expected to have future effects, and to identify income/loss which does not arise from, or is not necessarily representative of, the corporation's operations. *Item 303(a), Instruction 4.* In 1989, the SEC issued further interpretive releases on the MD & A requirements. These releases note the rationale for requiring MD & A disclosure. Without the MD & A, financial statements "may be insufficient [for] an investor to judge the quality of earnings and the likelihood that past performance is indicative of future performance. MD & A is intended to give the investors an opportunity to look at the company through the eyes of management by providing both a short and long-term analysis …." We note "the MD & A requirements are intentionally flexible and general …." The Release mandates disclosure when (i) the known event is reasonably likely to come to fruition, or (ii) the event's likelihood is indeterminable, but it would have a material financial effect should it occur. *MD & A Release Par. III.B.* Here,[the SEC] finds Caterpillar's (D) failure to include CBSA's information in MD & A violated the MD & A requirements by denying investors the opportunity to see the company "through the eyes of management." Specifically, Caterpillar (D) violated *Exchange Act § 13a, Rule 13a-1,* and *Rule 13a-13* by (i) failing, in its Form 10-K Annual Report, to provide adequate discussion of CBSA's 1989 operations' impact on Caterpillar's (D) financial statements, and (ii) failing, in its Form 10Q Quarterly Report, to adequately disclose known uncertainties reasonably likely to have material effects on Caterpillar's (D) future performance, due to CBSA's questionable ability to repeat its performance. This information was material, given the magnitude of CBSA's contribution to Caterpillar's (D) overall earnings. Further, the MD & A should have discussed certain factors which contributed to CBSA's earnings, including currency gains. Management must have known that CBSA's current and future earnings would affect materially Caterpillar's (D) finances, since it discussed these concerns with the directors weeks before filing. [Offer in settlement accepted.]

Analysis:

This administrative proceeding is critical because it was republished by the SEC as its official and authoritative position interpreting the MD & A requirement and Rule 175, it is believed the SEC, generally displeased with MD & A disclosure, singled out Caterpillar (D) in this test case. Of course, the exact items that must be disclosed in MD &A are necessarily broad. At a minimum, this release shows such disclosure must include (i) anomalous/unsustainable earnings; (ii) unusual operations results at individual subsidiaries; (iii) forward-looking predictions of future financial contingencies, if reasonably likely to occur, or if capable of having material effects; and (possibly) (iv) any major concerns management discloses to the directors. Note that the SEC adopts communications between the management and directors as the measure of what management knew, and thus presumably what should be reflected in filings. Note also this measure may give management bad incentives to overgeneralize or avoid disclosure to the board.

■ CASE VOCABULARY

MD & A: "Management's Discussion and Analysis of Financial Condition and Results of Operations," a necessary component of the annual report, required by *Regulation S-K Item 303.* Its broad mandate requires management to disclose enough to give investors an accurate portrait of current and future profitability ("an opportunity to look at the company through the eyes of management").

J.I. Case Co. v. Borak

(Corporation) v. *(Shareholder)*

377 U.S. 426, 84 S.Ct. 1555, 12 L.Ed.2d 423 (1964)

PROXY RULE VIOLATIONS PERMIT PRIVATE SUITS SEEKING DAMAGES AND RESCISSION

■ **INSTANT FACTS** When a shareholder sues a corporation for deceptive proxy solicitation, the corporation claims the proxy rules allow no private remedial relief.

■ **BLACK LETTER RULE** The *Exchange Act § 14(a)* proxy solicitation rules permit federal courts to grant remedial relief in private suits, including damages and/or rescission of transactions secured through misleading proxies.

■ **PROCEDURAL BASIS**

In shareholder derivative action seeking damages and/or rescission of merger, appeal from appellate judgement for plaintiff, on writ of certiorari.

■ **FACTS**

Shareholder Borak (P) owned stock in J.I. Case (D). Case (D) proposed to merge with American Tractor Corp. (ATC). Borak (P) believed Case's (D) proxy materials regarding the merger were false/misleading [the case omits why], and that the transaction was self-dealing by the directors. Borak (P) sued Case (D) to enjoin the merger, but the injunction was denied, and the merger was consummated. Afterwards, Borak (P) sued Case (D) for, among others, issuing false and misleading proxy materials, in violation of *Exchange Act § 14(a)*, in a derivative class action seeking rescission or damages. At trial, the court held (i) federal courts were powerless to redress *§ 14(a)* violations other than with declaratory relief, (ii) a Wisconsin statute, requiring small shareholders to post security before starting derivative action's (to defray legal expenses) applied and required Borak (P) to post $75K bond. Borak (P) appealed. On appeal, the court reversed, holding the district court could grant relief, and the security statute was inapplicable. Case (D) appeals. The Supreme Court granted certiorari, to determine whether *Exchange Act § 27* authorizes a federal cause of action for rescission or damages to a shareholder from a consummated merger authorized pursuant to proxy materials which were false and misleading, in violation of *§ 14(a)*.

■ **ISSUE**

Does *Exchange Act § 27* authorize a federal cause of action for rescission/damages to shareholders from a consummated merger authorized pursuant to proxy materials which were false or misleading, in violation of *§ 14(a)*?

■ **DECISION AND RATIONALE**

(Clark, J.) Yes. The *Exchange Act § 14(a)* proxy solicitation rules permit federal courts to grant remedial relief in private suits, including damages and/or rescission of transactions secured through misleading proxies. It appears clear private parties may bring suit under *§ 27* for *§ 14(a)* violations. Indeed, *§ 27* specifically grants district courts jurisdiction over "all suits in equity and . . . law brought to enforce any liability or duty created" under the *Exchange Act.* Case (D) contends Congress made no specific reference to a private right of action, and any such right would not extend to derivative suits and should be limited to prospective relief only [i.e., the court could have enjoined the transaction before it happened, but not rescinded it afterwards]. While Borak (P) contends his claim is not derivative, we need not decide the issue, since we believe a right of action exists for both derivative and direct causes. *§ 14(a)*'s purpose is to prevent management or others from obtaining authorization for corporate action by deceptive or inadequate disclosure in proxy solicitation. Legislative history shows Congress's purpose was to permit meaningful corporate suffrage, prevent recurring abuses, and require proxies to disclose the real nature of the questions for which votes are sought. *§ 14(a)*'s language reveals a broad remedial purpose, making it "unlawful for any person . . . to solicit or permit the use of his name to solicit any proxy or consent or authorization in respect of any [public] security . . . in contravention of such rules and regulations as the [SEC] may prescribe as necessary or appropriate in the public interest *or for the protection of investors*." While this language makes no specific reference to private suits, its chief purpose is "the protection of investors," which implies the availability of judicial relief where necessary to achieve that result. The injury which shareholders suffer from corporate action through deceptive proxies ordinarily flows from the damage to the corporation, rather than damage inflicted directly on the shareholder. The damage suffered results not from the deceit on any 1 shareholder, but from deceit upon the shareholders as a whole. Thus, to deny *§ 14(a)* derivative actions is to deny private relief. Private enforcement of proxy rules provides a most effective weapon, and a necessary supplement to SEC action. The SEC advises it reviews over 2,000 proxies annually, and cannot investigate all of them. Thus, we believe under the circumstances here that courts have a duty to provide remedies necessary to effectuate Congress's purpose. It is well-settled from prior caselaw "where legal rights have been invaded, and a federal statute provides for a general right to sue for such invasion, federal courts may use any available remedy to make good the wrong . . . ." *§ 27* grants district courts jurisdiction "of all suits in equity and . . . law brought to enforce any liability or duty created by [*§ 14*]." Prior caselaw, in analyzing almost identical language in the *Securities Act*, found it sufficient to imply the remedy to rescind fraudulent sales and obtain restitution. Case (D) contends such remedies are limited to prospective relief, because the availability of state law on this matter makes this basically a state law question, but we disagree. This remains a federal law question, despite the presence of some state law issues. If the state law happens to attach no liability for misleading proxy statements, *§ 14(a)*'s whole purpose would be violated if federal law were held subordinate to state law. Further, the hurdles plaintiff shareholders would face from such state laws—e.g., separate suits, security for expenses, etc.—might well prove insuperable for effective relief. Thus, we hold that federal courts have the power to grant all necessary remedial relief for § 14(a) actions, but make no finding on the appropriate relief here. Judgement for plaintiff affirmed and remanded.

Analysis:

Here, the Court held Rule 14a-9 implied a private right of action, which empowers courts to grant effective private remedies. As noted, this holding is necessary to permit effective private enforcement of the proxy rules, since the SEC alone cannot detect all dishonest proxy statements in time to enjoin the proposed corporate action. The same question—whether a private right of action is implied—has arisen under other securities laws. Later Supreme Court cases no longer follow *Borak*'s broad grant of power, which would effectively permit a private cause of action for any federal law, so while *Borak* remains good law supporting private claims and remedies for *§ 14a-9* proxy violations, its reasoning cannot be applied to all federal securities laws.

■ CASE VOCABULARY

DERIVATIVE ACTION: Suit brought by shareholder *on behalf of the corporation* (rather than himself).

TSC Indus., Inc. v. Northway, Inc.

(Corporation) v. *(Shareholder)*

426 U.S. 438, 96 S.Ct. 2126, 48 L.Ed.2d 757 (1976)

OMITTED FACTS ARE "MATERIAL" IF A REASONABLE SHAREHOLDER WOULD CONSIDER THEM IMPORTANT

■ **INSTANT FACTS** A shareholder sues a corporation for failing to disclose conflicts of interest in soliciting merger proxies, contending "material" facts are those which reasonable shareholders *might* consider important.

■ **BLACK LETTER RULE** Under § 14(a) proxy rules, an omitted fact is "material" if there is a substantial likelihood that a reasonable shareholder would consider it important in deciding how to vote, which is usually a question of fact.

■ PROCEDURAL BASIS

In shareholder action seeking damages and/or rescission, appeal from appellate grant of summary judgement for plaintiff.

■ FACTS

National Industries (D) acquired TSC Industries (D) gradually. First, National (D) purchased 34% from TSC's (D) founder, Schmidt. Consequently, National (D) was able to install 5 of its directors and a chairman into TSC (D). Later, TSC's (D) board agreed to sell TSC's (D) total assets to National (D), though the 5 dependent directors abstained. National (D) and TSC (D) issued a joint proxy statement, recommending approval of the sale. Shareholders approved. Shareholder Northway (P) sued National (D) and TSC (D), contending their joint proxy statement was incomplete and materially misleading, in violation of § 14(a), because it failed to disclose the degree of National's (D) control over TSC (D), and portrayed the sale as unrealistically favorable for shareholders. At trial, Northway (P) moved for summary judgement. The court denied Northway's (P) motion, holding it could not decide, as a matter of law, that the omissions were materially misleading. Northway (P) appealed. The appellate court granted Northway (P) summary judgement, holding that certain omissions of fact were material as a matter of law if there was incomplete disclosure of "all facts which a reasonable shareholder might consider important." National (D) and TSC (D) appeal. The Supreme Court granted certiorari.

■ ISSUE

Under § 14(a) proxy rules, is an omitted fact "material" if a reasonable shareholder might consider it important?

■ DECISION AND RATIONALE

(Marshall, J.) No. Under § 14(a) proxy rules, an omitted fact is "material" if there is a substantial likelihood that a reasonable shareholder *would* consider it important in deciding how to vote, which is usually a question of fact. *Exchange Act § 14(a)* was intended to promote shareholder voting by ensuring proxies are solicited with "explanation to the stockholder of the real nature of the questions for which authority to cast his vote is sought." *Borak* held § 14(a)'s broad remedial purpose implied a private right of action for proxy violations. *Mills v. Electric Auto-Lite Co.* (S.Ct. 1970) [solicitation failed to mention directors who approved merger had conflict of interest] clarified the elements of a private cause of action for *§ 14(a)* violations; a claim exists if (i) the misstatement or omission was material, and (ii) "the proxy solicitation itself . . . was an essential link in the accomplishment of the transaction." There is no need to demonstrate the alleged defect actually had a decisive effect on voting. It is universally agreed the question of materiality is objective, involving the significance of omitted or misrepresented facts to a reasonable investor. However, there is a circuit split: some courts hold material facts include "all facts which a reasonable investor *might* consider important;" other courts reject this formulation as too low a threshold. In formulating a standard, we are guided by *§ 14(a)*'s broad remedial purpose, which ensures disclosure by corporate management is sufficient to enable shareholders to make informed choices. Ideally, courts should determine whether the proposal would in fact have been approved absent any misstatement or omission, but in fact such matters are often indeterminate, and it is appropriate any doubts be resolved in favor of the shareholders the statute was designed to protect. We are aware that some information is of dubious significance, and that settling a low disclosure threshold may make managers liable for insignificant errors, or encourage them to avoid liability by deluging shareholders in an avalanche of trivial information. Thus, we reject the "might" formulation, which suggests that a mere possibility, however unlikely, should void a transaction. The better standard is this: an omitted fact is "material" if there is a substantial likelihood that a reasonable shareholder would consider it important in deciding how to vote. Put another way, there must be substantial likelihood that disclosure of the omitted fact would have been viewed by reasonable investors as having significantly altered the "total mix" of available information. However, this standard does not require proof that disclosure of the omitted fact would have caused a reasonable investor to change his vote. The issue of materiality is a mixed question of law and fact, and summary judgement is only appropriate if the established omissions are "so obviously important to an investor, that reasonable minds cannot differ on the question of materiality." Here, none of the omissions were material. [reasoning omitted in casebook.] Summary judgement for plaintiff reversed, and remanded.

Analysis:

This case defines what constitutes a "material" fact warranting judicial remedy under *§ 14(a)*. The Supreme Court granted certiorari to resolve a circuit split on the meaning of the world "material." Previously, some courts held an omitted fact was "material" if knowing it *might* strike reasonable shareholders as important, but the Court rejected this formulation as overbroad. TSC's rule tries to apply the "reasonable person" standard, saying basically that a fact is material if a reasonable shareholder would think it material. Notably missing is the element of causation. The Court does not require this element on policy concerns that plaintiffs, having proven false and misleading proxy communications, would usually be unable to prove how all shareholders would have voted had they known the truth.

Virginia Bankshares, Inc. v. Sandberg

(*Corporation*) v. (*Shareholder*)

501 U.S. 1083, 111 S.Ct. 2749, 115 L.Ed.2d 929 (1991)

OPINIONS IN PROXY STATEMENTS MAY BE ACTIONABLE, BUT PLAINTIFFS WHOSE VOTE WAS NOT REQUIRED FOR TRANSACTION LACK STANDING

■ **INSTANT FACTS** After a corporation asks minority shareholders to ratify a merger with proxy statements opining the buyout price is "high" and "fair," a dissenting shareholder sues under *§ 14(a)*, contending the opinion is misleading and actionable.

■ **BLACK LETTER RULE** False or misleading opinions, reasons, beliefs, or conclusory proxy statements are actionable under *§ 14(a)* if (i) they are false or misleading, (ii) they are material, (iii) the plaintiff can produce extrinsic evidence of falsity, and (iv) either the plaintiff-shareholder was of a class whose vote was legally required to enact the transaction, or the misstatement deprived the plaintiff-shareholder of a remedy under state law.

■ **PROCEDURAL BASIS**

In shareholder action alleging *§ 14(a)* violations, appeal from appellate judgement for plaintiff, on writ of certiorari.

■ **FACTS**

First American Bankshares, Inc. ("FABI") (D) began a "freeze-out" merger, in which First American Bank of Virginia ("Bank") merged into FABI's (D) wholly-owned subsidiary, Virginia Bankshares, Inc. ("VBI") (D). Afterwards, Bank (D) was owned 85% by VBI (D) and 15% by minority shareholders. Then, FABI (D) offered a merger proposal, which would buy out the minority shareholders at $42 per share, which its bankers' opined was fair. Under Virginia corporate law, such transactions could be approved without proxy, by circulating an informational statement to shareholders at the shareholders' meeting and calling a vote. Nevertheless, Bank (D) solicited shareholder proxies for the merger. [This was because VBI (D) and FABI (D) wanted a show of shareholder support to avoid bad publicity, and because 1 director had a conflict of interest, which could be ratified by shareholder approval. Under Virginia law, if the shareholders approve the self-interested transaction by majority vote, no dissenting shareholder may sue claiming the transaction was unfair]. Bank's directors' (D) solicitation stated the merger would give minority shareholders a "high" value and a "fair" price. The minority shareholders approved the merger. Ms. Sandberg (P), a shareholder who voted against, sued FABI (D), Bank's directors (D), and VBI (D), contending (i) Bank's directors (D) never believed $42 per share was "high" or "fair," but said so simply to remain on the board, violating *§ 14(a) and Rule 14a-9*, (ii) Bank's directors (D) and others breached fiduciary duties to minority shareholders, violating state law. The defendants defended, contending the statements were non-actionable opinions, and that Sandberg (D) lacked standing to sue because minority shareholders' votes were not legally required to approve the merger. At trial, Sandberg (P) obtained a jury instruction that she need not prove she relied on the misstatements to recover, as long as they were "material" and the proxy solicitation was an "essential link" in the merger's approval, under *Mills*. The jury found for Sandberg (P), finding the defendants' proxies were misleading, and finding Sandberg's (P) stock should have been worth $60 per share. The defendants appealed. On appeal, the appellate court affirmed, finding the directors' statements materially misleading, and holding Sandberg (P) had standing even though the merger could have been approved without the minority shareholders' vote. The defendants appealed again. Supreme Court granted cert.

■ ISSUE

Are misleading opinions or conclusory proxy statements actionable under *§ 14(a)* if the plaintiff-shareholder's vote was not required to enact the transaction?

■ DECISION AND RATIONALE

(Souter, J.) Yes. False or misleading opinions, reasons, beliefs, or conclusory proxy statements are actionable under *§ 14(a)* if (i) they are false or misleading, (ii) they are material, (iii) the plaintiff can produce extrinsic evidence of falsity, and (iv) either the plaintiff-shareholder was of a class whose vote was legally required to enact the transaction, or the misstatement deprived the plaintiff-shareholder of a remedy under state law. First, we consider the actionability per se of statements of reasons, opinion, or belief. That such statements may be materially significant is unquestioned, but we must consider if they are statements "with respect to . . . material fact[s]" within *Rule 14a-9*'s strictures. We assume the jury verdict expresses a finding that the directors' statements were made with knowledge they did not hold the beliefs/opinions expressed. Directors' statements of reasons or belief are factual in 2 senses: (i) as statements the directors are acting for the reasons given, or hold the beliefs stated, and (ii) as statements about the subject of the reason/belief. This applies to reasons or beliefs on valuation. It is irrelevant that the valuation expresses value in indefinite terms, like "high" and "fair," rather than definite values, because such conclusory terms in commercial contexts are understood to rest on a factual basis which makes them factually either accurate or inaccurate. However, plaintiff-shareholders wishing to challenge directors' opinions must do so based on independent evidence, such as the corporate record, minutes, directors' statements, and circumstantial evidence bearing on the facts which underly the reasons claimed and the honesty of any statement; such evidence cannot be controlled or readily manufactured by the plaintiffs. Here, whether $42 was "high" and "fair" depends on provable facts about Bank's (D) assets and actual/potential operations which substantiated a value of $42, more, or less. Here, Sandberg (P) adduced evidence showing the statement was misleading about its subject and a false expression of the directors' reasons: whereas the proxy statement described the $42 price as offering a premium above book value and share price, this premium was illusory, since it was based on ignoring Bank's (D) real estate's appreciated value. There was also evidence Bank's (D) bankers considered Bank (D) to have some market power and "going concern" value over $60 per share, which was not disclosed. Also, there is evidence the directors knew they would be replaced if they voted against, and may have given false opinions to save their jobs. Thus, Bank's (D) opinion that the price was "high" and "fair" is open to attack based on evidence. Thus, under *§ 14(a)*, plaintiffs may prove specific statements or reasons to be knowingly false or misleadingly incomplete, even when stated in conclusory terms. However, if a statement is challenged as false/misleading on the basis the speaker does not truly believe in what he says, we hold that proof of mere disbelief or belief undisclosed should not create liability under *§ 14(a)*.

Thus, if the directors here did not actually believe $42 was in the minority shareholders' interest, but merely voted that way to retain their seats on the board, that itself would not be actionable. However, misleading statements must be not only deceptive, but also material, to be actionable. Sometimes, misleading statements may lose their deceptive edge by being mixed with true statements which discredit them, but the rectifying effect must be obvious to [the average shareholder], not just to financial analysts, since the point of proxy statements is to inform shareholders. Thus, misleading statements are deemed *im*material only when their presentation together with true statements "would exhaust the misleading conclusion's capacity to influence the reasonable shareholder." Here, the defendant directors contend the rest of their disclosure—e.g., that they would keep their seats if they approved, etc.—neutralized the misleading statements, but we find it consisted of half-truths even more misleading. Second, we consider whether shareholders whose votes are not required by corporate law or bylaw to authorize the transaction may demonstrate causation sufficient to sue under *§ 14(a)*, an issue which *Mills* and *J.I. Case* left open. The recognition of any private right of action for violating federal statutes must ultimately rest on congressional intent to provide a private remedy; once the right is recognized, its breadth should not grow beyond the scope Congress intended. Here, we find Congress never intended to provide a private cause of action to shareholders whose votes are not required.   Examining the *Exchange Act's* legislative history provides little insight, so we look to policy reasons.   We reject the contention that desire to avoid minority shareholders' ill will creates causation, since this would create much protracted litigation on the hazy issue of what the corporation's directors would have done without the minority shareholders' approval.   Sandberg (P) also contends the proxy vote should be deemed "necessary" because, under Virginia corporate law, the fact a vote was held deprives dissenting shareholders of their corporate law right to sue for damages by claiming the transaction was unfair.   We recognize a private federal right of action exists where the misleading proxy actually deprived a shareholder of a right provided by state corporate law.   We need not decide this here, because if the vote was in fact solicited by materially misleading statements, Virginia law provides the vote is void, and dissenting shareholders retain their right to challenge the transaction as unfair.   Judgement for plaintiffs reversed.

■ CONCURRENCE

(Scalia, J.) I agree with the majority's reasoning, but believe the statements here were of facts rather than opinions, and are misleading under existing caselaw.   I also believe the majority's disallowance of claims for misrepresentation of belief is true to Congress's intent.

■ CONCURRENCE AND DISSENT

(Stevens, J.) I agree with the majority that statements of opinion/belief may be actionable under *§ 14(a)*, but believe shareholders should have a private cause of action for false/misleading proxy statements if management believed a proxy vote was necessary for either legal or practical reasons, since there is a strong interest in providing a remedy for shareholders injured by unfair transactions.

■ CONCURRENCE AND DISSENT

(Kennedy, J.) I agree with the majority that statements of opinion/belief may be actionable under *§ 14(a)*, but believe its denial of a cause of action to minority shareholders is unsupported by law or policy.   Here, under Virginia law, the minority shareholders were empowered to vote down the merger [because they could refuse to ratify the conflict of interest], and our decision should not take away the right to recover for a transaction approved by improper solicitations.   Here, there is sufficient evidence that, had the minority shareholders not approved the merger, management would have abandoned it.

Analysis:

Virginia Bankshares' main point is that opinions or predictions contained in proxy statements are actionable if misleading or intentionally false, even if those opinions are vague (i.e., that the price is "fair" or "high").   The Court properly notes that such statements, while couched as opinion, are understood by investors to be based on fact and relied upon as such.   If such opinions are made in bad faith, they are as misleading and dishonest/reckless as misstatements of fact, and policy dictates they should be actionable.   Secondarily, *Virginia Bankshares* offers a safe harbor for misleading statements, which is small but interesting: mistatements may be misleading, but are not actionable if contradicted by so much true proxy information that a reasonable (individual) shareholder would tend to disregard the misstatement.

■ CASE VOCABULARY

BOOK VALUE: The value of an asset, as indicated on its balance sheet.   For personal property, book value is reduced for depreciation.   Here, the controversy revolves around the book value of land.   While land's book value is not depreciated, the contention here is that the land value reflected on the latest balance sheet had not yet been updated to reflect appreciation in the land's price, and so was outdated and misleading.

"FREEZE-OUT" MERGER: Merger in which minority shareholders are forced to sell their shares, and have no ownership of the combined company.   By law, shareholders frozen out have a statutory right to demand a fair price for their shares, as determined by judicial appraisal.

Rauchman v. Mobil Corp.

(Shareholder) v. *(Corporation)*

739 F.2d 205 (6th Cir. 1984)

CORPORATIONS MAY EXCLUDE FROM PROXY SOLICITATIONS SHAREHOLDER PROPOSALS WHICH WOULD INFLUENCE DIRECTORIAL ELECTIONS

■ **INSTANT FACTS** After an oil company elects a Saudi Arabian to its board, a shareholder proposes to amend the bylaws to bar citizens of OPEC nations to the board, but the company excludes the proposal.

■ **BLACK LETTER RULE** Corporations may exclude from their proxy statements any shareholder proposals which would prohibit the election/reelection of any current candidate/director.

■ **PROCEDURAL BASIS**

In shareholder suit seeking injunction (forcing corporation to include shareholder's proposal on proxy), appeal from summary judgement for defendant.

■ **FACTS**

Mr. Rauchman (P) owned shares of Mobil Corp. (D). Rauchman (P) submitted a proposal for inclusion in Mobil's (D) proxy statement: to amend Mobil's (D) bylaws to exclude citizens of OPEC nations from Mobil's (D) board. Rauchman's (P) supporting statement explained that Mobil (D) recently appointed a Saudi Arabian citizen [Suliman Olayan] with ties to the Saudi government, which uses its oil supply to influence politics improperly. Mobil (D) wished to exclude Rauchman's (P) proposal, and wrote the SEC, that the proposal was excludable as relating to an election to the board (i.e., the right to reelect Olayan), under *Rule 14a-8(c)(8)*, and requested a no-action letter. The SEC issued a no-action letter, opining the proposal is excludable because it effectively questions Olayan's qualification for reelection, and thus could be deemed an effort to oppose management's solicitation on behalf of Olayan's reelection. Rauchman (P) sued Mobil (D) to require inclusion of his proposal. Mobil (D) moved for summary judgement. At trial, the District Court assumed Rauchman (P) had a private right of action under *Exchange Act § 14(a)* and *Rule 14a-8*, but found Mobil (D) properly excluded Rauchman's (P) proposal, since it related to an election to office. Rauchman (P) appeals.

■ **ISSUE**

May a corporation exclude from its proxy statement a shareholder proposal banning citizens of certain nations from its board?

■ **DECISION AND RATIONALE**

(Engel, J.) Yes. Corporations may exclude from their proxy statements any shareholder proposals which would prohibit the election/reelection of any current candidate/director. We conclude, with "substantial reservations," that a private cause of action exists for *Rule 14a-8* violations. Here, we conclude the district judge did not err in granting Mobil (D) summary judgement. It is undisputed Olayan, a Saudi Arabian citizen, was running for reelection to Mobil's (D) board. Rauchman's (P) proposed amendment would forbid his election by making him ineligible to sit on the board. Rauchman's (P) proposed comment unmistakably refers to Olayan, although not by name. In our view,

---

this circumstance sufficiently supports the trial judge's holding that the proposal related to an election to office, and is excludable under SEC rules. It is suggested the proposal has only incidental impact on Olayan's reelection, but we disagree, since Mobil's (D) shareholders could not vote for Rauchman's (P) proposal and at the same time ratify Olayan's nomination. Rauchman's (P) proposal, which forces shareholders to choose between ratifying it and reelecting Olayan, could clearly be viewed as an "effort to oppose management's solicitation on behalf of" Olayan's reelection, and thus is excludable. It is a form of electioneering which Mobil (D) was not required to include in its proxy statement. Rauchman (P) argues that, even so, the remedy would be for the court to include a "grandfather clause" excluding Olayan, but we are not disposed to act on that suggestion at this late date and level, since Rauchman (P) apparently never suggested this to Mobil (D) or the district court. Mobil (D) also argues the proposed bylaw is excludable under *Rule 14a-8(c)(2)*, which permits a corporation to omit proposals which, if implemented, would "require the issuer to violate any state . . . or federal law," contending Rauchman's (P) proposed bylaw would violate the laws of Mobil's state of incorporation (Delaware), and the laws of its principal place of business (New York) [because it discriminates on the basis of national origin]. However, we need not decide that issue.

Analysis:

The relevant SEC rule prohibits shareholder proposals that are an "effort to oppose management's solicitation on behalf of" candidates. Some argue that, since the right to elect directors is the shareholders' greatest power, they should be allowed to vote on proposals that influence elections. However, it appears the rule is not intended to impede shareholders' right to vote freely, but rather to prevent shareholders from using proxy proposals to campaign for their candidates. The SEC rule apparently recognizes that, since shareholders may vote against any candidate proposed, it is unnecessary to also allow proposals that would influence elections. However, shareholders still lack the ability to nominate their own candidates to the board.

■ CASE VOCABULARY

NO-ACTION LETTER: Statement from the SEC that, based on facts submitted by an applicant corporation, the SEC will take no enforcement action if the applicant does what it proposes. Here, the letter requested would state that, if Mobil (D) excluded Rauchman's (P) proposal from its proxy, the SEC would not deem it a violation.

CHAPTER ELEVEN

Duty of Care and the Business Judgment Rule

Litwin v. Allen

Instant Facts: When a corporation approved a sham purchase of bonds, and granted the seller an option to buy back at the same price for 6 months, a shareholder sued the corporation's directors for losses on the bonds.

Black Letter Rule: Corporate directors who exercised reasonable prudence in approving/ ratifying/participating in corporate transactions are not personally liable for any losses proximately caused by those transactions, if they also made the decision in good faith and without self-dealing.

Shlensky v. Wrigley

Instant Facts: When a baseball park owner refuses to install lights or play night games over concerns about deteriorating the neighborhood, a minority shareholder sues to force changes.

Black Letter Rule: Majority shareholders have exclusive control of corporate policy through the directors, absent fraud, illegality, conflict of interest, or similar wrongdoing.

Smith v. Van Gorkom

Instant Facts: When a corporate CEO convinces the Directors to sell the corporation without calculating its value, shareholders allege they breached their duty of care.

Black Letter Rule: Corporate directors who sell the corporation without determining its true value have breached their duty of care.

In re Caremark Intern. Inc. Derivative Litigation

Instant Facts: When a corporation charged with health care bribery is forced to pay $250 million and promise better management in a settlement with government agencies, angry shareholder request the court reject the settlement and permit them to sue the directors for negligently permitting bribery.

Black Letter Rule: Corporate directors have a duty to make good faith efforts to institute a corporate monitoring system they believe will alert them of material events, but are not liable if the system fails to detect wrongdoing.

Stone v. Ritter

Instant Facts: After the corporation's banks were assessed significant fines for employee misconduct, shareholders initiated a derivative action but failed to make a demand on the board prior to filing suit.

Black Letter Rule: To excuse the statutorily required pre-suit demand on directors, a court must determine whether the particularized factual allegations of a derivative stockholder complaint create a reasonable doubt that, as of the time the complaint was filed, the board of directors could have properly exercised its independent and disinterested business judgment in responding to a demand.

Malone v. Brincat

Instant Facts: Several shareholders of a corporation brought a state law claim of breach of fiduciary duty against the corporation's board of directors, asserting that the directors had breached their fiduciary duties by overstating the corporation's earnings in their periodic reports to the shareholders.

Black Letter Rule: A director who knowingly disseminates false information that results in corporate injury or damage to an individual stockholder violates his fiduciary duty to the corporation or shareholder and may be held accountable under state law.

Gall v. Exxon Corp.

Instant Facts: When a corporation discovered its officers bribed foreign politicians, its directors recommended not filing suit against the officers. A shareholder sues to enjoin the board to sue them.

Black Letter Rule: Corporate directors who discover wrongdoing by corporate officers may elect not to file derivative suit against those officers, and shareholders cannot compel them, unless the refusal to prosecute is based on the directors' fraud, collusion, self-interest, dishonesty, or other misconduct akin to breach of trust, and unless their judgement was grossly unsound.

Zapata Corp. v. Maldonado

Instant Facts: A shareholder filed derivative suit against most of a corporation's directors. The directors created a litigation committee of 2 independent directors, which claims its business judgement permits it to dismiss the suit.

Black Letter Rule: If a shareholder files a derivative suit without the need to make demand on the board, the corporation's litigation committee may dismiss the suit if it (i) makes a thorough objective investigation, (ii) moves to dismiss the complaint, (iii) proves the committee was independent, acted in good faith, made reasonable investigation, and can justify the basis of its conclusions, and (iv) the court determines, de novo, that the derivative suit should be dismissed, considering the merits, the corporation's interest in avoiding suit, and public policy.

Aronson v. Lewis

Instant Facts: When the directors approve a generous compensation package for an aging major shareholder, a shareholder files derivative suit and contends demand would be futile.

Black Letter Rule: Demand is deemed futile, and thus excused, only where the complaint alleges facts which create a reasonable doubt that the directors' action qualified under the business judgement rule, with sufficient particularity.

In re Oracle Corp. Derivative Litigation

Instant Facts: Oracle shareholders filed a derivative suit against Oracle directors, which an Oracle special litigation committee sought to dismiss.

Black Letter Rule: A director's independence turns on whether the director is, for any substantial reason, incapable of making a decision with only the best interests of the corporation in mind.

Cuker v. Mikalauskas

Instant Facts: When a Pennsylvania utility's shareholders file derivative suits against directors for not collecting overdue bills, the litigation committee decides against suit, but it is unclear whether Pennsylvania has a business judgement rule.

Black Letter Rule: In Pennsylvania, directors or their litigation committee may dismiss shareholder derivative suits if they qualify for the business judgement rule, as codified by ALI Principles of Corporate Governance §§ 7.02–7.10 and § 7.13.

Litwin v. Allen

(Shareholder [On Corporation's Behalf]) v. *(Directors)*

25 N.Y.S.2d 667 (Supr. Ct. 1940)

CORPORATE DIRECTORS ARE NOT LIABLE FOR BAD BUSINESS DECISIONS IF MADE WITH REASONABLE CARE

■ **INSTANT FACTS** When a corporation approved a sham purchase of bonds, and granted the seller an option to buy back at the same price for 6 months, a shareholder sued the corporation's directors for losses on the bonds.

■ **BLACK LETTER RULE** Corporate directors who exercised reasonable prudence in approving/ ratifying/participating in corporate transactions are not personally liable for any losses proximately caused by those transactions, if they also made the decision in good faith and without self-dealing.

■ **PROCEDURAL BASIS**

Derivative suit seeking damages.

■ **FACTS**

In 1929–1930, Alleghany Corporation, a railroad, needed $10M to pay for real estate purchases. Allegheny could not borrow the funds, since it had reached its charter-imposed borrowing limit. Instead, Alleghany proposed to raise money by selling some of the investment securities it held. Alleghany agreed to sell $3M of (another company's) debentures to its banker J.P. Morgan & Co. (D), which would then resell them to Guarantee Trust Company ("Trust Co.") (D), a corporation which often did business with Alleghany. Under the purchase, seller Alleghany retained an 6-month option to repurchase the bonds at the original price. [This was done to make the transaction seem more like a sale than a disguised loan, and avoid legal challenges under Alleghany's charter. Also, the transaction was apparently done to bail out Alleghany, since Morgan (D) had invested heavily in its affiliates, and encouraged its affiliate Trust Co. (D) to keep it afloat. Also, Trust Co. (D) was entitled to 5% interest for those 6 months.] Trust Co. (D) had committed to buying the bonds from Morgan (D) for $3M after the option expired. However, the debentures' price started falling due to the 1929 stock market crash and ensuing recession, continued falling when Trust Co.'s (D) Directors (D) approved the purchase, and later lost 81% of its value while held, for longer than 6 months, by Trust Co. (D). Trust Co. (D) shareholder Litwin (P) filed a derivative suit against Trust Company (D), its Directors (D), J.P. Morgan (D), and others, contending the Directors (D) breached their duties of care in purchasing securities whose value was falling and likely to fall further.

■ **ISSUE**

Are corporate directors who approve unwise business transactions personally liable for losses?

■ **DECISION AND RATIONALE**

(Shientag, J.) No. Corporate directors who exercised reasonable prudence in approving/ratifying/participating in corporate transactions are not personally liable for any losses proximately caused by those transactions, if they also made the decision in good faith and without self-dealing. The main transactions attacked in this case took place in October 1930. There had been a market crash in October 1929, but in April 1930 there was an upswing, which analysts mistakenly believed would continue. The second crash was largely unforeseeable. To judge the transactions complained of, we must attempt to take ourselves back to the time when these events occurred and try to put ourselves in the position of whose who approved them. Generally, directors are trustees, in the sense they owe fiduciary duties to the company, and are bound to act in good faith and without selfishness. A director owes undivided loyalty to the company, and any adverse interest by him is subjected to a scrutiny rigid and uncompromising. He may not profit at his corporation's expense, and may not divert the company's opportunities to himself. He is required to use his independent judgement. Here, there is no evidence of any improper influence, bad faith, or conflict of interest. Directors must, of course, act honestly and in good faith, but that is not enough; they must also exercise some degree of skill and prudence and diligence. The Court of Appeals previously stated directors should "know of and [direct] the general affairs of the [corporation] and its business policy, and have general knowledge of the manner in which the business is conducted, the character of the investments, and the employment of the resources. No custom ... can make a directorship a mere position of honor devoid of responsibility ...." In other words, directors are liable for negligence in performing their duties. But since directors are not insurers, they are not liable for errors of judgement which are made while acting with reasonable skill and prudence. It has been said directors are required to conduct the corporation's business with the same degree of fidelity and care as an ordinarily prudent man would exercise in managing personal affairs of similar magnitude and importance. Yet in the last analysis, whether or not a director met his duty of care depends upon the facts, including the kind of corporation involved, its size and financial resources, the transaction's magnitude, and the immediacy of the problem. Bank directors are held to stricter accountability than those of ordinary corporations, because bank directors are entrusted with depositors' funds, but even bank directors are not liable if they use the degree of care ordinarily exercised by prudent bankers. Finally, in deciding whether a director was negligent, we must "look at the facts as they exist at the time of their occurrence," not hindsight. Although there is no case on point, it seems that if it is against public policy for banks, anxious to dispose of securities, to agree to buy them back at the same price, then it is even more so where a bank purchases securities and gives the seller the option to buy them back at the same price, since this makes the bank liable for loss without possibility of gain, and also inflates the bank's balance sheet with securities which are not yet owned. Here, I find liability in this transaction because it was so improvident, unusual, and unnecessary as to be contrary to fundamental conceptions of prudent banking practice. As for damages, negligent directors are liable only for losses proximately caused by their own negligence. Here, the Directors (D) are liable for losses attributable to the improper repurchase option itself, until the date this option expired. Here, Trust Co. (D) incurred further losses by electing to hold the bonds, but this was a separate business judgement, not proximately caused by the option itself. The matter is referred to a Referee for assessment of damages to determine what price could have been obtained for the bonds had defendants sold them when the option expired. The next question is: which defendants are liable? All directors who were present and voted at the board meeting which approved the option are liable. Even if the directors merely ratified a transaction already consummated by corporate officers, they remain liable, since ratification is equivalent to prior acquiescence, and here, ratification was essential to complete the transaction. Directors who did not actually vote, but actively participated and acquiesced in the transaction are also liable. Officers who participated actively in the transaction are also liable. However, directors of affiliated corporations are not liable, even if they knew of the transaction, unless the matter was brought before the affiliated corporation's board.

Analysis:

This case sums up the doctrine of what would later be called the "business judgement rule": directors who make a business decision in good faith, with reasonable prudence, and without conflicted interests, are not liable for any losses caused by the decision. The case also details some guidelines for deciding whether a decision should be deemed prudent. The decision involves considering directors' knowledge *at the time they made the decision*, without the benefit of hindsight, and they are held to the "reasonable person" standard. Directors of corporations that hold others' funds in trust—e.g., banks, insurers, trust companies, etc.—are held to a slightly higher standard of care. The case also presents one of the few kinds of transactions that are deemed imprudent per se: a transaction that has no chance of benefitting the corporation, but carries a risk of loss.

Shlensky v. Wrigley

(Shareholder) v. *(Corporation's President and Corporation)*

95 Ill.App.2d 173, 237 N.E.2d 776 (1968)

MINORITY SHAREHOLDERS CANNOT CHALLENGE DIRECTORS' BUSINESS DECISIONS ABSENT FRAUD, ILLEGALITY, SELF-DEALING, OR WRONGDOING

■ **INSTANT FACTS** When a baseball park owner refuses to install lights or play night games over concerns about deteriorating the neighborhood, a minority shareholder sues to force changes.

■ **BLACK LETTER RULE** Majority shareholders have exclusive control of corporate policy through the directors, absent fraud, illegality, conflict of interest, or similar wrongdoing.

■ **PROCEDURAL BASIS**

In shareholder derivative suit seeking damages and injunction, appeal from dismissal of plaintiff's complaint.

■ **FACTS**

Shlensky (P) owned stock in Chicago National League Ball Club, Inc. ("Ball Club") (D), which owned and managed the Chicago Cubs pro baseball team, operated the Cubs' home park Wrigley Field, and arranged/broadcast games. Most ball parks played games at night, in lighted parks, to increase attendance. Shlensky (P) proposed that Wrigley Field should install lights to allow the Cubs to play games at night, to increase attendance. Shlensky (P) noted the Cubs were losing money due to poor attendance at daytime games, but did better at their road games, which were played at night. Shlensky (P) contends that, while the lights' installation cost would be readily recouped from increased attendance, park owner Philip Wrigley (D), who owned 80% of Ball Club (D), opposed the idea because he personally believes baseball is a "daytime sport," and, especially, that installing lights would deteriorate the neighborhood. Shlensky (P) filed suit against Wrigley (D), Ball Club (D), and Directors (D), contending Wrigley (D) was motivated by personal views rather than the corporation's best interests, and that the Directors (D), in acquiescing, negligently mismanaged the corporation and wasted corporate assets. Shlensky (P) contended this mismanagement created a valid basis for derivative suit. Defendants (D) contended their decision reflects their honest business judgement, which cannot be challenged absent fraud, illegality, or conflicted interests. At trial, the trial court dismissed Shlensky's (P) complaint. Shlensky (P) appeals.

■ **ISSUE**

May minority shareholders force the majority shareholder to change corporate policy?

■ **DECISION AND RATIONALE**

(Sullivan, J.) No. Majority shareholders have exclusive control of corporate policy through the directors, absent fraud, illegality, conflict of interest, or similar wrongdoing. Our courts have pronounced ground rules applicable here. Prior case law holds that the majority shareholder may control the corporation in his discretion, absent charter violation, illegality, corruption, or self-dealing. Delaware cases also hold that directors have discretion over corporate policy, and their judgement is presumed final unless tainted with fraud. Directorial discretion is challenged occasionally. For example, in *Dodge v. Ford*

Motor Co. (Mich), a plaintiff shareholder was able to force additional dividends when he proved that Ford's motive in retaining dividends was to benefit the general public by creating more jobs. The *Dodge* court found that, not only did this impoverish shareholders, but also amounted to a change in the corporation's purpose [to a philanthropy], in violation of its charter. Here, Shlensky (P) argues the Directors (D) act for reasons unrelated to the Cubs' financial interests. However, we are not convinced Wrigley's (D) motives are contrary to the corporation's and shareholders' best interest. For example, the Directors (D) may be proper in considering the effect of lighting on attendance if lighting creates an unsafe neighborhood, discouraging attendees. Furthermore, the Ball Club's (D) long-term interest might be to not let the neighborhood deteriorate, to preserve Wrigley Field's property value. We cannot opine whether their decision is correct or not; that is beyond our jurisdiction and ability. By law, courts should not interfere in directorial decisions unless they show fraud, illegality, conflict of interest, or conduct bordering on one of those. Also, we feel the plaintiff's complaint fails to allege the corporation was damaged by lack of lights. There is no allegation that other teams' night games generate higher profits, and no allegation that installing lights would increase overall revenues, considering the extra cost of maintaining lights. Shlensky (P) claims Ball Club's financial losses are caused by poor attendance, but it also states other possible causes. Finally, Shlensky (P) contends Directors (D) were negligent in failing to follow other clubs' example in scheduling night games, but courts cannot require directors, chosen for their independent business judgement, to follow other companies' policy. Proving directorial negligence requires a clear showing of specific directors' dereliction of duty, and mere failure to "follow the crowd" is no dereliction. Affirmed.

Analysis:

As *Shlensky* demonstrates, courts are extremely reluctant to overturn directors'/majority shareholders' honest business decisions/policies on the ground that better policies exist and should be adopted. Among the reasons for this reluctance: (i) the understanding that shareholders elect directors for their generally good overall business judgement and intended to give the directors discretion; (ii) the understanding by majority shareholders, or by minority shareholders buying into a corporation dominated by a majority shareholder, that the majority shareholder will set policies; and (iii) the reluctance of judges, who are not businessmen and have no particular knowledge of the industry, to try to guess which of 2 proposed policies will best benefit the corporation. Courts occasionally intervene when the majority is not even attempting to maximize shareholder profit and basically using corporate money for personal philanthropy/projects. Here, however, the judge apparently believed that not holding night games might be an attempt to maximize long-term profits, by maintaining a neighborhood attractive to fans and Wrigley Field's property value.

Smith v. Van Gorkom

(Shareholders, As Class) v. *(Chairman–CEO & Directors)*

488 A.2d 858 (Del. Supr. 1985)

BEFORE SELLING CORPORATION, DIRECTORS MUST DETERMINE ITS VALUE

■ **INSTANT FACTS** When a corporate CEO convinces the Directors to sell the corporation without calculating its value, shareholders allege they breached their duty of care.

■ **BLACK LETTER RULE** Corporate directors who sell the corporation without determining its true value have breached their duty of care.

■ **PROCEDURAL BASIS**

Appeal from judgement for defendants in shareholder class action seeking rescission or damages.

■ **FACTS**

Trans Union Corporation stood to lose tax benefits if it could not raise its taxable income. CEO Van Gorkom (D) and other Directors (D) considered a leveraged buy-out (LBO) [which would merge Trans Union into another higher-income corporation, allowing its tax credits to offset the combined corporation's taxable income]. The CFO (D) made [extremely] preliminary calculations showing an LBO would be profitable if the company were valued at $50 per share, but unprofitable at $60. There was no agreement Trans Union was actually worth $50 or $60 per share. Van Gorkom (D) secretly approached LBO financier Pritzker (D) and offered to permit an LBO for $55 per share. Van Gorkom (D) may have wanted to cash out his shares at $55 immediately, since he was approaching mandatory retirement and the market share price was only $38. Pritzker (D) agreed, but gave Trans Union only 3 days to accept. Trans Union's senior managers felt $55 was too low. Nevertheless, Van Gorkom (D) called an immediate Board meeting to present the LBO's general terms, without reading the LBO agreement. The Directors (D) received no prior notice an LBO was contemplated, never saw the merger agreement, and were never told how the $55 price was computed. The CFO (D) suggested he had done a study valuing the company at $55 to $65 per share, though he never showed this study to the Directors (D), and it is unclear whether the study was done. Under the LBO's terms, Trans Union would "auction" itself; it could accept, but not solicit, competing bids, and could disclose only limited information to other bidders. If another bidder prevailed, Trans Union would sell Pritzker (D) 1 million shares at $38. [This "poison pill" discouraged other bidders, who, if they won, would immediately have to sell 1 million shares, bought at $55+, for $38 to a large hostile shareholder.] Trans Union's attorney (D) told the Directors (D) they may be sued for failing to accept. The Directors (D) accepted the agreement after 2 hours of deliberation, though it is unclear if they demanded the right to accept higher bids and share information with bidders. Trans Union immediately issued a press release announcing Trans Union had entered into a "definitive" merger agreement with Pritzker (D). Facing protest, Trans Union recanted, retaining investment bankers to solicit bids and noting that in a press release, but also announcing Pritzker (D) had already arranged financing [thus arguably binding Trans Union to accept] and purchased 1 million shares. Van Gorkom (D) then asked the Directors (D) to approve changes to the LBO agreement purportedly allowing a freer auction, and the Directors (D) agreed, without seeing the changes. Van Gorkom (D) signed the revised agreement Pritzker (D) presented, apparently unaware it actually *impaired* Trans Union's ability to accept other bids or reject Pritzker, and was more onerous than he had represented to the Directors (D). Van Gorkom (D) and Pritzker (D) also discouraged the bidders, who withdrew. Eventually, the Directors (D) approved Pritzker's (D) offer. The shareholders also voted to approve by a 69.9% majority. Smith, (P) a shareholder, filed a class action to rescind the LBO or recover damages, contending (I) the Directors breached their duty of care by selling the company without proper valuation, and (ii) the shareholder vote was invalid because shareholders were misinformed. The Directors (D) contended their decision was reasonable because (I) the $55 offer was above the $38 market value, (ii) it still allowed them to accept higher offers, (iii) the Directors (D) were experienced and knowledgeable about the company's value, and (iv) they relied on Trans Union's attorney's (D) recommendation that they accept. The trial court found that (I) the Directors (D) acted upon information sufficient to invoke the business judgement rule, and (ii) the shareholder vote should not be set aside because the shareholders (P) were "fairly informed." The shareholders (P) appealed.

■ ISSUE

Have corporate directors who sell the corporation without determining its true value breached their duty of care?

■ DECISION AND RATIONALE

(Horsey, J.) Yes. Corporate directors who sell the corporation without determining its true value have breached their duty of care. The trial court was clearly erroneous in concluding the Director's (D) decision was eligible for the business judgement presumption, because the Directors (D) were grossly negligent in informing themselves before deciding. Under case law, a properly informed decision is one where directors inform themselves of "all material information reasonably available to them," and directors are liable only if grossly negligent. Here, the Directors (D), were grossly negligent in approving the initial LBO agreement, because they (i) did not examine Van Gorkom's (D) role in negotiating and pricing the sale, (ii) never calculated Trans Union's intrinsic value, (iii) adopted their decision after only 2 hours' consideration, without prior notice and without any need for rush, and (iv) relied solely on Van Gorkom's (D) presentation without examining the documents. Delaware statutory corporate law permits directors to rely on officers' "reports" in good faith, and case law construes "reports" to include summaries of informal personal investigations. Here, however, Van Gorkom's (D) presentation was not a reliable "report," because Van Gorkom (D) himself never knew the LBO agreement's terms, never supported his valuation with any study, and never presented documentation, which should have put the Directors (D) on inquiry notice. That a buyout offer pays a premium over current market value is not legally sufficient to make it fair. Here, Trans Union's stock was depressed at the time, so its then-market value did not reflect its true value, and the Directors (D) were required to assess the true value. We do not hold that a proper company valuation necessarily requires external valuations or an investment banker's fairness opinion, but it does require *some* study. The Directors' (D) contention the ensuing "auction" period presented a "market test," which proved no other buyer would offer more, proves nothing, because it is unclear the LBO agreement actually permitted an auction. That the defendants inexplicably refuse to produce the agreement permits inference that it does not. "The directors' unfounded reliance on both the premium and the market test as the basis for accepting the Pritzker [(D)] proposal undermines [their] remaining contention that . . . [their] collective experience and sophistication was a sufficient basis for" finding their decision reasonable. We conclude that Trans Union's Board (D) was grossly negligent in initially approving the LBO agreement, and again in approving the LBO revisions without reading them, as was Van Gorkom (D). The documents he actually signed effectively foreclosed any auction, so the alleged "market test" does not indicate the price or procedure was reasonable. Legally, careless directorial decisions may be "cured" of liability if approved through informed shareholder vote. Here, however, the shareholders (P) were improperly informed, [reasons omitted] so their vote does not absolve the Directors (D) of liability. Reversed and remanded to determine damages.

■ DISSENT

(McNeilly, J.) In this case, the business judgement rule should apply, since the evidence sufficiently shows the Directors (D) deliberated carefully by discussing Trans Union's value and tax problems months before the LBO, listening to Trans Union's attorney (D), and insisting the final agreement allow them to accept higher bids. Further, the Directors (D), both inside and outside, were very capable and experienced, and not likely to fall for a "fast shuffle."

Analysis:

Van Gorkom is usually cited as a landmark decision on directors' duty of care, but its holding does not clearly delineate what constitutes "due care." *Van Gorkom* explicitly holds that, when directors are about to sell a corporation, they cannot assume that any price above the current market price is necessarily "fair." Thus, the case unambiguously obligates directors, prior to selling a corporation, to attempt *some* sort of valuation of their company. However, it is unclear just what kind of valuation is required, since the case specifically declines to specify a reasonable procedure or set bright-line rules for how long directors must deliberate, what they must consider, how exact their valuation must be, etc. Though the case says that the valuation need not be done by an independent auditor/appraiser, in practice, *Van Gorkom* has driven almost all directors to commission an independent investment banker's valuation and "fairness opinion" prior to selling the corporation as a shield against liability for damages from faulty valuations. *Van Gorkom* was an extremely unpopular decision among practitioners, who believed it imposed crushing liability on independent and eminent outside directors, simply because the Court believed they moved too fast and failed to consider that the directors' long collective experience may have made even a fast decision reasonable.

■ **CASE VOCABULARY**

LEVERAGED BUY-OUT (LBO): Purchase of controlling interest in a corporation using money borrowed (leveraged) from investors or bankers, and usually secured by the corporation's assets.

POISON PILL: In a merger/acquisition, a contractual provision which favors a preferred partner/buyer buy requiring all other buyers, should they prevail, to pay a penalty, usually to the preferred partner.

In re Caremark Intern. Inc. Derivative Litigation

(Shareholders, for Corporation) v. *(Directors)*

698 A.2d 959 (Del. Ch. 1996)

CORPORATE DIRECTORS MUST IMPLEMENT MONITORING SYSTEM TO ELIMINATE ILLEGAL ACTS OF EMPLOYEES

■ **INSTANT FACTS** When a corporation charged with health care bribery is forced to pay $250 million and promise better management in a settlement with government agencies, angry shareholders request the court reject the settlement and permit them to sue the directors for negligently permitting bribery.

■ **BLACK LETTER RULE** Corporate directors have a duty to make good faith efforts to institute a corporate monitoring system they believe will alert them of material events, but are not liable if the system fails to detect wrongdoing.

■ **PROCEDURAL BASIS**

Motion to approve settlement of derivative action.

■ **FACTS**

Caremark Corporation (P), a large decentralized corporation, operated health care centers and prescription drug programs. Caremark (P) and its predecessor often awarded contracts and grants to physicians who prescribed Caremark's (P) services to patients, which may have violated the federal Anti-Referral Payments Law ("ARPL") prohibiting "kickbacks." Eventually, Caremark was investigated by federal and state agencies. Caremark's Directors (D) and managers attempted to curb these payments and improve supervision, though many Directors (D) remained unsure whether the payments were illegal. The Directors (D) (i) revised Caremark's (P) employee guides to be ARPL-compliant, (ii) required payments to be approved by managers, (iii) disclosed the investigations in financial statements, (iv) hired auditors to assess its control structure, (v) reviewed compliance policies, and (vi) trained employees in compliance. Nevertheless, after 4 years of investigations, it was discovered that at least some of the payments were outright bribes, and Caremark (P) was ordered to adopt further safeguards and paid $250 million to settle various civil/criminal charges, most of which began in the predecessor corporation but continued throughout the Directors' cleanup attempt. Under the settlement, the government stipulated that no senior executives at Caremark (D) ignored or participated in wrongdoing. Shareholders (P) filed several derivative suits, consolidated here, alleging that the Directors (D) breached their duty of care by (*unintentionally*) failing to supervise employees or institute effective controls, causing the fines. Caremark proposed in a settlement with state and federal agencies, which would bar Shareholders' (P) suits, that, in the future, Caremark would (i) have employees stop paying referral fees, (ii) discuss compliance regularly with physicians, (iii) disclose to patients any financial incentives paid to their doctors, (iv) establish a compliance committee with outside directors, and (v) review its contracts—existing and future—to ensure compliance. This settlement was submitted for court approval, as required.

■ **ISSUE**

Should the court allow a settlement which dismisses charges against directors for negligently failing to institute corporate controls which could have prevented fines?

■ DECISION AND RATIONALE

(Allen, J.) Yes. Corporate directors have a duty to make good faith efforts to institute a corporate monitoring system they believe will alert them of material events, but are not liable if the system fails to detect wrongdoing. Courts deciding whether to approve derivative litigation settlements must decide whether the settlement offered is fair compensation for the corporation and its absent shareholders. In doing so, courts should not determine contested facts, but should evaluate the parties' relative claims and defenses, to substitute for an adversarial process. The parties proposing the settlement bear the burden of persuading the court it is fair and reasonable. Directors may be liable in negligence for either (i) making ill advised decisions not protected by the business judgement rule, or (ii) failure to monitor reasonably, if monitoring would have prevented losses. In suits for failure to monitor, directors may be held liable for negligently but unintentionally failing to monitor other employees' actions/decisions. Despite an old case, *Graham v. Allis-Chalmers* (Del. 1963) [directors not liable for not discovering employees' antitrust violations, absent grounds for suspicion], suggesting otherwise, we now hold the law to require directors have a duty to make good faith efforts to institute an effective corporate monitoring system (which would alert them to material events and noncompliance), even if they have no reason to suspect wrongdoing. The level of detail necessary for this informational system is a question of business judgement, and directors are obviously not liable every time a reasonable system fails to detect wrongdoing. Our holding stems from (i) our belief the Delaware Supreme Court would today require this of directors, considering recent cases' imposition of greater duties on corporate boards, (ii) public policy choices, founded on recent events demonstrating the large damages, reputational and monetary, that unsupervised employees can cause, and (iii) the increasing risks of large Federal penalties for corporate criminal liability. Here, we find the settlement fair and reasonable. While the changes demanded by the settlement are small, since they were largely adopted in Caremark's ongoing cleanup effort, they are fully adequate consideration for dismissing the claims against the directors, since the evidence suggests the directors will have the claims against them dismissed. Here, Shareholders (P) would have to prove the Directors (D) (i) knew/should have known about the violations, (ii) took no good faith steps to prevent them, and (iii) proximately caused the losses. Claims of directorial liability for negligent failure to monitor must allege sustained or systematic failures to exercise oversight or create an information system, which would suggest bad faith. Here, the evidence suggests the Directors (D) made good faith efforts to inform themselves. Approving this settlement would dismiss an "extremely weak" claim in return for modest assurances of better management in the future. Finally, I will award plaintiffs' (P) attorneys $816K in attorney's fees for negotiating the settlement, in light of the amount and sophistication of legal services required, and the slight contingency faced. Settlement approved.

Analysis:

This case sets a sort of "business judgement rule" for corporate monitoring: directors are responsible for instituting a reasonable corporate monitoring system, but are not held personally liable each time the reasonable system fails to detect wrongdoing. Here, the decision to foreclose shareholder suits seems fair in light of evidence the directors made honest and reasonable efforts to avoid liability. Bear in mind many of the practices seem to have predated the directors' (D) appointment, so that even if they could have immediately stopped all of the suspect payments, the company would still remain liable for past payments that had already occurred before the directors' (D) tenure. Here, it would have been especially unfair to impose liability because there was apparently real legal uncertainty—among Caremark directors (D), employees, and even their lawyers—as to whether some types of payments, such as research grants, were actually prohibited as "kickbacks" (though it is admitted that at least some of the payments were intentional bribes).

■ CASE VOCABULARY

DERIVATIVE LITIGATION: Lawsuit filed by corporate shareholders suing on behalf of the corporation for damages done to the corporation. Here, the shareholders are claiming the Directors' (D) crimes harmed the corporation by causing the imposition of $250 million in fines.

Stone v. Ritter

(Shareholders) v. *(Director)*

911 A.2d 362 (Del. 2006)

WITHOUT RED FLAGS, DIRECTORS HAVE NO REASON TO SUSPECT WRONGDOING

■ **INSTANT FACTS** After the corporation's banks were assessed significant fines for employee misconduct, shareholders initiated a derivative action but failed to make a demand on the board prior to filing suit.

■ **BLACK LETTER RULE** To excuse the statutorily required pre-suit demand on directors, a court must determine whether the particularized factual allegations of a derivative stockholder complaint create a reasonable doubt that, as of the time the complaint was filed, the board of directors could have properly exercised its independent and disinterested business judgment in responding to a demand.

■ **PROCEDURAL BASIS**

Appeal from a trial court ruling against the plaintiffs.

■ **FACTS**

AmSouth Bank and a subsidiary paid a total of $50 million in fines and penalties for the failure of bank employees to file suspicious activity reports relating to money laundering. AmSouth shareholders brought a derivative action against the directors, alleging that they failed in their duty of oversight, which failure led to the employee misconduct and financial penalties. The plaintiffs filed their suit without making demand on the board, and the chancery court held that they failed to adequately plead that such a demand would have been futile, so their case could not proceed. The plaintiffs appealed.

■ **ISSUE**

Were the plaintiffs excused from making a demand that the directors initiate suit against AmSouth for their own alleged lack of oversight?

■ **DECISION AND RATIONALE**

(Holland, J.) No. To excuse the statutorily required pre-suit demand on directors, a court must determine whether the particularized factual allegations of a derivative stockholder complaint create a reasonable doubt that, as of the time the complaint was filed, the board of directors could have properly exercised its independent and disinterested business judgment in responding to a demand. Here, the plaintiffs allege that because the directors face significant potential liability in this lawsuit, they cannot reasonably be expected to initiate it themselves. In reality, however, the individual directors likely are not liable.

Based on the *Caremark* decision, corporate directors face no liability for failing to ferret out wrongdoing that they have no reason to suspect. The duty of directors to act in good faith and stay informed does not require them to possess detailed information about all aspects of the operation of the enterprise. Only a systematic failure of oversight, or an utter failure to attempt to assure that a reasonable information and reporting system exists, will establish the lack of good faith that is a necessary

---

condition to liability. Imposition of liability requires a showing that the directors *knew* they were not discharging their fiduciary obligations.

In the absence of red flags alerting corporate directors to misconduct, good faith is measured by the directors' actions to assure that a reasonable reporting and information system exists, not by second-guessing after the occurrence of employee misconduct. A bad outcome does not equal bad faith. Here, the evidence shows that the directors took steps to ensure that a reasonable reporting system did exist. Accordingly, the trial court properly applied *Caremark* and dismissed the plaintiffs' complaint for failure to excuse demand by alleging particularized facts that created reason to doubt whether the directors acted in good faith in exercising their oversight responsibilities. Affirmed.

Analysis:

The court here made it clear that *Caremark* continues to be good law in Delaware, holding that "*Caremark* articulates the necessary conditions predicate for director oversight liability: (a) the directors utterly failed to implement any reporting or information system or controls; or (b) having implemented such a system or controls, consciously failed to monitor or oversee its operations thus disabling themselves from being informed of risks or problems requiring their attention. In either case, imposition of liability requires a showing that the directors knew that they were not discharging their fiduciary obligations." Claims like those presented in this case have come to be generally referred to as "*Caremark* claims."

Malone v. Brincat

(Shareholder) v. *(Director)*

722 A.2d 5 (Del. 1998)

DELAWARE SUPREME COURT FINDS A BREACH OF FIDUCIARY DUTY RESULTING FROM DIRECTOR MISSTATEMENTS

■ **INSTANT FACTS** Several shareholders of a corporation brought a state law claim of breach of fiduciary duty against the corporation's board of directors, asserting that the directors had breached their fiduciary duties by overstating the corporation's earnings in their periodic reports to the shareholders.

■ **BLACK LETTER RULE** A director who knowingly disseminates false information that results in corporate injury or damage to an individual stockholder violates his fiduciary duty to the corporation or shareholder and may be held accountable under state law.

■ **PROCEDURAL BASIS**

Appeal of a dismissal with prejudice by the Delaware Court of Chancery of an action for breach of fiduciary duty under state corporate law.

■ **FACTS**

Doran Malone ("Malone") (P) and other shareholders of Mercury Finance Company ("Mercury") filed a suit against John Brincat ("Brincat") (D) and the other directors of Mercury alleging that Brincat (D) and the directors breached their fiduciary duty of disclosure by intentionally overstating Mercury's earnings on repeated occasions over a four-year period in documents issued to the company's shareholders. Malone (P) and the shareholders sought certification as a class action on behalf of themselves and all persons who owned Mercury stock over that four-year period. Malone (P) and the shareholders alleged simply that as a direct result of the false disclosures, Mercury had lost all or virtually all of its $2 billion value. The Delaware Court of Chancery dismissed the complaint with prejudice for failure to state a claim on which relief could be granted, accepting the directors' argument that directors have no fiduciary duty of disclosure under Delaware law in the absence of a request for shareholder action. The Chancery Court held that the only remedy a shareholder could pursue under such circumstances was a federal remedy. The shareholders appealed to the Delaware Supreme Court.

■ **ISSUE**

Has a director, who knowingly disseminates false information that results in corporate injury or damage to an individual stockholder, violated his state law fiduciary duty to the corporation or shareholder?

■ **DECISION AND RATIONALE**

(Holland, J.) Yes. This court has previously held that a board of directors is under a fiduciary duty to disclose material information when seeking shareholder action. This case requires us to decide if there may be a cause of action for disclosure violations only where directors seek shareholder action. We hold that directors who knowingly disseminate false information that results in corporate injury or damage to an individual stockholder violate their fiduciary duty and may be held accountable. Equitable principles act to protect beneficiaries who are not in a position to protect themselves.

Fiduciary duties are imposed on the directors of Delaware corporations to regulate their conduct when they manage the business of a corporation for the benefit of its shareholders. Directors stand in a fiduciary relationship to both the stockholders and the corporation on whose board they serve. Shareholders are entitled to rely on their elected directors to discharge their fiduciary duties at all times. Whenever directors communicate publicly or directly with shareholders about the corporation's affairs, with or without a request for shareholder action, directors have a fiduciary duty to shareholders to exercise due case, good faith, and loyalty. Dissemination of false information could violate one of those duties. Directors must be honest with their shareholders. When directors are not seeking shareholder action, but are deliberately misinforming shareholders about the business of the corporation, there is a violation of fiduciary duty which may result in a derivative claim on behalf of the corporation or a cause of action for damages. Here, the complaint alleges an egregious violation of fiduciary duty by the directors in knowingly putting out materially false information about earnings. Then it alleges that the corporation lost about $2 billion dollars as a result. This allegation that the corporation lost all of its value, seems to be some kind of claim of injury to the corporation, but Malone (P) and the shareholders never expressly assert a derivative claim on behalf of the corporation in their complaint. If they assert such a derivative claim, they should be permitted to replead their complaint to assert such a claim on behalf of the corporation or replead to assert any individual cause of action that may be appropriate on behalf of the named plaintiffs or a properly recognizable class. Without well-pleaded allegations stating a derivative, class, or individual cause of action and a properly assertable remedy, the Chancery Court was right to dismiss the claim. Nevertheless, we disagree with the Chancery Court that such a claim cannot be articulated on these facts. Malone (P) and the plaintiffs should have been permitted to amend their complaint, if possible, to state a cognizable cause of action. Thus, the Chancery Court should have dismissed the complaint *without* prejudice. Affirmed as to dismissal. Reversed as to dismissal with prejudice.

Analysis:

In holding that directors may violate their fiduciary duties by materially misstating the corporation's financial condition, even though the corporation does not engage in any specific transactions with shareholders or investors, the Delaware Supreme Court here finds a fiduciary duty of disclosure that some commentators have suggested parallels federal duties under Rule 10b-5, which makes it unlawful to defraud or deceive a person in connection with the purchase or sale of securities. In previous cases, the court had held that there was a fiduciary duty of disclosure when the corporation was seeking shareholder action or approval. Here, the court clarified that the obligation of honesty exists whenever the corporation communicates with its shareholders. Given the large number of public corporations incorporated in Delaware, the fiduciary duty of disclosure found by the court could potentially become a competitor to Rule 10b-5 as a method of attacking director fraud.

■ CASE VOCABULARY

DISMISSAL WITH PREJUDICE: A court order disposing of a case and barring any future right to bring a suit on the same claim or cause of action.

DISMISSAL WITHOUT PREJUDICE: A court order that removes a case from proceeding further, but permits a new suit to be filed for the same cause of action, usually on the basis of amended pleadings.

Gall v. Exxon Corp.

(Shareholder) v. *(Corporation)*

418 F.Supp. 508 (S.D.N.Y. 1976)

DIRECTORS WHO DISCOVER INTERNAL WRONGDOING HAVE DISCRETION WHETHER TO FILE DERIVATIVE SUIT

■ **INSTANT FACTS** When a corporation discovered its officers bribed foreign politicians, its directors recommended not filing suit against the officers. A shareholder sues to enjoin the board to sue them.

■ **BLACK LETTER RULE** Corporate directors who discover wrongdoing by corporate officers may elect not to file derivative suit against those officers, and shareholders cannot compel them, unless the refusal to prosecute is based on the directors' fraud, collusion, self-interest, dishonesty, or other misconduct akin to breach of trust, and unless their judgement was grossly unsound.

■ **PROCEDURAL BASIS**

In shareholder derivative action seeking injunction, motion for summary judgement for defendant.

■ **FACTS**

Exxon Corp. (D) found its officers diverted $59M of corporate funds to pay bribes and political contributions to Italian politicians, to secure illegal political favors. The Board of Directors, upon learning of it, established a Special Committee on Litigation to investigate. The investigation confirmed Exxon (D) officials paid $39M in secret payments (bribes) to Italian political parties, and another $20 in political contributions disguised as fictitious payments. Some Exxon (D) Directors (D) were aware of the political contributions, some were informed of them, and some had urged the political payments be phased out. A few directors were also aware of the secret payments. However, the Committee recommended against filing suit against any Exxon (D) officer, citing, inter alia, the difficulty of winning, the cost of litigation, interruption of business operations and demoralization. Shareholder Gall (P) sued to force Exxon's (D) Directors (D) to file suit against officers involved in bribery. Exxon (D) moved for summary judgement, contending the decision to litigate was a proper business judgement, reserved for them alone.

■ **ISSUE**

May a shareholder demand that directors who discover wrongdoing by corporate officers file a derivative suit against those officers?

■ **DECISION AND RATIONALE**

(Carter, J.) No. Corporate directors who discover wrongdoing by corporate officers may elect not to file a derivative suit against those officers, and shareholders cannot compel them, unless the refusal to prosecute is based on the directors' fraud, collusion, self-interest, dishonesty, or other misconduct akin to breach of trust, and unless their judgement was grossly unsound. There is no question the rights to be vindicated here are those of Exxon (D), not those of Gall (P) suing derivatively. Since the corporation's interests are at stake, it is the directors' responsibility to determine whether action should be brought on the corporation's behalf. It follows that the directors' decision on whether or not to sue rests within management's sound business judgement. The principle has become known as the business judgement rule. Previously, the Supreme Court held "whether or not a corporation shall seek to enforce ... a [claim] for damages is, like other business questions, ordinarily a matter of internal management, ... left to the discretion of the directors. Courts ... seldom [interfere] ..., except where the directors are guilty of misconduct equivalent to a breach of trust, or where they stand [have a conflict of interest] which prevents ... unprejudiced ... judgement." *United Copper Securities Co. v. Amalgamated Copper Co.* (S.Ct. 1917). It is clear that courts should not interfere with corporate officers' judgement at the instigation of a single shareholder, absent allegations of directorial fraud, collusion, self-interest, dishonesty, or other misconduct akin to breach of trust, and absent allegations the business judgement was grossly unsound. Recently, the legality and morality of foreign political contributions and bribes paid by American corporations is widely debated, but it is not for the courts to decide the issue or set corporate policy. However, Gall (D) calls into question the Special Committee's disinterestedness and bona fides, suggesting Committee members may have been involved personally, or at least interested enough in the wrongdoing to impair their business judgement. Thus, I conclude granting summary judgement at this stage is premature. Gall (P) must be given an opportunity to test the Special Committee's independence and bona fides through discovery and, if necessary, at plenary hearing. Issues of intent, motivation, and good faith are particularly inappropriate for summary judgement. Summary judgement denied without prejudice.

Analysis:

Litigation committees, such as Exxon's, are a common device instituted to deal with threats of shareholder derivative suits. If a shareholder files or threatens derivative suits, the committee steps in to decide whether the corporation will file the suit on its own behalf or elect not to litigate. The committee may elect not to pursue even valid suits, if, for example, the suit is too costly or disruptive. Theoretically, this may prevent the diversion of corporate resources into suits that are unjustified or likely unproductive. However, there is also an incentive for the directors on the committee to protect their colleagues or corporation from punishment by quashing valid claims, to shareholders' detriment. If such a litigation committee is in place, the dissenting shareholder has a difficult burden to overcome in forcing suit, since the committee's decision is given the benefit of the business judgement rule.

■ CASE VOCABULARY

BONA FIDES: Good faith.

PLENARY HEARING: A full hearing.

Zapata Corp. v. Maldonado

(*Corporation*) v. (*Shareholder*)

430 A.2d 779 (Del. 1981)

WHERE DERIVATIVE SUIT DOES NOT REQUIRE DEMAND TO BOARD, LITIGATION COMMITTEE DECISION TO DISMISS IS NOT ENTITLED TO BUSINESS JUDGEMENT RULE

■ **INSTANT FACTS** A shareholder filed derivative suit against most of a corporation's directors. The directors created a litigation committee of 2 independent directors, which claims its business judgement permits it to dismiss the suit.

■ **BLACK LETTER RULE** If a shareholder files a derivative suit without the need to make demand on the board, the corporation's litigation committee may dismiss the suit if it (i) makes a thorough objective investigation, (ii) moves to dismiss the complaint, (iii) proves the committee was independent, acted in good faith, made reasonable investigation, and can justify the basis of its conclusions, and (iv) the court determines, de novo, that the derivative suit should be dismissed, considering the merits, the corporation's interest in avoiding suit, and public policy.

■ **PROCEDURAL BASIS**

In shareholder derivative action, appeal from denial of defendant corporation's motion to dismiss.

■ **FACTS**

Zapata Corp.'s (D) Directors (D) adopted a stock option plan, granting certain officers and directors stock options at $12.15 per share, in five installments. As the final installment approached, Zapata (D) was planning a tender offer (share buyback) at $25/share, which was above the market price of $18–19. Zapata's (D) Directors (D) realized that, if they exercised their options after the tender offer, they would owe more taxes on the options. To avoid this, the Directors (D) accelerated the options' exercise date, requested the NYSE suspend trading pending "an important announcement," then announced the tender offer. In response, the share price rose to $24.50. Shareholder Maldonado (P) filed derivative suit against certain of Zapata's (D) Officers (D) and Directors (D) for breach of fiduciary duty. Maldonado (P), before filing suit, did not demand the Directors (D) bring the derivative suit, stating such demand was futile since the Directors (D) were named defendants and participated in the breach. Later, the Directors (D) created an Independent Investigation Committee, composed of two newly-appointed outside directors, which rejected the derivative suit as "inimical to the Company's best interests." Zapata (D) moved to dismiss Maldonado's (P) complaint. The Chancery Court denied Zapata's (D) motion, holding "business judgement" does not apply to permitting directors to dismiss derivative actions which shareholders have an individual right to maintain. Zapata (D) filed an interlocutory appeal.

■ **ISSUE**

Is the business judgement rule applicable to litigation committees' efforts to dismiss shareholders' derivative suits?

■ **DECISION AND RATIONALE**

(Quillen, J.) No. If a shareholder files a derivative suit without the need to make demand on the board, the corporation's litigation committee may dismiss the suit if it (i) makes a thorough objective investigation, (ii) moves to dismiss the complaint, (iii) proves the committee was independent, acted in good faith, made reasonable investigation, and can justify the basis of its conclusions, and (iv) the court determines, de novo, that the derivative suit should be dismissed, considering the merits, the corporation's interest in avoiding suit, and public policy.   In this interlocutory appeal, we limit our review to whether Zapata's (D) Committee could cause this action to be dismissed.   We begin by comparing the Chancery Court's holding in a tangential case, *Maldonado v. Flynn* (Del. Ch. 1980) ["business judgement" does not grant authority to dismiss derivative actions], with the decisions of several federal courts, applying Delaware law, which hold the opposite.   Corporations, existing by legislative grace, possess the authority granted by the legislature.   Delaware corporations' directors derive their managerial decision-making power (which includes decisions to initiate or forbear litigation) from *8 Del.C. § 141(a)*, which states, "The business and affairs of every corporation ... shall be managed by or under the direction of a board of directors."   The "business judgement rule" is a judicial creation that presumes the board's decision is proper under certain circumstances.   It does not create authority, but is generally used as a defense to attacks on the decision's soundness.   However, this legislative grant and judicial creation are related, because the "business judgement" rule evolved to grant deference to directors's business expertise when exercising their managerial power under *141(a)*.   Here, though Zapata's (D) decision to terminate the suit resulted from an exercise of directorial discretion, as delegated to the Committee, the question of "business judgement" would not become relevant unless that decision was attacked as improper.

Below, the Chancery Court found that shareholders, after making unsuccessful demands to the board to initiate suit, possess an independent individual right to continue a derivative suit for fiduciary breach, over the corporation's objection, but we find this erroneous.   Under the settled case law of *McKee v. Rogers* (Del. Ch. 1931), the general rule is that "a [shareholder] cannot be permitted ... to invade the discretionary field committed to the judgement of the directors and sue in the corporation's behalf when the managing body refuses."   However, under *McKee*, the board's refusal is not always determinative.   Directors, owing well-established fiduciary duties to the corporation, will not be allowed to cause a derivative suit to be dismissed when it would breach their fiduciary duties.   Consistent with the purpose of requiring demand, a board decision to dismiss a derivative suit as detrimental to the corporation, *after a demand was made*, will be respected unless wrongful.   In other words, when shareholders, after making demand and having their suit rejected, attack the board's decision as improper, the board's decision falls under the "business judgement" rule, and will be respected if taken in good faith, without conflicted interests, and with reasonable deliberation.   Absent a wrongful refusal, the shareholder simply lacks legal managerial power to pursue suit.

Yet *McKee* presents a settled exception to the general rule: "[a shareholder] may sue in equity in his derivative right to assert a [claim on] behalf of the corporation, *without prior demand* upon the directors to sue, when it is apparent a demand would be futile, that the officers are under an influence that sterilizes discretion and [they] could not be proper persons to conduct the litigation."   However, the shareholder's individual right to bring the action does not ripen unless he shows a demand would be futile.   However, if the shareholder *sues properly without demand*, may the board cause the suit to be dismissed?   Policy dictates that corporations should be able to rid themselves of detrimental litigation under *141(a)*, since otherwise a single shareholder might control the entire corporation's destiny.   It is clear that, since *141(c)* lets the board delegate all its authority to a committee, an independent committee so authorized has the power to move for dismissal or summary judgement.   This seems so even if no demand was made to the board; it still retains its power to oppose the suit.   The question now is whether Zapata's (D) board, tainted by its majority's self-interest, could legally delegate its authority to a committee of two disinterested directors.   Delaware statute clearly says this is proper, since *§ 141(c)* expressly authorizes committees to exercise the board's full authority if so delegated, and the analogous *8 Del.C. § 141* [concerning interested directors] is designed to permit disinterested directors to act for the board.   We do not think the board's majority's interest taint is per se a legal bar to delegating its powers to an independent disinterest committee.   Policy demands a balance: corporations should be able to rid themselves of meritless/harmful suits, but should not wrest actions away from well-meaning plaintiffs.   Some courts have accomplished this by giving the committee's decision the "business judgement" presumption, making it binding absent proof of self-interest, bad faith, or unreasonable investigation.

However, we are not satisfied that the "business judgement" presumption is proper at this point. Here, demand on the board was properly excused, and the suit was initiated properly, and we have to be concerned about the creation of an "Independent Investigation Committee" *four* years later, after electing two new outside directors, since, after years of vigorous litigation, committees may move to dismiss for reasons unconnected with the merits. Moreover, while Delaware law permits the board to delegate its powers to a committee, we must be mindful directors are passing judgement on fellow directors, and on those who appointed them to the committee, and consider whether empathy might not play a role. In our view, the best policy is to allow the courts to determine whether a litigation committee may dismiss a shareholder's derivative suit. The proper procedure is this: If a shareholder demands a derivative suit, an independent litigation committee must make an objective thorough investigation, and, if it decides dismissal is in the corporation's best interest, it may then cause the corporation to file a pretrial motion to dismiss. The motion should include a thorough written record of the investigation, its findings, and its recommendations. Each side should be entitled to present proof, and the movant must meet the proof burden of *Rule 56* [no genuine issue of material fact, and entitled to dismiss as a matter of law]. The court should apply a two-step test: first, the court should inquire into the committee's independence, good faith, reasonable investigation, and the basis of its conclusions. The committee should bear the proof burden. If the court determines the committee in not independent, not acting in good faith, or has not shown reasonable basis for its conclusions, it shall deny the motion. Otherwise, the court may proceed to the next step: the court must determine, *in its own judgement*, whether the motion to dismiss should be granted, giving special consideration to the action's merits, the corporation's interest in avoiding suit, and public policy. Interlocutory order reversed and remanded.

Analysis:

This case was critical in curbing the power of litigation committees to dismiss shareholders' valid derivative suits. Previous decisions interpreting Delaware case law held that the litigation committee's decision to dismiss a derivative suit was given the benefit of the "business judgment" presumption, meaning it was unreviewable unless the shareholder-plaintiff could prove the committee members acted in bad faith, had conflicted interests, or failed to make reasonable investigation before deciding. The obvious problem is that even independent directors are often loath to prosecute wrongdoing among their peers, especially if this could expose further wrongdoing or create bad press, and giving them free reign to act or not invites favoritism and abuses of discretion. *Zapata* provides a partial solution. When the plaintiff-shareholder is not required to first make a demand on the board to pursue the suit (because the directors are interested, or defendants, etc.), the litigation committee may dismiss only through a full showing to the court, without the benefit of the business judgment rule.

■ CASE VOCABULARY

DERIVATIVE SUIT: Lawsuit, brought by shareholder, to enforce the corporation's (not the shareholder's) rights, usually against someone who breached a fiduciary duty owed to the corporation. Any recovery from the wrongdoer goes to the corporation.

INTERLOCUTORY APPEAL: Appeal of an order/motion, rather than of a final judgement. Here, Zapata (D) appeals the denial of its right to dismiss Maldonado's (P) lawsuit.

TENDER OFFER: Offer to the public to purchase a corporation's shares, at a premium above market price. Usually done to buy voting shares and launch a takeover of another corporation. Here, Zapata Corp. (D) bought back its own shares from shareholders.

Aronson v. Lewis

(*Corporation and Directors*) v. (*Shareholder*)

473 A.2d 805 (Del. 1984)

DEMAND NOT DEEMED FUTILE UNLESS COMPLAINT SPECIFICALLY ALLEGES WHY DIRECTORS CANNOT MAKE FAIR DECISION

■ **INSTANT FACTS** When the directors approve a generous compensation package for an aging major shareholder, a shareholder files derivative suit and contends demand would be futile.

■ **BLACK LETTER RULE** Demand is deemed futile, and thus excused, only where the complaint alleges facts which create a reasonable doubt that the directors' action qualified under the business judgement rule, with sufficient particularity.

■ **PROCEDURAL BASIS**

In derivative action seeking contract rescission and damages, appeal from denial of defendant's motion to dismiss.

■ **FACTS**

Meyers Parking System (D) was a spinoff of Prudential Building Maintenance Corp. Meyers (D) hired Prudential's 75-year-old retired CEO, Leo Fink (D), as a consultant, to fulfill an earlier agreement between Prudential and Fink (D). Meyers's (D) Directors (D) approved an employment contract for Fink (D), under which Fink (D) got a 5-year consulting contract, at $150K/year plus profit-sharing, followed by a lifetime consulting contract, earning $100K-$150K annually for each year he lived. Fink (D) agreed to devote best efforts and substantially all his time to working for Meyers (D). The contract provided Fink (D) would be paid even if unable to work; (he was 75, though not in [especially] poor heath). Also, Meyers (D) loaned Fink (D) $225K, interest free, though these loans were later repaid. Shareholder Harry Lewis (P) filed derivative suit against the Directors (D) and Fink (D), contending Fink's (D) contract and loan had "no valid business purpose," the transaction wasted corporate assets by paying Fink (D) excessive compensation, and that Fink (D) performed few services because of his age and could not employ "best efforts" for Meyers (D) because of his prior consulting agreements with Prudential. Lewis's (P) complaint alleged no demand had been made on the board, because it would be futile, since (i) all the Directors (D) are defendants and had ratified the contract, (ii) all the Directors (D) were selected and controlled by Fink (D), who owns 47% of shares, and (iii) the demand would ask the Directors (D) to sue themselves. At trial, the Directors moved to dismiss, for failure to make such demand. The Chancery Court denied the motion, finding Lewis's (P) allegations raised a "reasonable inference" the Directors' (D) action was unprotected by the business judgement rule, and the board could not have considered the demand impartially.

■ **ISSUE**

Is demand excused when the plaintiff's complaint alleges the directors participated in the wrongdoing?

■ **DECISION AND RATIONALE**

(Moore, J.) No. Demand is deemed futile, and thus excused, only where the complaint alleges facts which create a reasonable doubt that the directors' action qualified under the business judgement rule, with sufficient particularity. *Zapata* left unanswered a crucial issue: when is a shareholders demand upon a board of directors, to redress an alleged wrong to the corporation, excused as futile? Below, the court denied dismissal, ruling the complaint's allegations raised a "reasonable inference" the board could not have acted impartially on the demand. We cannot agree with this formulation. Demand can only be excused where facts are alleged with particularity which create a reasonable doubt that the directors action was entitled to the protections of the business judgement rule. To hold otherwise would make demand futility automatic when based on conclusory allegations, and reasonable inferences drawn from them. Our view is that, in determining demand futility, a court must determine whether the particularized facts alleged create a reasonable *doubt* that (i) the directors are disinterested and independent, and (ii) the transaction challenged was otherwise made by a valid business judgement. An "interested" or self-dealing director transaction is deemed to create demand futility. The mere threat of personal liability for approving a transaction is not itself sufficient to challenge either independence or disinterestedness, unless the transaction is so prima facie egregious that director liability is substantially likely. Here, Lewis (P) claims demand futility because Fink (D) dominates and controls the Directors (D) because (i) he owns 47% of Meyer's (D) shares, which constitutes control because other shareholders are small, (ii) he "personally selected" each Director (D), (iii) the fact the Directors (D) approved Fink's (D) contract illustrates Fink's (D) domination. However, under Delaware law, such contentions do not support an inference that directors lack independence. Prior cases held that "[s]tock ownership alone, at least … less than a majority, is not sufficient proof of domination or control." *Kaplan v. Centex Corp.* (Del. Ch. 1971). Even majority ownership does not strip directors of the presumptions of independence and good faith in the demand context, absent factual allegations the directors are beholden to the controlling person through personal or other relationships. *Mayer v. Adams* (Del. 1961).

There is a strong presumption that directors' decisions were the product of their business judgement on the merits, and it is not enough to rebut that presumption to allege the director was elected at the behest of the majority shareholder(s), since this is the usual way one becomes a director. A director's independence is determined by his care, attention, and individual responsibility, not the method of his election. We conclude that, to invoke demand futility based on domination/control, plaintiffs must allege particularized facts manifesting "a direction of corporate conduct [so as to] comport with the wishes or interests of the [person] doing the controlling." We stress that the plaintiff need only allege specific facts, and need not plead evidence until after full discovery. Here, Lewis (P) has not alleged facts sufficient to support a claim of control, since the personal-selection-of-directors allegation is unsupported by facts. Lewis (P) also claims demand is futile because the Directors (D) all ratified Fink's (D) wasteful agreement, but this is conclusory, because there are no factual allegations showing why the agreement is wasteful, and the complaint may not even state a claim against the directors, considering their broad discretion to set compensation. Lewis's (P) final argument is that demand is excused because the directors are being asked to sue themselves, but this argument was rejected by other courts, because it would weaken directors' managerial powers. [Probably not the single stupidest doctrine handed down by the Delaware Supreme, but a top contender.] Denial of dismissal reversed, remanded with leave to amend complaint.

Analysis:

Aronson's broad holding is theoretically correct: demand should be excused when the complaint alleges facts showing the directors' response would not qualify for the business judgment presumption (i.e., the directors acted in bad faith, have an interest in the transaction they ratified, etc.). As the court notes, holding otherwise would make the demand requirement freely waivable, since it could be satisfied by a simple conclusory allegation that the directors tend to protect each other or colluded. However, the court's rejection of seemingly damning facts in the Lewis's (P) complaint here seems to set an impossibly high bar for what the court will accept as evidence rebutting business judgment.

■ CASE VOCABULARY

DEMAND FUTILITY: In derivative suits, allegation that demanding the board file the suit would be futile, usually because the directors themselves participated in the wrongdoing. If demand is deemed futile, it is not required, and the shareholder may institute derivative suit without permission from the board.

STRIKE SUIT: Derivative suit brought by shareholder to create a nuisance or force managerial policy with the threat of litigation.

In re Oracle Corp. Derivative Litigation

(*Corporation*) v. (*Directors*)

824 A.2d 917 (Del. Ch. 2003)

DIRECTORS WITH INDIRECT PERSONAL OR PROFESSIONAL TIES TO ACCUSED WRONGDOERS ARE NOT INDEPENDENT DECISIONMAKERS

■ **INSTANT FACTS** Oracle shareholders filed a derivative suit against Oracle directors, which an Oracle special litigation committee sought to dismiss.

■ **BLACK LETTER RULE** A director's independence turns on whether the director is, for any substantial reason, incapable of making a decision with only the best interests of the corporation in mind.

■ PROCEDURAL BASIS

Chancery court consideration of a motion to dismiss.

■ FACTS

Oracle shareholders (P) brought a shareholder derivative suit against four Oracle board members (the "Trading Defendants") for insider trading. In response, Oracle formed a special litigation committee (SLC) to determine whether the company should act on the shareholders' complaint. The SLC was made up of two Stanford University professors, Grundfest and Garcia–Molina, who participated in the investigation.

After conducting a thorough investigation, the SLC issued a lengthy report recommending that Oracle not act on the complaint and moved to dismiss. In discovery, the derivative plaintiffs learned of material ties between Oracle, the Trading Defendants, and Stanford University, which were not disclosed in the SLC's report. First, one of the Trading Defendants, Michael Boskin (D), was a Stanford professor and Grundfest's former teacher as a Ph.D. candidate. While Boskin (D) was not Grundfest's advisor, the two remained in contact and spoke occasionally on matters of public policy. Moreover, both were senior fellows serving as committee members at the Stanford Institute of Economic Policy Research (SIEPR). Next, another Trading Defendant, Lucas (D), was a loyal Stanford alumnus, making significant financial contributions to the Law School and SIEPR. Finally, Oracle's CEO, Ellison (D), was one of the nation's wealthiest men, making considerable charitable contributions to Stanford, including an endowment for a graduate interdisciplinary studies program.

In filing its motion to dismiss, the SLC had the burden of demonstrating its independence from Oracle and the Trading Defendants. It offered that, even assuming the connections with Stanford University, none of the Trading Defendants were in a position to affect Grundfest's and Garcia–Molina's tenured positions, either directly or through Stanford University. Such economically inconsequential relationships could not make them non-independent.

■ ISSUE

Did the SLC establish its independence from the Oracle board and its directors?

■ DECISION AND RATIONALE

(Strine, Vice Ch.). No. A director's independence turns on whether the director is, for any substantial reason, incapable of making a decision with only the best interests of the corporation in mind. Because the ties between the SLC, the Trading Defendants, and Stanford University are so strong, the SLC has not proven its independence. Not only did Grundfest and Garcia–Molina have the difficult decision whether to press insider trader claims against fellow board members, but there was the complicating factor that Boskin (D) was a fellow professor. The mere possibility that the three may encounter one another in an academic setting calls their partiality into question. Grundfest was nearly certain to encounter Boskin (D), as they serve together on the SIEPR committee and share an academic past. An understanding of human nature instructs that Grundfest and Garcia–Molina are more likely than not to unintentionally view the facts in his favor. Likewise, a recommendation to pursue the claims against Lucas (D) would require Grundfest to accuse the SIEPR Advisory Board Chair and significant contributor of wrongdoing. Certainly, both Grundfest and Garcia–Molina understand the importance of academic contributions and their value to the prestige and well-being of the institution. They would naturally consider the effect the claims would have on Lucas's (D) donations. Whether they knew the substance of his donations or not, surely such informed academics would understand the magnitude of his generosity.

As for Ellison (D), he is one of the most influential businessmen in Silicon Valley. That alone creates social awkwardness for anybody accusing him of wrongdoing. Moreover, his consideration of a sizeable endowment to Stanford University at the time Grundfest and Garcia–Molina were named to the board contributes to the question of independence. If Ellison's (D) ties with Stanford were not known before the report was issued, they should have been, because of the SLC's full and complete investigation. The SLC has not carried its burden of demonstrating independence. Motion denied.

Analysis:

Independence is a sticky concept when considering the composition of a board of directors. It would indeed be rare for an individual to serve on a board of directors without having some personal or professional relationship with other officers and directors serving on the board. Over time, service on the board breeds new relationships or animosity among board members, which undoubtedly affects one's judgment. Even placing financial interests aside, a director's true independence may always be suspect when he or she is called upon to judge the actions of fellow directors.

■ CASE VOCABULARY

DERIVATIVE ACTION: A suit by a beneficiary of a fiduciary to enforce a right belonging to the fiduciary; especially, a suit asserted by a shareholder on the corporation's behalf against a third party (usually a corporate officer) because of the corporation's failure to take some action against the third party.

Cuker v. Mikalauskas

(Shareholder) v. *(Director and Corporation)*

547 Pa. 600, 692 A.2d 1042 (1997)

PENNSYLVANIA ADOPTS PURE BUSINESS JUDGEMENT RULE ALLOWING LITIGATION COMMIT-
TEES TO DISMISS DERIVATIVE SUITS

■ **INSTANT FACTS** When a Pennsylvania utility's shareholders file derivative suits against directors for not collecting overdue bills, the litigation committee decides against suit, but it is unclear whether Pennsylvania has a business judgement rule.

■ **BLACK LETTER RULE** In Pennsylvania, directors or their litigation committee may dismiss shareholder derivative suits if they qualify for the business judgement rule, as codified by *ALI Principles of Corporate Governance §§ 7.02–7.10 and § 7.13.*

■ **PROCEDURAL BASIS**

In shareholder derivative action seeking damages, appeal from denial of defendants motion for summary judgement.

■ **FACTS**

Pennsylvania-based PECO Energy Company (D) underwent an audit, which produced a report criticizing PECO (D) for mismanaging its bill collections. Following the report, several shareholders, including Cuker (P), demanded PECO (D) authorize suit against those responsible for the losses, including some directors. PECO (D) created a litigation committee, composed of 3 new outside directors, and investigated the billing practices with the assistance of its lawyers and outside auditor. It found that, while PECO (D) often failed to terminate deadbeats' service and lost out on payments, this tactic ingratiated PECO (D) with regulators and allowed more generous rate increases. The committee concluded the practices were not in bad faith, and [surprise!] recommended no lawsuit. Thus, PECO (D) moved to dismiss Cuker's (P) derivative suit. At trial, the court denied PECO's (D) motion, holding the business judgement rule had never been applied in Pennsylvania to terminate derivative suits, and holding the rule frustrated public policy. PECO (D) sought extraordinary relief under the Pennsylvania Supreme Court's "King's Bench" powers.

■ **ISSUE**

In Pennsylvania, does the business judgement rule allow directors to terminate derivative suits?

■ **DECISION AND RATIONALE**

(Flaherty, J.) Yes. In Pennsylvania, directors or their litigation committee may dismiss shareholder derivative suits if they qualify for the business judgement rule, as codified by *ALI Principles of Corporate Governance §§ 7.02–7.10* and *§ 7.13* [i.e., if they (i) acted without fraud or self-dealing, (ii) did not exceed their authority, (iii) exercised reasonable diligence, and (iv) honestly and rationally believed their acts were in the corporation's best interests.] [We conclude Pennsylvania case law creates a business judgement rule, which permits directors of Pennsylvania corporations to terminate shareholders' derivative actions.] Ironically, this court has never used the term "business judgement rule" in corporate contexts [what other context is there?], nor has it ever explicitly adopted it, but a review of Pennsylvania decisions establishes the business judgement doctrine is the law of Pennsylvania [in other words, they just made it up yesterday].   The practical effect of our holding needs elaboration; assuming an independent board may terminate shareholder derivative actions, we need a procedural mechanism for judicial review of the board's decision.   The court should determine the validity of the board's decision to terminate litigation; if the decision was made under appropriate standards, the court should dismiss the derivative action without considering the merits.   The business judgement rule should insulate officers/directors if (i) they acted without fraud or self-dealing, (ii) their decision was within their authority, (iii) they exercised reasonable diligence, and (iv) they honestly and rationally believed their acts were in the corporation's best interests.   To make this determination, the court might stay the derivative action, or order limited discovery or evidentiary hearings to examine the board's decision.   Factors bearing on the board's decision include: (i) whether it/its litigation committee was disinterested, (ii) whether it was assisted by counsel, (iii) whether it prepared written reports, (iv) whether it was independent, (v) whether it conducted adequate investigation, and (vi) whether it acted in good faith (rationally believed its decision was in the corporation's best interests).   If all these criteria are met, the business judgement rule applies, and the court should dismiss the derivative action. These considerations and procedures are encompassed in the *ALI Principles of Corporate Governance, Part VII, Ch. 1*.   We specifically adopt *§§ 7.02–7.10* and *§ 7.13*.   These principles are largely codified in New York and Delaware, but we reject Delaware's "demand excused" cases, where courts apply their own business judgement to determine whether to honor the directors' decision to terminate litigation. Order reversed and remanded.

Analysis:

This case basically announces that Pennsylvania has adopted the "mainstream" business judgment rule for deciding whether directors may dismiss derivative suits and specifically codified parts the ALI Principles of Corporate Governance.   Apparently, the ALI's rule is not much different from the general judicial approach in New York and Delaware.   Pennsylvania's law is somewhat less generous than Delaware's, since it disallows the court to make a de novo review of the directors' motivations if demand is futile or excused.

■ CASE VOCABULARY

EXTRAORDINARY REMEDY: Remedy not generally available unless necessary to preserve rights not protected by standard remedies.   E.g., writ of mandamus (court order to compel government officer to perform required duties), writ of habeas corpus (order to bring imprisoned person to trial).

KING'S BENCH: Historically, a jurisdiction's highest law court.   Here, the King's Bench powers mentioned seem to be the Pennsylvania Supreme Court's power of judicial review.

CHAPTER TWELVE

Duty of Loyalty and Conflict of Interest

Marciano v. Nakash

Instant Facts: A corporate director loaned money to the corporation, when the corporation liquidated it sought to disclaim liability for the loan claiming that a self-interested loan from a director is voidable as a matter of law.

Black Letter Rule: A self-interested transaction between a director and a corporation is not void as a matter of law.

Heller v. Boylan

Instant Facts: A shareholder claimed that exorbitant salaries for directors amounted to corporate waste and sued to force the directors to refund the payments.

Black Letter Rule: Majority shareholders may not give away or waste corporate property without the consent of the minority.

Brehm v. Eisner

Instant Facts: Shareholders (P) sued Disney (D) after it agreed to give its president an extravagant compensation package, and then, after only 14 months, an even more extravagant severance package.

Black Letter Rule: Payment of an extravagant compensation and severance package to a corporate executive does not constitute waste unless it is so one-sided that no business person of ordinary, sound judgment could conclude that the corporation has received adequate consideration.

Brehm v. Eisner

Instant Facts: The chancery court determined that the Disney compensation committee did not breach its fiduciary duty by approving an unfavorable termination agreement.

Black Letter Rule: A director's action will not be labeled "bad faith" unless it involves an intentional dereliction of his duty or a conscious disregard for his responsibilities.

Sinclair Oil Corporation v. Levien

Instant Facts: A minority shareholder in a wholly owned subsidiary sued the parent corporation for causing the subsidiary to pay out excessive dividends and for breach of contract.

Black Letter Rule: When the transaction involves a parent and a subsidiary, with the parent controlling the transaction and fixing the terms, the test of intrinsic fairness, with its resulting shift of the burden of proof, is applied.

Weinberger v. UOP, Inc.

Instant Facts: A shareholder is suing a corporation claiming that its directors breached their duty of loyalty when they withheld information and agreed to sell the corporation too cheaply.

Black Letter Rule: A corporate director owes the same uncompromising duty of loyalty to each corporation the director serves.

Northeast Harbor Golf Club, Inc. v. Harris

Instant Facts: A country club sued one of its former directors claiming that the director's efforts to purchase and develop land adjacent to the club amounted to a breach of her fiduciary duty to refrain from taking a corporate opportunity for herself.

Marciano v. Nakash

(Corporation) v. *(Director)*
535 A.2d 400 (Del. 1987)

A SELF-INTERESTED TRANSACTION BETWEEN A DIRECTOR AND A CORPORATION WILL NOT BE VOIDED IF IT IS INTRINSICALLY FAIR TO THE CORPORATION

■ **INSTANT FACTS** A corporate director loaned money to the corporation, when the corporation liquidated it sought to disclaim liability for the loan claiming that a self-interested loan from a director is voidable as a matter of law.

■ **BLACK LETTER RULE** A self-interested transaction between a director and a corporation is not void as a matter of law.

■ **PROCEDURAL BASIS**

Appeal to Supreme Court of Delaware from Delaware Court of Chancery.

■ **FACTS**

Ari, Joe and Ralph Nakash (the Nakashes) (D) loaned $2.5 million to Gasoline, Ltd. (Gasoline). The Nakashes (D) owned fifty percent of Gasoline and the Marciano family (Marcianos) (P) owned the other fifty percent. The Marcianos (P) opposed the loan and, because of the deadlock among the board of directors, the corporation was placed in the custody of the courts and liquidated. In a liquidation proceeding before the Delaware Court of Chancery, the Marcianos (P) argued that, as a self-dealing transaction, the Nakashes' (D) loan to Gasoline should be considered void as a matter of law. The Vice Chancellor ruled that Gasoline's debt to the Nakashes (D) was valid and enforceable notwithstanding the self-dealing origin of the loan. The Marcianos (P) appealed the Vice Chancellor's ruling claiming first, that the debt was voidable as a matter of law, and second that, even if the debt was not voidable, the Nakashes (D) failed to meet their burden of establishing that the loan was fair to the corporation.

■ **ISSUE**

In the absence of shareholder ratification, is a self-interested transaction between a director and a corporation voidable as a matter of law?

■ **DECISION AND RATIONALE**

(Walsh, J.) No. The Vice Chancellor properly rejected the Marcianos (P) assertion that the Nakashes' (D) loan to Gasoline should, as a self-interested transaction, be voidable as a matter of law. A transaction between a corporate director and a corporation is not voidable simply because the transaction contains an element of self-interest. The test for whether a court will void a self-interested transaction is *intrisic fairness.* The Marcianos (P) argue that common law required a court to void a self-interested transaction as a matter of law. Additionally, the Marcianos (P) assert that self-interested transactions are voidable as a matter of law under Section 144 of Delaware General Corporation Law (144 GCL) unless it can be shown that there is a statutory exception for the transaction. [Section 144 of Delaware General Corporation Law provides that no transaction shall be voidable for reasons of self-dealing if at least one of three circumstances exist] The Marcianos (P) are however incorrect on both points. It is a common misconception that the common law required courts to find self-interested transactions void simply by virtue of the conflict of interest between the director and the corporation.

Though it is true that courts have always viewed such transactions with skepticism, historically, interested director transactions have been deemed voidable only after an examination of the fairness of the transaction as it relates to non-interested shareholders. Similarly, 144 GCL provides that a self-interested transaction shall be voidable unless the parties can demonstrate that there has been compliance with a statutory provision, such as independent shareholder ratification, which would remove the taint of self interest. The Marcianos (P) argue that, because the Nakashes (D) failed to demonstrate a statutory exception under 144 GCL, the transaction is voidable as a matter of law. Compliance with 144 GCL is not however the sole basis for avoiding the *per se* rule of voidability. Neither common law nor 144 GCL require a court to void a transaction for the simple reason that it was self-interested. There is no bright line test as to when a self-interested transaction is or is not void, rather, the court's ultimate question on the issue of voidability of self-interested transactions is one of *intrinsic fairness.* If a transaction is intrinsically fair to the corporation, it should not be voided for the simple reason that it did not comport with a narrow statutory exception; such an approach would be myopic and contrary to the corporate interest. We find therefore, that the Court of Chancery was correct when it found that the Nakashes' (D) loan to Gasoline was not voidable as a matter of law; the Court properly applied the intrinsic fairness test to the facts of this case. Affirmed.

Analysis:

The court in this case rejects the application of any simple bright line test to answer the question of when a self-interested transaction between a director and a corporation should be considered void. Such a bright line approach, suggests the court, would be both impractical and contrary to corporate interests. Rather than apply a rule of *per se* voidability, the court took a broader approach and asked whether the transaction was intrinsically fair to the corporation. If a transaction is intrinsically fair to the corporation, a court will not void the transaction simply because it is self-dealing. The intrinsic fairness test allows corporations to take advantage of business opportunities while at the same time preventing directors or other insiders from taking advantage of the corporation.

■ CASE VOCABULARY

INTRINSIC FAIRNESS: A director who enters into a self-dealing transaction has the burden of showing that the transaction is intrinsically fair to the corporation, in other words, that the terms of the transaction are fair and reasonable and that the director has not used his or her position to take advantage of the corporation.

Heller v. Boylan

(Shareholder) v. *(Director)*

29 N.Y.S.2d 653 (Sup. Ct. 1941)

MAJORITY SHAREHOLDERS MAY NOT GIVE AWAY CORPORATE ASSETS OVER THE PROTESTS OF MINORITY SHAREHOLDERS

■ **INSTANT FACTS** A shareholder claimed that exorbitant salaries for directors amounted to corporate waste and sued to force the directors to refund the payments.

■ **BLACK LETTER RULE** Majority shareholders may not give away or waste corporate property without the consent of the minority.

■ **PROCEDURAL BASIS**

Derivative action heard by the Supreme Court of New York.

■ **FACTS**

Seven minority shareholders of the American Tobacco Company (American) brought an action to recover bonus payments which had been made to the company's directors over a period of several years. Another minority shareholder, Richard Rogers, had previously challenged the bonus system and the U.S. Supreme Court had ruled in Roger's favor finding that the bonuses were so large that they constituted waste. In order to settle Roger's lawsuit, American agreed to restructure the bonus payment structure and also to pay Rogers a large fee. In a nearly unanimous vote, American's shareholders approved the restructured compensation plan. Even with the revisions to the compensation plan however, American's payments to its corporate directors remained exceedingly generous. Consequently, a new shareholder action was brought where the plaintiffs, including Heller (P), argued that the restructured compensation plan should be invalidated and American reimbursed by the directors. Heller (P) and the others argued that the settlement following Roger's court victory was not made in good faith and that the payment to Rogers constituted a bribe. Citing the U.S. Supreme Court's opinion in the earlier shareholder action, Heller (P) argued that the payments to American's directors were so large as to constitute waste. Majority shareholders, claimed Heller (P), did not have the power to give away corporate property against the protest of the minority. The Supreme Court of New York heard the case.

■ **ISSUE**

Are there limitations on how corporate directors may utilize corporate assets even if they have approval from a majority of shareholders?

■ **DECISION AND RATIONALE**

(Collins, J.) Yes. Corporate law is designed, as much as anything, to protect minority shareholders against the tyranny of the majority. The simple fact that corporate directors have the approval of a majority of shareholders does not entitle them to do as they please with corporate assets. In the earlier shareholder action initiated in response to American's generous executive compensation, the U.S. Supreme Court held that majority shareholder approval cannot be used to justify salaries which are so large that they in effect amount to "spoliation or waste of corporate property." Majority shareholders, held the Court, do not have the power to give away or waste corporate property over the objection of the minority. Bonus payments which have no relation to the value of the service rendered qualify as corporate waste. In this instance, there can be no doubt that American's payments to the directors were extraordinarily large but the question for us is not whether the payments were large but whether they amounted to corporate waste. Unfortunately, on the question of whether American's payments to its directors constituted waste, Mr. Heller (P) has not proffered any testimony or any other evidence to support his charge. Mr. Heller (P) offers only the size of the payments themselves in support of his position and, while we agree that the payments at issue are staggeringly large, they are not, on their own, evidence of waste. It should be remembered that the executive compensation plan that Mr. Heller (P) complains of, fantastic as it may be, was approved by a near unanimous vote of corporate shareholders. While this court may disagree with or even be offended by the sums advanced to American's directors, it is not this court's place to substitute its judgment for that of the corporation's shareholders. Courts are concerned that corporations be honestly and fairly operated by their directors, with the observance of the formal requirements of the law; what is reasonable compensation for directors, however, is for shareholders to decide. This is not to say that a corporate director backed by a majority of shareholders enjoys unlimited power; as fiduciaries, directors may not abuse or waste corporate assets. We simply cannot find that American's directors abused their fiduciary duties simply because they took large amounts of compensation from the corporation. While we do not approve of the sums paid to American's directors, we will not interfere the shareholders' rights to pay their directors as they see fit. Judgment for the defendants.

Analysis:

The court in this case is clearly appalled by the amount of money American paid to its directors. Yet, even while it acknowledges the excessive nature of the compensation, the court restrains itself from interfering. Shareholders should be granted broad discretion in matters related to running the corporation, states the court. Because the shareholders had approved the director's compensation in this case and there was no clear evidence that the directors had abused their roles as fiduciaries by wasting corporate assets, the court held the compensation to be lawful. While there are, no doubt, limitations on the powers of corporate directors, even those acting with the approval of their shareholders, this case makes clear that courts will be reluctant to substitute their judgment for that of shareholders absent some compelling evidence of abuse.

Brehm v. Eisner

(Shareholder) v. *(Chairman and CEO)*

746 A.2d 244 (Del. 2000)

"A BOARD'S DECISION ON EXECUTIVE COMPENSATION IS ENTITLED TO GREAT DEFERENCE": EVEN EXTRAVAGANT COMPENSATION WILL RARELY CONSTITUTE WASTE

■ **INSTANT FACTS** Shareholders (P) sued Disney (D) after it agreed to give its president an extravagant compensation package, and then, after only 14 months, an even more extravagant severance package.

■ **BLACK LETTER RULE** Payment of an extravagant compensation and severance package to a corporate executive does not constitute waste unless it is so one-sided that no business person of ordinary, sound judgment could conclude that the corporation has received adequate consideration.

■ **PROCEDURAL BASIS**

Appeal from dismissal of derivative action for breach of fiduciary duty.

■ **FACTS**

In 1995, the Walt Disney Company (Disney) (D) hired Michael Ovitz as president, according to an employment agreement that CEO Michael Eisner (D) negotiated and the 1995 Board (Old Board) (D) approved. Although Ovitz lacked experience managing a diversified public company like Disney (D), Eisner (D) and the Old Board (D) judged him valuable enough to be worth a base salary of $1 million per year plus a discretionary bonus and 5 million shares worth of stock options. The contract also included a termination contract that provided Ovitz a severance package if he left Disney (D) and it was not his fault. This severance package included a lump sum of $10 million, his remaining salary, and probable unpaid installments of his bonus. The Old Board (D) consulted a compensation expert about this contract, but he did not calculate the total cost of the severance package in the event of a non-fault termination. Problems with Ovitz's work soon surfaced, and before his first year was over Ovitz sent Eisner (D) a letter expressing his desire to leave Disney (D). A few months later Eisner (D) agreed to arrange for Ovitz to leave Disney (D) on a non-fault basis. The 1996 Board (New Board) (D) consented, and sent Ovitz a letter stating that, pursuant to their employment agreement, he would receive $38,888,230.77 plus an option to purchase 3,000,000 shares of stock. Thus, after working only 14 months, Ovitz left with a severance package worth more than $140 million. Brehm (P) and other shareholders (Shareholders) (P) sued Disney (D) and its Directors (D) for breach of fiduciary duty. Shareholders (P) claim that the Old Board (D) breached its duty by approving an employment contract with Ovitz that was so extravagant as to constitute waste, and that the New Board (D) breached its duty in consenting to a non-fault termination of this contract, triggering payment of a similarly extravagant severance package.

■ **ISSUE**

Does payment of an extravagant compensation and severance package to a corporate executive necessarily constitute waste?

■ DECISION AND RATIONALE

(Veasey, J.) No. Shareholders (P) argue that the Ovitz employment contract constituted waste ab initio because it gave Ovitz an incentive to seek an early non-fault termination, which would net him more money than working. As the Court of Chancery held, this theory does not meet the stringent requirements of the waste test. To constitute waste, a transaction must be "so one-sided that no business person of ordinary, sound judgment could conclude that the corporation has received adequate consideration." A board's decision on executive compensation is inherently a matter of business judgment and is entitled to great deference. There may be waste in unconscionable cases where directors irrationally squander or give away corporate assets. However, if the corporation receives substantial consideration, and if there is a good faith judgment that the transaction is worthwhile, there should be no finding of waste. The Court of Chancery inferred that the Old Board (D) decided that Ovitz would be valuable to Disney (D) and that it had to offer an expensive compensation package to attract him. The Court also found that the vesting schedule of the options was a disincentive for Ovitz to leave Disney (D). Shareholders (P) argue that the Old Board (D) did not exercise "substantive due care." However, with respect to business judgments, courts look only at process due care. Shareholders (P) argue that the Old Board (D) failed to properly inform itself about the costs of the employment contract, particularly the severance package. As the Court of Chancery held, the standard for judging the informational component of the directors' decisionmaking does not require them to be informed of every fact, but only to consider material facts that are reasonably available. Certainly the total cost of the Ovitz contract was material and reasonably available. However, the fact that the Old Board's (D) expert did not quantify the potential severance benefits to Ovitz for terminating on a non-fault basis does not create a reasonable inference that the Old Board (D) failed to consider this potential cost. Even if the Old Board (D) did fail to calculate this cost, this allegation fails to create a reasonable doubt that the Old Board (D) failed to exercise due care. The Old Board (D) is presumed to have exercised its business judgment in deciding whether to approve the employment contract. It is the essence of the business judgment rule that the court will not apply 20/20 hindsight to second guess a board's decision, except in rare cases in which the decision is so egregious on its face that it cannot meet the test of business judgment. The Old Board's (D) reliance on a compensation expert and that expert's decision to not fully calculate the amount of the severance package do not rise to the level of such egregiousness. If a board is fully informed about the manner in which a severance payout would be calculated, it fulfills its duty of care, even if it does not know the exact amount of a severance payout. A board is not required to be informed about every fact, but only to be reasonably informed. The Old Board (D) is also entitled to the business judgment presumption with respect to its good faith reliance on its compensation expert. Further, this compensation expert is presumed to be an expert on whom the Old Board (D) was entitled to rely to be "fully protected" under *Del. G.C.L. § 141(e)* [directors are "fully protected" in relying in good faith on experts they have selected with reasonable care]. To survive a motion to dismiss, Shareholders (P) must allege particularized facts that, if proved, would rebut these presumptions. For example, Shareholders (P) might show that the Old Board (D) did not actually rely on the expert; that its reliance was not in good faith; that it did not reasonably believe the expert's advice was within his sphere of competence; that it did not select the expert with reasonable care; that material and reasonably available information was so obvious that its failure to consider it was grossly negligent regardless of expert advice; or that its decision was so unconscionable as to constitute waste or fraud. Shareholders (P) also argue that the New Board's (D) approval of the severance package constituted waste because the sum was so large and because Disney (D) actually owed Ovitz nothing, either because he really resigned or because he was clearly subject to termination for cause. The New Board (D) is presumed to have exercised its business judgment in deciding whether Ovitz actually resigned or breached his contract. Shareholders (P) did not allege facts sufficient to prove gross negligence or malfeasance, which would be necessary to show that Ovitz was subject to termination for cause. Shareholders (P) also fail to meet the waste test here because they did not allege with particularity facts showing that no business person would have decided these matters as the New Board (D) did. Affirmed.

Analysis:

As generous as many executive compensation packages are, some argue that corporate pay is not generally a big shareholder issue. Shareholders may find the value of the executives worth the money, and pay them well because they do not want to lose them. Executive compensation is an investment for the shareholders, and as great as that investment may be, they might find the return on their investment far greater. How much compensation a particular individual is worth to a company is a business judgment, and courts are therefore reluctant to interfere.

■ CASE VOCABULARY

AB INITIO: From the beginning.

Brehm v. Eisner

(Shareholder) v. *(Disney CEO)*
906 A.2d 27 (Del. 2006)

THE DUTY TO EXERCISE DUE CARE AND THE DUTY OF GOOD FAITH ARE DISTINCT

■ **INSTANT FACTS** The chancery court determined that the Disney compensation committee did not breach its fiduciary duty by approving an unfavorable termination agreement.

■ **BLACK LETTER RULE** A director's action will not be labeled "bad faith" unless it involves an intentional dereliction of his duty or a conscious disregard for his responsibilities.

■ **PROCEDURAL BASIS**

On appeal to review the chancery court's judgment for the defendants.

■ **FACTS**

After Disney shareholders filed a shareholder derivative suit against the company's board for waste and breach of fiduciary duty, the Delaware Supreme Court found that the board did not waste corporate funds and remanded the case. On remand, the chancery court determined that, although the board failed to follow best practices, it breached no duty in approving the terms of the Ovitz termination.

■ **ISSUE**

Did the chancery court err in deciding that the board sufficiently knew the financial consequences of its approval of the termination provisions of the employment agreement and in determining that the directors acted with due care and not in bad faith?

■ **DECISION AND RATIONALE**

(Jacobs, J.) No. A director's action will not be labeled "bad faith" unless it involves an intentional dereliction of his duty or a conscious disregard for his responsibilities. First, the chancery court concluded that the compensation committee members had been informed of the financial consequences of Ovitz's no-fault termination when it approved his contract. The committee members were informed of the possible size of the termination package by virtue of similar benchmark options that were similarly granted to other directors. Additionally, the members understood that the termination package was calculated to compensate Ovitz for his lost commissions that would have reasonably accrued in his former job should his position at Disney not work out. Based on these two sources of information, the members were sufficiently informed to make a reasoned business decision.

Second, the chancery court concluded that, because the members' decisions were not made in bad faith, the business judgment rule protects them from any liability. In so ruling, the chancery court defined "bad faith" as an "intentional dereliction of duty, a conscious disregard for one's responsibilities." While the duty of good faith is important in corporate governance, little precedent exists to define its scope.

The duty of good faith concerns three categories of fiduciary behavior potentially labeled as bad faith. The first is "subjective bad faith," which is conduct motivated by the actor's actual intent to cause harm. Because the case involves no allegations of intent to harm, no discussion of this category is necessary.

The second category involves a lack of due care, such as fiduciary conduct that involves gross negligence, but no malevolent intent. Although the chancery court correctly determined that the members engaged in no gross negligence, it bears discussing whether such conduct can constitute bad faith. The duty to exercise due care and the duty of good faith are two distinct principles. This is illustrated in the Delaware statutes. First, Delaware statutes allow corporations to exculpate directors from damages for a breach of the duty of care, but specifically exclude "acts or omissions not in good faith" from the exculpatory power. Second, Delaware's indemnification statute permits a corporation to indemnify persons for liability for damages if they acted in good faith and in the best interests of the corporation. These statutes recognize that conduct amounting to gross negligence is entitled to certain corporate protections, while bad faith is not. Accordingly, grossly negligent conduct, while evincing a breach of the duty of due care, is insufficient to establish bad faith.

Finally, the third category of conduct—intentional dereliction of duty, a conscious disregard for one's responsibilities—*does* constitute bad faith. Whether or not such intentional misconduct is disloyal to the corporation, it is more culpable than gross negligence and necessitates sufficient protection of the corporate interests thereby threatened. Moreover, Delaware law suggests that conscious disregard—actions that surpass gross negligence but do not rise to the level of intentional—is likewise included in the class of conduct that is ineligible for corporate exculpation and indemnification. Accordingly, the Chancellor's definition of fiduciary bad faith is correct.

Lastly, the shareholders (P) claim that even if the members' decisions were protected by the business judgment rule, their payment of the severance amount constituted corporate waste. To constitute waste, the plaintiffs must prove that the payment was "so one sided that no business person of ordinary, sound judgment could conclude that the corporation has received adequate consideration." Waste occurs only in the rare occasions when directors have squandered or given away corporate assets. Here, the corporation was under a contractual obligation to pay the severance package upon Ovitz's termination. It cannot be said that they were wasteful, unless the contractual agreement itself was wasteful, which was determined *not* to be the case. Simply put, the members had a rational business purpose for approving the agreement and paying Ovitz's severance package. Affirmed.

Analysis:

The notion that an intentional omission to act or a conscious disregard of a director's duties constitutes bad faith is not a new legal principle. Many courts consider an intentional blind eye when action should be taken as damaging as intentionally harmful actions. Yet, a conscious disregard for one's duties generally fell within corporate exculpatory and indemnity clauses and subjected directors to no liability. This decision opens the door for director liability when they should reasonably act, but neglect to do so.

■ CASE VOCABULARY

FIDUCIARY: One who owes to another the duties of good faith, trust, confidence, and candor.

Sinclair Oil Corporation v. Levien

(Parent Company) v. *(Subsidiary's Shareholder)*
280 A.2d 717 (Del. 1971)

WHEN A PARENT COMPANY ENGAGES IN SELF-DEALING WITH ITS SUBSIDIARY, THE PARENT HAS THE BURDEN OF PROVING THE INTRINSIC FAIRNESS OF THE CHALLENGED TRANSACTION

■ **INSTANT FACTS** A minority shareholder in a wholly owned subsidiary sued the parent corporation for causing the subsidiary to pay out excessive dividends and for breach of contract.

■ **BLACK LETTER RULE** When the transaction involves a parent and a subsidiary, with the parent controlling the transaction and fixing the terms, the test of intrinsic fairness, with its resulting shift of the burden of proof, is applied.

■ **PROCEDURAL BASIS**

Appeal from an order of the Court of Chancery, requiring a parent company to account for damages sustained by its subsidiary as a result of excessive dividends paid by the subsidiary, and a breach of contract between the parent and the subsidiary.

■ **FACTS**

Levien (P), a shareholder of Sinclair Venezuelan Oil Company (Sinven), brought a derivative action against Sinclair Oil Corporation (Sinclair) (D), owner of 97% of Sinven's stock. Levien (P) alleging that Sinclair (D) caused Sinven to pay excessive dividends, denied Sinven opportunities to develop and expand, and breached a requirements contract with Sinven. As a parent company, Sinclair (D) nominated the members of Sinven's board of directors, all of whom were directors or employees of Sinclair (D). For a period of six years Sinven paid out dividends that exceeded earnings in the amount of $38,000,000. Levien (P) claimed that the dividends were paid in order to infuse Sinclair (D) with cash. Levien (P) also claimed that Sinclair (D)'s policy of pursuing development through other subsidiaries denied Sinven any opportunity to expand its operations. Levien's (P) final claim stemmed from a requirements contract between Sinven and International, one of the Sinclair (D) subsidiaries. Levien (P) alleged that International breached the contract by consistently being late on payments and by purchasing less oil than the contract's minimum.

■ **ISSUE**

Should challenged transactions between a parent company and its subsidiary be tested by the business judgment rule?

■ **DECISION AND RATIONALE**

(Wolcott, C.J.) No. When the transaction involves a parent and a subsidiary, with the parent controlling the transaction and fixing the terms, the test of intrinsic fairness, with its resulting shift of the burden of proof, is applied. A parent does owe a fiduciary duty to its subsidiary when there are parent-subsidiary dealings. However, this alone will not invoke the intrinsic fairness standard. This standard will be applied only when the fiduciary duty is accompanied by self-dealing—the situation where a parent is on both sides of the transaction. Self-dealing occurs when the parent, by virtue of its domination of the subsidiary causes the subsidiary to act in such a way that the parent receives something from the subsidiary to the exclusion and detriment of the minority stockholders of the subsidiary. Applying this rule to the facts we find that the excessive payment of dividends did not involve self-dealing because both, Sinclair (D) and the minority shareholders received a proportionate share. Thus, the business judgment rule should have applied, and Sinclair's (D) motives are immaterial, unless the payments amounted to waste. As to the claim of denied expansion, Levien (P) has not pointed to any particular opportunities that were presented to Sinven, and usurped by Sinclair (D). Sinclair (D) was under no duty to actively seek expansion opportunities for Sinven. We do find, however, the contract between International and Sinven was self-dealing. Sinclair (D), through its subsidiary, received the products but failed to comply with the terms of the contract, all to the detriment of Sinven's minority shareholders. As a result, Sinclair (D) was required to prove that the contract was intrinsically fair. This, it failed to do. Affirmed in part and reversed in part.

Analysis:

This opinion provides an overview of the fiduciary duty owed by a controlling shareholder (or parent company) to the corporation and minority shareholders. The court first notes that a parent company owes a fiduciary duty to its subsidiary *when there are parent-subsidiary dealings.* The court then goes on to hold that this limited duty is breached when self-dealing occurs, i.e., when the parent stands on both sides of the transaction and there is a disproportionate transfer of assets in favor of the parent. Without self-dealing, any parent-subsidiary transaction is subject to business-judgment protection. According to the court, the major consequence of self-dealing is not that the transaction is voided, but that the parent or subsidiary's board of directors must prove that the transaction was intrinsically fair to the minority shareholders.

Weinberger v. UOP, Inc.

(Shareholder) v. *(Corporation)*

457 A.2d 701 (Del. 1983)

A CORPORATE DIRECTOR OWES AN EQUAL DUTY OF LOYALTY TO EACH CORPORATION ON WHOSE BOARD THE DIRECTOR SITS

■ **INSTANT FACTS** A shareholder is suing a corporation claiming that its directors breached their duty of loyalty when they withheld information and agreed to sell the corporation too cheaply.

■ **BLACK LETTER RULE** A corporate director owes the same uncompromising duty of loyalty to each corporation the director serves.

■ **PROCEDURAL BASIS**

Appeal to Delaware Supreme Court from Court of Chancery's judgment that defendant did not breach its duty of loyalty to the plaintiff.

■ **FACTS**

Mr. Weinberger (P), a minority shareholder in UOP, Inc. (UOP) (D) sued UOP (D) and Signal Companies, Inc. (Signal) alleging that certain directors of Signal and UOP (D) had not acted in the best interests of UOP's (D) minority shareholders when they negotiated an offer for Signal to purchase UOP (D). The deal that Mr. Weinberger (P) complained of had its origins in an earlier deal where Signal purchased 50.5 percent of UOP's (D) stock. As a majority shareholder, Signal placed seven directors on UOP's (D) thirteen-member board of directors. Several of the directors Signal placed on UOP's (D) board were also directors of Signal. After it had purchased its majority stake in UOP (D) and placed it directors on UOP's (D) board, Signal decided to investigate the possibility of purchasing the remaining shares in the company. Signal appointed several of it directors who were also concurrently serving as directors of UOP (D) to study the feasibility of a Signal buyout of UOP (D). After conducting their study, the directors advised Signal's senior management that it would be a good investment for Signal to purchase the remaining shares of UOP (D) at any price of up to $24 a share. Signal's senior management considered the findings of their colleagues study and concluded that an offer of $20 to $21 a share for the remaining shares in UOP (D) would be a fair and reasonable offer for both parties and also in keeping with Signal's fiduciary obligations to UOP. The Signal senior management then proposed the $20 to $21 a share offer to UOP's (D) directors who immediately agreed that it was a fair price. The negotiations that followed Signal's initial suggestion that $20 to $21 a share would be a fair price for UOP's (D) shares could be described as cursory at best: Lehman Brothers rendered a hastily crafted ''fairness opinion'' which concluded that the offer price was indeed fair and there was some discussion of assurances being given to key UOP (D) personnel in order to maintain stability at the company. At no point did the parties discuss the possibility of an offer above $21 a share. The UOP (D) shareholders were told that Signal and UOP (D) had arrived at the $21 a share price after ''discussions'' but they were never informed of the hurried method by which Lehman Brothers reached its fairness opinion. Most significantly, Signal never revealed to UOP (D) the results of the feasibility study which concluded that the purchase of UOP (D) shares at any price up to $24 would still represent good value for Signal. Consequently, UOP (D) shareholders approved the sale of their shares to Signal at a price of $21 a share. Soon after, Mr. Weinberger (P) sued to rescind the sale claiming that the terms of the sale were not fair. The trial court found in favor of Signal and Mr. Weinberger (P) appealed.

■ ISSUE

Does a person who serves as a director of more than one corporation owe an equal duty of loyalty to each corporation?

■ DECISION AND RATIONALE

(Moore, J.)   Yes.   A director who sits on the board of more than one corporation owes the same uncompromising duty of loyalty to each corporation.   A corporate director's uncompromising duty of loyalty requires the director to deal with the corporation with complete candor.   The corporate director may not withhold knowledge from the corporation nor may the director refrain from doing something which might deprive the corporation of a profit or advantage.   Corporate directors who sit on both sides of a transaction are required to demonstrate their utmost good faith and to act in the best interest of each corporation.   In this instance, it is clear that the Signal directors who also sat on the board of UOP (D) breached their duty of loyalty to UOP (D).   As dual directors, the directors were required to deal with each of the corporations on whose boards they sat with complete candor.   Rather than dealing with each corporation with complete candor however, the dual Signal/UOP (D) directors withheld information from UOP (D) to the benefit of Signal.   Though the dual directors were aware that Signal considered a price of $24 a share for UOP (D) to be a good investment, they did not share this critical information with UOP's (D) outside directors.   Neither did the dual directors reveal to UOP (D) the hurried circumstances under which the Lehman Brothers fairness report was prepared.   It is clear from the circumstances of the transaction that the dual directors withheld knowledge to the detriment of UOP (D) and thereby breached their duty of loyalty as directors.   In many instances, it is impossible for a dual director to act in the best interest of corporations on opposite sides of a transaction.   In such circumstances, it may either be necessary to establish an independent negotiating structure or for the directors to abstain from any participation in the transaction.   Because the dual directors played an active role in this transaction however and, because they did not act in the best interest of UOP (D), a corporation on whose board they sat, this court must find the transaction was not fair to the shareholders of UOP (D).   Accordingly, the trial court is reversed.

Analysis:

Almost by definition, loyalty requires a corporate director to act with complete candor when dealing with the corporation.   As the court stated here, a director's duty of loyalty requires the director to share with the corporation any information that might be used to the corporation's profit or advantage.   Conversely, the duty of loyalty also requires a director to refrain from taking any action that might injure the corporation.   Consequently, had the dual directors in this case informed UOP (D) that Signal was willing to pay a higher price for UOP (D) than it originally offered, they would arguably have been violating their duty of loyalty to Signal.   It seems then that, by sitting on both sides of the transaction, the dual directors could not avoid violating their duty to a least one of the parties to the transaction.   Signal or UOP (D).   The court recognized this dilemma and suggested that, in order to avoid breaching their duty of loyalty to one of the corporations, the directors would have to either completely abstain from any involvement in the transaction or an independent negotiating structure would need to be developed.

■ CASE VOCABULARY

DUTY OF LOYALTY: The corporate director's duty of loyalty requires the director to deal with the corporation with complete candor, to refrain from doing anything which would harm to the corporation or would deprive the corporation of an advantage or profit.

Northeast Harbor Golf Club, Inc. v. Harris

(Corporation) v. *(Former Director)*

661 A.2d 1146 (Me. 1995)

DIRECTORS AND OFFICERS ARE PROHIBITED FROM USURPING FOR THEMSELVES A BUSINESS OPPORTUNITY THAT RIGHTFULLY BELONGS TO THE CORPORATION

■ **INSTANT FACTS** A country club sued one of its former directors claiming that the director's efforts to purchase and develop land adjacent to the club amounted to a breach of her fiduciary duty to refrain from taking a corporate opportunity for herself.

■ **BLACK LETTER RULE** A director must make a full disclosure prior to taking advantage of any corporate opportunity, and failure to do so is a per se breach of the director's fiduciary duty.

■ **PROCEDURAL BASIS**

Appeal to the Supreme Judicial Court of Maine challenging the trial court's finding that no breach of a fiduciary duty had occurred.

■ **FACTS**

Nancy Harris (D) was president of the Northeast Harbor Golf Club (Club) (P) from 1971 to 1990, when she was asked to resign. In 1979, Harris (D) was informed by a listing agent that property adjacent to the Club (P) was up for sale. The agent testified that he contacted Harris (D) because he thought the club might be interested in buying the property to prevent development. Harris (D) did not disclose this to members of the Club's (P) board. Instead, Harris (D) purchased the property on her own behalf. Harris (D) later disclosed her purchase to the board, but told the board members that she did not plan to develop the property. In 1984, while playing golf with the postmaster, Harris (D) learned that another parcel adjacent to the Club (P) might be available for purchase. After making the necessary inquiries, Harris (D) also purchased this parcel. Harris (D) formally disclosed this purchase at a 1985 board meeting. Once again, Harris (D) stated she had no plans for development. But in 1988, Harris began the process of development. Harris then resigned as president. After an unsuccessful challenge to the subdivision, the Club (P) instituted this law suit claiming Harris breached her fiduciary duty by purchasing the lots without providing notice and an opportunity for the Club (P) to purchase the property. The trial court found Harris (D) did not usurp a corporate opportunity because real estate was not in the Club's (P) line of business, and the Club (P) lacked the financial ability to purchase the real estate.

■ **ISSUE**

Does the corporate opportunity doctrine require a director or officer to disclose only those business opportunities that are in the corporation's line of business and that the corporation is financial able to undertake?

■ **DECISION AND RATIONALE**

(Roberts, J.) No. This case requires us to define the scope of the corporate opportunity doctrine in Maine. Various courts have embraced different versions of the corporate opportunity doctrine. The trial court adopted the "line of business" test, which defines a corporate opportunity as any business opportunity which the corporation is financially able to undertake and is in the line of the corporation's business, such that the self-interest of the director or officer is will be brought into conflict with the corporation. The problem with this formulation is that is suffers from two major weaknesses. First, as this case points out, the question of what is the corporation's line of business may prove difficult to answer. Here, the Golf Club (P) was in the business of running a golf course, but there is no doubt that the club had a significant interest in preventing development around the golf course. A second weakness inherent in the "line of business" test is its focus on the corporation's financial ability to undertake the opportunity. Reliance on this factor will cause officers and directors to refrain from solving financial difficulties in favor of the corporation. Other courts have developed a "fairness test" which requires an application of ethical standards to the facts of the case. The uncertainty involved with this type of inquiry is patent, for it provides no guidance to directors and officers who are seeking to measure their obligations. A third test has sought to combine these two tests. Under that approach the court first determines whether the opportunity was within the corporation's line of business, and then scrutinizes the equitable considerations surrounding the case. This third approach merely piles the uncertainty of the fairness test on top of the weaknesses of the line of business test. We choose instead to adopt the version adopted by the American Law Institute (ALI).

The ALI approach first requires the corporation to prove that the opportunity is a corporate opportunity by showing: 1) That the opportunity was offered to the director or officer in his official capacity under circumstances which should reasonably lead him to believe that the offeror expects the opportunity to be offered to the corporation; 2) the director became aware of the opportunity through the use of corporate information or property, if the opportunity is one that the director should believe is of interest to the corporation; or 3) that the senior executive knows the opportunity is closely related to a business in which the corporation is engaged or expects to engage. After showing that the opportunity is a corporate opportunity, the corporation must show that it was either not offered the opportunity by the director, or the corporation did not properly reject the offer. If the offer was not properly rejected, the director may defend on the basis that the taking of the opportunity was fair to the corporation. If the director did not disclose the opportunity, the director has violated her fiduciary duty and may not defend in any case. This disclosure oriented approach provides a clear procedure whereby a corporate officer may insulate herself from a legal challenge by making a full disclosure. Since we have adopted a new legal standard, fairness demands that we remand for a new trial so the parties may have an opportunity to adequately develop the record.

Analysis:

The ALI version of the corporate opportunity doctrine differs in several respects from those approaches adopted by other courts, all of which the Maine court rejects here. The first major difference lies in the efforts to define "corporate opportunity." The line of business test, the fairness test, and the hybrid approach take a subjective approach by scrutinizing the substance of the opportunity. The ALI approach on the other hand, focuses on an objective evaluation of the director or officer's conduct, knowledge, and state of mind: If the director or officer becomes aware of the opportunity in his capacity or through the use of corporate property and he should reasonably know that the corporation has an interest in the opportunity, then it is a "corporate opportunity." The ALI approach also differs with respect to what is required of a director or officer who is confronted with a corporate opportunity. Basically, he is under an absolute duty to disclose it. Any failure to do so constitutes a breach of his duty of loyalty under the ALI approach. Under the other approaches disclosure is merely a factor in determining whether the director or officer breached his duty.

CHAPTER THIRTEEN

Transactions in Shares: Rule 10b–5, Insider Trading and Securities Fraud

In re Enron Corporation Securities, Derivative & Erisa Litigation

Instant Facts: A group of investors who purchased Enron stock between October 1998 and November 2001 filed a class action lawsuit against certain sellers and promoters of the stock, alleging that they had engaged in fraud and deceit with respect to the sale and promotion of the stock.

Black Letter Rule: In a lawsuit over alleged securities laws violations, a complaint which alleges that more than on defendant participated in a scheme to defraud must allege with specificity a primary violation of § 10(b) by each defendant.

Securities and Exchange Comm'n v. Texas Gulf Sulphur Co.

Instant Facts: Several officers and other employees of Texas Gulf Sulphur Co. (D1) purchased the company's stock and accepted stock options after learning of a very rich ore discovery no one else was informed of.

Black Letter Rule: 1) Under Rule 10B–5, before trading in securities affected by material inside information, persons in possession of the material inside information must disclose it in a manner sufficient to insure its availability to the investing public. 2) Members of a corporation's top management must disclose material insider information to the officials issuing stock options before accepting those options.

Chiarella v. United States

Instant Facts: An employee of a financial printing company appealed a criminal conviction for having violated § 10(b) of the Securities Exchange Act of 1934 by trading in the stock of several companies that were to be acquired, on the basis of information about the impending acquisitions he had learned from merger announcement documents.

Black Letter Rule: Under § 10(b) of the Securities Exchange Act of 1934, a duty to disclose material nonpublic corporate information or abstain from trading in the stock of the corporation which is the subject of that information requires a fiduciary relationship with the corporation that is the subject of the stock trade.

United States v. O'Hagan

Instant Facts: O'Hagan (R), an attorney, was working for a law firm that was hired to represent a corporation making a tender offer for another company. O'Hagan (R) discovered the impending tender offer through his employment with the firm and used the information to profit in the stock market.

Black Letter Rule: 1) One who uses misappropriated, nonpublic, material information, in breach of a fiduciary duty to the information's source, in order to profit from securities transactions is in violation of § 10(b) and SEC Rule 10b–5. 2) The SEC, under § 14(e), may prohibit any act, not itself fraudulent under the common law or § 10(b), so long as the prohibition is reasonably designed to prevent acts and practices that are fraudulent, including the prohibition of trading on undisclosed information in the tender offer setting, even absent a duty to disclose.

Dirks v. Securities and Exchange Commission

Instant Facts: An investment analyst appealed his administrative censure for allegedly violating SEC Rule 10b–5 by disclosing material nonpublic information about fraudulent activity at an insurance company which he learned from corporate insiders at the insurance company to his investor clients, who sold their stock in the insurance company before the information became public.

Black Letter Rule: A person receiving a stock tip from a corporate insider violates SEC Rule 10b–5 when the corporate insider has breached his fiduciary duty to the corporation's shareholders by tipping information for his own personal benefit and the person receiving the tip knows or should know that the tip was a breach of the corporate insider's fiduciary duty.

United States v. Chestman

Instant Facts: Stockbroker Chestman (R) received confidential information about a pending sale of a corporation from a client whose relative controlled the corporation. Chestman (P) used this information to make profitable stock trades on his own and his clients' behalf.

Black Letter Rule: In order to be liable for insider trading under the misappropriation theory there must be a fiduciary relationship or similar relationship of trust and confidence between the information's source and the person appropriating the information.

Basic, Inc. v. Levinson

Instant Facts: Basic, Inc. (D) issued three public statements disclaiming what in fact were its ongoing merger talks with another corporation. Several shareholders sold the company's stock in reliance on the statement and now sue Basic, Inc. (D) under Rule 10b–5.

Black Letter Rule: 1) The standard of materiality applicable under Rule 10b–5 in preliminary merger discussions is that a fact is material if there is a substantial likelihood that a reasonable shareholder would consider it significant or important in deciding whether to purchase or sell securities. 2) An investor's reliance on any public misrepresentation of a material fact may be presumed for the purposes of a Rule 10b–5 lawsuit.

Mdcm Holdings, Inc. v. Credit Suisse First Boston Corporation

Instant Facts: A group of internet and other technology related companies filed a class action lawsuit alleging breach of contract and breach of fiduciary duty against the company that agreed to underwrite their initial public offerings of stock.

Black Letter Rule: The Securities Litigation Uniform Standards Act (SLUSA) provides for federal preemption of class action lawsuits which, among other things, contain allegations of misrepresentation or omission of a material fact or any manipulative or deceptive device or contrivance in connection with the purchase or sale of a covered security.

In Re Enron Corporation Securities, Derivative & ERISA Litigation

(Purchasers of Enron Stock) v. *(Sellers of Enron Stock)*

235 F.Supp.2d 549 (S.D. Tex. 2002)

SECONDARY ACTORS SUCH AS BANKS, ACCOUNTANTS, AND LAWYERS CAN BE HELD LIABLE FOR VIOLATIONS OF RULE 10b-5

■ **INSTANT FACTS** A group of investors who purchased Enron stock between October 1998 and November 2001 filed a class action lawsuit against certain sellers and promoters of the stock, alleging that they had engaged in fraud and deceit with respect to the sale and promotion of the stock.

■ **BLACK LETTER RULE** In a lawsuit over alleged securities laws violations, a complaint which alleges that more than one defendant participated in a scheme to defraud must allege with specificity a primary violation of § 10(b) by each defendant.

■ **PROCEDURAL BASIS**

A group of sellers and others involved in the sale of Enron stock filed a motion to dismiss in a Rule 10b-5 class action lawsuit filed against them.

■ **FACTS**

A group of investors (P) who purchased Enron stock between October 1998 and November 2001 filed a class action lawsuit against certain sellers and promoters (D) of the stock, claiming that they engaged in fraud and deceit with respect to the promotion of the stock. Specifically, it was asserted that these entities participated in a massive "Ponzi scheme" which involved illusory profits, illicit partnerships, violations of accounting principles and SEC rules, and the making of materially misleading financial statements for the purpose of inflating Enron's reported revenue and concealing growing debts. The complaint further contended that this was all accomplished while the corporation continued to raise money from public offerings of Enron and related securities. Finally, the complaint contended that a number of outside accountants, law firms, and banks participated in the fraudulent scheme. The complaint made the following defendant-specific allegations: (1) Banks. The purchasers (P) alleged that a number of banks participated in the scheme for the purposes of achieving personal enrichment, salvaging financial investments, and limiting exposure to risk. Specifically, it was alleged that the banks advanced funds to various Enron-created Special Purpose Entities (SPE's) at key times to allow them and Enron to complete bogus transactions just prior to year or quarter-end, in order to create fake profits and to conceal billions in unreported debt. The Plaintiffs further alleged that the banks (D) made loans to a financially-fragile Enron to ensure its liquidity and continued operation, while simultaneously assisting in the sale of securities to public investors so that Enron could continue to pay down its short-term debt and keep the scheme afloat.

The banks (D) also assisted in the inflation of Enron stock by issuing misleading financial reports. For the most part, the charges against the banks (D) involved cookie-cutter contentions unique only to a few Defendants. The complaint did, however, include specific allegations against CitiGroup (D). It asserted that CitiGroup (D) enjoyed large underwriting and other fees, interest, and commitment charges, and that some of its executives were permitted to invest in one of the fraudulent SPE's for very lucrative returns. It alleged that CitiGroup (D) participated in the scheme by making over $4 billion in loans to Enron, by helping Enron raise over $2 billion through the sale of securities, by assisting Enron in structuring and financing some of the illicit partnerships or SPE's used to inflate earnings and conceal debt, and by engaging in disguised loans to Enron that allowed the corporation to falsify its financial situation. It was alleged that CitiGroup (D) also made misleading statements in both the Registration Statements and Prospectuses for Enron securities and in other financial documents. (2) Law Firms. The complaint alleged that Vinson & Elkins (V&E), Enron's outside general counsel, also participated in the fraudulent scheme. It alleged that V&E (D) participated in writing and reviewing Enron's SEC filings, shareholder reports, and other financial statements, and in the creation of nearly all of the illicit SPE's and other illicit partnerships with knowledge that they were manipulative devices designed to move debt off of Enron's books, inflate earnings, and falsify financial reports. V&E (D) also allegedly provided false true sale and other opinions that were critical in the continuation of the scheme. Finally, the complaint alleged that V&E (D) disregarded a clear conflict of interest and assisted Enron in covering-up allegations of fraud that V&E (D) knew to be true. (3) Accountants/Auditors. The complaint charged that Arthur Anderson (AA) (D) abandoned its responsibilities to investors and violated professional standards in perpetrating a massive accounting fraud. The complaint maintained that AA knew that the critical factor to increasing the enormous amount of fees that it was collecting from Enron was to maintain Enron's investment-grade credit rating, which required a careful balance between creating outside entities to hold assets and the debt Enron was incurring to finance them and making it appear that Enron was not controlling these entities to avoid consolidation of their assets and debts into Enron's financial statements. The complaint also alleged that AA (D) operated its consulting services in a manner that revealed its lack of independence in audits and reviews, and that AA was aware of the excessive use of complicated partnerships, many with no business purpose other than to conceal debt and losses, and offshore tax haven entities. Finally, the complaint alleged that AA (D) knew about yet covered up or ignored numerous fraudulent accounting practices.

■ ISSUE

Will a complaint which contains only general allegations of fraud and deceit in the promotion and sale of securities survive a motion to dismiss?

■ DECISION AND RATIONALE

(Harmon, J.) No. In *Central Bank of Denver, N.A. v. First Interstate Bank of Denver, N.A.*, the Supreme Court held that while § 10(b) and Rule 10b-5 do not permit private plaintiffs to bring aiding and abetting claims against those who give aid to parties who commit § 10(b) violations, secondary actors such as lawyers, accountants, and banks are not immune from liability. It wrote: "Any person . . . who employs a manipulative device or makes a material misstatement (or omission) on which a purchaser or seller of securities relies may be liable as a primary violator under 10b-5 [if] all of the requirements for primary liability . . . are met." The SEC's proposed rule for primary liability of a secondary party requires that the secondary party "act with the requisite scienter;" the SEC has further determined that the party need not be "the initiator of a misrepresentation in order to be a primary violator." In short, to survive a motion to dismiss, a complaint which alleges that more than one defendant participated in a scheme to defraud must allege a primary violation of § 10(b) by each defendant. Defendants (D) have objected to the plaintiffs' use of boiler-plate allegations repetitively applied to each defendant, but rather than focus on deficiencies in the complaint, the Court examines what the plaintiffs have specifically pled against each defendant so as to determine whether it adequately states a claim with specificity and raises an inference of the requisite scienter necessary to survive a motion to dismiss. As a factor common to all, the Court initially finds that the scienter pleading requirement is partially satisfied by allegations of a regular pattern of repeated conduct involving the creation of unlawful Enron-controlled SPE's and the sale of unwanted Enron assets to these entities in non-arm's length transactions in order to shift debt off Enron's balance sheet and sham profits onto its books at critical times, often followed by the undoing of the deals once the reports were made.

These transactions were deliberate, repeated actions with shared characteristics that were part of an alleged common scheme through which Defendants all profited. The very pattern that is alleged undermines claims of unintentional or negligent behavior and supports allegations of intent to defraud. Similarly, conclusory allegations asserted against all or most of the secondary actor defendants, such as the long-term and extensive relationships with Enron and daily interaction with its executives, open access to nonpublic information, and involvement in formulating and funding key aspects of Enron's business, raise the specter of opportunities to learn about and take an active role in Enron's financial affairs. Defendants (D) have further complained that they are being targeted for performing the normal functions of their businesses. Regular business conduct within the bounds of the law would not support a claim of a securities law violation; instead the allegations must demonstrate that they knowingly or with reckless disregard stepped outside the bounds of legitimate activities in performing fraudulent acts. Viewing the specific allegations together, the Court finds that the plaintiffs have stated a claim against CitiGroup (D) because it knowingly or with severe recklessness engaged in a course of conduct that operated as a fraud upon Enron investors. With respect to Vinson & Elkins (V&E) (D), the complaint alleges that it participated in a plan in which it made material misrepresentations or omissions, employed a scheme to defraud, or engaged in a course of conduct that operated as a fraud in order to establish and perpetuate a scheme that made it rich. Among the complaint's specific allegations of acts in furtherance of the scheme are the firm's involvement in negotiation and structuring of illicit partnerships and off-the-books SPE's, whose formation documents it drafted.

Had V&E (D) remained silent publicly, the attorney/client relationship might protect it from liability to non-clients, but the complaint goes into great detail to demonstrate that V&E (D) did not remain silent, but chose to make public statements about Enron's financial situation. V&E (D) was essentially a co-author of the documents it created for public consumption, and it deliberately or with severe recklessness directed those public statements toward investors in order to influence investors to purchase more securities, credit agencies to keep Enron's credit high, and banks to continue providing loans to keep the scheme afloat. Therefore, V&E (D) had a duty to be truthful, and plaintiffs have alleged numerous inadequate disclosures by V&E (D) that breached that duty. For these reasons, the plaintiffs' have stated a claim under § 10(b) against V&E (D). Finally, the plaintiffs have alleged specific facts that give rise to a strong inference of scienter with respect to Arthur Anderson (AA) (D). AA's (D) comprehensive accounting, auditing, and consulting services to Enron necessarily made it intimately privy to the smallest details of Enron's alleged fraudulent activity. Plaintiffs have described several similar prior fraudulent audits of other companies, establishing a pattern of such conduct. Plaintiffs have also alleged details of a February 2001 meeting of senior AA (D) partners in which they discussed material concerns at the heart of the complaint and decided to continue doing business with Enron because that business was so lucrative. In the weeks following that meeting, AA (D) issued a clean audit opinion on the 2000 financial statements. Moreover, the plaintiffs have described e-mails and other memoranda that reflect AA's (D) knowledge and intent to continue in the fraudulent scheme. Because the plaintiffs have alleged numerous violations of generally accepted accounting principles and have pleaded facts giving rise to a strong inference of scienter, they have pleaded a securities fraud claim against AA (D). The defendants' motion to dismiss is denied.

Analysis:

In *Central Bank of Denver, N.A. v. First Interstate Bank of Denver,* decided in 1994, the United States Supreme Court held that "[t]he absence of § 10(b) aiding and abetting liability does not mean that secondary actors in the securities markets are always free from liability under the securities acts. Any person or entity, including a lawyer, accountant, or bank, who employs a manipulative device or makes a material misstatement (or omission) on which a purchaser or seller of securities relies may be liable as a primary violator under Rule 10b-5, assuming all of the requirements for primary liability under Rule 10b-5 are met." The present case, *In Re Enron Corporation*, is one of the first post-*Central Bank of Denver* cases to address the liability of secondary actors such as those listed by the Supreme Court. As the general nature of the court's opinion makes apparent, whether a secondary actor can be held liable for a violation of Rule 10b-5 is a fact-specific determination. As such, each case will have to be looked at individually to determine whether the requirement of scienter has been pled with respect to each and every named defendant. The *Enron* opinion is important because it shows what types of facts are relevant in determining whether a complaint claiming primary liability for secondary actors is sufficient, and it can therefore serve as a guide for future cases.

■ CASE VOCABULARY

DEBT SECURITY: A security such as a bond or a note which represents money borrowed from the holder of the security.

EQUITY SECURITY: A security such as a share of stock which represents an ownership interest in a corporation.

PONZI SCHEME: A fraudulent investment scheme in which financial contributions by later investors are used to create artificially high dividends for early investors for the purpose of attracting additional investments to further the scheme.

SCIENTER: Knowingly or with intent to defraud.

Securities and Exchange Comm'n v. Texas Gulf Sulphur Co.

(Federal Government) v. *(Mining Company)*

401 F.2d 833 (2d Cir. 1968)

THOSE POSSESSING MATERIAL INSIDE INFORMATION MUST RELEASE IT TO THE PUBLIC BEFORE TRADING OR REFRAIN FROM TRADING

■ **INSTANT FACTS** Several officers and other employees of Texas Gulf Sulphur Co. (D1) purchased the company's stock and accepted stock options after learning of a very rich ore discovery about which no one else was informed.

■ **BLACK LETTER RULE** 1) Under *Rule 10B-5*, before trading in securities affected by material inside information, persons in possession of the material inside information must disclose it in a manner sufficient to insure its availability to the investing public. 2) Members of a corporation's top management must disclose material insider information to the officials issuing stock options before accepting those options.

■ **PROCEDURAL BASIS**

Appeal to the Federal Circuit Court of Appeals from a ruling by the Federal District Court dismissing the suit after holding the inside information was not material.

■ **FACTS**

Texas Gulf Sulphur Co. (TGS) (D1) conducted mineral explorations in Canada. These explorations led to the discovery of very rich copper, zinc, and silver deposits. The people who discovered the deposits are Mollison (D2), a mining engineer and a vice president of TGS (D1), Holyk (D3), the chief geologist, Clayton (D4), an electrical engineer and geophysicist, and Darke (D5), a geologist (the aforementioned individual defendants make up the exploration group). In order to secure the rights to mine these minerals, TGS (D1) sought to purchase the land the deposits were found on or secure the mining rights for the land. To this end, Stephens (D6), one of TGS' (D1) vice presidents, instructed the exploration group to keep the discovery confidential. Additional defendants are Kline (D7) and Fogarty (D8), both upper-level executive managers at TGS (D1). In the period between the exploratory drilling, November 12, 1963, and the resumption of drilling at the site, March 31, 1964, certain of the individual defendants and persons said to have received "tips" from them, purchased TGS stock or calls thereon. Prior to these transactions these persons had owned 1135 shares and possessed no calls; thereafter they owned 8235 shares and possessed 12,300 calls. On February 20, 1964, also during this period, TGS (D1) issued stock options to 26 of its officers and employees, five of whom were the individual defendants Stephens (D6), Fogarty (D8), Mollison (D2), Holyk (D3), and Kline (D7). Only Kline (D7) was unaware of the detailed results of the test drilling made to confirm the deposits, but he, too, knew that the results were very favorable. At this time, neither the TGS (D1) Stock Option Committee nor the Board of Directors knew of the favorable results of the exploration, presumably because of the pending land acquisition program that required confidentiality. All of the defendants accepted the options granted them. [As all of this was going on, rumors leaked out that TGS (D1) had made a major mineral discovery. TGS (D1) issued a press release downplaying the explorations, but issued another release four days later admitting the import of the discovery.] As the process continued TGS stock rose steadily from 17 3/8 on November 8, 1963, when drilling began to 58 ¼ on May 15, 1964, one month after the announcement regarding the discovery. [Additional defendants are Crawford (D9) and Coates

(D10), apparently recipients of the insider tips.] Crawford's (D9) purchase of TGS stock was ordered about midnight on April 15, 1964, and again at 8:30 a.m. on April 16, just before the second press release later that morning.

■ ISSUE

1) May individuals in possession of material inside information act on that information by trading in securities affected by the information before the information has been effectively disseminated to the investing public? 2) May a corporation's top management accept stock options from the corporation without first informing those administering the option plan of material inside information unknown to that administration?

■ DECISION AND RATIONALE

(Waterman, Cir. J.) 1) No. 2) No. *Rule 10b-5* was promulgated to prevent inequitable and unfair practices and to generally insure fairness in security transactions. The *Rule* is based in policy on the justifiable expectation of the securities marketplace that all investors trading on impersonal exchanges have relatively equal access to material information. While the *Rule* obviously applies to insiders who are directors or managers, it also applies to persons possessing the information who may not be strictly termed an "insider." Thus, anyone in possession of material inside information must either disclose it to the investing public, or abstain from trading in or recommending the securities concerned while such inside information remains undisclosed, no matter the reason for it remaining undisclosed. We turn now to the question of whether the information at issue was material information. We believe it was. An insider is not always precluded from trading in his own company merely because he knows more than outsiders. The duty to disclose information or abstain from trading arises only in those situations which are essentially extraordinary in nature and which are reasonably certain to have substantial effect on the market price of the security if the situation is disclosed. The only regulatory objective is that access to material information be enjoyed equally, but this objective requires nothing more than the disclosure of basic facts so that outsiders may draw upon their own expertise in making their own decisions with knowledge equal to that of the insiders. Our survey of the facts shows that knowledge of the mineral discovery would have been important to a reasonable investor and might have affected the stock price. A major factor in making this determination is the importance attached to the drilling results by those who knew about it. The timing of the stock and short-term call purchases by those in the know—in some cases individuals who had never before purchased TGS calls or even stock— virtually compels the inference that the insiders were influenced by the drilling results. This is highly pertinent evidence and the only truly objective evidence of the materiality of the discovery. Some shout that our decision here today may have the effect of depleting the ranks of capable corporate managers by taking away an incentive to accept such employment.

The incentive though is, in essence, a form of secret corporate compensation derived at the expense of the uninformed investing public. Moreover, properly administered stock option and employee purchase plans already can provide adequate incentives for managers. In any event, the normal motivation induced by stock ownership, i.e. the identification of an individual with corporate progress, is ill promoted by the sort of insider activity found here. At the core of *Rule 10b-5* is the idea that all investors should have equal access to the rewards of participating in securities transactions and be subject to identical market risks. The insiders here were not trading on an equal footing with outside investors. Only they could invest safely, knowing that if the discovery panned out their stock would rise, and if it did not pan out the price of TGS stock would stay about the same. We hold, therefore, that all transactions in TGS stock or calls by individuals apprised of the drilling results were made in violation of *Rule 10b-5,* as were purchases by individuals who were told by Darke (D5) that TGS stock was a "good buy." By "tipping" these individuals on the outlook for TGS stock, Darke (D5) violated *Rule 10b-5(3).* Because the lower court ruled the information non-material, we remand for an appropriate remedy with respect to these "tippees." The next issue is when an insider may act on material information without running afoul of the securities laws. Both Crawford (D9), who ordered the purchase of TGS stock just before the April 16 announcement, and Coates (D10), who placed orders immediately after the announcement, admit they were in possession of material information. They claim, however, that their purchases are legal because the news had already been effectively disclosed. We disagree. The disclosure that is claimed to have put Crawford (D9) and Coates (D10) in the clear are the abbreviated announcement to the Canadian press at 9:40 a.m. on the 16th by the Ontario

Minister of Mines and the report carried by The Northern Miner, parts of which had sporadically reached New York on the morning of the 16th. But these disclosures are surely not the equivalent of the official 10–15 minute announcement, which was not released to the American financial press until after 10:00 a.m. Crawford's (D9) orders had been placed before that.

Coates' (D10) order was placed at 10:20 a.m. on April 16, after the announcement had been made even though the news could not be considered already a matter of public information. Neither of these purchases comports with the requirement that before insiders may act upon material information, such information must have been effectively disclosed in a manner sufficient to insure its availability to the investing public. Crawford (D9) clearly jumped the gun, and at a minimum Coates (D10) should have waited until the news could reasonably have been expected to appear over the media of widest circulation, the Dow Jones broad tape, rather than hastening to insure an advantage to himself. The final issue is whether the acceptance of stock options by insiders Fogarty (D8), Mollison (D2), Holyk (D3), and Kline (D7), without any of them informing the Stock Options Committee of the material information, violates securities laws. The stock options in question were accepted on February 20, 1964. The trial court held that Kline (D7) had no detailed knowledge of the discovery and that Holyk (D3) and Mollison (D2) could reasonably assume that their superiors, Stephens (D6) and Fogarty (D8), who were directors of the corporation, would report the results if that was advisable. Therefore, the trial court concluded, only Stephens (D6) and Fogarty (D8), of the top management, would have violated the *Rule* by accepting stock options without disclosure, but they did not because the information was held to be non-material. In light of our holding that the information was material, we also hold that Stephens (D6) and Fogarty (D8) violated the *Rule* by accepting the options. Also, contrary to the ruling of the trial court that Kline (D7) had no duty to disclose before accepting the options, we believe that he, a vice president, who had become the general counsel of TGS (D1) in January 1964, was a member of top management and under a duty before accepting his option to disclose any material information he may have possessed. Because this did not occur, we direct rescission of the option Kline (D7) received. With respect to Holyk's (D3) and Mollison's (D2) acceptance of options, their cases have not been appealed and we leave the ruling below as to them undisturbed. Affirmed in part, reversed in part and remanded.

■ CONCURRENCE

(Friendly, Cir. J.) The novel problem in this case is to define the responsibility of officers when a directors' committee running a stock option plan proposes of its own initiative to make options available to them and others at a time when they know that the option price did not reflect a substantial price increase likely to be realized in short order and was therefore unfair to the corporation. To require a minor officer to reject an option so tendered would not comport with the realities either of human nature or of corporate life. If the SEC (P) had appealed the ruling dismissing this portion of the complaint as to Holyk (D3) and Mollison (D2), I would have upheld the dismissal entered below. These two were entitled to believe that their superiors had reported the facts to the option committee unless they had information to the contrary. Stephens (D6), Fogarty (D8), and Kline (D7) stand on a different basis; as senior officers they had a duty to inform the Options Committee that this was not the correct time to grant options at 95% of the current price. The corporate need for secrecy does not excuse their failure. A recommendation from the President, the Executive Vice President, and the Vice President and General Counsel to postpone the plan would not normally be questioned by non-management directors, such as those on the committee. Also, it should be possible for communication to occur between these people without a breach of confidentiality. Hence, I am not at all sure that a company in the position of TGS (D1) might not have a claim against top officers who've failed to disclose such information for the entire damage suffered as a result of the untimely issuance of options, rather than the mere remedy of rescission of the options issued to them.

Analysis:

Before modern day securities laws were passed, the common law provided the means for redress of claims of fraud in securities transactions. Under the common law of fraud and deceit, an individual claiming that corporate officials took unfair advantage of inside information could institute legal action. The first element of a fraud and deceit claim is a false or misleading statement of material fact. But in an insider trading case, the complaint is that a statement was not made to inform the investing public. Thus, the argument is that the silence, alone, is fraud. Traditionally, courts have relied on the principle of caveat emptor—let the buyer beware—in dealing with claims of silence equaling fraud. Things have changed, however, so that in recent times many jurisdictions have allowed claims of fraud predicated upon silence in several different situations. Among these is a situation in which a defendant knows facts of which the plaintiff is unaware and custom has placed a duty to inform upon the defendant.

■ CASE VOCABULARY

CALL: An option to purchase a security at a previously fixed price regardless of its current trading price.

MATERIAL: Important, significant, or essential to an issue.

OPTION: The right to purchase or sell certain securities or other assets at a previously fixed price for a fixed period of time.

RESCISSION: The unilateral disposal or cancellation of a contract that restores the parties to their previous, pre-contract positions.

Chiarella v. United States

(Financial Printer) v. *(Federal Government)*

445 U.S. 222, 100 S.Ct. 1108 (1980)

U.S. SUPREME COURT REJECTS SECOND CIRCUIT'S EQUAL ACCESS THEORY AND NARROWS THE "DISCLOSE OR ABSTAIN" RULE

■ **INSTANT FACTS** An employee of a financial printing company appealed a criminal conviction under § 10(b) of the Securities Exchange Act of 1934 which was based on his buying and selling stocks on the basis of information about impending corporate acquisitions that he had learned from merger announcement documents.

■ **BLACK LETTER RULE** Under § 10(b) of the Securities Exchange Act of 1934, a duty to disclose material nonpublic corporate information or abstain from trading in the stock of the corporation which is the subject of that information arises only when there exists a fiduciary relationship with the corporation that is the subject of the stock trade.

■ **PROCEDURAL BASIS**

Appeal following a grant of certiorari by the U.S. Supreme Court of a federal appeals court's affirmance of a criminal conviction based upon violations of § 10(b) of the Securities Exchange Act of 1934 and SEC Rule 10b-5.

■ **FACTS**

Vincent Chiarella ("Chiarella") (D) worked as a financial printer for a company that was often hired by major corporations to print announcements of their mergers. When merger announcements were sent to the printer by the acquiring companies, the identities of the acquiring and target companies were left blank, to be filled in by the printer just before the final printing was to be done. Chiarella (D), however, was able to deduce the names of the companies from other information contained in the documents. Without disclosing his knowledge of the impending deals, Chiarella (D) bought stock in the target companies he had identified and then sold the stock immediately after the mergers were announced, realizing a sizeable profit. The Securities and Exchange Commission ("SEC") investigated Chiarella's (D) trading activities and Chiarella subsequently entered into a consent decree with the SEC in which he agreed to give up all of his trading profits. He also lost his job with the printing company. The United States Attorney (P) ultimately indicted Chiarella (D) for violating § 10(b) of the Securities Exchange Act of 1934 [legislation enabling the SEC to regulate the use of manipulative and deceptive devices in connection with purchase or sale of securities] and SEC Rule 10b-5 [regulation making it unlawful to defraud or deceive a person in connection with the purchase or sale of securities]. The trial court instructed the jury that Chiarella (D) should be found guilty if he traded on the basis of material nonpublic information, knowing that the other people trading in the market did not have access to the same confidential information. The jury convicted Chiarella (D) and the Second Circuit Court of Appeals affirmed his conviction. Chiarella (D) appealed to the U.S. Supreme Court, which granted certiorari.

■ **ISSUE**

Does a duty to disclose material nonpublic corporate information or abstain from trading in the stock of the corporation which is the subject of that information arise under § 10(b) of the Securities Exchange

Act of 1934 without the existence of a fiduciary relationship between the person trading and the corporation that is the subject of the stock trade?

■ DECISION AND RATIONALE

(Powell, J.)   No.   The trial court instructed the jury to convict Chiarella (D) if it found that he willfully failed to inform sellers of target company stock that he knew of an impending takeover bid that would make their shares more valuable.   Chiarella (D) was not a corporate insider and he received no confidential information from the target company in whose stock he traded.   At common law, one who fails to disclose material information prior to the consummation of a transaction commits fraud only when he is under a duty to disclose.   That duty arises because of a fiduciary or other similar relation of trust and confidence between the parties.   Chiarella's trades on the basis of information about the acquiring company was not fraud under § 10 of the Securities Exchange Act of 1934, unless he was subject to an affirmative duty to disclose the information before trading.   The trial court's instructions failed to specify any such duty.   In effect, the court instructed the jury that Chiarella (D) owed a duty to everyone; to all sellers and the market as a whole.   The lower court ruling rested on the belief that the federal securities laws have created a system of equal access to investment information and that the use by anyone of material information that is not generally available is fraudulent because it gives certain buyers and sellers unfair advantages in the market.   Not every instance of financial unfairness, however, constitutes fraudulent activity under § 10(b).   Moreover, the element required to make silence fraudulent, a duty to disclose, is absent in this case.   There can be no fraud absent a duty to speak.   Here, no duty could arise from Chiarella's relationship with the sellers of the target companies' stock because Chiarella (D) had no prior relationship with them.   He was not their agent, fiduciary, or anyone in whom those sellers had placed their trust.   He was a stranger dealing with them only through impersonal market transactions.   We cannot affirm the conviction here without finding a general duty for all market participants to forgo trading on material nonpublic information.   Formulation of such a broad duty would depart from established doctrine that duty arises from a specific relationship between two parties and should not be undertaken in the absence of some evidence of explicit congressional intent.   Neither Congress nor the SEC has ever adopted a rule of equal access to information.   We hold that a duty to disclose does not arise from the mere possession of nonpublic market information.   The United States (P) has offered an alternative theory to support the conviction, arguing that Chiarella (D) breached a duty to the acquiring corporations when he acted on information he obtained through his position as an employee of a printer employed by the acquiring corporations.   We need not decide whether such a theory has merit because it was never submitted to the jury and thus we will not speculate as to whether such a duty exists.   Reversed.

■ DISSENT

(Burger, C.J.)   I would read § 10(b) and Rule 10b-5 to mean that a person who has misappropriated material nonpublic information has an absolute duty to disclose that information or refrain from trading.   The majority leaves this issue open, apparently concluding that this theory of the case was not submitted to the jury.   I believe that the jury instructions did properly charge a violation of § 10(b) and Rule 10b-5.   By their terms, those provisions reach any person engaged in any fraudulent scheme.   This broad language negates the majority's suggestion that congressional concern was limited to trading by corporate insiders or to deceptive practices related to information obtained from within the corporation.   The antifraud provisions were designed to assure that dealing in securities is fair and without undue advantages among investors.   An investor who purchases stock on the basis of misappropriated nonpublic information possesses such an undue trading advantage.   His conduct clearly serves no useful function except his own enrichment at the expense of others.   Chiarella (D) stole valuable nonpublic information entrusted to him in confidence and then exploited his ill-gotten informational advantage by buying stock in the market.   I would affirm the conviction.

■ DISSENT

(Blackmun, J.) Although I agree with much of what The Chief Justice says in Part I of his dissenting opinion, I feel it is unnecessary to rest Chiarella's (D) conviction on a "misappropriation" theory.   I would find Chiarella's (D) conduct fraudulent within the meaning of § 10(b) and Rule 10b-5, even if his employers had given him permission to use the merger information to make money in the stock market. It matters not whether Chiarella (D) did or did not get such permission;   his brand of manipulative trading lies close to the heart of what the securities laws are intended to prohibit. The new requirement of a fiduciary relationship carved out by the Court here today finds no mandate in the language of the statute or its legislative history. Yet the Court fails even to attempt a justification of its ruling in terms of the securities laws, or to square that ruling with the long-standing principle that the securities laws are to be construed flexibly rather than with narrow technicality. Chiarella's (D) conduct fits squarely within the meaning of the Rule. He occupied a relationship to the takeover companies giving him intimate access to material information—information intended to be available only for a corporate purpose and not for the personal benefit of anyone. Chiarella (D) took virtually riskless advantage by selling the stocks right after the takeovers were announced. By any definition, this trading was inherently unfair. This misuse of confidential information was clearly placed before the jury and Chiarella's (D) conviction should stand.

Analysis:

In this case, Justice Powell and Chief Justice Burger set the stage for a lively debate among the justices that continued in several subsequent cases regarding the scope of the duty to disclose material nonpublic information about a corporation under § 10(b) and Rule 10b-5 or abstain from trading in that corporation's stock. Justice Powell's opinion narrowed the scope of the Second Circuit's reading of Rule 10b-5 by finding that in order for a "disclose or abstain" duty to apply, there must be some kind of fiduciary relationship between the person possessing the material nonpublic information and the corporation that is the subject of the information and the stock trading. Since Chiarella (D) had no fiduciary relationship with the target corporations whose stock he was buying and selling, the majority believed that there was no basis to impose a "disclose or abstain" duty upon him. In dissent, Chief Justice Burger adopted what has since come to be known as "misappropriation theory," arguing that a "disclose or abstain" duty should apply to anyone who "misappropriates" (steals) nonpublic information, regardless of a fiduciary relationship.

■ CASE VOCABULARY

JURY INSTRUCTIONS: The directions given by a trial judge to the jury regarding how they should apply the law to the facts of the case. The jury is required to follow the statement of the law the judge gives to them.

United States v. O'Hagan

(Federal Government) v. *(Attorney-Investor)*

521 U.S. 642, 117 S.Ct. 2199 (1997)

RULE 10b-5 PROSCRIBES THE USE OF MISAPPROPRIATED MATERIAL NONPUBLIC INFORMATION FOR SECURITIES TRADING

■ **INSTANT FACTS** O'Hagan (R), an attorney, was working for a law firm that was hired to represent a corporation making a tender offer for another company. O'Hagan (R) discovered the impending tender offer through his employment with the firm and used the information to profit in the stock market.

■ **BLACK LETTER RULE** 1) One who uses misappropriated, nonpublic, material information, in breach of a fiduciary duty to the information's source, in order to profit from securities transactions, is in violation of § 10(b) and SEC Rule 10b-5. 2) The SEC, under § 14(e), may prohibit any act, not itself fraudulent under the common law or § 10(b), so long as the prohibition is reasonably designed to prevent acts and practices that are fraudulent, including the prohibition of trading on undisclosed information in the tender offer setting, even absent a duty to disclose.

■ **PROCEDURAL BASIS**

Appeal to the U.S. Supreme Court of the Circuit Court of Appeals' reversal of numerous district court convictions.

■ **FACTS**

James Herman O'Hagan (R) was a partner in the law firm of Dorsey & Whitney (Dorsey) in Minneapolis, MN. Dorsey was retained by Grand Metropolitan PLC (Grand Met) in July 1988 as local counsel for a potential tender offer for the stock of the Pillsbury Company. Both Grand Met and Dorsey took precautions to protect the confidentiality of Grand Met's plans. O'Hagan (R) did not do any work on the tender offer. Dorsey's representation of Grand Met ended on September 9, 1988 and less than a month later, on October 4, 1988, Grand Met announced its tender offer for Pillsbury stock. On August 18, 1988, O'Hagan (R) started to purchase call options for Pillsbury stock and continued to buy options until, by the end of September he held 2,500 options, apparently more than any other single investor. In addition, O'Hagan (R) purchased some 5,000 shares of Pillsbury stock for just under $39 per share during this period. After the tender offer was announced Pillsbury stock rose to nearly $60 a share. O'Hagan (R) sold his options and stock for a profit in excess of $4.3 million. A Securities and Exchange Commission (SEC) (P) investigation into O'Hagan's (R) transactions culminated in a 57 count indictment alleging that O'Hagan (R) defrauded his firm and its client, Grand Met, by using for his own trading purposes material, nonpublic information about the planned tender offer. O'Hagan (R) was charged with 20 counts of mail fraud; 17 counts of securities fraud, in violation of § 10(b) of the Securities and Exchange Act of 1934, and SEC Rule 10b-5; 17 counts of fraudulent trading in connection with a tender offer, in violation of § 14(e) of the Exchange Act and SEC Rule 14e-3; and 3 counts of violating federal money laundering statutes. [In other words, they threw the book at him.] A jury convicted O'Hagan (R) on all counts and he was sentenced to 41 months in prison [probably club fed]. The Eighth Circuit Court of Appeals reversed all of the convictions because, it held, liability under Rule 10b-5 may not be grounded on the "misappropriation theory" on which the prosecution relied.

The Court also held that Rule 14e-3, which prohibits trading while in possession of material, nonpublic information relating to a tender offer, exceeds the SEC's (P) § 14e rulemaking authority because the rule contains no requirement for breach of fiduciary duty.

■ ISSUE

1) Is it a violation of § 10(b) and SEC Rule 10b-5 for a person to trade in securities for profit, using confidential information misappropriated in breach of a fiduciary duty to the information's source? 2) Was the SEC (P) properly within its authority when it adopted Rule 14e-3 proscribing the trading on undisclosed information in the tender offer setting, even when there is no duty to disclose?

■ DECISION AND RATIONALE

(Ginsburg, J.) 1) Yes. 2) Yes. First we address the reversal of O'Hagan's (R) convictions under § 10(b) and Rule 10b-5. We hold that criminal liability under § 10(b) may be predicated on the misappropriation theory. Section 10(b) of the Exchange Act proscribes (1) using any deceptive device (2) in connection with the purchase or sale of securities. This provision does not define its coverage to deception of a purchaser or seller of securities. Rather, it reaches any deceptive device used "in connection with the purchase or sale of any security." Under the "traditional" or "classical" theory, § 10(b) and Rule 10b-5 are violated when a corporate insider trades in the securities of his corporation on the basis of material, nonpublic information. Such trading qualifies as a "deceptive device" under § 10(b), because a relationship of trust and confidence exists between the shareholders of a corporation and those insiders who have obtained confidential information by reason of their position with that corporation. The "misappropriation theory" holds that a person commits fraud "in connection with" a securities transaction, and thereby violates § 10(b) and Rule 10b-5, when he misappropriates confidential information for securities trading purposes, in breach of a duty owed to the source of the information. The theory thus premises liability on a fiduciary-turned-trader's deception of those who entrusted him with access to confidential information, rather than on the fiduciary relationship between company insider and purchaser or seller of the company's stock. The misappropriation theory is therefore designed to protect the integrity of the markets against abuses by 'outsiders' to a corporation who have access to confidential information that will affect the corporation's security price when revealed, but who owe no fiduciary or other duty to that corporation's shareholders. Misappropriation, as just defined, satisfies § 10(b)'s requirement that chargeable conduct involve a "deceptive device or contrivance" used "in connection with" the purchase or sale of securities. First, misappropriators deal in deception by pretending loyalty to the principal while secretly converting the principal's information for personal gain—by "duping" or defrauding the principal.

The confidential information taken is property to which the company has a right of exclusive use, and the misappropriation of which is similar to embezzlement, which is the fraudulent appropriation to one's own use of the money or goods entrusted to one's care by another. Our holding is consistent with our previous decision in *Santa Fe Industries, Inc. v. Green* underscoring that § 10(b) is not an all purpose breach of fiduciary duty ban; rather, it trains on conduct involving manipulation or deception. Therefore, full disclosure as to the source of the information by the would-be misappropriator forecloses liability under the misappropriation theory. We turn next to the § 10(b) requirement that the deceptive use of the information be "in connection with the purchase or sale of a security." This element is satisfied because the fiduciary's fraud is consummated, not when the fiduciary gains the confidential information, but when, without disclosure to his principal, he uses the information to purchase or sell securities. The securities transaction and the breach of duty thus coincide. This is so even though the person or entity defrauded is not the other party to the trade, but is, instead, the source of the nonpublic information. The dissent's charge that the misappropriation theory is incoherent because information, like funds, can be put to multiple uses misses the point. The point is that when such information is capitalized on through its use in securities transactions, § 10(b) is violated. Other uses will not fail under the ambit of § 10(b) because they do not get at the purpose of § 10(b), to insure honest securities markets and promote investor confidence. In sum, the misappropriation at issue here was properly made the subject of a § 10(b) charge because it meets the statutory requirement that there be "deceptive" conduct "in connection with" securities transactions. Vital to our decision approving the misappropriation theory, we emphasize, are two sturdy safeguards Congress has provided regarding scienter. To establish a criminal violation of Rule 10b-5, the Government must prove that a person "willfully" violated the provision. Furthermore, a defendant may not be imprisoned for violating Rule 10b-5 if he proves that he had no knowledge of the rule.

O'Hagan's (R) charge that the misappropriation theory is too indefinite to permit the imposition of criminal liability thus fails because the theory is limited to those who breach a recognized duty, and because of the requirement of culpable intent. We next consider whether the SEC (P), as the Court of Appeals held, exceed its rulemaking authority under § 14(e) when it adopted Rule 14e-3(a) without requiring a showing that the trading at issue entailed a breach of fiduciary duty? We hold that the SEC (P) did not exceed its authority. The pertinent provision of § 14(e) of the Exchange Act reads: "It shall be unlawful for any person . . . to engage in any fraudulent, deceptive, or manipulative acts or practices, in connection with any tender offer. The SEC (P) shall, for the purposes of this subsection, by rules and regulations define, and prescribe means reasonably designed to prevent, such acts and practices as are fraudulent, deceptive or manipulative." Relying on § 14(e)'s rulemaking authorization, the SEC (P), in 1980, promulgated Rule 14e-3(a), a "disclose or abstain from trading" requirement. The Rule is violated when one trades on the basis of material nonpublic information concerning a pending tender offer that he knows or has reason to know has been acquired 'directly or indirectly' from an insider of the offeror or issuer, or someone working on their behalf. The Rule creates a duty in those traders who fall within its ambit to abstain or disclose, without regard to whether the trader owes a pre-existing fiduciary duty to respect the confidentiality of the information. This Rule does not exceed the SEC's (P) powers under § 14(e). Rule 14e-3(a), as applied to cases of this genre, qualifies under § 14(e) as a "means reasonably designed to prevent" fraudulent trading on material, nonpublic information in the tender offer context. We hold that under § 14(e), the SEC (P) may prohibit acts, not themselves fraudulent under the common law or § 10(b), if the prohibition is "reasonably designed to prevent acts and practices [that] are fraudulent." We need not reexamine the Court of Appeals' reversal of O'Hagan's (R) mail fraud convictions as our reversal of the other convictions requires that we also reinstate the mail fraud convictions. Reversed and remanded.

■ CONCURRENCE AND DISSENT

(Scalia, J.) I disagree with Part II of the Court's opinion, containing its analysis of O'Hagan's (R) conviction under § 10(b) and Rule 10b-5. It does not matter whether the SEC's (P) promulgation of Rule 10b-5 is supported by the reasons that the SEC (P) has set forth because O'Hagan's (R) actions either violated § 10(b) and Rule 10b-5, or they did not—regardless of the reasons the Government (P) gave. While the Court's explanation of the scope of § 10(b) and Rule 10b-5 would be entirely reasonable in some other context, it does not seem to accord with the principle of lenity we apply to criminal statutes. In light of that principle, it seems to me that the unelaborated statutory language of § 10(b)—"to use or employ in connection with the purchase or sale of any security . . . any manipulative or deceptive device or contrivance"—must be construed to require the manipulation or deception of a party to a securities transaction.

■ CONCURRENCE AND DISSENT

(Thomas, J.) Central to the majority's holding is the need to interpret § 10(b)'s requirement that a deceptive device be "use[d] or employ[ed], in connection with the purchase or sale of any security." Because the SEC's (P) misappropriation theory fails to provide a coherent and consistent interpretation of this essential requirement for liability under § 10(b), I dissent. In particular, I cannot accept the SEC's (P) interpretation of when a deceptive device is "use[d] . . . in connection with" a securities transaction. The majority's attempts to clear the confusion up only serves to cause more confusion. I also disagree with the majority's decision to sustain O'Hagan's (R) convictions under § 14(e) and Rule 14e-3(a) regardless of whether O'Hagan (R) violated a fiduciary duty to anybody. I dissent because, while § 14(e) does allow regulations prohibiting nonfraudulent acts as a prophylactic measure against certain fraudulent acts, neither the majority nor the SEC (P) identifies any relevant underlying fraud against which Rule 14e-3(a) reasonably provides protection.

Analysis:

The Court had to make two key holdings in order to reinstate O'Hagan's (R) convictions under Rule 10b-5 in this case: (1) the Court had to find that the misappropriation of Information can equal fraud, and (2) it had to hold that the fraud was "in connection with the purchase or sale of a security." The second step is part of what caused the dissents by Justices Scalia and Thomas. The majority relied on the view that the act by which O'Hagan (R) misappropriated information was the stock purchase itself, and the fraud was therefore in connection with the purchase of a security. The first step—a finding of fraud—cannot be overlooked, however. Here, the court adopted what some have called the "sneaky theft" theory, whereby a person who has a fiduciary relationship to another either expressly or implicitly represents to the other that he will remain loyal and not misuse information entrusted to him. If the person misuses the information without disclosing the intent to do so to the owner of the information, the fiduciary has violated the express or implicit promise of loyalty, thereby defrauding the other party.

■ **CASE VOCABULARY**

TENDER OFFER: A public offer by one party to purchase a certain number or percentage of a corporation's shares at a certain price, usually over the current market value, in order to gain control over the corporation.

Dirks v. Securities and Exchange Commission

(*Investment Analyst*) v. (*Government Agency*)

463 U.S. 646, 103 S.Ct. 3255 (1983)

U.S. SUPREME COURT EXPLAINS TIPPEE LIABILITY UNDER RULE 10b-5

■ **INSTANT FACTS** An investment analyst appealed his administrative censure for allegedly violating SEC Rule 10b-5 by disclosing to his investor clients material nonpublic information about fraudulent activity at an insurance company which he learned from corporate insiders at the insurance company.

■ **BLACK LETTER RULE** A person who receives a stock tip from a corporate insider violates SEC Rule 10b-5 when the corporate insider has breached his fiduciary duty to the corporation's shareholders by tipping information for his own personal benefit and the person receiving the tip knows or should know that the giving of the tip was a breach of the corporate insider's fiduciary duty.

■ **PROCEDURAL BASIS**

Appeal to the U.S. Supreme Court of an appeals court's affirmance of an investment analyst's SEC disciplinary censure for violations of SEC rules.

■ **FACTS**

Raymond Dirks ("Dirks") (D) was an investment analyst for a brokerage company. He specialized in the analysis of insurance company stocks for institutional investors. Dirks (D) was given information by Ronald Secrist ("Secrist"), a former officer of Equity Funding, an insurance company, that the company had vastly overstated its assets and engaged in fraudulent activities. Secrist urged Dirks (D) to investigate the charges and disclose the fraud. Dirks conducted an investigation, visiting Equity Funding and interviewing several employees who corroborated the fraud charges. While neither Dirks (D) nor his brokerage firm owned or traded any Equity Funding stock, during his investigation, Dirks discussed the information he had obtained with several clients and other investment analysts who subsequently sold all of their Equity Funding stock. Dirks urged the Wall Street Journal to write a story on the alleged fraud, but the newspaper did not believe that such extensive fraud was possible and would not print the story. Over the two-week period of Dirks' investigation, Equity Funding's stock price fell sharply. Eventually, the New York Stock Exchange halted trading of the stock and California authorities impounded Equity Funding's records, uncovering direct evidence of the fraud. The Securities and Exchange Commission ("SEC") (P) then filed a complaint against Equity Funding, which went into receivership. Subsequently, the SEC (P) investigated Dirks' (D) role in the exposure of the fraud. After an administrative disciplinary hearing, the SEC (P) ruled that Dirks (D) had aided and abetted violations of Rule 10b-5 [SEC (P) regulation making it unlawful to defraud or deceive a person in connection with the purchase or sale of securities] by repeating the fraud allegations to his clients and other investors who later sold their Equity Funding stock. The SEC (P) concluded that those who receive a selective disclosure of material inside information that they know is confidential and that they know or should know came from a corporate insider must publicly disclose that information or abstain from trading. Recognizing Dirks' (D) role in bringing the fraud to light, the SEC (P) merely censured him. Dirks (D) appealed that censure to the D.C. Court of Appeals, which affirmed the SEC's (P) ruling. Dirks (D) then appealed to the U.S. Supreme Court, which granted certiorari.

■ ISSUE

Does a person receiving a stock tip from a corporate insider violate SEC Rule 10b-5 when the corporate insider has breached his fiduciary duty to the corporation's shareholders by tipping information for his own personal benefit and the person receiving the tip knows or should know that the tip was a breach of the corporate insider's fiduciary duty?

■ DECISION AND RATIONALE

(Powell, J.) Yes. The SEC (P) asserts that a tippee inherits a corporate insider's obligation to shareholders whenever he receives inside information from an insider. This position conflicts with the principle set out in *Chiarella v. United States* [holding that a "disclose or abstain" duty requires a fiduciary relationship with the corporation that is the subject of the stock trade] that only some persons, under some circumstances, will be barred from trading while in possession of material nonpublic information. We reaffirm today that a duty to disclose arises from the relationship between parties and not merely from one's ability to get information because of his position in the market. This conclusion does not mean that tippees are always free to trade on the information they have received. The need for a ban on some tippee trading is clear. Insiders are forbidden by their fiduciary relationship from personally using undisclosed corporate information to their advantage and should also be unable to give such information to an outsider for the same improper purpose of exploiting the information for their personal gain. The tippee's "disclose or abstain" duty is derivative from that of the insider. A tippee assumes a fiduciary duty to the corporation's shareholders not to trade on material nonpublic information only when the tipper/insider has breached his fiduciary duty to the shareholders by disclosing the information to the tippee and the tippee knows or should know that there has been a breach. Whether the disclosure by the insider is a breach of his fiduciary duty will depend on the purpose of the disclosure. If the insider will directly or indirectly benefit personally from the disclosure, then there is a breach. Here, we find no violation by Dirks (D). Dirks (D) was a stranger to Equity Funding, with no direct fiduciary duty to shareholders. Unless the insiders breached their fiduciary duty to the shareholders in disclosing the material nonpublic information about the fraud to Dirks (D), he breached no duty by passing the information to investors and the press. Neither Secrist nor the Equity Funding employees who told Dirks (D) of the fraud violated their duty to the shareholders by tipping off Dirks (D). The tippers received no monetary or personal benefit for revealing the secrets and were not trying to make a gift of the information to Dirks (D). The facts show they were simply out to expose the fraud at the company. With no breach of duty by the insiders, Dirks (D) can have committed no derivative breach. Reversed.

■ DISSENT

(Blackmun, J.) In disclosing the fraud information to Dirks (D), Secrist intended that Dirks (D) would disseminate the information to his clients, those clients would unload their Equity Funding stock on the market, the price would fall precipitously, and that this would trigger a reaction from the SEC (P). No one questions that Secrist could not himself have traded on the inside information to the disadvantage of uninformed shareholders and purchasers of Equity Funding stock. Secrist had a fiduciary duty to them. The majority acknowledges that Secrist could not do by proxy what he was prohibited from doing personally. But this is exactly what Secrist did. He used Dirks (D) to disseminate information to Dirks' (D) clients, knowing they would dump their stock, and thus intending to injure the purchasers of Equity Funding stock to whom Secrist had a duty to disclose. The majority says that Dirks (D) is not liable because Secrist had no improper purpose of personal gain. I disagree with this new, subjective limitation on the scope of the duty owed by insiders to shareholders. The fact that the insider himself does not benefit from the breach does not eradicate the shareholder's injury. The insider's duty is addressed not to his own motives, but to the consequences of his actions on the shareholders. Personal gain is not an element of the breach of duty. In my view, Secrist violated his duty to the Equity Funding shareholders by giving material nonpublic information to Dirks (D) with the intent to cause Dirks' (D) clients to trade on that information. Dirks (D) was thus under a duty to disclose the Information or refrain from actions he knew would lead to trading at the expense of purchasers of Equity Funding stock. I would find that Dirks (D) violated Rule 10b-5 and affirm the appeals court.

Analysis:

The SEC's (P) approach in going after Dirks (D) was to argue that anyone who obtains information from an insider picks up the insider's duty to disclose the information or refrain from trading. The Supreme Court, however, refused to accept such a blanket prohibition, finding a "disclose or abstain" duty only when the tippee was acting as an after-the-fact participant in the insider's breach of his duty to the shareholders of the corporation. Noting that an insider cannot trade on the basis of material nonpublic corporate information, the Court believed that it should also be illegal for the insider to profit indirectly by passing the information to another person for their use. Thus, under the rule established in this case, a tippee violates Rule 10b-5 when the tipper/insider breaches his fiduciary duty to the shareholders by tipping information for his own personal benefit and the tippee knows or should know that the tip was a breach of the tipper/insider's fiduciary duty.

■ CASE VOCABULARY

CENSURE: An formal and official reprimand issued against a party by an administrative agency regulating that party. In general, such reprimands are viewed as a very minor form of punishment for wrongful behavior.

INSTITUTIONAL INVESTORS: Organizations such as mutual funds, pension plans, and labor unions that are significant investors of money they are employed to manage and invest in public corporations.

RECEIVERSHIP: When a court has appointed a person to control and preserve the assets of an insolvent corporation in order to preserve those assets for the benefit of the corporation's creditors.

TIPPEE: A person who receives information (a tip) from a person who provides the information with the expectation that the tippee will trade stock based on the information provided.

TIPPER: A person who provides information (a tip) to another person with the expectation that the other person will trade stock on the basis of that information.

United States v. Chestman

(Federal Government) v. *(Stockbroker)*

947 F.2d 551 (2d Cir. 1991)

THE MISAPPROPRIATION THEORY REQUIRES THAT THERE EXIST A FIDUCIARY RELATIONSHIP
BETWEEN THE USER AND PROVIDER OF THE CONFIDENTIAL INFORMATION

■ **INSTANT FACTS** Stockbroker Chestman (R) received confidential information about a pending sale of a corporation from a client whose relative controlled the corporation. Chestman (P) used this information to make profitable stock trades on his own and his clients' behalf.

■ **BLACK LETTER RULE** In order to be liable for insider trading under the misappropriation theory there must be a fiduciary relationship or similar relationship of trust and confidence between the information's source and the person appropriating the information.

■ **PROCEDURAL BASIS**

Appeal to the Second Circuit Court of Appeals sitting en banc from the same court's reversal of 31 counts of various securities law violations.

■ **FACTS**

Ira Waldbaum was the controlling shareholder of Waldbaum, Inc. In 1986, Ira agreed to sell the corporation to A & P and told his sister, Shirley Witkin, three of his children, and a nephew of the sale, and also admonished them to keep the information confidential. Shirley nevertheless told her daughter, Susan Loeb, who in turn told her husband, Keith Loeb. Keith Loeb then phoned Robert Chestman (R), a broker used by junior members of the family, and told him that Waldbaum, Inc. was going to be sold at a "substantially higher" price than the market price. Chestman (R) knew that Susan Loeb was a granddaughter of the Waldbaums. Chestman (R) executed several purchases of Waldbaum stock both for his own account and for those of several of his customers, including Keith Loeb. Chestman (R) was indicted and convicted on 31 counts of violations of Rule 10b-5, mail fraud, violations of Rule 14e-3(a), and one count of perjury. A panel of the Second Circuit set aside the conviction in its entirety.

■ **ISSUE**

May criminal liability under Rule 10b-5 be predicated upon the misappropriation theory without a showing of a fiduciary relationship or similar relationship of trust and confidence between the source of the information and the user of the information?

■ **DECISION AND RATIONALE**

(Meskill, C.J.) No. [The first portion of Judge Meskill's majority opinion upholds Chestman's (R) conviction on the Rule 14e-3(a) counts.] Chestman's (R) Rule 10b-5 convictions were based on the misappropriation theory, which provides that one who misappropriates nonpublic information in breach of a fiduciary duty and trades on that information to his own advantage violates § 10(b) and Rule 10b-5. With respect to the shares Chestman (R) purchased on behalf of Keith Loeb, Chestman (R) was convicted of aiding and abetting Loeb's misappropriation of nonpublic information in breach of a duty

---

Loeb owed to the Waldbaum family and to his wife Susan. As to the shares Chestman (R) purchased for himself and his other clients, Chestman (R) was convicted as the "tippee" of that same misappropriated information. Therefore, the alleged misappropriator was Keith Loeb and, thus, the government (P) agrees that Chestman's (R) convictions cannot be sustained unless there was sufficient evidence to show that (1) Keith Loeb breached a duty owed to the Waldbaum family or Susan Loeb based on a fiduciary or similar relationship of trust and confidence, and (2) Chestman (R) knew that Loeb had done so. Our central inquiry is, therefore, what constitutes a fiduciary or similar relationship of trust and confidence in the context of Rule 10b-5 criminal liability? To begin we note two principles. First, a fiduciary duty cannot be imposed unilaterally by entrusting a person with confidential information. The fact that confidential information is reposed in someone, without some sort of agreement or acknowledgment from them to keep it confidential, does not create a fiduciary relationship. Second, marriage or mere kinship does not, without more, create a fiduciary relationship. Rather, the existence of a confidential relationship must be determined independently of a preexisting family relationship. In sum, more than the gratuitous reposal of a secret to another who happens to be a family member is required to establish a fiduciary or similar relationship of trust and confidence. We take the criteria for deciding whether such a relationship exists from the common law and the securities fraud precedents. Under this criteria it is clear that the relationships involved in this case were not traditional fiduciary relationships. But the misappropriation theory requires us to also consider whether there exists a relationship of trust and confidence similar to a fiduciary relationship.

A fiduciary relationship is one where one person depends on another—the fiduciary—to serve his interests. It involves dependence and influence. It also involves entrusting the fiduciary with custody over some sort of property in order to serve the beneficiary's ends and binds the fiduciary in not appropriating the property for the fiduciary's own use. The fiduciary is subject to a duty of confidentiality in the use and possession of the beneficiary's confidential information. A similar relationship of trust and confidence consequently must share these qualities. In *United States v. Reed* a member of the board of the Amax Corporation, Gordon Reed, disclosed to his son on several occasions confidential information about a proposed tender offer for Amax. The son then purchased Amax stock call options. The indictment against the son was based on the breach of a fiduciary duty to the father, Gordon Reed, and was sustained by the district court. Neither party here challenges the holding of *Reed*. To remain consistent with our interpretation of a "similar relationship of trust and confidence," however, we limit *Reed* to its essential holding: the repeated disclosure of business secrets between family members may substitute for a factual finding of dependence and influence and thereby sustain a finding of the functional equivalent of a fiduciary relationship. We note, in this regard, that *Reed* repeatedly emphasized that the father and son "frequently discussed business affairs." Here the government (P) presented only two pieces of evidence on this point. The first was that Keith was an extended member of the Waldbaum family. Second is Ira Waldbaum's testimony that he frequently discussed business with family members and that they know never to speak about business outside the family, with family defined by Ira as his three children who were involved in the business. This evidence falls short of establishing the required relationship for a fiduciary relationship. Instead, it is clear that the critical information at issue was gratuitously communicated to Keith Loeb without any semblance of influence or reliance of any sort. The evidence thus does not support a finding that Keith Loeb and the Waldbaum family shared either a fiduciary relation or its functional equivalent.

The government's (P) theory that Keith breached a fiduciary duty of confidentiality to Susan suffers from similar defects. All that was demonstrated was that Keith and Susan were married; Susan admonished Keith not to discuss the tender offer; and the two had shared and maintained confidences in the past. But their status as husband and wife does not itself establish a fiduciary relationship. Nor does the coda—"don't tell"—without the prior existence of a fiduciary relationship or an express confidentiality agreement. That leaves only the testimony that Keith and Susan had shared and maintained generic confidences before. In the absence of evidence of an explicit acceptance by Keith of a duty of confidentiality, the context of the disclosure must be looked at. Acceptance can only be implied from a pre-existing fiduciary relationship between the parties. There was insufficient evidence from which to infer an implied acceptance. The government (P), therefore, failed to offer sufficient evidence to establish the functional equivalent of a fiduciary relation. In sum, because Keith owed neither Susan nor the Waldbaum family a fiduciary duty or its functional equivalent, he did not defraud them by disclosing news of the tender offer to Chestman (R). Absent a predicate act of fraud by Keith Loeb, the alleged misappropriator, Chestman (R) could not be derivatively liable as Loeb's tippee or as an aider or abettor. Therefore, Chestman's (R) Rule 10b-5 convictions must be reversed, as must the mail fraud convictions. We affirm the Rule 14e-3(a) convictions and reverse the Rule 10b-5 and mail fraud convictions.

■ CONCURRENCE AND DISSENT

(Winter, J.) I respectfully dissent from the reversals of Chestman's (R) convictions under § 10(b) and under the mail fraud statute. The difficulty this court has in resolving the issues in this appeal stems largely from the history of the development of the law in this area. The SEC's (P) treatment of the law has been without a recognizable purpose or direction. It is therefore not surprising that disagreements exist within this court sitting en banc. Nor is it surprising that the lower courts have added a misappropriation of information doctrine to the already existing case law. One commentator has attempted to explain the Supreme Court decisions in terms of the business property rationale for banning insider trading. This rationale says that information is one of the most precious commodities in commercial markets. It is expensive to produce and has a very high risk of being stolen for someone else's profit. Where the profit from any activity, including information gathering, is likely to be diverted, investment in that activity will decline. If the law fails to protect property rights in commercial information, therefore, less will be invested in generating such information. Insider trading may reduce the return on information in two ways. First, it creates incentives for insiders to generate or disclose information that may disregard the welfare of the corporation. That risk is not implicated in this case and will not be discussed further. Second, insider trading creates a risk that information will be prematurely disclosed by such trading, and the corporation will lose part or all of its property in that information. Although trades by an insider may rarely affect market price, it is the risk that others will notice the insider trading and piggyback on it that may end up affecting the market price of a corporation and possibly tipping people as to the nature of the inside information. Once the information is public knowledge it loses its value to those who gathered it. Too much of this and the information will cease to be gathered and accrued. While this analysis provides a policy rationale for prohibiting insider trading when property rights in information are violated by traders, the rationale stops short of prohibiting all trading on material nonpublic information.

Efficient markets depend on protection of property rights in information, but they also require that those who legitimately acquire information be able to profit from it. A rule commanding equal access would remove the profit motive in gathering independent information and would result in a market governed by relative degrees of ignorance. The pricing of securities would thus be less accurate. This may be why the Supreme Court stopped short of barring all trading on material nonpublic information. The misappropriation theory fits within this rationale because it involves the misuse of confidential information in a way that risks making information public in a fashion similar to trading by corporate insiders. When this analysis is applied to a family-controlled corporation, I believe the family members who have benefitted from the family's control are under a duty not to disclose confidential corporate information that comes to them in the ordinary course of family affairs. After all, it is inevitable that normal familial interactions will lead to the revelation of confidential corporate matters to various family members. Keith Loeb learned of the pending acquisition through precisely such interactions. His wife Susan told him of the development and admonished him not to leak the information because the family stood to make a lot of money on the deal. Susan Loeb indicated that she and Keith had shared confidences in the past and that on each such occasion they had indicated to each other that the confidences would be respected. Thereafter, Keith Loeb told Chestman (R) about the A & P acquisition in the hope of making a profit. I have little difficulty in concluding that Chestman's (R) convictions can be affirmed on either the *Dirks* breach of fiduciary duty rule or the misappropriation theory. The disclosure here was a result of ordinary familial communications that can be expected in the case of a family controlled corporation. Members of such a family have a duty not to disclose, based on a mutual understanding among the family members, owed to the family, the corporation, and the corporation's public shareholders. Because trading on inside information so acquired by family members is theft, the misappropriation theory also applies. Under the majority's theory, the disclosure of family corporate information can only be avoided by formal, express promises of confidentiality, or by refusals to discuss family business affairs. The critical gap, for the majority, was the lack in testimony by Susan that she and Keith had an express agreement on the matter or a pattern of prior confidential communications involving the Waldbaum's corporation. While it is difficult to draw lines here, the line they draw is unrealistic in that it expects family members to behave like strangers toward one another. I thus believe that a family member (i) who has received or expects benefits from family control of a corporation, here gifts of stock, (ii) who is in a position to learn confidential corporate information through ordinary family interactions, and (iii) who knows that under the circumstances both the corporation and the family desire confidentiality, has a duty not to use information so obtained for personal profit where the use risks disclosure.

■ CONCURRENCE

(Miner, J.) I concur in the comprehensive opinion of Judge Meskill. I write only to comment upon the "familial relationship" rule of insider trading proposed by Judge Winter at the end of his partially dissenting opinion. The apparent rationale for such a rule is that it would encourage family members to speak more freely on all matters pertaining to the family, knowing that the lips of those receiving confidential corporate information would be kept sealed. Without the rule, it is maintained, family members in this case would have been inhibited from discussing any family matters that would inevitably have lead to the disclosure of the corporate information. It seems to me though, that family discourse would be inhibited, rather than promoted, by a rule that would automatically assure confidentiality. What speaker, secure in the knowledge that a relative could be prosecuted for insider trading, would reveal to that relative anything remotely connected with corporate dealings? And what family member would want to receive such information? The difficulty in ascertaining those family members covered by the rule poses another problem with the proposed rule. It is not clear just who would be subject to the confidentiality requirement. Does it include grandchildren who have received a few shares of stock as a gift? In the case at bar we are dealing with an attenuated trail of family confidences in which information was received without any assurance of confidentiality from the receiver and without any prior sharing of business information within the family. It therefore makes little sense to imply assurances of confidentiality. Finally, to further extend the concept of confidential duty would be to take courts into an area of securities regulation not yet entered by Congress. This would give prosecutors the wrong signal in their continuing efforts to push against existing boundaries in the prosecution of securities fraud cases. I would await further instructions from Congress before sailing into this uncharted area.

Analysis:

Whether applying the classical or the misappropriation theory, liability under Rule 10b-5 usually turns on whether there has been a breach of duty. There are other concerns, however. For instance, the information disclosed must be material; that is, the information would have been important to a reasonable investor in making an investment decision. After all, there is no reason to protect information that is not material because it is, by definition, irrelevant to the stock trader. The information must also be nonpublic, as there can be no effect of disclosing information already known to the investing public because the markets have already digested such information. One other, less prominent, requirement is that the inside trader have the proper scienter.

■ CASE VOCABULARY

SCIENTER: The quality of having done an act knowingly or with intent to do the act.

Basic, Inc. v. Levinson

(Merger Candidate) v. *(Former Shareholder)*

485 U.S. 224, 108 S.Ct. 978 (1988)

THE ISSUANCE OF A MATERIALLY MISLEADING STATEMENT GIVES RISE TO A REBUTTABLE PRESUMPTION THAT A TRADER RELYING ON THE MARKET'S PRICE SETTING INTEGRITY HAS BEEN DEFRAUDED BY THE MISLEADING STATEMENT

■ **INSTANT FACTS** Basic, Inc. (D) issued three public statements disclaiming what in fact were its ongoing merger talks with another corporation. Several shareholders sold the company's stock in reliance on the statement and now sue Basic, Inc. (D) under Rule 10b-5.

■ **BLACK LETTER RULE** 1) The standard of materiality applicable under Rule 10b-5 in preliminary merger discussions is that a fact is material if there is a substantial likelihood that a reasonable shareholder would consider it significant or important in deciding whether to purchase or sell securities. 2) An investor's reliance on any public misrepresentation of a material fact may be presumed for the purposes of a Rule 10b-5 lawsuit.

■ **PROCEDURAL BASIS**

Appeal to the United States Supreme Court of Court's reversal of a grant of summary judgment in a securities fraud class action lawsuit.

■ **FACTS**

Before December 20, 1978, Basic, Inc. (D) was a publicly traded company engaged in manufacturing chemical refractories for the steel industry. Beginning in September 1976, Combustion Engineering, Inc. (Combustion), another maker of refractories, expressed interest in acquiring Basic (D). To this end Combustion representatives had meetings and phone conversations with Basic (D) officers and directors concerning a merger. During 1977 and 1978, Basic (D) made three public statements denying that it was engaged in merger negotiations. Then, on December 18, 1978, Basic (D) issued a release stating that it had been "approached" by another company concerning a merger. The next day Basic's (P) board endorsed Combustion's offer of $46 per share and on the following day publicly announced its approval of the tender offer for all outstanding shares. Levinson (P) represents a class of respondents who are former shareholders of Basic (D), who sold their stock after Basic's (P) first public statement. Levinson (P) asserts that Basic (D) issued three false or misleading public statements and thereby violated § 10 (b) and Rule 10b-5, thus injuring the class because they all sold their Basic shares at artificially depressed prices in a market affected by Basic's (P) misleading statements in reliance thereon. The district adopted a presumption that Levinson (P) and the others did rely on Basic's (P) public statements, but still entered summary judgment for Basic (D). The Court of Appeals reversed the summary judgment and remanded the case. An appeal followed.

■ **ISSUE**

1) Is an omitted fact in the case of a preliminary merger discussion material if there is a substantial likelihood that a reasonable shareholder would consider it important in deciding whether to purchase or sell securities? 2) Does a corporation's public misrepresentation of a material fact give rise to a

presumption that an investor relied on the misrepresentation in making transactions in the corporation's securities?

■ DECISION AND RATIONALE

(Blackmun, J.) 1) Yes. 2) Yes. This Court has previously addressed the various positive and common law requirements for a violation of § 10(b) or of Rule 10b-5. The Court has also explicitly defined, in *TSC Industries, Inc. v. Northway, Inc.*, a standard of materiality under the securities law, concluding in the proxy solicitation context that an omitted fact is material if there is a substantial likelihood that a reasonable shareholder would consider it important in deciding how to vote. That opinion further explained that to fulfill the materiality requirement "there must be a substantial likelihood that the disclosure of the omitted fact would have been viewed by the reasonable investor as having significantly altered the 'total mix' of information made available." We now expressly adopt the *TSC Industries* standard of materiality for the § 10(b) and Rule 10b-5 context. The application of this materiality standard is not self-evident. Where the event is contingent or speculative in nature, it is difficult to ascertain whether the "reasonable investor" would have considered the omitted information significant at the time. Merger negotiations, because of the ever-present possibility that the transaction will not close, fall into this category. Basic (D) urges the Court to adopt a standard holding that preliminary merger discussions are not material until an "agreement-in-principle" has been reached. The first rationale offered for this standard, that investors should not be overwhelmed by excessively detailed and trivial information, assumes that investors are nitwits unable to appreciate the intricacies and risk of merger negotiations. We soundly reject this rationale. The second, that merger negotiations need to be held in the strictest secrecy, seems irrelevant to the question of whether merger negotiations are important to investors in making decisions. The third rationale is that a bright-line rule is easier to follow for managers in merger negotiations. But ease of application alone is not an excuse for ignoring the purposes of the securities acts and Congress' policy decisions. A rigid formula will not serve these purposes. We therefore reject the standard proposed by Basic (D). Prior to our decision in *TSC Industries*, the Second Circuit explained the role of the materiality requirement of Rule 10b-5, with respect to contingent or speculative information or events, in a manner that gave that term a meaning independent of the other provisions of the Rule. Under such circumstances, materiality will depend at any given time upon a balancing of both the indicated probability that the event will occur and the anticipated magnitude of the event in light of the totality of the company activity. In a subsequent case, Judge Friendly used the Second Circuit's approach in the context of preliminary merger negotiations. Judge Friendly first acknowledged that materiality is something to be determined on the basis of the particular facts of each case. He then stated that since mergers are so important in a corporation's life, we think that inside information in this context can become material at an earlier stage than would be the case as regards lesser transactions, even though the mortality rate of mergers is high. We agree with this analysis.

Whether merger talks are material in any one case depends on the facts. In order to assess the probability that the event will occur, the factfinder will need to look at indicia of interest in the transaction at the highest corporate levels. Some important factors are board resolutions, instructions to investment bankers, and actual negotiations between principals or their intermediaries. To assess the magnitude of the transaction to the issuer of the securities allegedly manipulated, a factfinder will need to consider such facts as the size of the two corporate entities and of the potential premiums over market value. No event or fact, short of closing the deal, is controlling. Because the standard of materiality we endorse today is different from that used by the courts below, we remand the case for a consideration of whether summary judgment is appropriate on this record. We turn now to the question of reliance and the fraud on the market theory. The fraud on the market theory is based on the premise that, in an open and developed securities market, the price of a company's stock is determined by the available material information regarding the company and its business. Misleading statements will therefore defraud purchasers of stock even if the purchasers do not directly rely on the misstatements. We do not determine the validity of the theory, but only whether it was proper for the courts below to apply a rebuttable presumption of reliance, supported in part by the fraud on the market theory. Requiring proof of reliance from each member of the proposed plaintiff class effectively would have prevented a class action here. The district court found that the presumption of reliance created by the fraud on the market theory provided a good solution to the problem of balancing the reliance requirement with the procedural requirements for a class action. Basic (D) avers that use of the fraud on the market theory in such a way eliminates the requirement that reliance be proven. We agree that reliance is a required element, but there is more than one way to prove such a causal connection between the misinformation and the shareholder's loss. Explicit proof of reliance has been substituted by similar presumptions in the past.

The modern securities markets involve millions of transactions daily and differ from face to face transactions where reliance is easy to prove. Our understanding of Rule 10b-5's reliance requirement must take into account these differences. When one is dealing through an impersonal market, the market is performing a substantial part of the valuation process through its pricing mechanism. The market is, in effect, informing the investor that given all the information available to it, the value of the stock is the market price. Material misinformation affects the price of a stock in the market. When one buys the stock on the market, he is, therefore, indirectly relying on the misinformation. Another consideration is that the courts have traditionally relied on presumptions when direct proof, for whatever reason, is difficult to come by. The courts below realized that requiring a plaintiff to show a speculative state of facts would place an unnecessarily unrealistic evidentiary burden on the Rule 10b-5 plaintiff who has traded in an impersonal market. The presumption of reliance employed in this case is consistent with, and, by facilitating Rule 10b-5 litigation, supports, the congressional policy embodied in the 1934 act. Common sense and probability also support the presumption. Recent empirical studies have tended to confirm Congress' premise that the market price of shares traded on well-developed markets reflects all publicly available information, and, hence, any material misrepresentations. We therefore endorse the use of the fraud on the market theory to create a presumption of reliance in Rule 10b-5 actions. It must be noted, however, that the presumption may be rebutted by proof going to the basic facts giving rise to the presumption, or that the misrepresentation did not distort the price, or that the individual plaintiff traded or would have traded despite his knowing the statement was false. The judgment of the court of appeals is vacated, and the case is remanded for further proceedings consistent with this opinion.

■ CONCURRENCE AND DISSENT

(White, J.) The fraud on the market theory is a mere babe. Yet today, the Court embraces this theory with the sweeping confidence usually reserved for more mature legal doctrines. One element of the Court's decision I agree with, however, is the availability of means for rebutting the presumption given rise to by the theory. But even with this limitation, the pitfalls in the Court's approach are revealed by previous uses by the lower courts of the broader versions of the theory. Confusion and contradictions in court rulings are inevitable when traditional legal analysis is replaced with economic theorization by the federal courts. With no staff economists, no experts schooled in the "efficient-capital-market-hypothesis," no ability to test the validity of the empirical market studies, we are not well equipped to embrace novel constructions of a statute like § 10(b) based on contemporary microeconomic theory. The Congress, with its superior resources and expertise, is far better equipped than us for the task of determining how modern economic theory and global financial markets require that established legal notions of fraud be modified. Consequently, I cannot join the Court in its effort to reconfigure the securities laws, based on recent economic theories. Even if I was prepared to accept the premise that most persons dealing in securities do so in reliance on the market price, the fraud on the market theory goes further. In adopting a "presumption of reliance," the Court also assumes that buyers and sellers rely—not just on the market price—but on the "*integrity*" of that price. It is this aspect of the theory that most mystifies me. Indeed, many investors purchase or sell stock because they believe the price *inaccurately* reflects the corporation's worth. As we previously recognized, investors act on inevitably incomplete or inaccurate information; consequently there are always winners and losers; but those who have 'lost' have not necessarily been defrauded. Yet today, the Court allows investors to recover who can show little more than that they sold stock at a lower price than what might have been. Finally, the facts of this case make it an exceedingly poor candidate for the Court's fraud on the market theory, and illustrate the illogic achieved by the theory's application in many cases. It is indisputable that virtually every member of the class profited from his or her sale of Basic stock. The oddities of applying the theory in this case are manifest. First, there are the facts that the plaintiffs are the sellers and the class period is so lengthy—both are virtually without precedent in prior fraud on the market cases. Second, there is no indication that Basic (D) officials made the statements for the purpose of manipulating stock prices, or with any intent of engaging in underhanded trading of Basic stock. It is also difficult to square liability in this case with § 10(b)'s express provision that it prohibits fraud "*in connection with* the purchase or sale of any security." Third is the confusion about which investors can recover. Many did not purchase Basic stock until after the first public announcement. But such persons could still recover, even though they probably believed the announcement and even though they made a profit on the stock. Indeed, many if not most of those who bought or sold the stock during this period probably disbelieved the announcements. Why should such investors be able to recover? I would reverse the lower court's holding allowing the fraud on the market theory to create a presumption of reliance.

Analysis:

The controversial aspect of the *Basic* decision, as pointed out by Justice White, is the Court's endorsement of the fraud-on-the-market theory, not as such, but as a presumption-creating tool available to those investing in open, impersonal securities markets. In order to understand why the Court endorsed this means of proving reliance, one must first have a basic understanding of how markets work. Many corporations, both large and small, are actively traded on the various securities markets around the world. There are many things that go into determining the price of a share of any given corporation on these markets, many of which are not even fully understood by the world's best economists. Some variables affect all stock prices, like current interest rates, consumer and investor confidence, current prices of ubiquitous inputs (like energy), etc. Some variables will affect the stock prices of corporations in certain industries, like legislation dealing with the cable industry. Then there are variables that only affect the price of one company, as in *Basic.* Corporations are required to make public reports on various corporate statistics that provide investors with a snapshot of the company's health and prospects for the future. These reports are immediately—if not sooner—reflected in the corporation's stock price. Similarly, the fact that a corporation is considering a merger or buyout will affect the corporation's price on the market. So in the case of *Basic*, the information that there were no merger talks ongoing, when digested by the market, had the affect of quelling investor excitement, which, in turn, had the effect of artificially depressing Basic stock. Thus the market was reflecting the misrepresentations made by Basic's (P) officials.

■ CASE VOCABULARY

MERGER: The joining of two companies by the absorption of one by the other, with all assets and liabilities being assumed by the resulting company.

REBUTTABLE PRESUMPTION: When certain basic facts give rise to an inference of a secondary fact or facts that may be overcome by the introduction of evidence contradicting either the basic facts or the presumed facts.

MDCM Holdings, Inc. v. Credit Suisse First Boston Corporation

(Corporation Issuing Stock) v. *(IPO Underwriter)*

216 F.Supp.2d 251 (S.D.N.Y. 2002)

THE SECURITIES LITIGATION UNIFORM STANDARDS ACT PROVIDES FOR FEDERAL PREEMPTION OF MOST SECURITIES-RELATED CLASS ACTION LAWSUITS

■ **INSTANT FACTS** A group of internet and other technology related companies filed a class action lawsuit alleging breach of contract and breach of fiduciary duty against the company that agreed to underwrite their initial public offerings of stock.

■ **BLACK LETTER RULE** The Securities Litigation Uniform Standards Act (SLUSA) provides for federal preemption of class action lawsuits which, among other things, contain allegations of misrepresentation or omission of a material fact or any manipulative or deceptive device or contrivance in connection with the purchase or sale of a covered security.

■ **PROCEDURAL BASIS**

Credit Suisse First Boston Corporation (D), an underwriter, sought to have the court dismiss a lawsuit filed against it which alleged breach of an underwriting agreement.

■ **FACTS**

In August of 1999, Mortgage.com (P), an internet mortgage business, entered into an underwriting agreement with Credit Suisse (D), one of the nation's largest underwriting firms, for the purpose of making an initial public offering of stock. Following the execution of that agreement, shares of Mortgage.com (P) were issued to the public and began to be traded under the symbol MDCM. The offering of MDCM stock grossed $59.5 million for Mortgage.com (P), $4,167,450 of which went to Credit Suisse (D) per the underwriting agreement. Specifically, under that agreement, Credit Suisse purchased 7,441,875 shares of MDCM at a price of $7.44, 7% less than the public offering price of $8.00 per share. In May of 2001, Mortgage.com (P), then known as MDCM Holdings, Inc. (P), along with other technology companies that had used the same underwriter, filed a class action lawsuit against Credit Suisse (D). In general, the complaint alleged that Credit Suisse (D) used MDCM's increase in value to enrich itself by requiring that customers who wanted to purchase IPO shares pay it the prospectus price plus a share of the profits that the customers realized and that Credit Suisse (D) purposely under-priced certain securities in order to guarantee a rise in value once they were issued. Specifically, Count I of the complaint alleged that Credit Suisse (D) breached the underwriting agreement by selling the IPO shares to favored customers and not to the public as the agreement required and by selling the shares at a higher price than that provided in the prospectus. Count II alleged that Credit Suisse (D) violated implied covenants of good faith and fair dealing by under-pricing the IPO shares so that it could allocate undervalued shares to favored clients and receive additional compensation, meaning the issuers received deficient and overpriced underwriting services. Count III alleged that Credit Suisse (D) violated its fiduciary duties of loyalty, due care, and fair dealing—owed because it had knowledge of confidential information and acted as an agent to the issuers—by allocating shares to favored customers and sharing in the profits made by those customers. Finally,

---

Count IV alleged unjust enrichment on the ground that the issuers conferred benefits upon Credit Suisse (D) in connection with the IPO's which it would be inequitable for Credit Suisse (D) to retain.

■ ISSUE

Does SLUSA per se provide for federal preemption in lawsuits alleging breach of an underwriting agreement?

■ DECISION AND RATIONALE

(Scheindlin, J.)   No.   Credit Suisse (D) argues that MDCM's (P) complaint should be dismissed because its state law claims are barred by the Securities Litigation Uniform Standards Act of 1998 (SLUSA).   Congress enacted the Private Securities Litigation Reform Act of 1995 (PSLRA) to raise the bar for bringing class actions under the Securities Act of 1933 and the Securities Exchange Act of 1934. Among other things, the PSLRA heightened pleading standards, generally required courts to stay discovery pending resolution of a motion to dismiss, and placed limits on recovery.   In the aftermath of the PSLRA, plaintiffs increasingly filed securities class actions in state courts under state law theories of liability.   Congress responded in 1998 by enacting SLUSA, which seeks to "prevent plaintiffs from seeking to evade the protections that Federal law provides against abusive litigation by fling suit in State court."   The purpose of SLUSA was to make federal court the exclusive venue, and federal law the exclusive remedy, for most securities class actions.   SLUSA provides for federal preemption of any claim that meets four prerequisites.   Specifically, the lawsuit must be: (1) a covered class action, (2) based on state law, (3) in which the plaintiff has alleged either a "misrepresentation or omission of a material fact" or "any manipulative or deceptive device or contrivance," (4) "in connection with the purchase or sale of a covered security."   Because MDCM (P) does not allege the third element of SLUSA, the statute does not preempt their class action.   When determining whether SLUSA preempts a lawsuit, a court is directed to look at what the private party is alleging.   MDCM (P) only alleges that Credit Suisse (D) signed numerous contracts which it breached.   A breach of contract does not constitute fraud unless the defendant secretly intended not to perform or knows that he could not perform.   MDCM (P) has made no such allegation and therefore only needs to prove that Credit Suisse (D) did not satisfy the requirements laid out in the underwriting agreements, a claim which does not involve allegations of misrepresentation or omissions by Credit Suisse (D).   Credit Suisse (D) argues that other courts have disregarded state law labels and dismissed similar claims under SLUSA. However, the cases relied on by Credit Suisse (D) involve explicit allegations of misrepresentation or material omission, and therefore are distinguishable from MDCM's (P) claims.   Credit Suisse's (D) motion to dismiss is denied.

Analysis:

MDCM Holdings provides an example of how the Delaware carve-out exception to the Securities Litigation Uniform Standards Act of 1998 (SLUSA) works when applied to real lawsuits.   As stated by the Court in the *MDCM* opinion, the purpose of SLUSA is to provide federal preemption in the majority of securities-related class action lawsuits and thereby limit the ability of plaintiffs to do an end-around federal law in state court. The drafters of SLUSA determined that when a securities-related class action claim has a greater basis in contract or corporate law (i.e., breach of contract or breach of fiduciary duty) than in fraud, that claim should be litigated in state court rather than federal court.   This exception to federal preemption, generally referred to as the Delaware carve-out, was enacted so that the predictability of state corporations law—particularly that of the state of Delaware—might be retained and the expertise of state law courts in litigating these types of cases—the Delaware Chancery Court in particular—might not be wasted.

■ CASE VOCABULARY

DELAWARE CARVE-OUT: An exception to the doctrine of federal preemption contained in SLUSA which allows for securities-related class actions to be filed in state court when the true cause of action is breach of contract or breach of fiduciary duty as opposed to fraudulent misrepresentation.

FEDERAL PREEMPTION: A principle of constitutional law which holds that federal law supersedes any inconsistent state regulation or law.

INITIAL PUBLIC OFFERING: A corporation's first or initial sale of stock to the public.

PSLRA: Private Securities Litigation Reform Act of 1995: A piece of federal legislation which heightened the requirements for bringing securities-related class action lawsuits by raising pleading standards, limiting discovery pending resolution of a motion to dismiss, and placing limits on recovery.

SLUSA: Securities Litigation Uniform Standards Act of 1998: A piece of federal legislation which makes federal court the exclusive venue and federal law the exclusive remedy for most securities-related class action lawsuits.

UNDERWRITING AGREEMENT: An agreement between a company issuing stock and the investment bank underwriting the IPO.

CHAPTER FOURTEEN

Indemnification and Insurance

Merritt–Chapman & Scott Corp. v. Wolfson

Instant Facts: Corporate directors and officers who were charged with violating and conspiring to violate federal securities laws, sought to have the corporation indemnify them for their expenses incurred in successfully defending four out of the five charges.

Black Letter Rule: A director or officer of a corporation need not be found innocent on all charges in order to be eligible for mandatory indemnification for those charges he does successfully defend.

McCullough v. Fidelity & Deposit Co.

Instant Facts: Federal regulators filed a declaratory judgment action to determine whether a bank's insurer had received sufficient notice of the potential claim for a claim made by the regulator against the directors and officers who were to be indemnified by the insurance policy.

Black Letter Rule: A "claims made" policy requires the insured.

Merritt-Chapman & Scott Corp. v. Wolfson

(*Corporation*) v. (*Directors*)

321 A.2d 138 (Del. Super. 1974)

A DIRECTOR OR OFFICER WHO IS ONLY PARTIALLY SUCCESSFUL IN DEFENDING A CRIMINAL CHARGE IS, NEVERTHELESS, ENTITLED TO INDEMNIFICATION FOR THOSE CHARGES HE SUCCESSFULLY DEFENDS

■ **INSTANT FACTS** Corporate directors and officers who were charged with violating and conspiring to violate federal securities laws, sought to have the corporation indemnify them for their expenses incurred in successfully defending four out of the five charges.

■ **BLACK LETTER RULE** A director or officer of a corporation need not be found innocent on all charges in order to be eligible for mandatory indemnification for those charges he does successfully defend.

■ **PROCEDURAL BASIS**

Decision of the trial court ruling on motions for summary judgment.

■ **FACTS**

Louis Wolfson (P), Elkin Gerbert (P), Joseph Kosow (P), and Marshal Staub (P) were all charged with conspiring to violate federal securities laws. Wolfson (P) and Gerbert (P) were also charged with perjury before the SEC and, along with Staub (P), filing false reports with the SEC and New York Stock Exchange. After several trials and one appeal, the charges were settled. Wolfson (P) pled *nolo contendere* to one count of filing false reports; Gerbert (P) agreed not to appeal his conviction for perjury, in exchange for having all other charges dropped and a suspended sentence; and all charges against Kosow (P) and Staub (P) were dropped. Each then sought indemnification from Merritt-Chapman & Scott Corp. (MCS) (D) for expenses incurred in defending those charges of which they were not convicted. All parties moved for summary judgment.

■ **ISSUE**

Must a director or officer successfully defend every charge against him in order to be eligible for mandatory indemnification?

■ **DECISION AND RATIONALE**

(Balick, J.) No. A director or officer of a corporation need not be found innocent on all charges in order to be eligible for mandatory indemnification for expenses incurred in connection with those charges he does successfully defend. Section 145 of the Delaware Corporation Code expressly requires that a corporation indemnify its director, officer, employee or agent, who has been successful on the merits or otherwise in defense of any criminal proceeding, or in defense of any issue or matter therein, for the expenses incurred in connection with the defense. The purpose of such indemnification is two-fold. First, it encourages corporate officials to defend against unjustified suits and claims. Also, indemnification encourages responsible and capable persons to serve as directors. MCS argues that indemnification should not be required where the charges are dropped for prosecutorial convenience, rather than outright acquittal. But the statute requires indemnification for success on the merits or *otherwise*. Any result other than conviction is success. Furthermore, the statute does not require complete success. It allows for indemnification for success in defending any issue or matter. Wolfson's (P) plea of *nolo contendere* and Gerbert's (P) conviction establish that they were in derelict of performance of their duty, and they are not entitled to indemnification against expenses incurred in defending those charges. However, they are entitled to be indemnified for those expenses incurred in successfully defending four charges.

Analysis:

Most states mandate that a corporation indemnify directors and officers for successfully defending civil, criminal, or administrative claims arising out of their conduct as corporate agents. Mandatory indemnification is justified, primarily, on two grounds. It is doubtful that legislators intended to indemnify officers and directors who were adjudged guilty of criminal conduct. It would seem to violate public policy to require that the victim must pay for the wrongdoers' legal expenses. However, as the court points out, the plain language of the statute required indemnification for success on any issue or matter within a claim. In response to this holding the Model Business Corporation Act was amended to require that a director or officer be *wholly* successful before he becomes entitled to indemnification as a matter of statutory right.

■ CASE VOCABULARY

NOLO CONTENDERE: A plea whereby the defendant does not contest the charges; except for purposes of res judicata, it has the same effect as a guilty verdict.

McCullough v. Fidelity & Deposit Co.

(Not Provided) v. *(Insurance Co.)*

2 F.3d 110 (5th Cir. 1993)

PRIOR TO THE EXPIRATION OF A CORPORATION'S DIRECTOR AND OFFICER INSURANCE, THE INSURER MUST BE NOTIFIED DURING THE POLICY PERIOD OF SPECIFIC ACTS, WHICH POTENTIALLY FORM THE BASIS OF CLAIMS COVERED BY THE POLICY

■ **INSTANT FACTS** Federal regulators filed a declaratory judgment action to determine whether a bank's insurer had received sufficient notice of the potential claim for a claim made by the regulator against the directors and officers who were to be indemnified by the insurance policy.

■ **BLACK LETTER RULE** A "claims made" policy requires the insured to give notice of specified wrongful acts of officers and directors to trigger coverage.

■ **PROCEDURAL BASIS**

Appeal to the Fifth Circuit Court of Appeals challenging the decision of the trial court to grant summary judgment for the defendant in a declaratory judgment action.

■ **FACTS**

Fidelity & Deposit Co. (F & D) (D) issued director and officer (D & O) liability policies to Harris County Bankshares, Inc. and three of its subsidiaries. The policies covered only claims made against the insured directors and officers during the policy period. This limitation notwithstanding, coverage was extended to claims made after expiration of the policy period if, prior to such expiration, F & D (D) was notified of "any act, error, or omission" which could subsequently give rise to a claim against the officers and directors for a "specified Wrongful Act." In conjunction with renewal of the policy, the banks provided their annual report, which, in a footnote, referred to a cease and desist order issued to one of the subsidiary banks by the Office of the Comptroller of the Currency (OCC). When banks began to experience financial problems, F & D (D) requested that it receive certain reports and other information. The OCC declared the banks insolvent and declared the FDIC (P) as Receiver. The FDIC (P) then filed suit against the banks' officers and directors, alleging the improper or illegal administration and collection of loans. The FDIC (P) then sought a declaratory judgment declaring that F & D (D) was liable for the directors' and officers' legal expenses. The trial court granted summary judgment for F & D (D).

■ **ISSUE**

Does awareness of a bank's worsening financial condition place the bank's insurer on notice that specified wrongful acts giving rise to a potential claim have occurred?

■ **DECISION AND RATIONALE**

(Davis, Cir. J.) No. A "claims made" policy requires the insured to give notice of specified wrongful acts of officers and directors to trigger coverage. This conclusion is supported by the express language of the policy, which states that coverage will be provided if F & D (D) is notified of "any act, error, or omission which may subsequently give rise to a claim being made against Directors or Officers, or any of them, for a specified wrongful act." If the policy requirement for notice is relaxed, then coverage expands under the policy. For example, if notice that an attorney has a poor docket control system suffices as notice of a wrongful act, then his malpractice insurance would cover any suit arising from missed deadlines. We also conclude that adequate notice was not given in this instance. The reference to the cease and desist order and the information provided to F & D regarding the banks' financial condition do not, alone or together, provide adequate notice. F & D (D) was not notified of the particular subsidiary involved, the particular agents, officers or directors involved, the time period when the events occurred, the identity of potential claimants, or the specific unsound practices making the basis of the cease and desist order. Furthermore, notice of a bank's worsening condition is not notice of an officer's or director's act, error or omission. Affirmed.

Analysis:

D & O insurance is usually issued under a "claims made" policy, rather than one that is occurrence based. In other words, D & O policies insure against claims made during the policy's term. In contrast, occurrence based insurance, such as that for automobiles, protect the insured against suits arising out of conduct occurring during the term of the policy, regardless of when the claim is made. This obviously leaves open the possibility that directors and officers will be uninsured at the time a particular claim is made. In order to ameliorate the harsh effects of claims based policies, insurers include "awareness" clauses, such as the one at issue here. Under these clauses, a claims based policy will insure against those claims that arise after the policy has expired if, prior to the expiration, the insurer is made aware of the conduct from which claims can be expected.

CHAPTER FIFTEEN

Takeovers

CTS Corporation v. Dynamics Corp. of America

Instant Facts: Dynamics (P) claimed that the Indiana Act was preempted by the Williams Act, and, additionally, that the Act violates the Commerce Clause of the Federal Constitution.

Black Letter Rule: The Control Share Acquisitions Chapter of the Indiana Business Corporation Law is not preempted by the Williams Act, nor is it in violation of the Commerce Clause of the Federal Constitution.

Moran v. Household International, Inc.

Instant Facts: A corporate director who had voted against the adoption of a "poison pill" defensive measure sued to invalidate the plan after he lost the vote 14 to 2.

Black Letter Rule: A board of directors can adopt a poison pill plan as a defensive measure in response to its reasonable fear of a possible future hostile takeover of the corporation.

Mentor Graphics v. Quickturn Design Systems, Inc.

Instant Facts: After commencing a hostile takeover, the acquiring company sought to challenge the "no-hand" poison pill, adopted by the target company's board of directors, which prevented every member of a newly elected board from redeeming rights to facilitate an acquisition.

Black Letter Rule: A board of directors fails to meet its burden of demonstrating the reasonableness of a shareholders' rights plan, if the plan's operative terms cannot be reconciled with the directors' stated justification for adopting it.

International Brotherhood of Teamsters v. Fleming Companies

Instant Facts: A shareholder sought to include in the company's annual proxy materials a proposed amendment to the corporation's bylaws which would require any rights plan implemented by the board of directors to be put to the shareholders for a majority vote.

Black Letter Rule: Unless the articles of incorporation state otherwise, a board of directors does not have exclusive authority to adopt a shareholder rights plan and shareholders are not precluded from proposing resolutions or amendments regarding such plans.

CTS Corporation v. Dynamics Corp. of America

(Target Corporation) v. *(Buying Company)*

481 U.S. 69, 107 S.Ct. 1637, 95 L.Ed.2d 67 (1987)

THE INDIANA CONTROL SHARES ACQUISITION CHAPTER IS NEITHER PREEMPTED BY THE WILLIAMS ACT NOR IN CONFLICT WITH THE COMMERCE CLAUSE

■ **INSTANT FACTS** Dynamics (P) claimed that the Indiana Act was preempted by the Williams Act, and, additionally, that the Act violates the Commerce Clause of the Federal Constitution.

■ **BLACK LETTER RULE** The Control Share Acquisitions Chapter of the Indiana Business Corporation Law is not preempted by the Williams Act, nor is it in violation of the Commerce Clause of the Federal Constitution.

■ **PROCEDURAL BASIS**

Appeal from the Court of Appeals' affirmance of the District Court's judgment for the plaintiff.

■ **FACTS**

On March 4, 1986, the Governor of Indiana signed a revised Indiana Business Corporation Law, *Ind.Code* Sec. 23–1–17–1 et seq. (Supp.1986). That law included the Control Share Acquisitions Chapter (Indiana Act or Act). Beginning on August 1, 1987, the Act will apply to any corporation incorporated in Indiana, unless the corporation amends its articles of incorporation or bylaws to opt out of the Act. Before that date, any Indiana corporation can opt into the Act by resolution of its board of directors. The Act focuses on the acquisition of "control shares" in an issuing public corporation. On March 10, 1986, Dynamics Corporation of America (P) owned 9.6% of the common stock of CTS Corporation (D), an Indiana corporation. On that day, six days after the Act went into effect, Dynamics (P) announced a tender offer for another million shares in CTS (D); purchase of those shares would have brought Dynamics' (P) ownership interest in CTS (D) to 27.5%. Also on March 10, Dynamics (P) filed suit alleging that CTS (D) had violated the federal securities laws. On March 27, the Board of Directors of CTS (D) elected to be governed by the provisions of the Act. Four days later, on March 31, Dynamics (P) moved for leave to amend its complaint to allege that the Act is preempted by the Williams Act, and violates the Commerce Clause. Dynamics (P) sought a temporary restraining order, a preliminary injunction, and declaratory relief against CTS's (D) use of the Act. On April 9, the District Court ruled that the Williams Act preempts the Indiana Act and granted Dynamics' (P) motion for declaratory relief. A week later, on April 17, the District Court issued and opinion accepting Dynamics' (P) claim that the Act violates the Commerce Clause. CTS (D) appealed the District Court's holdings on these claims to the Court of Appeals for the Seventh Circuit. On April 23, the Court of Appeals issued an order affirming the judgment of the District Court.

■ **ISSUE**

Is the Control Share Acquisitions Chapter of the Indiana Business Corporation Law preempted by the Williams Act, or in violation of the Commerce Clause of the Federal Constitution?

■ **DECISION AND RATIONALE**

(Powell, J.) No. The first question in this case is whether the Williams Act preempts the Indiana Act. As we have stated frequently, absent an explicit indication by Congress of an intent to preempt state law, a state statute is preempted only where compliance with both federal and state regulations is a physical impossibility, or where the state law stands as an obstacle to the accomplishment and execution of the full purposes and objectives of Congress. Because it is entirely possible for entities to comply with both the Williams Act and the Indiana Act, the state statute can be preempted only if it frustrates the purposes of the federal law. The Court of Appeals based its finding of preemption on its view that the practical effect of the Indiana Act is to delay consummation of tender offers until 50 days after the commencement of the offer. As did the Court of Appeals, Dynamics (P) reasons that no rational offeror will purchase shares until it gains assurance that those shares will carry voting rights. Because it is possible that voting rights will not be conferred, until a shareholder meeting 50 days after commencement of the offer, Dynamics (P) concludes that the Act imposes a 50-day delay. This, it argues, conflicts with the shorter 20-business day period established by the SEC as the minimum period for which a tender offer may be held open. We find the alleged conflict illusory. The Act does not impose an absolute 50-day delay on tender offers, nor does it preclude an offeror from purchasing shares as soon as federal law permits. If the offeror fears an adverse shareholder vote under the Act, it can make a conditional tender offer, offering to accept shares on the condition that the shares receive voting rights within a certain period of time. The Williams Act permits tender offers to be conditioned on the offeror's subsequently obtaining regulatory approval. We also note that the Williams Act would preempt a variety of state corporate laws of hitherto unquestioned validity if it were construed to preempt any state statute that may limit or delay the free exercise of power after a successful tender offer. In our view, the possibility that the Indiana Act will delay some tender offers is insufficient to require a conclusion that the Williams Act preempts the Act. The longstanding prevalence of state regulation in this area suggests that, if Congress had intended to preempt all state laws that delay the acquisition of voting control following a tender offer, it would have said so explicitly. The regulatory conditions that the Act places on tender offers are consistent with the text and the purposes of the Williams Act. Accordingly, we hold that the Williams Act does not preempt the Indiana Act. As an alternative basis for its decision, the Court of Appeals held that the Act violates the Commerce Clause of the Federal Constitution. We now address this holding. The principal objects of dormant Commerce Clause scrutiny are statutes that discriminate against interstate commerce. The Indiana Act is not such a statute. It has the same effects on tender offers whether or not the offeror is a domiciliary or resident of Indiana. Thus, it visits its effects equally upon both interstate and local business.

Dynamics (P) nevertheless contends that the statute is discriminatory because it will apply most often to out-of-state entities. This argument rests on the contention that, as a practical matter, most hostile tender offers are launched by offerors outside of Indiana. But this argument avails Dynamics (P) little. The fact that the burden of a state regulation falls on some interstate companies does not, by itself, establish a claim of discrimination against interstate commerce. Because nothing in the Indiana Act imposes a greater burden on out-of-state offerors than it does on similarly situated Indiana offerors, we reject the contention that the Act discriminates against interstate commerce. The Court of Appeals rested its decision that the Act was unconstitutional on its view of the Act's potential to hinder tender offers. However, it is an accepted part of the business landscape in this country for States to create corporations, to prescribe their powers, and to define the rights that are acquired by purchasing their shares. A State has an interest in promoting stable relationships among parties involved in the corporations it charters, as well as in ensuring that investors in such corporations have an effective voice in corporate affairs. There can be no doubt that the Act reflects these concerns. The primary purpose of the Act is to protect the shareholders of Indiana corporations. It does this by affording shareholders, when a takeover offer is made, an opportunity to decide collectively whether the resulting change in voting control of the corporation, as they perceive it, would be desirable. The autonomy provided by allowing shareholders collectively to determine whether the takeover is advantageous to their interests may be especially beneficial where a hostile tender offer may coerce shareholders into tendering their shares. Dynamics' (P) argument that the Act is unconstitutional ultimately rests on its contention that the Act will limit the number of successful tender offers. There is little evidence that this will occur, but even if true, this result would not substantially affect our Commerce Clause analysis. On its face, the Indiana Control Share Acquisitions Chapter evenhandedly determines the voting rights of shares of Indiana corporations. The Act does not conflict with the provisions or purposes of the Williams Act. To the limited extent that the Act affects interstate commerce, this is justified by the State's interests in defining the attributes of shares in its corporations and in protecting shareholders.

Congress has never questioned the need for state regulation of these matters. Nor do we think such regulation offends the Constitution. Accordingly, we reverse the judgment of the Court of Appeals.

■ CONCURRENCE

(Scalia, J.) I do not share the Court's apparent high estimation of the beneficence of the state statute at issue here. But a law can be both economic folly and constitutional. The Indiana Control Shares Acquisition Chapter is at least the latter. I therefore concur in the judgment of the Court.

■ DISSENT

(White, J.) I disagree with the conclusion that the Indiana Act is neither preempted by the Williams Act nor in conflict with the Commerce Clause. The Indiana Act undermines the policy of the Williams Act by effectively preventing minority shareholders, in some circumstances, from acting in their own best interests by selling their stock. In addition, the Indiana Act will substantially burden the interstate market in corporate ownership, particularly if other States follow Indiana's lead as many already have done The Indiana Act, therefore, directly inhibits interstate commerce, the very economic consequences the Commerce Clause was intended to prevent.

Analysis:

Every State in this country has enacted laws regulating corporate governance. By prohibiting certain transactions, and regulating others, such laws necessarily affect certain aspects of interstate commerce. This necessarily is true with respect to corporations with shareholders in states other than the state of incorporation. The beneficial free market system depends at its core upon the fact that a corporation is organized under, and governed by, the law of a single jurisdiction, traditionally the corporate law of the state of its incorporation. The Indiana Act involved in this case does not prohibit any entity, resident or nonresident, from offering to purchase, or from purchasing, shares in Indiana corporations, or from thereby gaining control. It only provides regulatory procedures designed for the better protection of the corporations' shareholders. The Court therefore concluded that the Act does not offend the Commerce Clause. Since this case was decided, other states have jumped on the bandwagon and adopted similar legislation.

■ CASE VOCABULARY

ET SEQ.: "And the following"; most commonly used in denominating page reference and statutory section numbers.

INTERSTATE COMMERCE: The purchase, sale, and exchange of commodities across state lines.

PLURALITY: An opinion agreed to by less than a majority of the court, but the result of which is agreed to by the majority.

PREEMPTION: A judicial doctrine asserting the supremacy of federal legislation over state legislation of the same subject matter.

Moran v. Household International, Inc.

(Director) v. *(Corporation)*

500 A.2d 1346 (Del. 1985)

CORPORATE BOARD MAY EMPLOY A POISON PILL PLAN TO COUNTER A GENERAL THREAT OF A COERCIVE TAKEOVER

■ **INSTANT FACTS** A corporate director who had voted against the adoption of a "poison pill" defensive measure sued to invalidate the plan after he lost the vote 14 to 2.

■ **BLACK LETTER RULE** A board of directors can adopt a poison pill plan as a defensive measure in response to its reasonable fear of a possible future hostile takeover of the corporation.

■ **PROCEDURAL BASIS**

Appeal of a judgment of the Delaware Court of Chancery.

■ **FACTS**

The board of directors of Household International, Inc. ("Household") (D) adopted a "poison pill" plan. Under the plan, if either a bidder made a tender offer for 30 percent of Household's (D) shares and then merged with Household (D), or, a single entity or group acquired 20 percent of Household's (D) shares and then merged with Household (D), the Household (D) shareholders would have a right to purchase stock in the surviving corporation at half price. The plan was thus designed to deter a takeover of Household (D) not supported by the Household (D) board. Although John Moran ("Moran") (P1), a Household (D) director and chairman of Dyson-Kissner-Moran Corporation ("D-K-M") (P2), the largest single stockholder in Household (D), had begun discussions concerning a possible leveraged buy-out of Household (D) by D-K-M (P2), the "poison pill" plan was not adopted as a specific response to a corporate raider, but instead as a general preventative mechanism to ward off any possible future hostile takeover attempts, with which the board was generally concerned. The board approved the plan by a vote of 14 to 2. The board consisted of ten outside directors and six members of Household's (D) management. Moran (P1) was one of the two board members to vote against the plan. Following its adoption, Moran (P1) and D-K-M (P2) brought suit to invalidate the "poison pill" plan. The Delaware Chancery Court upheld the plan as a legitimate exercise of business judgment by the Household (D) board. Moran (P1) and D-K-M (P2) appealed.

■ **ISSUE**

Can a board of directors adopt a poison pill plan as a defensive measure in response to its reasonable fear of a possible future hostile takeover of the corporation?

■ **DECISION AND RATIONALE**

(McNeilly, J.) Yes. In *Unocal Corp. v. Mesa Petroleum Co.* [permitting a discriminatory self-tender offer by a corporation as a defensive measure in response to a hostile tender offer by a corporate shareholder], we held that a discriminatory self-tender offer was a reasonable response by the corporate board in that case to a pending coercive and inadequate tender offer made by one of the corporation's shareholders. Here, we have a defensive mechanism adopted to ward off possible future advances and not a specific threat as occurred in *Unocal*. This difference does not result in the board of directors losing the protection of the business judgment rule. To the contrary, pre-planning for the possibility of a hostile takeover might actually reduce the chance that management will fail to exercise reasonable judgment under the pressure of a hostile bid. Moran (P1) and D-K-M (P2) contend that no provision of Delaware law authorizes a board to adopt a "poison pill" plan. They assert that, while Delaware corporate law provides for the issuance of options to purchase shares, the legislature intended this power to apply only as a device to finance the corporation and not for use as a defensive measure to a takeover bid. We disagree. Nothing in the statutes limits the right to issue such options only to the purpose of corporate financing. Without affirmative evidence showing that the legislature meant to confine the statute to corporate financing, we decline to impose such a limit on a board. Moran (P1) and D-K-M (P2) also assert that the "poison pill" plan would effectively block any hostile tender offer. Again, we disagree. The plan is not absolute. When the board is faced with a hostile tender offer, they will not be able to arbitrarily reject the offer. They will be held to the same fiduciary standards any other board of directors would be held to in deciding to adopt a defensive mechanism, the same standard they were held to in initially approving the "poison pill" plan. *Unocal* says that the board must show that it had reasonable grounds for believing a danger to corporate policy and effectiveness existed, but can do this by showing good faith and reasonable investigation. The board must also show that the defensive mechanism established was reasonable in relation to the threat posed. That proof is materially enhanced where, as here, a majority of the board favoring the proposal consisted of outside independent directors. Here, there is no claim of bad faith or that the board took its action in order to preserve its own power. Household (D) has adequately demonstrated that the adoption of the "poison pill" plan was a reaction to what it perceived to be the threat in the marketplace of coercive two-tier tender offers. The board reviewed adequate information to make its decision. Their response was reasonable. We conclude that the board receives the benefit of the business judgment rule in the adoption of this defensive measure. Affirmed.

Analysis:

"Poison pills" (or shareholder rights plans as they are euphemistically referred to by corporations) are measures adopted by a board of directors to ward off the threat of hostile takeovers. The major problem with poison pills is that a decision by the board to implement a shareholder rights plan carries an inherent conflict of interest between the board and the shareholders. Poison pills make it more difficult to take over a company and effect a change in the makeup of the board of directors. Consequently, there is a danger that the directors will employ such defensive measures solely to preserve their positions. The interest in maintaining their position may conflict with the shareholders' interest in obtaining a generous offer for their stock. Recognizing that this conflict exists, courts scrutinize poison pills somewhat differently than other decisions made by a board of directors. In *Unocal Corporation v. Mesa Petroleum Co.* [a case involving a board of directors' decision to adopt a poison pill to ward off an actual takeover attempt] the Delaware Court had held that the business judgment rule applied to a decision to employ a poison pill, if the board established that it reasonably perceived a threat to the corporation's interests and the measures adopted were reasonably related to the perceived threat. The court here extends this rule to a situation where the board of directors implements a poison pill to discourage takeovers in general, rather than to ward off a particular attempt.

■ CASE VOCABULARY

FLIP-OVER POISON PILL: A device adopted by a target (or potential target) corporation in which, in the event of a takeover of the target corporation in which the bidder merges with the target, the target's shareholders will have the right to purchase the stock of the surviving corporation at a bargain price.

POISON PILL: A device adopted by a corporation to make its stock less attractive to a potential takeover bidder. In general the idea is to make more difficult and expensive for a bidder to acquire the corporation than it would be without the existence of the device.

Mentor Graphics v. Quickturn Design Systems, Inc.

(Target Company) v. *(Acquirer)*

728 A.2d 25 (Del. Ch. 1998)

A BOARD OF DIRECTORS IS RESTRICTED FROM LIMITING THE POWER OF A SUBSEQUENTLY ELECTED BOARD TO REDEEM POISON PILLS

■ **INSTANT FACTS** After commencing a hostile takeover, the acquiring company sought to challenge the "no-hand" poison pill, adopted by the target company's board of directors, which prevented every member of a newly elected board from redeeming rights to facilitate an acquisition.

■ **BLACK LETTER RULE** A board of directors fails to meet its burden of demonstrating the reasonableness of a shareholders' rights plan, if the plan's operative terms cannot be reconciled with the directors' stated justification for adopting it.

■ **PROCEDURAL BASIS**

Not provided.

■ **FACTS**

In an effort to gain control over emulation patents held by Quickturn Design Systems, Inc. (Quickturn) (D), Mentor Graphic Corporation (Mentor) (P) initiated a takeover of Quickturn (D). Pursuant to its takeover plan, Mentor (P) announced a cash tender offer for all outstanding shares of Quickturn at $12.125 per share, a price representing a 50% premium over the current market price and a 20% discount from the stocks' 52-week high. Once consummated, Mentor's (P) tender offer would be followed by a second-step merger in which the remaining shareholders in Quickturn (D) would receive $12.125 for each of their shares. Mentor (P) also announced its intent to seek proxies to replace Quickturn's (D) current board of directors. In response, Quickturn's (D) board of directors decided to recommend that the shareholders reject Mentor's (P) tender offer as an inadequate price. The board also adopted two defensive measures. First, it amended the company's by-laws to require that the board fix the record date for any special meeting called by the shareholders between 90 and 100 days after receipt of the shareholder's request. Second, the board amended the shareholder rights plan, to include a Deferred Redemption Plan (DRP), under which no member of a newly elected board could redeem the rights plan for at least six months after taking office, if the purpose of the redemption would be to facilitate a transaction with the party who supported election of the new directors. Both provisions delayed any acquisition of Quickturn (D) by Mentor (P) for at least nine months.

■ **ISSUE**

May the board of directors of the target of a hostile takeover adopt a poison pill that restricts the ability of a newly elected board to redeem the pill?

■ **DECISION AND RATIONALE**

(Jacobs, V.C.) No. A board of directors may not a adopt a poison pill that cannot be redeemed by a newly elected board for some time unless there is a reason justifying such a restriction. Although most decisions of a board of directors are protected by the business judgment rule, actions taken to resist or defend against a hostile takeover are reviewed under a different standard, which essentially requires the board to establish two things before it is afforded the protections of the business judgment rule. First, the board carries the burden of proving that it had reasonable grounds to believe the takeover threatened corporate policy and effectiveness. Second, the board must prove that the defensive measures adopted were reasonable in proportion to the perceived threat. The evidence shows that Quickturn's (D) board was concerned that the company's shareholders might, without knowing Quickturn's (D) true value, accept Mentor's (P) inadequate offer and elect a board that would prematurely sell the company to Mentor (P) without having time to inform itself of Quickturn's (D) fair value. I conclude that the board perceived these events as reasonable threats. However, the plan adopted by the board was disproportionate to the threat posed. The board attempts to justify its adoption of the DRP by asserting that it wanted to force a new elected board to take sufficient time to familiarize itself with Quickturn's (D) true value. However, this justification is at odds with the terms of the plan. The DRP does not create a six-month pill redemption delay where the newly nominated board seeks to sell the company to someone other than Mentor (P). Therefore, the terms of the DRP cannot be reconciled with the justification for adopting it. Furthermore, the board has failed to establish why a waiting period of six months was necessary. The length of time seems arbitrary. For these reasons the DRP cannot survive scrutiny.

Analysis:

Since not all takeovers are inimicable to the interests of the target corporation, most poison pills are accompanied by a redemption provision, which gives the board of directors the power to redeem the poison pill at a nominal cost to the corporation. In this case, Quickturn's (D) Board of Directors enacted a "no-hand" poison pill, a variation of the "dead-hand" poison pill used to prevent an acquiring company from engaging in a proxy fight to replace the target company's existing board of directors in order to redeem the poison pill. Whereas a dead-hand provision creates two classes of directors, one with and one without the power to redeem the poison pill, a no-hand poison pill restricts redemption by a newly elected board for some time or indefinitely. Like many defensive tactics, however, redemption provisions carry with them the danger that they are being used for "entrenchment" purposes. On appeal, the Supreme Court of Delaware held that, under the Delaware General Corporations Law, delayed redemption provisions are invalid because they prevent a newly elected board of directors from exercising its fiduciary duty to protect the interests of the corporation and its shareholders. The court seemed to hold that a board of directors cannot deprive a newly elected board of its power to run the corporation. This holding has cast doubt over whether dead-hand or no-hand poison pills are valid at all.

■ CASE VOCABULARY

DEAD-HAND POISON PILL: A poison pill with a redemption provision that gives the right of redemption to only those directors who enacted the provision, depriving newly elected board members of the power to redeem the poison pill.

ENTRENCHMENT: The adoption of corporate policy by directors whose primary motive it is to prevent the board's ouster by way of a takeover, proxy fight or other means.

NO-HAND POISON PILL: A variation of the dead-hand poison pill which restricts redemption by any board member, regardless of his identity; it essentially handcuffs the corporation completely.

International Brotherhood of Teamsters v. Fleming Companies

(Shareholder) v. *(Board of Directors)*

975 P.2d 907 (Okla. 1999)

SHAREHOLDERS HAVE THE RIGHT TO RESTRICT THE BOARD FROM ADOPTING A POISON PILL

■ **INSTANT FACTS** A shareholder sought to include in the company's annual proxy materials a proposed amendment to the corporation's by-laws which would require any rights plan implemented by the board of directors to be put to the shareholders for a majority vote.

■ **BLACK LETTER RULE** Unless the articles of incorporation state otherwise, a board of directors does not have exclusive authority to adopt a shareholder rights plan and shareholders are not precluded from proposing resolutions or amendments regarding such plans.

■ **PROCEDURAL BASIS**

On appeal, in an action brought under the federal proxy rules, the Tenth Circuit certified to the Supreme Court of Oklahoma the question of whether a board of directors has exclusive authority to create shareholder rights plans.

■ **FACTS**

The International Brotherhood of Teamsters (the Teamsters) (P), a shareholder in the Fleming Companies (Fleming) (D) sought to have the company include in its annual proxy materials a proposal for amending the bylaws to require shareholder ratification of all shareholder rights plans—i.e., poison pills. Fleming's (D) board of directors refused to include the resolution in the company's proxy materials on the ground that the proposal was not a subject for shareholder action under the law of Oklahoma. The Teamsters (P) then brought an action in federal district court to require the board to include the proposal. The district court found in favor of the Teamsters (P). Fleming's (D) board of directors appealed. In the meantime, Fleming (D) was forced to include in its proxy materials the proposed amendment, which passed by a 60 percent vote. The Tenth Circuit then certified to the Oklahoma Supreme Court the question of whether such proposals were a proper subject for shareholder action.

■ **ISSUE**

Is a board of directors vested with exclusive authority to create and implement shareholder rights plans or are shareholders proscribed from proposing by-law amendments or resolutions regarding such plans?

■ **DECISION AND RATIONALE**

(Simms, J.) No. Unless the articles of incorporation state otherwise, a board of directors does not have exclusive authority to adopt a shareholder rights plan and shareholders are not precluded from proposing resolutions or amendments regarding such plans. Although a board of directors is given authority over corporate governance, that authority is subject to shareholder oversight. The Oklahoma Corporation Statute provides that "every *corporation* may create and issue...rights or options entitling the holders thereof to purchase...any shares of its capital stock...." Fleming (D) would have us read the term corporation to mean only the board of directors. However, the statue itself defines corporation and director differently. Furthermore, the same statutory sub-section contains the term *board of directors*. We do not believe the legislature intended to use the two terms interchangeably. Fleming's position is further undercut by case law holding that shareholders have a right to require ratification of stock option plans. After all, what is a shareholder rights plan besides a variety of stock option plan? Fleming also argues that only the certificate of incorporation can limit the board's authority to implement such a plan. While we might agree that the certificate of incorporation could preclude the Teamsters (P) from proposing the by-law amendment at issue, there is no evidence showing that Fleming's (D) certificate contains such a limitation. Finally, while some states have enacted statutes permitting the board to act with relative autonomy when it comes to shareholder rights plans, Oklahoma has no such provision.

Analysis:

In this case, the Oklahoma Court held that the board of directors did not have exclusive authority to create and implement poison pills and that, by amending the by-laws, shareholders may require that poison pills be submitted for ratification unless the certificate of incorporation provides otherwise. The court based its holding on two grounds, The first being statutory language that gives the *corporation*, a term the court interpreted to mean either the board or the shareholders, the power to create and issue the right to purchase stock. The court also based its holding on precedent giving the shareholders the right to ratify stock option plans.

CHAPTER SIXTEEN

Corporate Books and Records

Thomas & Betts Corporation v. Leviton Manufacturing Co., Inc.

Instant Facts: While attempting to takeover a corporation in which it held shares, a company demanded to inspect a list of the target's corporate records on the grounds that the shareholder was investigating possible waste and mismanagement and attempting to value its shares.

Black Letter Rule: A court need not blindly accept a shareholder's proffered reasons for requesting inspection of corporation books and records.

Saito v. Mckesson HBOC, Inc.

Instant Facts: Shareholder of corporation formed after merger sought to review corporate books and records predating his purchase of stock in order to investigate wrongdoing on the part of the board of directors.

Black Letter Rule: Limitation on who may bring a derivative suit has no bearing on shareholder's right to inspect corporate records.

Parsons v. Jefferson–Pilot Corp.

Instant Facts: Relying on her common law right to inspect corporate books and records, a shareholder sought to inspect her corporation's accounting records, despite a statutory provision restricting shareholders' right to inspect such records of publicly held companies.

Black Letter Rule: The North Carolina Business Corporation Act, which grants shareholders certain rights regarding inspection of corporate books and records, does not abrogate a shareholder's common law right to such inspection.

Thomas & Betts Corporation v. Leviton Manufacturing Co., Inc.

(Shareholder) v. *(Corporation)*

681 A.2d 1026 (Del. 1996)

A COURT MAY DISREGARD A SHAREHOLDER'S STATED PURPOSES FOR REQUESTING INSPECTION OF CORPORATE RECORDS AND EXAMINE THE TRUE MOTIVE FOR THE REQUEST

■ **INSTANT FACTS** While attempting to takeover a corporation in which it held shares, a company demanded to inspect a list of the target's corporate records on the grounds that the shareholder was investigating possible waste and mismanagement and attempting to value its shares.

■ **BLACK LETTER RULE** A court need not blindly accept a shareholder's proffered reasons for requesting inspection of corporation books and records.

■ **PROCEDURAL BASIS**

Appeal to the Supreme Court of Delaware challenging the decision of the Court of Chancery circumscribing a shareholder's inspection of corporate records.

■ **FACTS**

In an effort to acquire Leviton Manufacturing Co., Inc. (Leviton) (D), the Thomas & Betts Corporation (P) obtained a minority interest in Leviton (D) by purchasing 29.1 percent of its outstanding shares from Leviton's (D) Group Vice President. Leviton's (D) majority stockholder, Harold Leviton, resisted all overtures from Thomas & Betts (P) to establish an amicable relationship. Thomas & Betts (P) eventually served Leviton (D) with a formal demand seeking inspection of: (1) a list of stockholders, (2) the minutes of shareholder and directors meetings, (3) audited financial statements, (4) internal financial statements for the current year, (5) tax returns, (6) organizational charts of the company and its subsidiaries, (7) documents relating to interested party transactions, (8) "key man" life insurance documents, (9) material contracts between the company and its subsidiaries, and (10) real estate and equipment lease documents. Thomas & Betts' (P) CEO then offered to purchase the balance of Leviton's (P) stock for $250 million. Leviton (D) refused the offer and inspection demand. Thomas & Betts (P) then brought an action to compel inspection. Because Thomas & Betts (P) failed to meet a "greater than normal evidenciary burden," the trial court determined that Thomas & Betts' (P) actual purpose for demanding inspection was to gain leverage in efforts to acquire the company and that such purpose ran counter to Leviton's (D) interests. Nevertheless, the trial court permitted a narrowly circumscribed inspection because Thomas & Betts (P) was entitled to value its shares after such a fundamental change of circumstances.

■ **ISSUE**

Must a shareholder seeking to inspect corporate records meet a heightened burden of proving that it has a proper purpose for demanding inspection?

■ **DECISION AND RATIONALE**

(Veasey, C.J.) No. A shareholder seeking to inspect corporate records has a normal, not heightened, burden of proving he has a proper purpose. It is well settled that, when a stockholder seeks to inspect

---

corporate books and records, he carries the burden of demonstrating that his purpose is proper. We have previously held that investigation of waste and management is a proper purpose for inspection of books and records. In order to meet his burden of proof, a stockholder has the burden of presenting specific and credible allegations sufficient to warrant a suspicion of waste and mismanagement. The Court of Chancery seemingly articulated the wrong standard when it stated that Thomas & Betts (D) was required to meet a "greater-than-normal evidentiary burden." However, we find that what the court meant was that, when there is substantial evidence showing that a shareholder's motive for inspection is improper, he must overcome that evidence with sufficient proof of his own. In other words, Thomas & Betts (D) had to overcome the evidence against them. Furthermore, the court's decision turned, in large part, on the Vice Chancellor's determination that Thomas & Betts' (P) witnesses were not credible. These findings of fact establish that Thomas & Betts (D) failed to meet even the normal burden. The facts also establish that Thomas & Betts (P) was motivated by its efforts at acquisition. These motives cast serious doubt on the genuineness of its claim that it sought to inspect books and records for investigatory purposes. We have been given no reason to revisit these factual findings. Thomas & Betts (P) argues that the trial court abused its discretion by circumscribing inspection after it found that inspection was justified due to changed circumstances and Thomas & Betts' (P) position as a locked-in minority shareholder. We must reject this contention because the plain language of the statute gives the trial court the discretion to limit or condition such inspection. This discretion is supported by a recognition that the interest of the corporation must be balanced with those of the inspecting shareholder. Here, the court found those interests here diametrically opposed. This finding is sufficient to justify the curtailment of Thomas & Betts' right to inspect. Affirmed.

Analysis:

Shareholders are granted a statutory qualified right to inspect lists of shareholders, financial records and minutes and records of meetings and actions taken by the board of directors. The qualification is that shareholders have a "proper purpose" for inspection. Courts generally hold that a proper purpose is anything affecting a shareholder's interests in the corporation, but this standard is rarely helpful. Rather, as this case illustrates, it is a fact-intensive inquiry that determines whether a particular shareholder has a proper purpose. As the court stated, a request is proper if it is aimed at facilitating a shareholder's investigation of corporate mismanagement. Courts will not hesitate to look beyond the shareholder's stated purpose and examine the true motive for requesting inspection of books and records.

Saito v. McKesson HBOC, Inc.

(Shareholder) v. *(Corporation)*

806 A.2d 113 (Del. 2002)

STANDING TO BRING DERIVIATIVE SUIT HAS NO BEARING ON SHAREHOLDER'S RIGHT TO INSPECT CORPORATE RECORDS

■ **INSTANT FACTS** Shareholder of corporation formed after merger sought to review corporate books and records predating his purchase of stock in order to investigate wrongdoing on the part of the board of directors.

■ **BLACK LETTER RULE** Limitation on who may bring a derivative suit has no bearing on shareholder's right to inspect corporate records.

■ **PROCEDURAL BASIS**

Appeal to the Supreme Court of Delaware of trial court's order denying access to corporate records.

■ **FACTS**

Saito (P), a shareholder in McKesson, sought to review several documents of McKesson, HBOC, a subsidiary of McKesson HBOC (D), and McKesson HBOC (D), the resulting corporation. Saito's (P) stated purpose was the investigation of the failure of the McKesson board to discover the accounting irregularities of HBOC prior to the merger. Concluding that § 327 of the Delaware Corporation Code would preclude Saito (P) from bringing a derivative action against McKesson, the trial court ruled that Saito (P) did not have standing to review the corporate records under § 220 of the Delaware Corporation Code in preparation for an action he was barred from bringing. Saito (P) appealed.

■ **ISSUE**

Must a shareholder have standing to bring a derivative suit in order to gain access to corporate books and records as part of an investigation into wrongdoing on the part of the board of directors?

■ **DECISION AND RATIONALE**

(Berger, J.) No. Generally speaking, a shareholder that demands inspection of corporate books and records for a proper purpose should be given access to all of the documents in the corporation's possession or control that are necessary to satisfy that proper purpose. In this case, the trial court denied Saito's (P) request to inspect records based on the date he purchased his shares. Under § 327, shareholders who bring derivative suits must allege that they were shareholders at the time of the transaction of which the suit complains. Since Saito (P) was not a shareholder of either HBOC or McKesson HBOC at the time of the merger, the trial court concluded that Saito (P) did not have a valid purpose for viewing the corporate records under § 220. Although we recognize the interplay between § 327 and § 220, the latter only requires that the shareholder's purpose be "reasonably related" to his interest as a shareholder. Obviously if a shareholder wanted to investigate wrongdoing that substantially predated his purchase of stock, a question would exist as to whether this purpose was reasonably related to the shareholder's interest. However, shareholders may use information for many purposes other than initiating a derivative action, including seeking a meeting with the board to discuss the problems and come up with a resolution or initiating a proxy fight to replace the board. Even where the shareholder's purpose is to gather information for a derivative suit, the date of the shareholder's

---

purchase of stock should not be used as an absolute cut-off date in a § 220 request. First, the potential lawsuit could involve a continuing wrong. Second, the alleged post-purchase wrongs could have at their foundation actions that predated the purchase, thereby making the pre-purchase information reasonably related to the shareholder's interest. Here Saito (P) wants to investigate McKesson's apparent failure to learn of HBOC's accounting irregularities prior to the merger. In this context, due diligence documents generated before the merger agreement may be essential to that investigation. Thus, if activities that occurred before the purchase date are reasonably related to the shareholder's interest, then the shareholder should be given access to records necessary to an understanding of those activities.

The trial court also denied Saito's (P) request for financial documents, apparently on the grounds that third party financial advisors prepared them. It is not clear from the record whether the trial court found that Saito (P) did not have a proper purpose in seeking these records or whether the trial court simply sought to exclude all third party documents. To the extent the trial court attempted to issue a blanket order covering all third-party documents, it was in error. The source of a corporation's documents does not control a shareholder's right to inspection. Instead, the issue is whether the documents are necessary and essential to satisfy the shareholder's proper purpose. Here, Saito (P) wants to investigate potential wrongdoing on the part of McKesson HBOC (D). Since McKesson and McKesson HBOC (D) relied on financial information and accounting advisors in evaluating HBOC's financial condition, those advisors' reports and related correspondence are critical to Saito's (P) investigation. Finally, the trial court also denied Saito (P) access to financial records in HBOC's possession on the grounds that Saito (P) has never been a shareholder of HBOC. To the extent this excluded documents never produced to McKesson or McKesson HBOC (D), we agree. However, while we recognize that a shareholder of a parent corporation does not have the right to inspect books and records of a subsidiary absent a showing of fraud or that the subsidiary is merely the alter ego of the parent company, in this case some of HBOC's records were provided to both McKesson and McKesson HBOC (D) for purposes of evaluating the merger. Those records would be essential to Saito's (P) investigation and should have been produced. This case is therefore affirmed in part and reversed in part and remanded for further proceedings.

Analysis:

The actual holding of the court in this case is fairly simple: the right of a shareholder to bring a derivative action does not control or affect the right of the shareholder to inspect corporate books and records. Rather, the test for inspection is (1) whether the shareholder has a proper purpose and (2) whether the documents are necessary and essential to that purpose. Prior to the accounting scandals that have rocked the corporate world since 2002, shareholder's inspections were often routine and easily determined. The post-Enron corporate environment has taken a toll on inspection rights. What is left is new legislation, like the Sarbanes-Oxley Act, and a policy of permitting inspection in more and more cases. The Sarbanes-Oxley Act, which attempts to fill in gaps left by other federal legislation and contains provisions making destruction of corporate records and other documents an obstruction of justice crime with stiff penalties even in anticipated matters, is the first attempt by Congress to regulate the attorney-client privilege.

■ CASE VOCABULARY

8 Del. C. § 220: Permits a shareholder to inspect a corporation's books and records upon a showing that such records are reasonably related to his interest as a shareholder and that he has a proper purpose for requesting an inspection.

8 Del. C. § 327: Requires a shareholder to prove that he was a shareholder at the time of the transaction of which he intends to complain in a derivative action in order to be entitled to bring such an action.

DERIVIATIVE SUIT: An action by a shareholder on behalf of the corporation alleging wrongdoing on the part of the board of directors.

Parsons v. Jefferson-Pilot Corp.

(Shareholder) v. *(Corporation)*

333 N.C. 420, 426 S.E.2d 685 (1993)

IN SOME STATES, SHAREHOLDERS HAVE BOTH A COMMON LAW AND STATUTORY RIGHT TO INSPECT CORPORATE BOOKS AND RECORDS

■ **INSTANT FACTS** Relying on her common law right to inspect corporate books and records, a shareholder sought to inspect her corporation's accounting records, despite a statutory provision restricting shareholders' right to inspect such records of publicly held companies.

■ **BLACK LETTER RULE** The North Carolina Business Corporation Act, which grants shareholders certain rights regarding inspection of corporate books and records, does not abrogate a shareholder's common law right to such inspection.

■ **PROCEDURAL BASIS**

Appeal to the Supreme Court of North Carolina challenging the decision of the Court of Appeals affirming in part and reversing in part the judgment of the trial court, which denied motions for summary judgment and sanctions.

■ **FACTS**

Louise Price Parsons (P), an owner of 300,000 shares of stock in Jefferson-Pilot Corp. (D), sent a formal letter requesting that Jefferson-Pilot (D) permit her to inspect and copy certain books and records that would enable her to communicate with other shareholders. Jefferson-Pilot (D) permitted Parsons (D) to inspect and copy certain books, but refused to provide a list of beneficial owners of stock, stating that it did not posses such a list. The company also refused to provide Parsons (P) with accounting records on the ground that such records were outside the scope of her statutory inspection rights. Parsons (P) filed a motion for injunctive relief, seeking an order directing Jefferson-Pilot (D) to provide accounting records and a list of beneficial owners of stock. The trial court denied Jefferson-Pilot's (D) motions for summary judgment and sanctions, concluding that Parsons (P) had a right to inspect the accounting records. However, the trial court also found that Jefferson-Pilot (D) was not required to provide a list of beneficial owners of stock because the company had no such list. The Court of Appeals affirmed the trial court's order with regard to the list of beneficial owners and with regard to the finding that Parsons (P) had described her purpose for inspection with "reasonable particularity." The appellate court reversed the trial court's order as to Parsons right to inspect accounting records. Both parties appealed.

■ **ISSUE**

Is a shareholder's right to inspect corporate books and records prescribed only by statute?

■ **DECISION AND RATIONALE**

(Mitchell, J.) No. The North Carolina Business Corporation Act, which grants shareholders certain rights regarding inspection of corporate books and records, does not abrogate a shareholder's common law right to such inspection. The statute, in pertinent part, provides shareholders with the

---

right to inspect and copy accounting records of the corporation upon written notice. That right is limited by a provision providing that shareholders of publicly held corporations do not have the right to inspect any accounting records of the corporation. We disagree with the Court of Appeals, which held that this provision abrogates any common law right to inspect accounting records. We have expressly held that shareholders have a common law right to make a reasonable inspection of its books to assure themselves of efficient management. Our conclusion is supported by the express language of the statute, which states that the power of a court to compel production of corporate records is not affected by the statute. In fact, the Official Comment to the statute states that the common law right to inspection is preserved. We do, however, agree with the Court of Appeals that Parsons (P) was not entitled to inspect a "NOBO" list—i.e., a list of non-objecting beneficial owners—because the company did not have such a list. We believe that the legislature intended to provide shareholders with a right to inspect records concerning the identity of shareholders so that they may have the same opportunity as the corporation to communicate with other shareholders. The legislative purpose is in no way furthered by requiring Jefferson-Pilot (D) to provide a list it neither possesses nor uses to communicate with shareholders. Finally, we agree with the Court of Appeals that Parsons (D) stated her purpose for inspection with "reasonable particularity," as required by the statute. Whether a shareholder has met this burden depends on the particular facts and circumstances. The question turns on the degree of knowledge possessed by the shareholder. Because Parsons (P) had no specific knowledge of corporate mismanagement or improper use of corporate assets, it was not feasible to state her purpose with any greater particularity that she did.

Analysis:

The Oklahoma Court here takes an expansive view toward the inspection rights of shareholders. By holding that a shareholder has a common law right to inspection in addition to any statutory right, the court undermines the purposes of the statute. After all, what good does the statutory restriction on inspection of accounting records do if the shareholder can circumvent the rule by relying on his common law right? This issue notwithstanding, many courts have held that the statutory right to inspection is independent of, and supplementary to, a shareholder's common law right to inspection. The court's holding with respect to the NOBO list—that a corporation need not provide records that it has no duty to keep and does not actually keep—is in line with the prevailing view.

■ CASE VOCABULARY

BENEFICIAL OWNER: A person who has title to the shares but who is not the registered owner of the shares.

NOBO LIST: Non-objecting beneficial owners list; a list of beneficial owners who do not object to having their names disclosed.